Reviewing
ENGLISH LANGUAGE ARTS

Perfection Learning®

Editorial Director Carol Francis
Editor Terry Ofner
Proofreading Coordinator Sheri Cooper
Art Director Randy Messer
Designer Tobi Cunningham
Cover Tobi Cunningham
Permissions Karyn Morrison

Please visit our Web site at:
www.perfectionlearning.com

When ordering this book, please specify:
ISBN 978-1-62974-690-6 or **14871**

3 4 5 6 BB 20 19 18 17 16

Printed in the United States of America

Table of Contents

To the Student

This book will help you review and strengthen core skills commonly assessed on English Language Arts Exit Exams. Through guided practice, focused tasks, and short assessments you will review the following key skills and concepts.

Close Reading—Questions and tasks will give you practice in the close reading of complex texts, including direct instruction and practice in—

- initial reading
- rereading
- marking up and annotating texts to identify evidence and record questions and insights
- synthesizing your ideas

Writing from Sources—Every chapter provides valuable practice in interpreting and writing about complex literary and informational texts and in using textual evidence for support.

Lesson Structure

In each chapter you will focus on one general topic through two or more lessons. Each lesson followe the same structure described below.

Review: In this brief section, you will be introduced to concepts and key terms related to the topic.

Check Understanding: In the reading chapters (Units 1 and 2), you will be presented with a text that has been partially marked up and annotated. You will be prompted to read the text closely and to mark up, annotate, and/or write a brief interpretation of the text and to share and discuss your response with a partner. In the writing chapters (Unit 3), you will be presented with a task related to the process of writing.

Try It: With this activity, you will be directed to answer several questions or be prompted to write short response paragraphs. Suggested answers and sample responses follow in the text.

Chapter Review: In Units 1 and 2 (Reading Literature and Reading Informational Texts), you will be presented with a reading selection followed by multiple-choice and short answer interpretive questions. In Unit 3 (Writing to Sources), you will be presented with several source documents and a writing prompt.

Other components of the lessons include Toolbars, Strategies, and Test-Taking Tips.

Toolbar: Here you will find valuable skills and hints specific to the topic.

Strategies: Check the strategies section for a summary of reading or writing strategies relevant to the focus of the chapter.

Test-Taking Tips: Here you will find tips for applying the skills and concepts of the chapter in testing situations.

Practice Test 1 and 2

There are two assessments at the end of the book. These two tests are similar to English Language Arts exit exams you will take sometime in your high school career. Each test is composed of three parts.

Reading Comprehension: This section of the text consists of three texts (fiction, poetry, and informational). Each is followed by 6–10 multiple-choice questions for a total of 24 questions.

Writing from Sources: This section consists of 4–6 related source documents on a controversial topic. You will be prompted to perform a close reading of the texts and to write a source-based argument.

Text Analysis: In this section, you will perform a close reading of a literary or informational selection and write a two- to three-paragraph analysis of a literary element or technique used by the author.

Your teacher may direct you take one of these tests before using the book to assess your understanding and skills and to determine the chapters and lessons that you need to focus on the most.

Unit 1 Reading Literature

Unit Focus

The focus of this unit is the close reading of fiction, poetry, and drama. Theme, setting, plot, narrative structures, and characterization will be addressed, as well as tone, figurative language, and irony.

Chapter 1 Close Reading of Literary Texts (RL.11–12.1)

If there is one key to understanding and enjoying literature, it is close reading. Taking time to focus your attention on a short story, poem, or play, you begin to make it your own. By sharing the unique perspective you gain through close reading, you take part in the creative process at the heart of the literary enterprise. This chapter addresses the following three aspects of close reading.

1.1 Analyzing explicit details and implicit meanings
1.2 Identifying and interpreting uncertainties
1.3 Citing strong and thorough textual evidence

1.1 Analyzing Explicit Details and Implicit Meanings

Review

Close reading is the careful interpretation of a text. There is no single right way to do a close reading. In general, however, the process can be divided into three stages: 1) First Reading, 2) Rereading, 3) Synthesizing.

In the *first reading,* focus on **explicit details**. In fiction and drama, determine the setting, main characters, and main events of the narrative. In poetry, determine the tone, imagery, and main message. In *rereading,* focus on the **implicit meanings** or inferences. Inferences are what you bring to the text. When you infer, you start with a detail from the text and combine it with knowledge that you already have. Based on this combination, you make an educated guess about the text. In *synthesizing,* you bring explicit details and implicit meanings together to form an interpretation of the text.

Key Terms

explicit detail: actual text of a work.

implicit meaning: an inference or interpretation based on the explicit text.

inference: an educated guess based on the explicit text, context, and prior knowledge.

Check Understanding

Notice the way one reader draws an inference from the excerpt below.

from A New England Nun

by Mary Wilkins Freeman

1. It was late in the afternoon, and the light was waning. There was a difference in the look of the tree shadows out in the yard. Somewhere in the distance cows were lowing, and a little bell was tinkling; now and then a farm-wagon tilted by, and the dust flew; some blue-shirted laborers with shovels over their shoulders plodded past; little swarms of flies were dancing up and down before the peoples' faces in the soft air.

Notes

The lowing cows and farm wagons establish a rural setting.

Activity 1.1 Reread the excerpt above. Highlight other details and write inferences based on them in the margin. Share your findings with a partner.

Toolbox

As you reread a text—

- Underline or highlight important passages and add inferences and connections in the margin. These details and notes will provide a way back into the text when you return to it.
- In a test situation, you will have to conserve time by combining stages. For example, by reviewing questions and prompts before reading, you will be able to focus on specific passages or aspects of the text addressed by the questions and prompts.

Try It

Directions: Read the opening paragraphs of the short story below and answer the questions.

from The Wife of His Youth

by Charles Chesnutt

1. Mr. Ryder was going to give a ball. There were several reasons . . . for such an event. Mr. Ryder might aptly be called the dean of the Blue Veins. The original Blue Veins were a little society of colored persons organized . . . shortly after the war. Its purpose was to establish and maintain correct social standards among a people whose social condition presented almost unlimited room for improvement. By accident, combined perhaps with some natural affinity, the society consisted of individuals who were . . . more white than black. Some envious outsider made the suggestion that no one was eligible for membership who was not white enough to show blue veins. The suggestion was readily adopted by those who were not of the favored few, and since that time the society . . . had been known . . . as the "Blue Vein Society," and its members as the "Blue Veins."

2. The Blue Veins did not allow that any such requirement existed for admission to their circle, but, on the contrary, declared that character and culture were the only things considered; and that if most of their members were light-colored, it was because such persons, as a rule, had had better opportunities to qualify themselves for membership. Opinions differed, too, as to the usefulness of the society. There were those who had been known to assail it violently as a glaring example of the very prejudice from which the colored race had suffered most. . . . Another alleged prerequisite for Blue Vein membership was that of free birth; and while there was really no such requirement, it is doubtless true that very few of the members would have been unable to meet it if there had been. If there were . . . older members who had come up from the South and from slavery, their history presented enough romantic circumstances to rob their servile origin of its grosser aspects.

Notes

1. Which inference is best supported by the text?

Ⓐ Mr. Ryder came up from the South.

Ⓑ Mr. Ryder is pretentious.

Ⓒ The Blue Vein Society is trying to emulate upper-class white society.

Ⓓ The narrator is unbiased in his presentation of the society.

2. Cite at least two details in the text that could be used to support your answer to question 1.

____

____

____

____

Question 1 asks you to select the inference that is best supported by the text. While choice A may be true, there is no evidence in the text to support it. Choice B may be true as well, but again, there is no definitive evidence in the text to support the claim. Choice C is the best answer. There is evidence that the Blue Vein Society is patterned after similar groups in white society. Choice D is not accurate; there is evidence that the narrator is not completely unbiased in his view of the Blue Vein Society.

Question 2 asks you to cite and explain two details from the text that could be used to support the inference you selected in question 1. Sample response: Objections by members of the Blue Vein Society aside, there is evidence that the group strives to emulate white society. There is the fact that most of the members appear "more white than black." Also, the group practices a similar form of prejudice against blacks who do not meet "correct social standards" as practiced by white society against all blacks.

1.2 Identifying and Interpreting Uncertainties

Review

Some implicit details, such as those noted in "The Wife of His Youth" above, are relatively easy to interpret—the connection between detail and inference is easy to make. But the interpretation of some details can be **uncertain**. That is, different people may interpret such details differently. Idioms, personifications, similes, and metaphors are often open to interpretation. Also, highly descriptive passages in prose or poetry may foreshadow events or mirror character traits in ways that are uncertain or **ambiguous**.

Key Terms

ambiguity: uncertainty or inexactness of meaning.

uncertainty: part of a text in which meaning is not clear. Multiple interpretations can be based on such passages.

Check Understanding

Notice how the student writer begins to interpret paragraphs 5 and 6 of "A New England Nun" on the next page.

5. In about half an hour Joe Dagget came. She heard his heavy step on the walk, and rose and took off her pink-and-white apron. Under that was still another white linen with a little cambric edging on the bottom; that was Louisa's company apron. She never wore it without her calico sewing apron over it unless she had a guest. She had barely folded the pink and white one with methodical haste and laid it in a table-drawer when the door opened and Joe Dagget entered.

6. He seemed to fill up the whole room. A little yellow canary that had been asleep in his green cage at the south window woke up and fluttered wildly, beating his little yellow wings against the wires. He always did so when Joe Dagget came into the room.

Notes

Joe Dagget's heavy step evokes the plodding field workers in the opening paragraph while Louisa is drawn in fine, careful lines. Even in haste, she is methodical.

Activity 1.2 Reread the excerpt above. Highlight at least one uncertainty and record a brief interpretation in the margin. Share your findings with a partner.

Toolbox

Literary Present Tense Notice how the writer used present tense in his notes above, even though the story is told in past tense. This is known as literary present tense. Creative works, such as fiction, drama, paintings, and film, are thought to exist in an eternal present. For this reason, critical essays are written in present tense. You should use past tense when discussing historical events.

Try It

Directions: Read the paragraphs from "The Wife of His Youth" and answer the questions that follow.

6. "I have no race prejudice," [Mr. Ryder] would say, "but we people of mixed blood are ground between the upper and the nether millstone. Our fate lies between absorption by the white race and extinction in the black. The one doesn't want us yet, but may take us in time. The other would welcome us, but it would be for us a backward step. 'With malice towards none, with charity for all,' we must do the best we can for ourselves and those who are to follow us. Self-preservation is the first law of nature."

7. His ball would serve by its exclusiveness to counteract leveling tendencies, and his marriage with Mrs. Dixon would help to further the upward process of absorption he had been wishing and waiting for.

Notes

3. Identify a detail from the story that is open to several possible interpretations. Write the passage on the lines below.

4. Write a brief interpretation of the passage you selected in question 3.

Question 3 asks you to identify a detail that is open to several possible interpretations. There are several possible answers. One is the sentence in paragraph 6 in which Mr. Ryder invokes Abraham Lincoln's second inaugural address.

"... 'With malice towards none, with charity for all,' we must do the best we can for ourselves and those who are to follow us. Self-preservation is the first law of nature."

Question 4 asks you to interpret the passage you selected in question 3. The meaning of the passage is uncertain. Why does Mr. Ryder quote directly from Lincoln's second inaugural address? To interpret such ambiguity, you can combine context with logical thinking and prior knowledge to come up with a logical explanation. Consider the response below.

Mr. Ryder is in the midst of a conflict between the white race and the black. Being of mixed blood (or at least, pretending to be), he and others in the Blue Vein Society find themselves between a future in which they are absorbed by the white race or, as he sees it, "extinction in the black (paragraph 6)." Caught in the middle of this racial conflict, Mr. Ryder invokes the famous words of Abraham Lincoln, who was seeking an end to the conflict between the North and the South.

1.3 Citing Strong and Thorough Textual Evidence

Review

The backbone of any literary analysis is the **evidence** you draw from a text to support your **interpretation**. Evidence can be direct quotations from the text, **paraphrases** of the text, or a combination of the two. Besides citing textual evidence, you must be prepared to explain how the evidence supports your interpretation.

Key Terms

evidence: direct quotation or paraphrase of a text used to support an interpretation.

interpretation: the meaning you get from a text.

paraphrase: a restatement of part of a text in your own words.

Check Understanding

Notice the use of textual evidence (highlighted) in the opening paragraph of this student draft essay on Freeman's short story.

The Uses of Imagery in "A New England Nun"

Mary Wilkins Freeman uses descriptive language and contrasting images throughout her short story "A New England Nun" to mirror the inner lives of her characters. The technique is evident in the opening scene, where Freeman establishes the setting of a farm community. She creates a rural scene through descriptions of "distant cows" lowing, "a farm-wagon" tilting by, and "blue-shirted laborers" plodding past. The verbs *low*, *tilt*, and *plod* evoke slow, heavy movement, as if the people, animals, and the land itself are tired after a long day's work. Against this backdrop, Freeman inserts a contrasting lighter note: "a little bell . . . tinkling." The little bell surrounded by heavy and muscular imagery mirrors Louisa's delicate, nun-like existence in the farm community.

Notes

Activity 1.3 Reread the student paper above and underline two interpretive statements. On the lines below, explain why you agree or disagree with the interpretation.

Toolbox

Assume your reader knows the work. In a critical essay, don't feel that you have to retell the work you are interpreting. Assume that your reader is familiar enough with the work that a brief descriptive phrase will locate him or her in the text: "In the opening scene. . .", "In the parlor scene. . .", etc.

Try It

Directions: Read paragraphs 8–10 of "The Wife of His Youth" and answer the questions that follow. Then compare your responses with those in the Review It section that follows.

Notes

8. The ball was to take place on Friday night. The house had been put in order, . . . ; and in the afternoon Mr. Ryder sat on his front porch, which the shade of a vine running up over a wire netting made a cool and pleasant lounging-place. He expected to respond to the toast "The Ladies," at the supper, and from a volume of Tennyson — his favorite poet — was fortifying himself with apt quotations. The volume was open at A Dream of Fair Women. His eyes fell on these lines, and he read them aloud to judge better of their effect: — "At length I saw a lady within call. Stiller than chisell'd marble, standing there; A daughter of the gods, divinely tall, And most divinely fair." He marked the verse, and turning the page read the stanza beginning, —

"O sweet pale Margaret,
O rare pale Margaret."

9. He weighed the passage a moment, and decided that it would not do. Mrs. Dixon was the palest lady he expected at the ball, and she was of a rather ruddy complexion, and of lively disposition and buxom build. So he ran over the leaves until his eye rested on the description of Queen Guinevere: —

10. "She seem'd a part of joyous Spring:
A gown of grass-green silk she wore,
Buckled with golden clasps before;
A light-green tuft of plumes she bore
Closed in a golden ring.

. . . .

"She look'd so lovely, as she sway'd
The rein with dainty finger-tips,
A man had given all other bliss,
And all his worldly worth for this,
To waste his whole heart in one kiss
Upon her perfect lips."

5. Cite two passages from paragraphs 8–10 that could be used as evidence to show the conflict Mr. Ryder faces in the passage.

6. Explain how the citations you selected for question 5 support your view of the conflict Mr. Ryder faces.

____

____

____

____

____

Question 5 asks you to select two passages from paragraphs 8–10 that could be used to show the conflict Mr. Ryder faces. Several passages answer the question:

He expected to respond to the toast "The Ladies," at the supper, and from a volume of Tennyson—his favorite poet—was fortifying himself with apt quotations.

He weighed the passage a moment, and decided that it would not do. Mrs. Dixon was the palest lady he expected at the ball, and she was of a rather ruddy complexion, and of lively disposition and buxom build.

Question 6 asks you to explain how the passages you selected in question 5 support your understanding of the conflict Mr. Ryder faces. Consider this response, which combines details and interpretation.

Mr. Ryder is in a conflict between his ideal self and his reality. In his ideal, he enjoys an upper-class white lifestyle with its refinement, elegance, and poetry (particularly the poetry of Alfred Noyes Tennyson—the great British poet). He finds it difficult, however, to find lines of poetry he can use to toast Mrs. Dixon. The poetry is full of references to the ideal white woman: chisell'd marble, divinely fair, and pale (paragraph 8). Unfortunately, Mrs. Dixon is of "ruddy complexion, and of lively disposition and buxom build" (paragraph 9). With some effort, Mr. Ryder finds some lines without reference to the ideal pale woman.

Strategies for Close Reading of Literary Text

Use the following strategies as you read closely and as you draw inferences and cite explicit and implicit meanings from text.

- Underline key details such as descriptions that reveal character and/or setting.
- Underline figurative language; such passages reveal mood, tone and the attitude of the narrator and/or characters.
- The margin is a good place to add notes such as inferences and brief interpretations.
- Mark places in the text where matters are uncertain.
- Once you make an inference, watch for new information that confirms or changes your conclusion.

Test-Taking Tips

- Good literature rarely includes unnecessary details. Think about the meaning of the details as you read. They may foreshadow what will happen later, provide important information about the characters, or introduce a theme.
- Make a short outline before you begin a written response, making sure to address each part of the question. Remember to use only those details that help explain your response.
- Get in the habit of using literary present tense when writing about fiction, drama, and poetry.

Chapter Review

Read the short story and answer the questions that follow.

Dead Men's Path

by Chinua Achebe

Notes

1. Michael Obi's hopes were fulfilled much earlier than he expected. He was appointed headmaster of Ndume Central School in January 1949.

2. It had always been an unprogressive school, so the Mission authorities decided to send a young and energetic man to run it. Obi accepted this responsibility with enthusiasm. He had many wonderful ideas and this was an opportunity to put them into practice. He had had sound secondary school education which designated him a "pivotal teacher" in the official records and set him apart from the other headmasters in the mission field. He was outspoken in his condemnation of the narrow views of these older and often less-educated ones.

3. "We shall make a good job of it, shan't we?" he asked his young wife when they first heard the joyful news of his promotion.

4. "We shall do our best," she replied. "We shall have such beautiful gardens and everything will be just modern and delightful . . ." In their two years of married life she had become completely infected by his passion for "modern methods" and his denigration of "these old and superannuated people in the teaching field who would be better employed as traders in the Onitsha market." She began to see herself already as the admired wife of the young headmaster, the queen of the school.

5. The wives of the other teachers would envy her position. She would set the fashion in everything . . . Then, suddenly, it occurred to her that there might not be other wives. Wavering between hope and fear, she asked her husband, looking anxiously at him.

6. "All our colleagues are young and unmarried," he said with enthusiasm which for once she did not share. "Which is a good thing," he continued.

7. "Why?"

8. "Why? They will give all their time and energy to the school."

9. Nancy was downcast. For a few minutes she became skeptical about the new school; but it was only for a few minutes. Her little personal misfortune could not blind her to her husband's happy prospects. She looked at him as he sat folded up in a chair. He was stoop-shouldered and looked frail. But he sometimes surprised people with sudden bursts of physical energy. In his present posture, however, all his bodily strength seemed to have retired behind his deep-set eyes, giving them an extraordinary power of penetration. He was only twenty-six, but looked thirty or more. On the whole, he was not unhandsome.

Notes

10. "A penny for your thoughts, Mike," said Nancy after a while, imitating the woman's magazine she read.

11. "I was thinking what a grand opportunity we've got at last to show these people how a school should be run."

12. Ndume School was backward in every sense of the word. Mr. Obi put his whole life into the work, and his wife hers too. He had two aims. A high standard of teaching was insisted upon, and the school compound was to be turned into a place of beauty. Nancy's dream-gardens came to life with the coming of the rains, and blossomed. Beautiful hibiscus and allamanda hedges in brilliant red and yellow marked out the carefully tended school compound from the rank neighborhood bushes.

13. One evening as Obi was admiring his work he was scandalized to see an old woman from the village hobble right across the compound, through a marigold flower-bed and the hedges. On going up there he found faint signs of an almost disused path from the village across the school compound to the bush on the other side.

14. "It amazes me," said Obi to one of his teachers who had been three years in the school, "that you people allowed the villagers to make use of this footpath. It is simply incredible." He shook his head.

15. "The path," said the teacher apologetically, "appears to be very important to them. Although it is hardly used, it connects the village shrine with their place of burial."

16. "And what has that got to do with the school?" asked the headmaster.

17. "Well, I don't know," replied the other with a shrug of the shoulders. "But I remember there was a big row some time ago when we attempted to close it."

18. "That was some time ago. But it will not be used now," said Obi as he walked away. "What will the Government Education Officer think of this when he comes to inspect the school next week? The villagers might, for all I know, decide to use the schoolroom for a pagan ritual during the inspection."

19. Heavy sticks were planted closely across the path at the two places where it entered and left the school premises. These were further strengthened with barbed wire.

20. Three days later the village priest of Ani called on the headmaster. He was an old man and walked with a slight stoop. He carried a stout walking-stick which he usually tapped on the floor, by way of emphasis, each time he made a new point in his argument.

21. "I have heard," he said after the usual exchange of cordialities, "that our ancestral footpath has recently been closed . . ."

22. "Yes," replied Mr. Obi. "We cannot allow people to make a highway of our school compound."

23. "Look here, my son," said the priest bringing down his walking-stick, "this path was here before you were born and before your father was born. The whole life of this village depends on it. Our dead relatives depart by it and our ancestors visit us by it. But most important, it is the path of children coming in to be born . . . "

24. Mr. Obi listened with a satisfied smile on his face.

25. "The whole purpose of our school," he said finally, "is to eradicate just such beliefs as that. Dead men do not require footpaths. The whole idea is just fantastic. Our duty is to teach your children to laugh at such ideas."

26. "What you say may be true," replied the priest, "but we follow the practices of our fathers. If you re-open the path we shall have nothing to quarrel about. What I always say is: let the hawk perch and let the eagle perch." He rose to go.

27. "I am sorry," said the young headmaster. "But the school compound cannot be a thoroughfare. It is against our regulations. I would suggest your constructing another path, skirting our premises. We can even get our boys to help in building it. I don't suppose the ancestors will find the little detour too burdensome."

28. "I have no more words to say," said the old priest, already outside.

29. Two days later a young woman in the village died in childbed. A diviner was immediately consulted and he prescribed heavy sacrifices to propitiate ancestors insulted by the fence.

30. Obi woke up the next morning among the ruins of his work. The beautiful hedges were torn up not just near the path but right round the school, the flowers trampled to death and one of the school buildings pulled down . . . That day, the white Supervisor came to inspect the school and wrote a nasty report on the state of the premises but more seriously about the "tribal-war situation developing between the school and the village, arising in part from the misguided zeal of the new headmaster."

Notes

Questions 1–7: Choose the best answer or write your response on the lines.

1. Which inference regarding Obi and his wife is best supported by the text?

   Ⓐ Obi and his wife are devoted to the goals of the mission.

   Ⓑ Obi and his wife are highly energetic and they like to garden.

   Ⓒ Obi and his wife are young, energetic, and somewhat arrogant.

   Ⓓ Obi and his wife are humbled by the task ahead of them.

2. Cite two sentences from the first five paragraphs that you could use as evidence to support your answer to question 1. Write them on the lines below.

3. Explain how the sentences you selected for question 2 support your answer to question 1.

4. Cite one passage from the text that could be used as strong evidence that Obi is unwilling to compromise with the old ways represented by the village priest.

5. Which of the following quotations could be used as evidence to support the claim that the village priest is more open-minded than Obi?

   Ⓐ "Look here, my son," said the priest bringing down his walking-stick, "this path was here before you were born and before your father was born."

   Ⓑ ". . . The whole life of this village depends on it. . . ."

   Ⓒ ". . . What I always say is: let the hawk perch and let the eagle perch."

   Ⓓ "I have no more words to say," said the old priest, already outside.

6. What meaning, if any, can you draw from the detail that both Obi and the village priest have a stoop? Write your answer on the lines below.

7. Using evidence from the text, explain why the school was attacked at the end of the story. Then, explain what might happen next.

Chapter 2 Theme

(RL.11–12.2)

The theme of a work of fiction, a drama, or a poem is rarely stated directly in the work. You must infer the theme through close reading and your prior knowledge. This chapter addresses the following aspects of theme.

2.1 Identifying themes
2.2 Analyzing the development of themes
2.3 Providing an objective summary

2.1 Identifying Themes

Review

Theme is the major idea or message of a literary work. Theme is the author's way of sharing an idea about life, human nature, or aspects of society. An author may include several themes in a literary work and both major and minor themes. A **major theme** is one of the most important ideas in a literary work; a **minor theme** is an idea that appears only briefly.

Do not confuse the theme of a literary work with its **subject**. The subject is the topic of the work, whereas the theme is an insight into, or idea about, that topic. For example, the subject of a poem might be love, whereas the theme of that same poem might be love conquers all.

A theme is rarely stated directly. It must be inferred through close reading. Much like interpreting a text, creating a theme statement is a creative act. For this reason, no single theme statement can fully "define" a work. Two people may see different themes at work in a poem or story. Indeed, the same person rereading a text after the passage of time may see very different themes at play.

Key Terms

major theme: an idea that appears throughout a literary work.

minor theme: an idea that appears briefly in a literary work.

subject: the topic about which an author has chosen to write.

theme: a major idea revealed through the setting, characters, and plot in a literary work.

Toolbox

- When writing about theme, don't be satisfied with one-word descriptors or trite overused phrases. If a story or poem suggests the theme of identity, dig deeper into the literature to determine the specific way the literature deals with the theme of identity.

Check Understanding

Notice the way one reader starts the process of identifying the theme in the poem on the next page.

The Latin Deli: An Ars Poetica

by Judith Ortiz Cofer

Presiding over a formica counter,
plastic Mother and Child magnetized
to the top of an ancient register,
the heady mix of smells from the open bins
of dried codfish, the green plantains
hanging in stalks like votive offerings,
she is the Patroness of Exiles,
a woman of no-age who was never pretty,
who spends her days selling canned memories
while listening to the Puerto Ricans complain
that it would be cheaper to fly to San Juan
than to buy a pound of Bustelo coffee here,
and to Cubans perfecting their speech
of a "glorious return" to Havana—where no one
has been allowed to die and nothing to change until then;
to Mexicans who pass through, talking lyrically
of *dólares* to be made in El Norte—

all wanting the comfort
of spoken Spanish, to gaze upon the family portrait
of her plain wide face, her ample bosom
resting on her plump arms, her look of maternal interest
as they speak to her and each other
of their dreams and their disillusions—
how she smiles understanding,
when they walk down the narrow aisles of her store
reading the labels of packages aloud, as if
they were the names of lost lovers; Suspir*os*,
Merengues, the stale candy of everyone's childhood.

She spends her days
slicing *jamón y queso* and wrapping it in wax paper
tied with string: plain ham and cheese
that would cost less at the A&P, but it would not satisfy
the hunger of the fragile old man lost in the folds
of his winter coat, who brings her lists of items
that he reads to her like poetry, or the others,
whose needs she must divine, conjuring up products
from places that now exist only in their hearts—
closed ports she must trade with.

Notes

A reference to Catholic religious imagery

votive offering: another religious reference.

Patroness of Exiles: her title makes her seem like a caring mother or grandmother.

Activity 2.1 Reread the poem. Highlight details that strike you as important. Then write a theme statement in the margin. Share your statement with a partner.

Try It

Directions: Read the excerpt below and answer the questions that follow.

from Snow Falling on Cedars

by David Guterson

Hatsue is the daughter of Japanese immigrants to the northwestern United States. In this scene, she is being taught how to be a proper Japanese lady.

Notes

1. Mrs. Shigemura, on Wednesday afternoons, taught Hatsue the intricacies of the tea ceremony as well as calligraphy and scene painting. She showed her how to arrange flowers in a vase and how, for special occasions, to dust her face with rice powder. She insisted that Hatsue must never giggle and must never look at a man directly. In order to keep her complexion immaculate—Hatsue, said Mrs. Shigemura, had skin as smooth as vanilla ice cream—she must take care to stay out of the sun. Mrs. Shigemura taught Hatsue how to sing with composure and how to sit, walk, and stand gracefully. It was this latter that remained of Mrs. Shigemura: Hatsue still moved with a wholeness of being that began in the balls of her feet and reached right through to the top of her head. She was unified and graceful.

. . .

2. Mrs. Shigemura taught Hatsue to sit without moving and claimed that she would not mature properly unless she learned to do so for extended periods. Living in America, she said, would make this difficult, because here there was tension and unhappiness. At first Hatsue, who was only thirteen, could not sit still for even thirty seconds. Then later, when she had stilled her body, she found it was her mind that would not be quiet. But gradually her rebellion against tranquility subsided. Mrs. Shigemura was pleased and claimed that the turbulence of her ego was in the process of being overcome. She told Hatsue that her stillness would serve her well. She would experience harmony of being in the midst of the changes and unrest that life inevitably brings.

3. But Hatsue feared, walking home over forest trails from Mrs. Shigemura's, that despite her training she was not be calmed. She dallied and sometimes sat under trees, searched for lady's slippers or white trilliums to pick, and contemplated her attraction to the world of illusions—her craving for existence and entertainment, for clothes, makeup, dances, movies. It seemed to her that in her external bearing she had succeeded only in deceiving Mrs. Shigemura; inwardly she knew her aspiration for worldly happiness was frighteningly irresistible. Yet the demand that she conceal this inner life was great, and by the time she entered high school she was expert at implying bodily a tranquility that did not in fact inhabit her. In this way she developed a secret life that disturbed her and that she sought to cast off.

1. Identify two details in the passage that could develop into major themes in the novel. Briefly explain your choices.

2. Write a sentence stating your interpretation of the theme of the passage.

Question 1 asks you to identify details in the passage that could develop into major themes. Several details could become major themes. One is how Hatsue must take a class in being Japanese. This hints at the notion that the Japanese community is not integrated into the American culture. Another detail is the contrast between Hatsue's external composure and grace and her internal turbulence.

Question 2 asks you to write a sentence stating the theme of the passage. Here is a sample answer:

A product of both Japanese and American influences, Hatsue is torn between two cultures.

2.2 Analyzing the Development of Themes

Review

Authors develop theme through word choice and figurative language, character, setting, plot, and structure.

Word choice and figurative language can help emphasize and develop the theme of a work. For example, in "The Latin Deli: An Ars Poetica," the word "votive" and the simile "as if / they were lost lovers" help develop the theme of homesickness.

A character's inner thoughts, conversations, and motives can provide important clues to the theme. In *Snow Falling On Cedars*, for example, the theme of conflicting cultures is heightened through Hatsue's inner thoughts and struggles.

Authors also use **setting** to develop theme. For instance, Ortiz Cofer sets her poem in a deli where Spanish is spoken and where familiar items are for sale, highlighting the themes of hospitality, exile, and longing for home.

The **plot** of a literary work can also provide clues to the theme. A story in which a character takes decisive action may suggest a theme of freedom from social norms; a story in which a character is hampered from taking action may suggest themes of oppression or injustice.

Authors may also use **structure** to develop theme. Structure may

Key Terms

character: an imaginary person represented in a literary work.

narrative structure: the overall organization of a narrative, including such elements as exposition, *in medias res* openings, flashbacks, and foreshadowing.

plot: the sequence of events in a literary work.

setting: the time, geographic location, and conditions in which a literary work takes place.

structure: the overall design of a work, such as chapters in a short story or the scenes in a play.

be conventional and rule-bound, as in the three quatrains and concluding couplet of the Shakespearean sonnet, or avant-garde and experimental, as in the multiple perspectives and shifting times found in some works by Virginia Woolf.

Check Understanding

Directions: Notice how one reader started to mark up the poem below by Walt Whitman.

Beat! Beat! Drums!

by Walt Whitman

"Beat! Beat! Drums!" was first published in Harper's Weekly *on September 28, 1861, a few months after the start of the American Civil War.*

Beat! beat! drums!—blow! bugles! blow!
Through the windows—through doors—burst like a ruthless force,
Into the solemn church, and scatter the congregation,
Into the school where the scholar is studying,
Leave not the bridegroom quiet—no happiness must he have now with his bride,
Nor the peaceful farmer any peace, ploughing his field or gathering his grain,
So fierce you whirr and pound you drums—so shrill you bugles blow.

Beat! beat! drums!—blow! bugles! blow!
Over the traffic of cities—over the rumble of wheels in the streets;
Are beds prepared for sleepers at night in the houses? no sleepers must sleep in those beds,
No bargainers' bargains by day—no brokers or speculators—would they continue?
Would the talkers be talking? would the singer attempt to sing?
Would the lawyer rise in the court to state his case before the judge?
Then rattle quicker, heavier drums—you bugles wilder blow.

Beat! beat! drums!—blow! bugles! blow!
Make no parley[1]—stop for no expostulation,
Mind not the timid—mind not the weeper or prayer,
Mind not the old man beseeching the young man,
Let not the child's voice be heard, nor the mother's entreaties,
Make even the trestles to shake the dead where they lie awaiting the hearses,
So strong you thump O terrible drums—so loud you bugles blow.

Notes

Whitman lived through the Civil War and wrote many poems about it.

The rhythm of the opening line matches that of beating drums.

In the first stanza, the persona appears to be preparing people for the sacrifices war will require.

---

1 parley: a meeting between opposing sides in a dispute to discuss terms for ending the conflict

Activity 2.2 Reread the poem on the previous page. Highlight details that you feel are important and annotate them in the margin. In the space below, write a brief statement about how the theme of the poem is developed.

Try It

Directions: Read a passage from Jamaica Kincaid's story "Girl" and answer the questions that follow.

from Girl

by Jamaica Kincaid

	Notes
1. Wash the white clothes on Monday and put them on the stone heap; wash the color clothes on Tuesday and put them on the clothesline to dry; don't walk barehead in the hot sun; cook pumpkin fritters in very hot sweet oil; soak your little cloths right after you take them off; when buying cotton to make yourself a nice blouse, be sure that it doesn't have gum on it, because that way it won't hold up well after a wash; soak salt fish overnight before you cook it; is it true that you sing benna[1] in Sunday school?; always eat your food in such a way that it won't turn someone else's stomach; on Sundays try to walk like a lady and not like the slut you are so bent on becoming; don't sing benna in Sunday school; you mustn't speak to wharf-rat boys, not even to give directions; don't eat fruits on the street—flies will follow you; but I don't sing benna on Sundays at all and never in Sunday school; this is how to sew on a button; this is how to make a button-hole for the button you have just sewed on; this is how to hem a dress when you see the hem coming down and so to prevent yourself from looking like the slut I know you are so bent on becoming.	

1 benna: Calypso music

3. How does the daughter respond to the orders her mother gives?

4. How does the structure of the selection hint at the theme of the piece?

____

____

____

____

____

____

Question 3 asks you to describe how the daughter responds to her mother's orders. It is nearly impossible to tell how the daughter may respond, given that the she is allowed to speak only one line. However, she does defend herself by stating that she doesn't sing benna in Sunday school. From this you might infer that the daughter may have already developed her own mind and personality and that she will find her own way.

Question 4 asks you to analyze the structure of the passage to identify a theme. The piece appears to be a list of advice given by a mother to her daughter. The list is punctuated by semicolons, giving it the feel of a nonstop rant. The daughter tries to defend herself against the accusation that she sings benna on Sunday, but she is given time for only one brief statement—a statement that is all but lost in the midst of the torrent. This structure suggests several possible themes:

> The mother's demands and criticism silence the girl and will likely lead the girl to reject her mother's ways.
>
> Children learn by imitation. If a mother is too busy talking and giving advice to listen to her daughter, the daughter will be too busy with her own thoughts to listen to the advice.

2.3 Providing an Objective Summary

Review

When you **summarize** a literary work, you provide a brief overview in your own words of its major ideas or events. You omit unimportant details, and focus instead on major ideas and key details that support these ideas.

A good summary is **objective**, or told without opinion statements. It can help you zero in on the major theme or themes of a literary work.

As you read a text, underline and write notes on the key ideas and details. Then retell these ideas and details in a brief summary.

> **Key Terms**
>
> **objective:** not influenced by personal feelings or opinions.
>
> **summarize:** condensing a literary work's main ideas and events into shorter paragraphs, sentences, or phrases.

Check Understanding

Notice the way one student underlines key details and jots down main ideas to prepare for writing a summary of a passage from the excerpt below.

from The Cherry Orchard

Anton Chekhov

1. **Anya**. What have you done to me, Peter? I don't love the cherry orchard as I used to. I loved it so tenderly, I thought there was no better place in the world than our orchard.

2. **Trofimov**. All Russia is our orchard. The land is great and beautiful, there are many marvelous places in it. [Pause] Think, Anya, your grandfather, your great-grandfather, and all your ancestors were serf-owners, they owned living souls. Now, doesn't something human look at you from every cherry in the orchard, every leaf and every branch? Don't you hear voices...? Oh, it's awful, your orchard is terrible; and when in the evening or at night you walk through the orchard, then the old bark on the trees sheds a dim light and the old cherry trees seem to be dreaming of all that was a hundred, two hundred years ago, and are oppressed by their heavy visions. Still, we've left those two hundred years behind us. So far we've gained nothing at all—we don't yet know what the past is to be to us–we only philosophize, we complain that we are dull, or we drink vodka. For it's so clear that in order to begin to live in the present we must first redeem the past, and that can only be done by suffering, by strenuous, uninterrupted labor. Understand that, Anya.

Notes

The cherry orchard is a symbol of Russia's past.

The past was a time of injustice owing to the institution of serfdom.

Activity 2.3 Reread the excerpt above. Highlight and annotate details. Then write a brief summary of the passage on the lines below. Share your summary with a partner.

Toolbox

The student writer in the example above zeros in on key points, leaving out unimportant details as well as personal opinions and ideas. These notes will later help the writer determine the main themes of the play. As you read literary works, underline significant details and jot down key words and phrases. Then create a brief summary of what you've read.

Try It

Directions: Read paragraphs 1 and 2 of Nadine Gordimer's story "The Moment the Gun Went Off" and answer the questions that follow. Then compare your responses with those in the Review It section that follows.

from The Moment the Gun Went Off

by Nadine Gordimer

Notes

1. Marais Van der Vyver shot one of his farm labourers, dead.

2. An accident. There are accidents with guns every day of the week: children playing a fatal game with a father's revolver in the cities where guns are domestic objects, and hunting mishaps like this one, in the country. But these won't be reported all over the world. Marais Van der Vyver knows his will be. He knows that the story of the Afrikaner farmer—a regional Party leader and Commandant of the local security commando—he, shooting a black man who worked for him will fit exactly their version of South Africa. It's made for them. They'll be able to use it in their boycott and divestment campaigns. It'll be another piece of evidence in their truth about the country. The papers at home will quote the story as it has appeared in the overseas press, and in the back-and-forth he and the black man will become those crudely-drawn figures on anti-apartheid banners, units in statistics of white brutality against the blacks quoted at United Nations—he, whom they will gleefully call "a leading member" of the ruling Party.

5. State in your own words two key details that reveal the narrator's attitude toward the farm worker's death.

____

____

____

____

____

6. Write an objective summary of paragraphs 1 and 2. Then use your summary to infer the main idea of the passage.

____

____

____

____

Question 5 directs you to retell in your own words two key details from the passage that reveal the narrator's attitude toward the farm worker's death. Two key details are:

The narrator compares the accident to other types of freak accidents involving guns to make it seem routine and insignificant.

The narrator exhibits little emotion about the death itself. He is more worried about the negative publicity the death of the farm worker will bring to the South African system of apartheid.

Question 6 directs you to provide a brief summary of the passage and tell what it reveals about the main idea. One possible response follows.

An Afrikaner farmer accidentally kills one of the black workers on his farm. The narrator of the story, who seems to be a friend, is more concerned with how the death of the farm worker will make South Africa look in the eyes of other countries than he is with the death itself. The main idea is the farm worker is ultimately the victim of the system of apartheid.

Strategies for Close Reading of Literary Text

Use the following strategies to successfully identify themes, analyze their development, and provide objective summaries of literary text.

- Look for and underline details in a text that strike you as insightful or profound.
- Underline details about time, place, and social conditions in a literary work.
- Take notes in the margin about the main characters, their inner thoughts, motives, and actions to help you draw conclusions about theme.
- Synthesize what you learn about the setting, character, and plot to determine the theme.
- Underline key details, words, and phrases to write brief summaries of text. Try to omit all personal feelings and opinions as you write.

Test-Taking Tips

- Get in the habit of supporting your answers with evidence from the text. Try to use a wide range of evidence to support your analysis.
- Reread the question after you have completed a response to make sure you have addressed each part of it. If you discover an omission, revise that section of your response.
- Try to avoid overused words and phrases in your response. Look for words that will enable you to be as specific as you can.
- Proofread your response to make sure it contains no punctuation, grammatical, or spelling errors.

Chapter Review

Directions: Read the excerpt from F. Scott Fitzgerald's story "Bernice Bobs Her Hair" and answer the questions that follow.

from Bernice Bobs Her Hair

by F. Scott Fitzgerald

Notes

1. After dark on Saturday night one could stand on the first tee of the golf-course and see the country-club windows as a yellow expanse over a very black and wavy ocean. The waves of this ocean, so to speak, were the heads of many curious caddies, a few of the more ingenious chauffeurs, the golf professional's deaf sister—and there were usually several stray, diffident waves who might have rolled inside had they so desired. This was the gallery.

2. The balcony was inside. It consisted of the circle of wicker chairs that lined the wall of the combination clubroom and ballroom. At these Saturday-night dances it was largely feminine; a great babel of middle-aged ladies with sharp eyes and icy hearts behind lorgnettes[1] and large bosoms. The main function of the balcony was critical. It occasionally showed grudging admiration, but never approval, for it is well known among ladies over thirty-five that when the younger set dance in the summer-time it is with the very worst intentions in the world, and if they are not bombarded with stony eyes stray couples will dance weird barbaric interludes in the corners, and the more popular, more dangerous, girls will sometimes be kissed in the parked limousines of unsuspecting dowagers.

3. But, after all, this critical circle is not close enough to the stage to see the actors' faces and catch the subtler byplay. It can only frown and lean, ask questions and make satisfactory deductions from its set of postulates, such as the one which states that every young man with a large income leads the life of a hunted partridge. It never really appreciates the drama of the shifting, semicruel world of adolescence. No; boxes, orchestra-circle, principals, and chorus are represented by the medley of faces and voices that sway to the plaintive African rhythm of Dyer's dance orchestra.

4. From sixteen-year-old Otis Ormonde, who has two more years at Hill School, to G. Reece Stoddard, over whose bureau at home hangs a Harvard law diploma; from little Madeleine Hogue, whose hair still feels strange and uncomfortable on top of her head, to Bessie MacRae, who has been the life of the party a little too long—more than ten years—the medley is not only the center of the stage but contains the only people capable of getting an unobstructed view of it.

5. With a flourish and a bang the music stops. The couples exchange artificial, effortless smiles, facetiously repeat "la-de-da-da dum-dum," and then the clatter of young feminine voices soars over the burst of clapping.

1 lorgnette: a pair of opera glasses held to one's eyes with a handle

6. A few disappointed stags caught in midfloor as they had been about to cut in subsided listlessly back to the walls, because this was not like the riotous Christmas dances—these summer hops were considered just pleasantly warm and exciting, where even the younger marrieds rose and performed ancient waltzes and terrifying fox trots to the tolerant amusement of their younger brothers and sisters.

7. Warren McIntyre, who casually attended Yale, being one of the unfortunate stags, felt in his dinner-coat pocket for a cigarette and strolled out onto the wide, semidark veranda, where couples were scattered at tables, filling the lantern-hung night with vague words and hazy laughter. He nodded here and there at the less absorbed and as he passed each couple some half-forgotten fragment of a story played in his mind, for it was not a large city and every one was Who's Who to every one else's past. There, for example, were Jim Strain and Ethel Demorest, who had been privately engaged for three years. Every one knew that as soon as Jim managed to hold a job for more than two months she would marry him. Yet how bored they both looked, and how wearily Ethel regarded Jim sometimes, as if she wondered why she had trained the vines of her affection on such a wind-shaken poplar.

8. Warren was nineteen and rather pitying with those of his friends who hadn't gone East to college. But, like most boys, he bragged tremendously about the girls of his city when he was away from it. There was Genevieve Ormonde, who regularly made the rounds of dances, house-parties, and football games at Princeton, Yale, Williams, and Cornell; there was black-eyed Roberta Dillon, who was quite as famous to her own generation as Hiram Johnson or Ty Cobb; and, of course, there was Marjorie Harvey, who besides having a fairylike face and a dazzling, bewildering tongue was already justly celebrated for having turned five cart-wheels in succession during the last pump-and-slipper dance at New Haven.

9. Warren, who had grown up across the street from Marjorie, had long been "crazy about her." Sometimes she seemed to reciprocate his feeling with a faint gratitude, but she had tried him by her infallible test and informed him gravely that she did not love him. Her test was that when she was away from him she forgot him and had affairs with other boys. Warren found this discouraging, especially as Marjorie had been making little trips all summer, and for the first two or three days after each arrival home he saw great heaps of mail on the Harveys' hall table addressed to her in various masculine handwritings. To make matters worse, all during the month of August she had been visited by her cousin Bernice from Eau Claire, and it seemed impossible to see her alone. It was always necessary to hunt round and find some one to take care of Bernice. As August waned this was becoming more and more difficult.

Notes

Notes

10. Much as Warren worshiped Marjorie, he had to admit that Cousin Bernice was sorta dopeless. She was pretty, with dark hair and high color, but she was no fun on a party. Every Saturday night he danced a long arduous duty dance with her to please Marjorie, but he had never been anything but bored in her company.

11. "Warren"—a soft voice at his elbow broke in upon his thoughts, and he turned to see Marjorie, flushed and radiant as usual. She laid a hand on his shoulder and a glow settled almost imperceptibly over him.

12. "Warren," she whispered, "do something for me—dance with Bernice. She's been stuck with little Otis Ormonde for almost an hour."

13. Warren's glow faded.

14. "Why—sure," he answered half-heartedly.

15. "You don't mind, do you? I'll see that you don't get stuck."

16. "'Sall right."

17. Marjorie smiled—that smile that was thanks enough.

18. "You're an angel, and I'm obliged loads."

19. With a sigh the angel glanced round the veranda, but Bernice and Otis were not in sight. He wandered back inside, and there in front of the women's dressing-room he found Otis in the center of a group of young men who were convulsed with laughter. Otis was brandishing a piece of timber he had picked up, and discoursing volubly.

20. "She's gone in to fix her hair," he announced wildly. "I'm waiting to dance another hour with her."

21. Their laughter was renewed.

22. "Why don't some of you cut in?" cried Otis resentfully. "She likes more variety."

23. "Why, Otis," suggested a friend, "you've just barely got used to her."

24. "Why the two-by-four, Otis?" inquired Warren, smiling.

25. "The two-by-four? Oh, this? This is a club. When she comes out I'll hit her on the head and knock her in again."

26. Warren collapsed on a settee and howled with glee.

27. "Never mind, Otis," he articulated finally. "I'm relieving you this time."

28. Otis simulated a sudden fainting attack and handed the stick to Warren.

29. "If you need it, old man," he said hoarsely.

30. No matter how beautiful or brilliant a girl may be, the reputation of not being frequently cut in on makes her position at a dance unfortunate. Perhaps boys prefer her company to that of the butterflies with whom they dance a dozen times an evening, but youth in this jazz-nourished generation is temperamentally restless, and the idea of fox-trotting more than one full fox trot with the same girl is distasteful, not to say odious. When it comes to several dances and the intermissions between she can be quite sure that a young man, once relieved, will never tread on her wayward toes again.

31. Warren danced the next full dance with Bernice, and finally, thankful for the intermission, he led her to a table on the veranda. There was a moment's silence while she did unimpressive things with her fan.

32. "It's hotter here than in Eau Claire," she said.

33. Warren stifled a sigh and nodded. It might be for all he knew or cared. He wondered idly whether she was a poor conversationalist because she got no attention or got no attention because she was a poor conversationalist.

34. "You going to be here much longer?" he asked, and then turned rather red. She might suspect his reasons for asking.

35. "Another week," she answered, and stared at him as if to lunge at his next remark when it left his lips.

36. Warren fidgeted. Then with a sudden charitable impulse he decided to try part of his line on her. He turned and looked at her eyes.

37. "You've got an awfully kissable mouth," he began quietly.

38. This was a remark that he sometimes made to girls at college proms when they were talking in just such half dark as this. Bernice distinctly jumped. She turned an ungraceful red and became clumsy with her fan. No one had ever made such a remark to her before.

39. "Fresh!"—the word had slipped out before she realized it, and she bit her lip. Too late she decided to be amused, and offered him a flustered smile.

40. Warren was annoyed. Though not accustomed to have that remark taken seriously, still it usually provoked a laugh or a paragraph of sentimental banter. And he hated to be called fresh, except in a joking way. His charitable impulse died and he switched the topic.

41. "Jim Strain and Ethel Demorest sitting out as usual," he commented.

42. This was more in Bernice's line, but a faint regret mingled with her relief as the subject changed. Men did not talk to her about kissable mouths, but she knew that they talked in some such way to other girls.

43. "Oh, yes," she said, and laughed. "I hear they've been mooning round for years without a red penny. Isn't it silly?"

44. Warren's disgust increased. Jim Strain was a close friend of his brother's, and anyway he considered it bad form to sneer at people for not having money. But Bernice had had no intention of sneering. She was merely nervous.

Notes

Questions 1–5: Choose the best answer or write your response on the lines.

1. Placed in the context of the rest of the text, the thematic purpose of the first three paragraphs is to

   Ⓐ draw a distinction between those who watch and those who act.

   Ⓑ draw a distinction between the older and younger generations.

   Ⓒ draw distinctions between the lower, middle, and upper classes of the town.

   Ⓓ show the overarching influence of jazz on the youth culture of the time.

2. Cite and explain two details that support your answer to question 1.

3. One of the themes common to the fiction of F. Scott Fitzgerald is that of youth. Based on evidence in the text, how would you describe the mood and lived experience of the young people at the heart of the story? Support your answer with evidence from the text.

4. Another theme at the heart of "Bernice Bobs Her Hair" is competition. Cite and explain two examples from the passage that foreshadow this theme.

5. Write an objective summary of the passage.

Chapter 3 Author Choices (RL.11–12.3)

An author has many choices as he or she starts to compose a story or drama. Where will the action take place? How will events be presented? How will characters be introduced and developed? The answers to these and other similar questions has great impact on the finished story. This chapter addresses the following aspects related to author choices.

3.1 Analyzing setting
3.2 Analyzing plot development
3.3 Analyzing character development

3.1 Analyzing Setting

Review

Setting is the time and place of a story or drama. The author may directly state the setting in the text or present clues about the setting through description and dialogue. Authors often choose settings that develop characters, themes, or the plot. For example, to explore the theme of self-reliance and survival, an author may choose to set the story in a harsh environment, such as a desert or a storm at sea.

Beside the physical environment, the setting will also establish the **cultural context**, or the society in which the characters live and how that society influences, or even determines the beliefs and actions of the characters. The cultural context is rarely stated directly.

For comic effect, an author may deliberately insert an **anachronism** into a story. An anachronism is a detail out of place for the setting. For example, a monk with a Brooklyn accent in a story set in medieval France would be anachronistic.

Setting is frequently used to establish the **mood** or atmosphere of a story or poem. The opening lines of Edgar Allan Poe's poem "The Raven," for example, establish a gloomy and melancholy mood common to so much of his poetry and fiction:

> Once upon a midnight dreary, while I pondered weak and weary,
> Over many a quaint and curious volume of forgotten lore,
> . . .
> Ah, distinctly I remember it was in the bleak December,
> And each separate dying ember wrought its ghost upon the floor.

Key Terms

anachronism: a detail out of place for the setting. Anachronisms are sometimes employed for comic purposes.

cultural context: the society in which the characters of the story belong.

mood: the atmosphere or impression that is evoked by a literary work.

Toolbox

As you read a text—

- Underline or highlight important details about the setting. These details and notes will help form a big picture of the story's time and place.
- Ask the following questions about the setting: What time period is shown? Where are the characters at the beginning of the story versus the end? What mood is suggested by the setting (e.g., ominous, mysterious, hopeful, etc.)? Does the setting somehow keep the characters from attaining their goals? Answering these questions will allow you to analyze how the setting impacts the story or drama.

Check Understanding

Notice the way one reader responds to the opening paragraphs of "The Reader" by Bernhard Schlink.

from The Reader

by Bernhard Schlink

1. When I was fifteen, I got hepatitis. It started in the autumn and lasted until spring. As the old year darkened and turned colder, I got weaker and weaker. Things didn't start to improve until the new year. January was warm, and my mother moved my bed out onto the balcony. I saw sky, sun, clouds, and heard the voices of children playing in the courtyard. As dusk came one evening in February, there was the sound of a blackbird singing.

2. The first time I ventured outside, it was to go from Blumenstrasse, where we lived on the second floor of a massive turn-of-the-century building, to Bahnhofstrasse.

3. That's where I'd thrown up on the way home from school one day the previous October. I'd been feeling weak for days, in a way that was completely new to me. Every step was an effort. When I was faced with stairs either at home or at school, my legs would hardly carry me. I had no appetite.

Notes

The scene starts in autumn.

The scene seems restful with the narrator hearing children playing and seeing the sky, sun, and clouds.

Activity 3.1 The time of the scene is autumn to spring. What hints about the place are supplied? Is there a distinctive mood? Share your responses with a partner.

Try It

Directions: Read the opening of the short story below and answer the questions that follow.

from The Kiss

by Kate Chopin

	Notes

1. It was still quite light out of doors, but inside with the curtains drawn and the smoldering fire sending out a dim, uncertain glow, the room was full of deep shadows.

2. Brantain sat in one of these shadows; it had overtaken him and he did not mind. The obscurity lent him courage to keep his eyes fastened as ardently as he liked upon the girl who sat in the firelight.

3. She was very handsome, with a certain fine, rich coloring that belongs to the healthy brune[1] type. She was quite composed, as she idly stroked the satiny coat of the cat that lay curled in her lap, and she occasionally sent a slow glance into the shadow where her companion sat.

1 brune: brunette

1. Which word or phrase best describes the mood?

Ⓐ indoors

Ⓑ dark

Ⓒ romantic

Ⓓ full of shadows

2. Cite at least two details from the text that contribute to the mood. Briefly explain your choice.

____

____

____

____

____

Question 1 asks you to identify the word that best describes the mood of the story. Choices A, B, and D are words that describe the setting, but they are not descriptive of the mood. Choice C, romantic, is the best choice because it describes the overall effect created by the details described by the other choices.

Question 2 asks you cite and explain two details from the text that contribute to the mood. One such detail is "inside with the curtains drawn and the smoldering fire sending out a dim, uncertain glow, the room was full of deep shadows." The drawn curtains and deep shadows in the room show an intimate setting. The glow of the firelight is another detail that adds to the mood. A darkened room, lit mainly by firelight, can suggest a romantic mood.

3.2 Analyzing Plot Development

Review

Plot is the sequence of significant events in a story. A typical plot follows a recognizable pattern of *beginning*, *complication*, *crisis*, and *ending*.

In the **beginning**, the scene is set and the routines of everyday life are described. In the **complication**, everyday life is disrupted, creating a **conflict**. After one or more dramatic turns and subplots, the conflict reaches its peak in the *crisis*, or **climax**. In the **ending**, or **denouement**, comes the resolution—the establishment of a "new normal" based on the fallout of the crisis.

Many stories are told in **chronological order** in which events occur in sequence. Frequently, however, authors employ techniques that disrupt normal time order. In a **flashback**, events that occurred before the time of the story are narrated—perhaps in the form of a memory, a dream, a story within a story, or direct narration. In **foreshadowing**, events to come are hinted at or prepared for. Foreshadowing is often employed to create anticipation or suspense.

Key Terms

conflict: a problem or issue a character must solve or overcome. A conflict may be internal or external.

flashback: an interruption of present action to describe events that transpired before the time of the story.

foreshadowing: hints about future events.

resolution: the ending, the point in a story or drama when the conflict is resolved and complications are unraveled. Also known as denouement.

story within a story: a literary device in which a character in a narrative tells a story.

Check Understanding

Notice how events moves the story forward in this excerpt from *The Reader*.

4. I was ashamed of being so weak. I was even more ashamed when I threw up. That was another thing that had never happened to me before. My mouth was suddenly full, I tried to swallow everything down again, and clenched my teeth with my hand in front of my mouth, but it all burst out of my mouth anyway straight through my fingers. I leaned against the wall of the building, looked down at the vomit around my feet, and retched something clear and sticky.

5. When rescue came, it was almost an assault. The woman seized my arm and pulled me through the dark entrance into the courtyard. Up above there were lines strung from window to window, loaded with laundry. Wood was stacked in the courtyard; in an open workshop a saw screamed and shavings flew. The woman turned on the tap, washed my hand first, and then cupped both of hers and threw water in my face. I dried myself with a handkerchief.

6. 'Get that one!' There were two pails standing by the tap: she grabbed one and filled it. I took the other one, filled it, and followed her through the entrance. She swung her arm, the water sluiced down across the walk and washed the vomit into the gutter. Then she took my pail and sent a second wave of water across the walk.

Notes

The narrator vomits for the first time near a building. He feels ashamed of his weakness.

The narrator describes his rescue as "almost an assault." This word choice makes the rescue seem sudden and forceful.

***Activity* 3.2** Highlight and annotate events that create suspense. Share your notes with a partner.

Toolbox

Plot and Character When considering the question of plot, look beyond the sequence of events. Look for the effects events have on the main characters. The heart of a story resides in the changes—or lack of changes—the main character experiences.

Try It

Directions: Read the paragraphs from "The Kiss" and answer the questions that follow.

from The Kiss

by Kate Chopin

1. She was very handsome, with a certain fine, rich coloring. . . . She was quite composed, as she idly stroked the satiny coat of the cat that lay curled in her lap, and she occasionally sent a slow glance into the shadow where her companion sat. They were talking low, of indifferent things which plainly were not the things that occupied their thoughts. She knew that he loved her—a frank, blustering fellow without guile enough to conceal his feelings, and no desire to do so. For two weeks past he had sought her society eagerly and persistently. She was confidently waiting for him to declare himself and she meant to accept him. The rather insignificant and unattractive Brantain was enormously rich; and she liked and required the entourage which wealth could give her.

2. During one of the pauses between their talk of the last tea and the next reception the door opened and a young man entered whom Brantain knew quite well. The girl turned her face toward him. A stride or two brought him to her side, and bending over her chair—before she could suspect his intention, for she did not realize that he had not seen her visitor—he pressed an ardent, lingering kiss upon her lips.

3. Brantain slowly arose; so did the girl arise, but quickly, and the newcomer stood between them, a little amusement and some defiance struggling with the confusion in his face.

4. "I believe," stammered Brantain, "I see that I have stayed too long. I—I had no idea— that is, I must wish you good-by." He was clutching his hat with both hands, and probably did not perceive that she was extending her hand to him, her presence of mind had not completely deserted her; but she could not have trusted herself to speak.

Notes

3. The main purpose for the background information in paragraph 1 is to—

Ⓐ establish the relationship between Brantain and the girl.

Ⓑ establish that the girl is only interested in Brantain's money.

Ⓒ explain the girl's position on marriage.

Ⓓ explain why Brantain is a good catch.

4. Identify events in the story that complicate the plot. Briefly explain.

____

____

____

____

____

____

Question 3 asks you to identify the purpose of the background information in paragraph 1. Although the paragraph describes the girl as wanting to marry Brantain for his wealth, this detail does not reveal the overall purpose of the paragraph. The paragraph includes the sentence, "For two weeks past he had sought her society eagerly and persistently." This sentence indicates that the purpose is to establish the relationship between the two characters. Choice A is the best choice.

Question 4 asks you to identify events in the story that complicate the plot. The first complication is when the young man enters the room and kisses the girl. This action flusters all of the characters in the story. The young man is confused but defiant about the kiss, the girl is speechless, and Brantain is reduced to a stutter. Brantain's hasty exit is the second complication. The girl reaches out her hand to him, but Brantain fails to see it or ignores it as he leaves the room.

3.3 Analyzing Character Development

Review

Characters are the people (or animals) in a story or drama. The main character is at the center of the plot; secondary characters play supporting roles. The plot usually revolves around the main character or *protagonist*. The main character in "The Reader" is the narrator.

Characters can be *flat* or *round*. A flat character is one who has one prominent trait such as greed, jealousy, or naiveté. As such, a flat character is usually predictable and does not change or develop during the course of a story. A round character, on the other hand, is complex, has many sides or aspects to his or her personality, and may change in surprising ways.

Characterization is the manner in which the author reveals information about characters. Characters can be presented through the narrator's description; through the character's thoughts, actions, and speeches; or through what other characters say and think about the character.

When analyzing a character, consider his or her *motivation*—that which drives him or her to act (or not to act). Also consider if and how the character changes. The changes and what the character learns (or fails to learn) provide key entry points to the heart of the story and the main message or theme.

Key Terms

characterization: the means by which the author reveals character.

flat character: a character in a story with one prominent trait. A flat character typically does not develop during the course of the story.

motivation: the reason a character acts or behaves in a certain way.

protagonist: the primary character or hero in a literary work.

round character: a complex character who has many aspects to his or her personality. A round character will typically change during the course of the story.

secondary character: a subordinate or minor character in a story.

Check Understanding

Notice how the author reveals details about the woman's character in this excerpt from *The Reader*.

1. When she straightened up, she saw I was crying. 'Hey, kid,' she said, startled, 'hey, kid' — and took me in her arms. I wasn't much taller than she was . . . I smelled the sourness of my own breath and felt a sudden sweat as she held me, and didn't know where to look. I stopped crying.

2. She asked me where I lived, put the pails down in the entrance, and took me home, walking beside me holding my satchel in one hand and my arm in the other. It's no great distance from Bahnhofstrasse to the Blumenstrasse. She walked quickly, and her decisiveness helped me to keep pace with her. She said goodbye in front of our building.

Notes

The woman's use of the word "kid" tells that she might be older.

Activity 3.3 Underline and annotate at least two instances of characterization in the paragraphs above.

> **Toolbox**
>
> **Read between the lines.** Readers must make inferences about characters based on their actions, thoughts, and interactions with other characters. How a character says something is often just as important as what a character says. For instance, if Character One uses soothing words and a gentle tone when addressing Character Two, you might infer that Character One is trying to avoid upsetting Character Two.

The way a character interacts with other characters reveals character relationships. For example, the fact that the woman calls the narrator "kid" suggests she is older than he is.

Try It

Directions: Read these paragraphs from "The Kiss" and answer the questions that follow.

from The Kiss

by Kate Chopin

1. "Hang me if I saw him sitting there, Nattie! I know it's deuced awkward for you. But I hope you'll forgive me this once—this very first break. Why, what's the matter?"

2. "Don't touch me; don't come near me," she returned angrily. "What do you mean by entering the house without ringing?"

3. "I came in with your brother, as I often do," he answered coldly, in self-justification. "We came in the side way. He went upstairs and I came in here hoping to find you. The explanation is simple enough and ought to satisfy you that the misadventure was unavoidable. But do say that you forgive me, Nathalie," he entreated, softening.

4. "Forgive you! You don't know what you are talking about. Let me pass. It depends upon—a good deal whether I ever forgive you."

Notes

Notes

5. At that next reception which she and Brantain had been talking about she approached the young man with a delicious frankness of manner when she saw him there.

6. "Will you let me speak to you a moment or two, Mr. Brantain?" she asked with an engaging but perturbed smile. He seemed extremely unhappy; but when she took his arm and walked away with him, seeking a retired corner, a ray of hope mingled with the almost comical misery of his expression. She was apparently very outspoken.

7. "Perhaps I should not have sought this interview, Mr. Brantain; but—but, oh, I have been very uncomfortable, almost miserable since that little encounter the other afternoon. When I thought how you might have misinterpreted it, and believed things"—hope was plainly gaining the ascendancy over misery in Brantain's round, guileless face— "Of course, I know it is nothing to you, but for my own sake I do want you to understand that Mr. Harvy is an intimate friend of long standing. Why, we have always been like cousins—like brother and sister, I may say. He is my brother's most intimate associate and often fancies that he is entitled to the same privileges as the family. Oh, I know it is absurd, uncalled for, to tell you this; undignified even," she was almost weeping, "but it makes so much difference to me what you think of—of me."

8. Her voice had grown very low and agitated. The misery had all disappeared from Brantain's face.

9. "Then you do really care what I think, Miss Nathalie? May I call you Miss Nathalie?" They turned into a long, dim corridor that was lined on either side with tall, graceful plants. They walked slowly to the very end of it. When they turned to retrace their steps Brantain's face was radiant and hers was triumphant.

5. Using details from the excerpt as support, describe how Brantain's feelings change. Write your answer on the lines below.

____

____

____

6. How does Nathalie influence Brantain's emotional change? Write your answer on the lines below.

____

____

____

____

Question 5 asks you to use details from the passage to show how Brantain's feelings change. Consider this response, which combines analysis of and details from the text.

> At first, Brantain is "extremely unhappy." However, after Nathalie takes him aside to explain that she and Mr. Harvy are like cousins, his feelings experience a turnaround: "The misery had all disappeared from Brantain's face." Brantain's feelings rebound from misery to radiant happiness by the end of the excerpt.

Question 6 asks you to explain how Nathalie influences Brantain's change of emotion. In this response, you must build upon your analysis of how Brantain's feelings change to explain how Nathalie affects this change. Consider this response, which combines references to details with interpretation.

> Nathalie has a direct effect on Brantain's feelings. When she sees Brantain at the reception, she asks him to grant her a private audience. At this point, "a ray of hope mingled with the almost comical misery of his expression." Already, Nathalie has had an effect on his feelings. After Nathalie explains her relationship with Mr. Harvy, Brantain appears much happier. In fact, the more upset Nathalie appears during her explanation, the happier Brantain becomes. Nathalie's voice is described as "low and agitated," while "[t]he misery had all disappeared from Brantain's face." In short, Nathalie and her explanation cause Brantain's change of heart.

Strategies for Analyzing Setting, Plot, and Character

Use the following strategies as you analyze the setting, plot, and characters in literary texts.

- Underline key details about the setting.
- Underline important events that move the plot forward.
- Underline descriptions and dialogue that reveal character.
- The margin is a good place to add notes such as inferences and brief interpretations.
- Once you understand the setting, plot, and characters in the text, watch for new information that confirms or changes your analyses.

Test-Taking Tips

- Good literature rarely includes unnecessary details. Think about the meaning of the details as you read. They may foreshadow what will happen later, provide important information about the setting, or describe characters' motivations.
- To understand the effect of the plot, setting, and character on a story, imagine what the story would be like if any these elements were changed.
- Make a short outline before you begin a written response, making sure to address each part of the question. Remember to use only those details that help explain your response.

Chapter Review

Read the short story and answer the questions that follow.

from A White Heron

by Sarah Orne Jewett

Notes

1. . . . It was a surprise to find so clean and comfortable a little dwelling in this New England wilderness. The young man had known the horrors of its most primitive housekeeping, and the dreary squalor of that level of society which does not rebel at the companionship of hens. This was the best thrift of an old-fashioned farmstead, though on such a small scale that it seemed like a hermitage. He listened eagerly to the old woman's quaint talk, he watched Sylvia's pale face and shining gray eyes with ever growing enthusiasm, and insisted that this was the best supper he had eaten for a month, and afterward the new-made friends sat down in the door-way together while the moon came up.

2. Soon it would be berry-time, and Sylvia was a great help at picking. The cow was a good milker, though a plaguy thing to keep track of, the hostess gossiped frankly, adding presently that she had buried four children, so Sylvia's mother, and a son (who might be dead) in California were all the children she had left. "Dan, my boy, was a great hand to go gunning," she explained sadly. "I never wanted for pa'tridges or gray squer'ls while he was to home. He's been a great wand'rer, I expect, and he's no hand to write letters. There, I don't blame him, I'd ha' seen the world myself if it had been so I could.

3. "Sylvy takes after him," the grandmother continued affectionately, after a minute's pause. "There ain't a foot o' ground she don't know her way over, and the wild creaturs counts her one o' themselves. Squer'ls she'll tame to come an' feed right out o' her hands, and all sorts o' birds. Last winter she got the jay-birds to bangeing here, and I believe she'd 'a' scanted herself of her own meals to have plenty to throw out amongst 'em, if I hadn't kep' watch. Anything but crows, I tell her, I'm willin' to help support—though Dan he had a tamed one o' them that did seem to have reason same as folks. It was round here a good spell after he went away. Dan an' his father they didn't hitch, —but he never held up his head ag'in after Dan had dared him an' gone off."

4. The guest did not notice this hint of family sorrows in his eager interest in something else.

5. "So Sylvy knows all about birds, does she?" he exclaimed, as he looked round at the little girl who sat, very demure but increasingly sleepy, in the moonlight. "I am making a collection of birds myself. I have been at it ever since I was a boy." (Mrs. Tilley smiled.) "There are two or three very rare ones I have been hunting for these five years. I mean to get them on my own ground if they can be found."

6. "Do you cage 'em up?" asked Mrs. Tilley doubtfully, in response to this enthusiastic announcement.

7. "Oh no, they're stuffed and preserved, dozens and dozens of them," said the ornithologist, "and I have shot or snared every one myself. I caught a glimpse of a white heron a few miles from here on Saturday, and I have followed it in this direction. They have never been found in this district at all. The little white heron, it is," and he turned again to look at Sylvia with the hope of discovering that the rare bird was one of her acquaintances.

8. But Sylvia was watching a hop-toad in the narrow footpath.

9. "You would know the heron if you saw it," the stranger continued eagerly. "A queer tall white bird with soft feathers and long thin legs. And it would have a nest perhaps in the top of a high tree, made of sticks, something like a hawk's nest."

10. Sylvia's heart gave a wild beat; she knew that strange white bird, and had once stolen softly near where it stood in some bright green swamp grass, away over at the other side of the woods. There was an open place where the sunshine always seemed strangely yellow and hot, where tall, nodding rushes grew, and her grandmother had warned her that she might sink in the soft black mud underneath and never be heard of more. Not far beyond were the salt marshes just this side the sea itself, which Sylvia wondered and dreamed much about, but never had seen, whose great voice could sometimes be heard above the noise of the woods on stormy nights.

11. "I can't think of anything I should like so much as to find that heron's nest," the handsome stranger was saying. "I would give ten dollars to anybody who could show it to me," he added desperately, "and I mean to spend my whole vacation hunting for it if need be. Perhaps it was only migrating, or had been chased out of its own region by some bird of prey."

12. Mrs. Tilley gave amazed attention to all this, but Sylvia still watched the toad, not divining, as she might have done at some calmer time, that the creature wished to get to its hole under the door-step, and was much hindered by the unusual spectators at that hour of the evening. No amount of thought, that night, could decide how many wished-for treasures the ten dollars, so lightly spoken of, would buy.

13. The next day the young sportsman hovered about the woods, and Sylvia kept him company, having lost her first fear of the friendly lad, who proved to be most kind and sympathetic. He told her many things about the birds and what they knew and where they lived and what they did with themselves. And he gave her a jack-knife, which she thought as great a treasure as if she were a desert-islander. All day long he did not once make her troubled or afraid except when he brought down some unsuspecting singing creature from its bough. Sylvia would have liked him vastly better without his gun; she could not understand why he killed the very birds he seemed to like so much. But as the day waned, Sylvia still watched the young man with loving admiration. She had never seen anybody so charming and delightful; the woman's heart, asleep in the child, was vaguely thrilled by a dream of love. Some premonition of that great power stirred and swayed these

Notes

young creatures who traversed the solemn woodlands with soft-footed silent care. They stopped to listen to a bird's song; they pressed forward again eagerly, parting the branches — speaking to each other rarely and in whispers; the young man going first and Sylvia following, fascinated, a few steps behind, with her gray eyes dark with excitement.

14. She grieved because the longed-for white heron was elusive, but she did not lead the guest, she only followed, and there was no such thing as speaking first. The sound of her own unquestioned voice would have terrified her — it was hard enough to answer yes or no when there was need of that. At last evening began to fall, and they drove the cow home together, and Sylvia smiled with pleasure when they came to the place where she heard the whistle and was afraid only the night before.

Notes

Questions 1–9: Choose the best answer or write your response on the lines.

1. The overall purpose of the description in the first paragraph is to

Ⓐ suggest a cause and effect.

Ⓑ foreshadow an event.

Ⓒ establish a relationship.

Ⓓ provide a motive.

2. What is the setting?

Ⓐ a farm in New England

Ⓑ an old house in the evening

Ⓒ an overgrown path

Ⓓ a swamp

3. Cite two details from the passage that you could use as evidence to support your answer to question 2. Write them on the lines below.

____

____

____

____

____

____

4. Placed in the context of the rest of the text, Sylvia's willingness to follow the young man around the woods (paragraph 13) reflects

Ⓐ the young man's search for the white heron.

Ⓑ Sylvia's desire to impress the young man.

Ⓒ the young man's inexperience with hunting.

Ⓓ Sylvia's new feelings toward the young man.

5. Explain your answer to question 4 using at least two details from the passage for support.

____

____

____

____

____

6. What complicates Sylvia's feelings toward the young man? Write your answer on the lines below.

____

____

____

____

____

7. In paragraph 2, the author presents Mrs. Tilley as a woman who is

Ⓐ melancholy.

Ⓑ miserable.

Ⓒ exhausted.

Ⓓ frazzled.

8. Which word best describes the character of Sylvia?

Ⓐ childish

Ⓑ dreamy

Ⓒ indifferent

Ⓓ innocent

9. Cite and explain two passages that support your answer to question 8.

Chapter 4 Language & Tone (RL.11–12.4)

Authors have a number of tools at their disposal as they craft their works, including the language itself. This chapter will focus on the following aspects of language that can be exploited in the craft of writing.

4.1 Figurative Language

Review

Figurative language is any use of language that departs from the usual literal meanings of words in order to add strength, fresh expression, imagery, or analogy to writing. Figurative language is often expressed through common **figures of speech**, such as **simile**, **metaphor**, **personification**, and **hyperbole**.

Simile and **metaphor** involve comparisons between two things that are unlike in most ways. In a simile, such as "She is as blind as a bat," a connecting word such as *like* or *as* is used to make the comparison. A metaphor is a direct comparison with no connecting word, as in "Time is a thief."

In **personification** an inanimate object or idea takes on human or animal attributes, as in "The moon waved to me."

Hyperbole is the use of exaggeration to emphasize a point. It is frequently used for comic effect, as in this excerpt from *Stiff Upper Lip, Jeeves* by P. G. Wodehouse. Note the use of a simile in the first hyperbolic description:

> . . . as I felt my way along the wall I collided with what turned out to be a grandfather clock, for the existence of which I had not budgeted, and it toppled over with a sound like the delivery of several tons of coal through the roof of a conservatory. Glass crashed, pulleys and things parted from their moorings, and as I stood trying to separate my heart from the front teeth in which it had become entangled, the lights flashed on and I beheld Sir Watkyn Bassett.

Key Terms

figurative language: language used to create images and to express ideas in vivid, surprising ways.

figure of speech: a literary device.

hyperbole: a figure of speech in which exaggeration is used for emphasis or effect.

metaphor: a figure of speech that makes an implied comparison between things.

personification: a figure of speech in which inanimate objects or ideas are given human or animal attributes.

simile: a figure of speech that makes an explicit comparison between two objects or things.

Toolbox

Identifying metaphors in a literary work can be more challenging than finding similes. Lacking signal words such as *like* or *as,* metaphors make the reader do the work of drawing the connection between unlike things. Get comfortable with metaphors by making a list of examples used in everyday speech, such as "He is the light of my life." Then challenge yourself to look for examples of metaphors as you read. Record them in a writer's notebook.

Check Understanding

Notice the way one reader responds to lines from *Macbeth* by William Shakespeare.

from Macbeth

by William Shakespeare

Lady Macbeth. Infirm of purpose!
Give me the daggers: the sleeping and the dead
Are but as pictures: 'tis the eye of childhood
That fears a painted devil. If he do bleed,
I'll gild the faces of the grooms withal;
For it must seem their guilt.
Knock within.
Macbeth. Whence is that knocking?
How is't with me, when every noise appalls me?
What hands are here? ha! they pluck out mine eyes.
Will all great Neptune's ocean wash this blood
Clean from my hand? No, this my hand will rather
The multitudinous seas incarnadine,
Making the green one red.
Enter Lady Macbeth.
Lady Macbeth. My hands are of your color; but I shame
To wear a heart so white. (*Knock.*) I hear a knocking
At the south entry: retire we to our chamber;
A little water clears us of this deed:
How easy is it, then! Your constancy
Hath left you unattended. (*Knock.*) Hark! more knocking.
Get on your nightgown, lest occasion call us,
And show us to be watchers. Be not lost
So poorly in your thoughts.

Notes

Hyperbole: exaggeration reveals the emotional toll the murder has had on Macbeth.

Activity 4.1 Reread the excerpt above. Highlight and explain at least one other figure of speech in the excerpt. Share your response with a partner.

Try It

Directions: Read the opening stanzas of the poem below and answer the questions that follow. As you read, keep in mind that Eliot uses figurative language to reveal the state of mind of Prufrock.

from The Lovesong of J. Alfred Prufrock

by T. S. Eliot

Notes

Let us go then, you and I,
When the evening is spread out against the sky
Like a patient etherized upon a table;
Let us go, through certain half-deserted streets,
The muttering retreats
Of restless nights in one-night cheap hotels
And sawdust restaurants with oyster-shells:
Streets that follow like a tedious argument
Of insidious intent
To lead you to an overwhelming question. . . .
Oh, do not ask, "What is it?"
Let us go and make our visit.
. . .
The yellow fog that rubs its back upon the window-panes,
The yellow smoke that rubs its muzzle on the window-panes,
Licked its tongue into the corners of the evening,
Lingered upon the pools that stand in drains,
Let fall upon its back the soot that falls from chimneys,
Slipped by the terrace, made a sudden leap,
And seeing that it was a soft October night,
Curled once about the house, and fell asleep.

1. Scholars agree that the poem reveals Prufrock's frame of mind. Based on the figurative language, which choice best expresses Prufrock's mental state?

Ⓐ That he is angry and bitter.

Ⓑ That he is friendly but shy.

Ⓒ That he is humble but vigorous.

Ⓓ That he is unable to act and is lost.

2. Cite evidence from the poem to support your answer to question 1.

3. Interpret the figure of speech in lines 14–21.

____

____

____

____

Question 1 asks you to select the choice that best illustrates Prufrock's inner state. Eliot's choice of words in the lines don't suggest that Prufrock is angry, or friendly or vigorous. Instead, they suggest that Prufrock feels paralyzed, like a patient about to be operated upon, and lonely, like half-deserted streets. Choice D is the best answer.

Question 2 asks you to cite evidence from the poem to support your answer to question 1. Lines 1–3 compare the evening to an etherized patient, that is, a person who is completely unaware and unable to move—unable to act. The simile in lines 4–10 compares the streets to an argument of "insidious intent" that ends not in clarity but in an overwhelming question, that is, that Prufrock is lost.

Question 3 asks you to interpret the figure of speech in lines 14–12. The yellow fog is compared to a cat, rubbing itself on objects, licking its tongue, and curling up to sleep. The image is bleak, in keeping with the sense of loss and paralysis introduced in the first stanza.

4.2 Word Choice

Review

Authors express themselves not only through the stories they choose to tell, but the ways they choose to tell them. Through the words she chooses (**diction**) and the way she uses them (**syntax**), a writer can establish all the rich textures of life, from the formal utterance of a courtroom to the colloquial slang of a playground. Connotation and multiple meaning words are two tools in the writer's diction toolbox.

Connotation refers to the emotional associations a word may carry. For example, the words *slim, svelte* and *scrawny* all have similar denotations, or dictionary meanings: *thin*. The connotations, however, are very different. *Slim* and *Svelte* have positive connotations and might be used to compliment someone who has started exercising at the gym. *Scrawny,* on the other hand, carries a negative connotation. It might be used to describe a person who appears unhealthy or malnourished.

A word's **context** can provide a clue to its connotation. For example, if the word *shady* is used in the context of a picnic spot, it has little if any implied meaning. In the context of a business deal, on the other hand, it carries the implied meaning of something dishonest or unlawful.

Key Terms

connotation: the implied meaning of a word.

context clues: hints provided by the sentences around a word that point to its meaning.

diction: the vocabulary (actual words) used in a piece of writing.

denotation: the literal or dictionary meaning of a word.

multiple meaning word: word with more than one meaning.

syntax: the way in which words are arranged to form phrases, clauses, and sentences.

Writers—especially poets—use **multiple-meaning words** to add subtlety and depth to a text. For example, the word *sleep* in the repeated line at the end of Robert Frost's famous poem "Stopping by Woods on a Snowy Evening" has multiple meanings. Taken literally, "miles to go before I sleep" means that the speaker has miles to go before he reaches a place where he can sleep for the night. The word *sleep* can also mean *death,* in which case the line takes on a more philosophical tone. Both meanings are valid. Indeed, the beauty of the poem is that both meanings exist together at the same time.

Check Understanding

Notice how one reader studies the word choices in the passage from Toni Morrison's novel *Beloved.*

from Beloved

by Toni Morrison

1. White people believed that whatever the manners, under every dark skin was a jungle. Swift unnavigable waters, swinging screaming baboons, sleeping snakes, red gums ready for their sweet white blood. In a way . . . they were right. . . . But it wasn't the jungle blacks brought with them to this place. . . . It was the jungle whitefolks planted in them. And it grew. It spread . . . until it invaded the whites who had made it. . . . Made them bloody, silly, worse than even they wanted to be, so scared were they of the jungle they had made. The screaming baboon lived under their own white skin; the red gums were their own.

Notes

"Jungle" has the literal meaning of "a land overgrown with dense vegetation." In this context the implied meaning is dangerous and violent emotions.

***Activity* 4.2** Reread the passage above. Highlight and interpret at least two other word choices and their impacts. Share your response with a partner.

Toolbox

Context Clues Look at the text that comes before and after a word to determine the intended meaning. Context can help you determine if an author is using a word for its literal meaning and/or for the emotional associations that it carries. For instance, the imagery in the second sentence of the excerpt from *Beloved* provides details of a literal jungle to heighten the effect of the figurative use of the word "jungle" in the first sentence.

Try It

Directions: Read the excerpt below from Arundhati Roy's *The God of Small Things,* a novel that describes the tragic fall of a village family in India. As you read, consider the meanings of the underlined words. Then answer the questions that follow.

from The God of Small Things

by Arundhati Roy

1. . . . he was offended by her eyes. They behaved as though they belonged to someone else. Someone watching. Looking out of the window at the sea. At a boat in the river. Or a passerby in the mist in a hat.

Notes

2. He was exasperated because he didn't know what that look *meant*. He put it somewhere between indifference and despair. He didn't know that in some places, like the country that Rahel came from, various kinds of despair competed for primacy. And that *personal* despair could never be desperate enough. That something happened when personal turmoil dropped by at the wayside shrine of the vast, violent, circling, driving, ridiculous, insane, unfeasible, public turmoil of a nation. That Big God howled like a hot wind, and demanded obeisance. Then Small God (cozy and contained, private and limited) came away cauterized, laughing numbly at his own temerity. Inured by the confirmation of his own inconsequence, he became resilient and truly indifferent. Nothing mattered much. Nothing much mattered. And the less it mattered, the less it mattered. It was never important enough. Because Worse Things had happened. In the country that she came from, poised forever between the terror of war and the horror of peace, Worse Things kept happening.

3. So Small God laughed a hollow laugh, and skipped away cheerfully. Like a rich boy in shorts. He whistled, kicked stones. The source of his brittle elation was the relative smallness of his misfortune. He climbed into people's eyes and became an exasperating expression.

Notes

4. Which definition best fits the use of the word "insane" as used in paragraph 2, sentence 5?

Ⓐ mentally ill

Ⓑ in a state of extreme distraction

Ⓒ extremely foolish

Ⓓ mentally unstable

5. Which word or phrase from the excerpt is the best context clue for answering question 4?

Ⓐ He was exasperated

Ⓑ hot wind

Ⓒ public turmoil of a nation

Ⓓ laughing numbly at his own temerity

6. The words "contained" and "cauterized" are used to define Small God. Use both the denotation and connotation of these words and the simile in paragraph 3 to write a brief character sketch of Small God.

Question 4 asks you to select the best definition of the word "insane" as used in the excerpt. All four choices can be found in a dictionary, however, choice B is the definition the best fits the context.

Question 5 asks you to select the context clue that best helps determine the answer to question 4. Choice C, public turmoil of a nation, is the best clue.

Question 6 asks you to write a brief character sketch based on the denotations and connotations of the words "contained" and "cauterized" and the simile in paragraph 3. A sample response:

> The Small God is both contained and cauterized. "Contained," as used in the excerpt, means "controlled, restrained." "Cauterized" describes a method of treating wounds in which the affected tissue is burned. The process stops bleeding but also causes the deadening of the tissue. Small God, therefore, has been burned by war. The cauterization has deadened his ability to feel to the point that he no longer cares. Like a rich boy in shorts, he ignores the pain all around him and pretends indifference.

4.3 Tone

Review

Tone refers to the attitude a writer takes toward the subject. Unlike **mood,** which refers to the overall feeling a work evokes in the reader, tone reflects the writer's feelings about a particular character, development, or topic.

The tone of a work can range from positive (admiring, jovial, nostalgic) to negative (angry, insolent, sarcastic). The tone can also be neutral (objective, questioning, meditative), as in a magazine article or the expository introduction of a novel.

Like many aspects of literature, an author's tone is rarely stated directly. It must be inferred from word choice, figurative language, and other context clues.

Tone plays a crucial role in giving the reader insight into how to interpret a work. A satiric tone, for example, may indicate that the author is criticizing an aspect of his or her society.

Key Terms

imagery: words and phrases that appeal to the reader's senses.

mood: the feeling a work evokes in the reader.

tone: a writer's implicit attitude toward a subject or audience.

Toolbox

If you're having trouble determining the tone of a work, try reading it aloud. Is the word choice formal or informal? Are the figures of speech forceful as in the passage by Toni Morrison or are they detached and distancing as in the last paragraph of the passage by Arundhati Roy?

Check Understanding

Notice the way one reader begins to interpret the tone of this passage from Amy Tan's *The Joy Luck Club*.

from The Joy Luck Club

by Amy Tan

1. Now the woman was old. And she had a daughter who grew up speaking only English and swallowing more Coca-Cola than sorrow. For a long time now the woman had wanted to give her daughter the single swan feather and tell her, 'This feather may look worthless, but it comes from afar and carries with it all my good intentions.' And she waited, year after year, until she could tell her daughter this in perfect American English.

Notes

The Coca-Cola detail gives the passage a playful, amusing tone

Activity 4.3 Reread the passage above. Describe the overall tone of the passage. Share your response with a partner.

Try It

Directions: Read the passage below from the short story "The Red Convertible" by Louise Erdrich and answer the questions that follow.

from The Red Convertible

by Louise Erdrich

1. I still see that picture now, as if it tugs at me, whenever I pass that closet door. The picture is very clear in my mind. It was so sunny that day Henry had to squint against the glare. Or maybe the camera Bonita held flashed like a mirror, blinding him, before she snapped the picture. My face is right out in the sun, big and round. But he might have drawn back, because the shadows on his face are deep as holes. There are two shadows curved like little hooks around the ends of his smile, as if to frame it and try to keep it there—that one, first smile that looked like it might have hurt his face. He has his field jacket on and the worn-in clothes he'd come back in and kept wearing ever since. After Bonita took the picture, she went into the house and we got into the car. There was a full cooler in the trunk. We started off, east, toward Pembina and the Red River because Henry said he wanted to see the high water.

Notes

7. Which set of words best describes the tone of the passage?

Ⓐ nostalgic, melancholic, relaxed

Ⓑ direct, fearful, uneasy

Ⓒ tense, fearful, solemn

Ⓓ placid, ambivalent

8. What details, syntax, and word choices help reveal the tone?

____

____

____

____

Question 7 asks you to select the choice that best describes the tone of the passage. Choices B and C are incorrect. There is nothing in the text to suggest fear. Choice D might fit the passage except there doesn't seem to be any ambivalence in the voice. Choice A is the best answer.

Question 8 asks you to point out diction and details that create the tone in the passage. The following helps reveal the tone: informal (Erdrich uses everyday language), nostalgic ("I still see that picture," "it tugs at me," "whenever I pass that closet door," "The picture is very clear in my mind"), melancholic ("the shadows on his face are deep as holes," "two shadows curved like little hooks," "first smile that looked like it might have hurt his face").

Strategies for Close Reading of Literary Text

Use the following strategies to identify and deepen your understanding of figures of speech, tone, and the connotative meanings of words.

- To locate similes in text, look for signal words such as *like* or *as*. For metaphors, search for direct comparisons (often the verb "to be" points to their presence: "The sun is a jewel in the sky").
- As you read, be aware of both the implied and literal meaning of words. Look for any emotional associations a writer might have intended to communicate.
- Search the context of the sentence or paragraph in which an unknown word appears for clues to its meaning(s).
- One way to find the right meaning(s) for a word with multiple meanings is to identify its part of speech. Knowing a word is being used as a noun rather than as a verb will help you nail down its correct meaning.
- Underline diction, images, and syntax that reveal tone in a piece of writing.

Test-Taking Tips

- When composing a written response, make sure to include evidence that supports your ideas.
- Powerful literature often includes figurative language. As you read, underline figures of speech and make notes about their meaning in the margin.
- As you review a written response, make sure that you have used varied syntax. Different types of clauses and sentence structures will make your writing more effective and appealing.

Chapter Review

Directions: Read the poem "Church Going" by Philip Larkin. Then answer the questions that follow.

Church Going

by Philip Larkin

Notes

Once I am sure there's nothing going on
I step inside, letting the door thud shut.
Another church: matting, seats, and stone,
And little books; sprawlings of flowers, cut
For Sunday, brownish now; some brass and stuff
Up at the holy end; the small neat organ;
And a tense, musty, unignorable silence,
Brewed God knows how long. Hatless, I take off
My cycle-clips in awkward reverence.

Move forward, run my hand around the font.
From where I stand, the roof looks almost new –
Cleaned, or restored? Someone would know: I don't.
Mounting the lectern, I peruse a few
Hectoring large-scale verses, and pronounce
'Here endeth' much more loudly than I'd meant.
The echoes snigger briefly. Back at the door
I sign the book, donate an Irish sixpence,
Reflect the place was not worth stopping for.

Yet stop I did: in fact I often do,
And always end much at a loss like this,
Wondering what to look for; wondering, too,
When churches will fall completely out of use
What we shall turn them into, if we shall keep
A few cathedrals chronically on show,
Their parchment, plate and pyx[1] in locked cases,
And let the rest rent-free to rain and sheep.
Shall we avoid them as unlucky places?

Or, after dark, will dubious women come
To make their children touch a particular stone;
Pick simples for a cancer; or on some
Advised night see walking a dead one?
Power of some sort will go on
In games, in riddles, seemingly at random;
But superstition, like belief, must die,
And what remains when disbelief has gone?
Grass, weedy pavement, brambles, buttress, sky,

1 pyx: a box or case used to carry the Eucharist to the sick.

A shape less recognizable each week,
A purpose more obscure. I wonder who
Will be the last, the very last, to seek
This place for what it was; one of the crew
That tap and jot and know what rood-lofts were?
Some ruin-bibber,[2] randy for antique,
Or Christmas-addict, counting on a whiff
Of gown-and-bands and organ-pipes and myrrh?
Or will he be my representative,

Bored, uninformed, knowing the ghostly silt
Dispersed, yet tending to this cross of ground
Through suburb scrub because it held unspilt
So long and equably what since is found
Only in separation – marriage, and birth,
And death, and thoughts of these – for which was built
This special shell? For, though I've no idea
What this accoutred frowsty[3] barn is worth,
It pleases me to stand in silence here;

A serious house on serious earth it is,
In whose blent air all our compulsions meet,
Are recognized, and robed as destinies.
And that much never can be obsolete,
Since someone will forever be surprising
A hunger in himself to be more serious,
And gravitating with it to this ground,
Which, he once heard, was proper to grow wise in,
If only that so many dead lie round.

Notes

2 bibber: one who indulges too much in something
3 accoutred frowsty: outfitted and musty

Questions 1–8: Choose the best answer or write your response on the lines.

1. Which word or phrase best describes the tone in stanza 1 (lines 1–10)?

Ⓐ reverent

Ⓑ secretive

Ⓒ informal

Ⓓ tense

2. Support your answer to question 1 with details from the first stanza.

____

____

____

____

____

3. The denotation of the word "hectoring" (line 14) is "bullying, browbeating, threating." What does this word choice reveal about the speaker's attitude toward the activities that take place in the church?

____

____

____

____

4. Consider the personification in line 16 in the context of the entire poem. Explain two possible meanings of the figure of speech.

____

____

____

____

____

5. Think about the precise meaning of the word "chronically" (line 24) and the details that follow in the next line. Together, what do they suggest about what will happen to the church?

Ⓐ The church will turn into a museum.

Ⓑ The church will turn into a recreation hall.

Ⓒ The church will become part of the natural world.

Ⓓ The church will continue to be a place for Christian worship.

6. The words "dubious" (line 28) and "simples" (line 30) both have multiple meanings. Which meanings do you think Larkin intended for these two words?

Ⓐ of uncertain outcome, foolish people

Ⓑ questionable, medicinal herbs

Ⓒ doubtful, easily understood

Ⓓ hesitant, unmixed things

7. The word "serious" is repeated three times in the poem (lines 55–63). What is the speaker saying about churches and their future through the repeated use of this word?

____

____

____

____

____

____

8. Why do you think Larkin chose the words "church" and "going" for the title of his poem?

____

____

____

____

Chapter 5 Structure of Literature (RL.11–12.5)

Writers of literature are confronted with many structural choices: *Where should I start? In what order should I present events? How and where should I end?* In making these and other decisions, writers need to consider not only the overall structure of a work but also the meaning they wish to convey and the effects they hope to achieve. In this chapter, we will examine structural decisions and their effects by addressing the following topics:

5.1 Plot openings and sequence of events

5.2 Climaxes and resolutions

5.1 Plot Openings and Sequence of Events

Review

Structure is the organizational pattern of a literary work. In narrative fiction and drama, the overall structure is the **plot**, the series of events centering around a conflict that a main character faces. Writers organize their plots not only to convey meaning but also to build suspense to keep their readers reading.

In a typical plot, **exposition** introduces the main characters and setting. The conflict begins with what is sometimes called the **narrative hook**, drawing the reader into the story. Events then generally proceed in chronological order, with each event adding complication to the conflict, building suspense. Writers may add to the suspense with **foreshadowing**, hinting at events to come.

Writers do not always follow the typical plot pattern. For instance, they may dispense with opening exposition and start ***in medias res***, or in the middle of the action. This technique quickens the **pacing** of a narrative and adds to the suspense by making the reader wonder about the characters and settings.

A writer may also provide exposition in the form of a **flashback**, interrupting the chronological order to reveal events from an earlier time.

A writer may use a **frame narrative**, a main narrative that establishes the setting for the telling of one or more **stories within a story.** A common frame story features a character who finds a journal or a series of letters that forms the story within the story.

Key Terms

exposition: background information identifying the main characters, the setting, and the basic situation.

flashback: an interruption of present action to narrate events that happened earlier.

foreshadowing: the use of hints about future events.

frame narrative: a device that creates the setting for the telling of one or more stories within a story.

in medias res: Latin for "in the midst of things," a term applied to works that open in the middle of the action.

narrative hook: a point in a plot in which the main conflict is introduced; called the *dramatic hook* in a play.

pacing: the speed at which a plot unfolds.

plot: the series of events in a narrative or drama

story within a story: a story told by a character in a frame narrative.

structure: the organizational pattern of a literary work.

Toolbox

As you read a text—

- Highlight opening exposition, identifying the main characters and setting.
- Highlight any narrative (or dramatic) hook, and identify the conflict.
- If a work opens *in medias res,* indicate that in the margin.
- Highlight passages that appear to foreshadow future events.

Check Understanding

Read the opening of this story by Russian author Anton Chekhov. Some of the structures have been indicated with notes in the margin.

from In Exile

by Anton Chekhov

In the nineteenth-century Russian empire, people found guilty of crimes were often sent into exile to Siberia.

1. Old Semyon, nicknamed Canny, and a young Tatar,[1] whom no one knew by name, were sitting on the river-bank by the camp-fire; the other three ferrymen were in the hut. Semyon, an old man of sixty, lean and toothless, but broad shouldered and still healthy-looking, was drunk; he would have gone in to sleep long before, but he had a bottle in his pocket and he was afraid that the fellows in the hut would ask him for vodka. The Tatar was ill and weary, and wrapping himself up in his rags was describing how nice it was in the Simbirsk province,[2] and what a beautiful and clever wife he had left behind at home. He was not more than twenty-five, and now by the light of the camp-fire, with his pale and sick, mournful face, he looked like a boy.

2. "To be sure, it is not paradise here," said Canny. "You can see for yourself, the water, the bare banks, clay, and nothing else. . . . Easter has long passed and yet there is ice on the river, and this morning there was snow."

3. "It's bad! it's bad!" said the Tatar, and looked round him in terror. . . .

4. "You will get used to it," said Semyon, and he laughed. "Now you are young and foolish, the milk is hardly dry on your lips, and it seems to you in your foolishness that you are more wretched than anyone; but the time will come when you will say to yourself: 'I wish no one a better life than mine.' You look at me. Within a week the floods will be over and we shall set up the ferry; you will all go wandering off about Siberia while I shall stay and shall begin going

Notes

Exposition: introduction of the two characters, and the frozen Siberian setting to which they have been exiled.

Narrative hook: The conflict of the young Tatar's struggle with exile is introduced.

1 Tatar: someone of Turkic background from the central Asian part of Russia.

2 Simbirsk province: central Asian province in the nineteenth-century Russian Empire

from bank to bank. I've been going like that for twenty-two years, day and night. The pike and the salmon are under the water while I am on the water. And thank God for it, I want nothing; God give everyone such a life."

5. The Tatar threw some dry twigs on the camp-fire, lay down closer to the blaze, and said:

6. "My father is a sick man. When he dies my mother and wife will come here. They have promised."

7. "And what do you want your wife and mother for?" asked Canny. "That's mere foolishness, my lad. It's the devil confounding you, damn his soul! Don't you listen to him, the cursed one. Don't let him have his way. He is at you about the women, but you spite him; say, 'I don't want them!' He is on at you about freedom, but you stand up to him and say: 'I don't want it!' I want nothing, neither father nor mother, nor wife, nor freedom, nor post, nor paddock; I want nothing, damn their souls! . . . If anyone gives way to the devil and listens to him, if but once, he is lost, there is no salvation for him: he is sunk in the bog to the crown of his head and will never get out.

8. "It is not only a foolish peasant like you, but even gentlemen, well-educated people, are lost. Fifteen years ago they sent a gentleman here from Russia. He hadn't shared something with his brothers and had forged something in a will. They did say he was a prince or a baron, but maybe he was simply an official—who knows? Well, the gentleman arrived here, and first thing he bought himself a house and land in Muhortinskoe.[3] 'I want to live by my own work,' says he, 'in the sweat of my brow, for I am not a gentleman now,' says he, 'but a settler.' 'Well, if you want to be happy,' says I, 'the chief thing is not to want anything. Yes, if,' says I, 'if Fate has wronged you and me cruelly it's no good asking for her favor and bowing down to her, but you despise her and laugh at her, or else she will laugh at you.' That's what I said to him. . . .

9. "Two years later I ferried him across to this side, and he was rubbing his hands and laughing. 'I am going to Gyrino to meet my wife,' says he. 'She was sorry for me,' says he; 'she has come. She is good and kind.' And he was breathless with joy. So a day later he came with his wife. A beautiful young lady in a hat; in her arms was a baby girl. And lots of luggage of all sorts. . . .

10. "The lady did not stay with him long. How could she? The clay, the water, the cold, no vegetables for you, no fruit. All around you ignorant and drunken people and no sort of manners, and she was a spoilt lady from Petersburg or Moscow. . . .

11. "He grew gray and bent, and yellow in the face, as though he was in consumption. If he talked to you he would go khee—khee—khee and there were tears in his eyes . . . for eight years, but now he has grown brighter and more cheerful again: he has found another whim to give way to. You see, his daughter has grown up. He looks

Notes

Complication: The conflict deepens with the young Tatar's desire for his wife and mother to join him in exile.

3 bought . . . Muhortinskoe: Exiles who could afford to were sometimes allowed to purchase land in Siberia

at her, and she is the apple of his eye. . . . They used to stand on the ferry, side by side, she would laugh and he could not take his eyes off her. 'Yes, Semyon,' says he, 'people can live even in Siberia. Even in Siberia there is happiness. Look,' says he, 'what a daughter I have got! I wager that you wouldn't find another like her for a thousand miles round.' 'Your daughter is all right,' says I, 'that's true, certainly.' But to myself I thought: 'Wait a bit, the girl is young, her blood is dancing, she wants to live, and there is no life here.' And she did begin to pine, my lad. She faded and faded, and now she can hardly crawl about. Consumption.[4]

12. . . . "So you see what Siberian happiness is, damn its soul! You see how people can live in Siberia. . . ."

Notes

4 consumption: tuberculosis

Activity 5.1 Highlight the beginning of a flashback and a passage that could foreshadow future events. Explain your choices in the margin. Share your findings with a partner.

Try It

Directions: Read the story opening below and answer the questions that follow.

from Peter
by Willa Cather

1. "No, Antone, I have told thee many times, no, thou shalt not sell it until I am gone."

2. "But I need money; what good is that old fiddle to thee? The very crows laugh at thee when thou art trying to play. Thy hand trembles so thou canst scarce hold the bow. Thou shalt go with me to the Blue to cut wood tomorrow. See to it thou art up early."

3. "What, on the Sabbath, Antone, when it is so cold? I get so very cold, my son, let us not go tomorrow."

4. "Yes, tomorrow, thou lazy old man. Do not I cut wood upon the Sabbath? Care I how cold it is? Wood thou shalt cut, and haul it too, and as for the fiddle, I tell thee I will sell it yet." Antone pulled his ragged cap down over his low heavy brow, and went out. The old man drew his stool up nearer the fire, and sat stroking his violin with trembling fingers and muttering, "Not while I live, not while I live."

5. Five years ago they had come here, Peter Sadelack, and his wife, and oldest son Antone, and countless smaller Sadelacks, here to southwestern Nebraska, and had taken up a homestead.

Notes

1. This story opens—

Ⓐ with a frame narrative.
Ⓑ with a flashback.
Ⓒ with a section of exposition.
Ⓓ *in medias res.*

2. Cite a passage from the opening that indicates a plot complication. Explain your choice.

____

____

____

____

____

____

3. Cite a passage from the opening that indicates a flashback and explain its purpose.

____

____

____

____

____

____

Question 1 asks you to identify the way in which the story opens. Choices A and B are incorrect. There is no frame narrative, and while there is a brief flashback near the end of the excerpt, the story does not open with that flashback. Choice C is also incorrect. There is no section introducing the main characters and setting. The correct answer is choice D. The story opens in the middle of the action, and readers must figure out who the main characters are from the dialogue and other details.

Question 2 asks you to identify and explain a plot complication. Sample response:

At the end of paragraph 4, the old man draws up close to the fire and mutters to himself, "Not while I live, not while I live," creating a conflict between the old man and Antone, who plans to sell the old man's fiddle.

Question 3 asks you to identify a flashback and to explain its purpose. Sample response:

Paragraph 5 flashes back to five years ago. Its purpose is to provide exposition, explaining some background of the characters and the setting.

Try It

Directions: Read the opening of this story by Katherine Anne Porter, and then answer the questions.

from The Jilting of Granny Weatherall

by Katherine Anne Porter

1. She flicked her wrist neatly out of Doctor Harry's pudgy careful fingers and pulled the sheet up to her chin. The brat ought to be in knee breeches.[1] Doctoring around the country with spectacles on his nose! "Get along now. Take your schoolbooks and go. There's nothing wrong with me."

2. Doctor Harry spread a warm paw like a cushion on her forehead where the forked green vein danced and made her eyelids twitch. "Now, now, be a good girl, and we'll have you up in no time."

3. "That's no way to speak to a woman nearly eighty years old just because she's down. I'd have you respect your elders, young man."

4. "Well, Missy, excuse me." Doctor Harry patted her cheek. "But I've got to warn you, haven't I? You're a marvel, but you must be careful or you're going to be good and sorry."

5. "Don't tell me what I'm going to be. I'm on my feet now, morally speaking. It's Cornelia. I had to go to bed to get rid of her."

6. . . . She meant to wave good-by, but it was too much trouble. Her eyes closed of themselves, it was like a dark curtain drawn around the bed. The pillow rose and floated under her, pleasant as a hammock in a light wind. She listened to the leaves rustling outside the window. No, somebody was swishing newspapers: no, Cornelia and Doctor Harry were whispering together. She leaped broad awake, thinking they whispered in her ear.

7. "She was never like this, *never* like this!" "Well, what can we expect?" "Yes, eighty years old . . ."

8. Well, and what if she was? She still had ears. It was like Cornelia to whisper around doors. She always kept things secret in such a public way. She was always being tactful and kind. Cornelia was dutiful; that was the trouble with her. Dutiful and good: "So good and dutiful," said Granny, "that I'd like to spank her." She saw herself spanking Cornelia and making a fine job of it.

9. "What'd you say, mother?"

10. Granny felt her face tying up in hard knots.

11. "Can't a body think, I'd like to know?"

12. "I thought you might like something."

13. "I do. I want a lot of things. First off, go away and don't whisper."

14. She lay and drowsed, hoping in her sleep that the children would keep out and let her rest a minute. It had been a long day. Not that she was tired. It was always pleasant to snatch a minute

1 knee breeches: short pants usually worn by young boys

Notes

now and then. There was always so much to be done, let me see: tomorrow.

15. Tomorrow was far away and there was nothing to trouble about. . . . The dust that lion could collect in twenty-four hours! The box in the attic with all those letters tied up, well, she'd have to go through that tomorrow. All those letters – George's letters and John's letters and her letters to them both—lying around for the children to find afterwards made her uneasy. Yes, that would be tomorrow's business. No use to let them know how silly she had been once.

16. While she was rummaging around she found death in her mind and it felt clammy and unfamiliar. She had spent so much time preparing for death there was no need for bringing it up again. Let it take care of itself for now. When she was sixty she had felt very old, finished, and went around making farewell trips to see her children and grandchildren, with a secret in her mind: This was the very last of your mother, children! Then she made her will and came down with a long fever. That was all just a notion like a lot of other things, but it was lucky too, for she had once and for all got over the idea of dying for a long time. Now she couldn't be worried. She hoped she had better sense now. . . .

Notes

1. This story opens—

Ⓐ with a frame narrative. Ⓒ with a section of exposition.

Ⓑ with a flashback. Ⓓ *in medias res.*

2. Which of these inferences can readers make about the identity of the characters?

Ⓐ The main character is an eighty-year-old woman; Cornelia is her daughter.

Ⓑ The main character is a sixty-year-old woman; Doctor Harry is her grandson.

Ⓒ The main character has three children: Cornelia, George, and John.

Ⓓ The main character is Cornelia; Granny Weatherall is her eighty-year-old grandmother.

3. Around what main conflict do the plot events in this portion of the story revolve?

Ⓐ Cornelia's struggle to save her mother's life

Ⓑ Granny Weatherall's struggle to reconcile with Cornelia

Ⓒ Granny Weatherall's struggle to reconcile with George and John

Ⓓ Granny Weatherall's struggle to face death

4. Which paragraph contains a brief flashback?

Ⓐ the first Ⓒ the next-to-last

Ⓑ the second Ⓓ the last

5. Identify the foreshadowing in paragraph 15. What main effect does the foreshadowing have on readers?

____

____

____

____

____

____

Question 1 asks you to identify the way in which the story opens. Choices A and B are incorrect. There is no frame narrative, and while there is a brief flashback near the end of the excerpt, the story does not open with that flashback. Choice C is also incorrect. There is no section introducing the main characters and setting. The correct answer is choice D. The story opens in the middle of the action, and readers must figure out who the main characters are from the dialogue and other details.

Question 2 asks about the inferences readers can make as they read the opening. Choice A is the correct answer. Granny mentions her age in the third paragraph and, as the focus of all the actions and thoughts, she is the main character. Cornelia is apparently her daughter, for she addresses her as mother and seems to be her chief caretaker. Choice B is incorrect. Nothing in the excerpt indicates that Doctor Harry is related to Granny; he seems to be merely her attending physician. Choice C is also incorrect. The relationships of George and John to Granny are not clarified in the excerpt, and from the details about their letters, it is more than possible than one of them is Granny's deceased husband or one or both of them is an old boyfriend. Choice D is incorrect because Granny is the main character and she seems to be Cornelia's mother, not grandmother.

Question 3 asks you to identify the conflict at the center of the plot. Choice A is incorrect. Cornelia is not the main character, and the events do not center on her actions. Choices B and C are also incorrect. There is no evidence that Granny wishes to reconcile with any of these characters, and it is not even clear that a reconciliation is necessary. Choice D is the correct answer. Granny is a sick old woman, probably dying, and most of the details in the excerpt show how she is facing death.

Question 4 asks you to identify the paragraph that contains a flashback. Choices A and B are clearly incorrect, for the paragraphs in those choices contain no flashbacks. Choice C is also incorrect. The second-to-last paragraph does bring up letters from the past but it does not jump to an earlier time. Choice D is the correct answer. The last paragraph briefly jumps back to the time when Granny was sixty.

Question 5 asks you to identify the foreshadowing in the next-to-last paragraph and explain its effects on readers. The foreshadowing is Granny Weatherall's thoughts about the letters: "All those letters—George's letters and John's letters and her letters to them both—lying around for the children to find afterwards made her uneasy. Yes, that would be tomorrow's business. No use to let them know how silly she once had been." Apparently she is uneasy about having her children or others see the letters after she dies because the letters reveal something embarrassing or shameful about her behavior that she does not want revealed. Obviously, the author mentions the letters to make readers curious about what they contain and will no doubt satisfy that curiosity later in the story.

5.2 Climaxes and Resolutions

Review

One of the most basic questions a writer must decide is how to resolve a story or drama. Should the ending be tragic, comic, or something else?

In a classic comedy, the resolution is a happy one. Lighthearted complication follows lighthearted complication as the plot builds to a **climax** in which, in a moment of **discovery**, a secret is revealed, a character opposing the main character has a change of heart, or some other obstacle is overcome. In the **comedic resolution** that follows, the main characters come to a happy end, social harmony is restored, and the viewer or reader is pleased by a happy outcome.

In a classic tragedy, a flawed but otherwise admirable **tragic hero** faces plot complications until events come to a turning point or crisis. In the **crisis**, the hero experiences a serious reversal of fortune or **catastrophe**—death, exile, loss of social position, etc. The hero's fall generally restores social order in some way. From it the viewer or reader usually comes to a better understanding of human nature.

Not all endings are clearly comic or tragic. Some works have mixed endings, comic, or happy in some ways, tragic in others. Some works have **unresolved endings** that leave the reader hanging. The unresolved ending is popular in serials such as television dramas, with episodes or season finales ending in a **cliffhanger**, hooking viewers into tuning in next time.

Also popular is the surprise ending featuring a twist at the end, usually created through situational irony. Note that a surprise ending may also be tragic, comedic, or mixed.

Key Terms

catastrophe: the tragic hero's serious reversal of fortune.

cliffhanger: an unresolved ending designed to hook viewers into watching the next episode.

climax: the point of highest tension in a plot.

comedic resolution: the happy ending of a dramatic, romantic, or other lighthearted comedy.

crisis: in the plot of a tragedy, the decisive point that determines the outcome of the conflict.

discovery: in the plot of a comedy, the climactic revelation, solution, or change of heart that leads to a happy resolution.

tragic hero: main character of a tragedy; usually a flawed but otherwise admirable figure whose flaw and/or fate brings about his or her downfall.

tragic resolution: the end of a tragedy, marked by catastrophe for the hero.

unresolved ending: an ending in which the conflict is not completely resolved or the outcome is unclear.

Check Understanding

Read the condensed version of Oscar Wilde's *The Importance of Being Earnest* that starts on the next page.

from The Importance of Being Earnest

by Oscar Wilde

Jack Worthing is a wealthy landowner of Hertfordshire with many responsibilities, including the guardianship of Cecily Cardew, the eighteen-year-old granddaughter of the late Thomas Cardew, who adopted Jack when he was a baby. To escape his cares, Jack pretends to have a dissolute brother in London named Ernest who frequently needs Jack to rescue him. In London, Jack in fact becomes Ernest, leading a double life as an idle man-about-town. His friend Algernon Moncrieff discovers the truth but says nothing to his cousin Gwendolen, since Jack and Gwendolen are in love.

1. **Gwendolen.** . . . The moment Algernon first mentioned to me that he had a friend called Ernest, I knew I was destined to love you. . . .

2. **Jack.** But you don't really mean to say that you couldn't love me if my name wasn't Ernest?

3. **Gwendolen.** But your name is Ernest.

4. **Jack.** Yes, I know it is. But supposing it was something else? . . . I must say that I think there are lots of other much nicer names. I think Jack, for instance, a charming name.

5. **Gwendolen.** Jack? . . . No, there is very little music in the name Jack, if any at all, indeed. It does not thrill. It produces absolutely no vibrations . . . The only really safe name is Ernest

6. **Jack.** Gwendolen, I must get christened at once—I mean we must get married at once. There is no time to be lost.

Before granting permission for her daughter to marry, Lady Bracknell, Gwendolen's mother, questions Jack about his family.

7. **Jack.** . . . I don't actually know who I am by birth. I was . . . well, I was found.

8. **Lady Bracknell.** Found!

9. **Jack.** The late Mr. Thomas Cardew, an old gentleman of a very charitable and kindly disposition, found me, and gave me the name of Worthing, because he happened to have a first-class ticket for Worthing in his pocket at the time. Worthing is a place in Sussex. It is a seaside resort.

10. **Lady Bracnell.** Where did the charitable gentleman who had a first-class ticket for this seaside resort find you?

11. **Jack.** [*Gravely.*] In a hand-bag.

12. **Lady Bracknell.** A hand-bag?

13. **Jack.** [*Very seriously.*] Yes, Lady Bracknell. I was in a hand-bag—a somewhat large, black leather hand-bag, with handles to it. . . . In the cloak-room at Victoria Station. It was given to him in mistake for his own.

14. **Lady Bracknell.** The cloak-room at Victoria Station?

15. **Jack.** Yes. The Brighton line.

Notes

Conflict: The plot centers around the main characters' struggles to marry those they love

Complication: Gwendolen wants to marry someone named Ernest, but that isn't Jack's real name.

16. **Lady Bracknell.** The line is immaterial. Mr. Worthing, I confess I feel somewhat bewildered by what you have just told me. To be born, or at any rate bred, in a hand-bag, whether it had handles or not, . . . could hardly be regarded as an assured basis for a recognized position in good society.

17. **Jack.** May I ask you then what you would advise me to do? I need hardly say I would do anything in the world to ensure Gwendolen's happiness.

18. **Lady Bracknell.** I would strongly advise you, Mr. Worthing, to try and acquire some relations as soon as possible, and to make a definite effort to produce at any rate one parent, of either sex, before the season is quite over.

Algernon mischievously visits the country, posing as Jack's brother Ernest. He and Cecily immediately fall in love; in fact, Cecily has long imagined meeting "Ernest" and falling in love with him.

19. **Cecily.** You must not laugh at me, darling, but it had always been a girlish dream of mine to love someone whose name was Ernest. [**Algernon** *rises,* **Cecily** *also.*] There is something in that name that seems to inspire absolute confidence. I pity any poor married woman whose husband is not called Ernest.

20. **Algernon.** But, my dear child, do you mean to say you could not love me if I had some other name?

21. **Cecily.** But what name?

22. **Algernon.** Oh, any name you like—Algernon—for instance . . . if my name was Algy, couldn't you love me?

23. **Cecily.** [*Rising.*] I might respect you, Ernest, I might admire your character, but I fear that I should not be able to give you my undivided attention.

24. **Algernon.** Ahem! Cecily! [*Picking up hat.*] Your Rector here is, I suppose, thoroughly experienced in the practice of all the rites and ceremonials of the Church?

25. **Cecily.** Oh, yes. Dr. Chasuble is a most learned man. He has never written a single book, so you can imagine how much he knows.

26. **Algernon.** I must see him at once on a most important christening—I mean on most important business.

Now Gwendolen arrives at the country house to visit the man she thinks is named "Ernest." Jack, who has followed her, is forced to admit the truth about his name. Then Algy appears, and Cecily learns that the man she loves is not named Earnest after all. The two women are angry at first, but then more forgiving, except for one thing—

27. **Gwendolen and Cecily.** [*Speaking together.*] Your Christian names are still an insuperable barrier. That is all!

28. **Jack and Algernon.** [*Speaking together.*] Our Christian names! Is that all? But we are going to be christened this afternoon.

29. **Gwendolen.** [*To* **Jack.**] For my sake you are prepared to do this terrible thing?

Notes

Complication: Lady Bracknell will not let her daughter marry someone of dubious ancestry.

Complication: Cecily wants to marry Algy's brother, whom she thinks is named Ernest, but Algy is only pretending to be Jack's brother named Ernest.

30. **Jack.** I am.

31. **Cecily.** [*To* **Algernon.**] To please me you are ready to face this fearful ordeal?

32. **Algernon.** I am!

33. **Gwendolen.** How absurd to talk of the equality of the sexes! Where questions of self-sacrifice are concerned, men are infinitely beyond us.

34. **Jack.** We are. [*Clasps hands with* **Algernon.**]

35. **Cecily.** They have moments of physical courage of which we women know absolutely nothing.

36. **Gwendolen.** [*To* **Jack.**] Darling!

37. **Algernon.** [*To* **Cecily.**] Darling! [*They fall into each other's arms.*]

Lady Bracknell arrives and, on learning Cecily is an heiress, approves of her marrying Algy. Jack, as Cecily's guardian, refuses to give permission for the marriage because Lady Bracknell will not allow Jack to marry Gwendolen. Happiness for the two couples appears to be out of reach, when Miss Prism, Cecily's governess, arrives, and Lady Bracknell recognizes her.

38. **Lady Bracknell.** [*In a severe, judicial voice.*] Prism! [*Miss Prism bows her head in shame.*] Come here, Prism! [*Miss Prism approaches in a humble manner.*] . . . Twenty-eight years ago, Prism, you left Lord Bracknell's house, Number 104, Upper Grosvenor Street, in charge of a perambulator that contained a baby of the male sex. You never returned. A few weeks later, through the elaborate investigations of the Metropolitan police, the perambulator was discovered at midnight, standing by itself in a remote corner of Bayswater. It contained the manuscript of a three-volume novel of more than usually revolting sentimentality. [*Miss Prism starts in involuntary indignation.*] But the baby was not there! [*Everyone looks at Miss Prism.*] Prism! Where is that baby? [*A pause.*]

39. **Miss Prism.** Lady Bracknell, I admit with shame that I do not know. I only wish I did. The plain facts of the case are these. On the morning of the day you mention, a day that is forever branded on my memory, I prepared as usual to take the baby out in its perambulator. I had also with me a somewhat old, but capacious hand-bag in which I had intended to place the manuscript of a work of fiction that I had written during my few unoccupied hours. In a moment of mental abstraction, for which I never can forgive myself, I deposited the manuscript in the bassinette, and placed the baby in the hand-bag.

40. **Jack.** [*Who has been listening attentively.*] But where did you deposit the hand-bag? . . .

41. **Miss Prism.** I left it in the cloak-room of one of the larger railway stations in London.

42. **Jack.** What railway station?

43. **Miss Prism.** [*Quite crushed.*] Victoria. The Brighton line. . . .

44. *Jack leaves and returns with a large black bag.*

45. **Jack.** [*Rushing over to Miss Prism.*] Is this the hand-bag, Miss Prism? Examine it carefully before you speak. The happiness of more than

Notes

Complication: Jack will not give permission for Cecily to wed Algy if Lady Bracknell refuses to give permission for Jack to wed Gwendolen.

one life depends on your answer.

46. **Miss Prism.** [*Calmly.*] It seems to be mine. . . . I am delighted to have it so unexpectedly restored to me. It has been a great inconvenience being without it all these years.

47. **Jack.** [*In a pathetic voice.*] Miss Prism, more is restored to you than this hand-bag. I was the baby you placed in it. . . . [*Embracing her.*] Yes . . . mother!

48. **Miss Prism.** [*Recoiling in indignant astonishment.*] Mr. Worthing! I am unmarried! . . . [*Pointing to* **Lady Bracknell.**] There is the lady who can tell you who you really are.

49. **Jack.** [*After a pause.*] Lady Bracknell, I hate to seem inquisitive, but would you kindly inform me who I am?

50. **Lady Bracknell.** . . . You are the son of my poor sister, Mrs. Moncrieff, and consequently Algernon's elder brother.

51. **Jack.** Algy's elder brother! Then I have a brother after all. I knew I had a brother! I always said I had a brother! Cecily—how could you have ever doubted that I had a brother? [*Seizes hold of* **Algernon.**] . . . Algy, you young scoundrel, you will have to treat me with more respect in the future. You have never behaved to me like a brother in all your life. . . . Aunt Augusta, . . . what name was I given? Let me know the worst.

52. **Lady Bracknell.** Being the eldest son you were naturally christened after your father.

53. **Jack.** [*Irritably.*] Yes, but what was my father's Christian name?

54. **Lady Bracknell.** [*Meditatively.*] I cannot at the present moment recall what the General's Christian name was. But I have no doubt he had one. . . .

55. **Jack.** Algy! Can't you recollect what our father's Christian name was?

56. **Algernon.** My dear boy, we were never even on speaking terms. He died before I was a year old.

57. **Jack.** His name would appear in the Army Lists of the period, I suppose, Aunt Augusta?. . . [*Rushes to bookcase and tears the books out.*] M. Generals . . . Mallam, Maxbohm, Magley, what ghastly names they have—Markby, Migsby, Mobbs, Moncrieff! Lieutenant 1840, Captain, Lieutenant-Colonel, Colonel, General 1869, Christian names, Ernest John. [*Puts book very quietly down and speaks quite calmly.*] I always told you, Gwendolen, my name was Ernest, didn't I? Well, it is Ernest after all. I mean it naturally is Ernest.

58. **Lady Bracknell.** Yes, I remember now that the General was called Ernest. I knew I had some particular reason for disliking the name.

59. **Gwendolen.** Ernest! My own Ernest! I felt from the first that you could have no other name!

60. **Jack.** Gwendolen, it is a terrible thing for a man to find out suddenly that all his life he has been speaking nothing but the truth. Can you forgive me?

61. **Gwendolen.** I can. For I feel that you are sure to change.

62. **Jack.** My own one! . . .

63. **Algernon.** Cecily! [*Embraces her.*] At last!

Notes

Irony: Jack and Algernon's lies turn out to be true.

64. **Jack.** Gwendolen! [*Embraces her.*] At last!
65. **Lady Bracknell.** My nephew, you seem to be displaying signs of triviality.
66. **Jack.** On the contrary, Aunt Augusta, I've now realized for the first time in my life the vital Importance of Being Earnest.
[*Final curtain.*]

Notes

Activity 5.2 Highlight and annotate the two discoveries that lead to the resolution of the play. In the space below, explain how the discoveries and the resolution support the claim that the play is a comedy. Share your explanation with a partner.

Try It

Directions: Reread the short story "Dead Men's Path" by Chinua Achebe on pages 10–12 (Chapter 1). Then answer the questions below.

6. What conflict heightens as the plot moves toward a climax?

7. Does Michael Obi qualify as a tragic hero? Cite evidence from the story to support your response.

8. Which of these events best qualifies as the climax of the story?

Ⓐ Obi and his wife beautify the school grounds.

Ⓑ Obi learns from one of his teachers the reason the villagers cross the school grounds.

Ⓒ Obi has the villagers' path blocked off with sticks and barbed wire.

Ⓓ Obi refuses to reopen the path and is blamed for the deaths of two villagers in childbirth.

9. The resolution of the story is—

Ⓐ tragic.

Ⓑ comedic.

Ⓒ unresolved.

Ⓓ mixed.

10. In addition to your answer to question 9, the story also has an ironic ending. Explain why.

____

____

____

____

11. Consider the effects of the story's structure, especially its climax and resolution. What better understanding of human experience does the story convey?

____

____

____

____

Question 6 asks you to identify the conflict that heightens as the plot moves toward a climax. Sample answer:

Obi's desire to make the school a modern showplace conflicts with the villagers' desire to walk across school grounds to their traditional burial site.

Question 7 asks you if Michael Obi qualifies as a tragic hero and to support your answer with evidence from the story. Sample answer:

Obi does qualify as a tragic hero. He is an admirable but flawed figure. In the exposition, he is described as "a young and energetic man" and he is designated as a "'pivotal teacher' in the official records." He has let his success go to his head, however. In paragraph 11, for example, Obi tells his wife boastfully, "I was thinking what a grand opportunity we've got at last to show these people how a school should be run." Pride in his abilities and single-minded focus on his mission blinds him to the beliefs and traditions of the villagers.

Question 8 asks you to identify the climax. Choices A and B are incorrect. They both happen fairly early in the plot and are not the point of highest tension. Choice C is also incorrect. Though it is a tense event, the tension continues to rise with the visit of the village priest. Choice D is the correct answer. The death of the two villagers is the point of highest tension that leads to the resolution.

Question 9 asks you about the type of ending. Choice A is the best answer. The story ends with the downfall of the main character. Choice B is incorrect. The story does not end happily for its main character. Choices C is incorrect because the ending is clear. Choice D is also incorrect because the story does not end happily for some and sad for others.

Question 10 asks you to explain why the story's ending is ironic. Sample answer:

> The supervisor whom Obi feared would give him a bad report if villagers used the school grounds actually gives him a bad report for failing to get along with the villagers.

Question 11 asks what better understanding of human experience the story gives readers. Sample answer:

> The story shows how cultural differences can lead to conflict. It also demonstrates how ambition and pride can lead to conflict and a reversal of fortune.

Strategies for Identifying and Analyzing Literary Text Structures

Use the following strategies as you read and analyze literary text structures.

- Underline or highlight any opening exposition and use it to identify the main characters and setting. If the text opens in medias res, underline details in the text from which you can infer the main characters and setting. If the text uses a frame narrative, identify main characters and settings of both the frame narrative and the story within the story.
- Underline or highlight key events (including any narrative hook as well as the climax), and use them to identify the conflict and formulate a chronological chain of events. Also underline or highlight any flashbacks and consider the information they provide.
- Underline or highlight any foreshadowing and consider its effects.
- Underline or highlight the resolution and consider its effects.

Test-Taking Tips

- Focus on the main conflict and its revolution, and consider how events relate to that conflict and resolution.
- As you read, formulate an idea about the overall meaning of the text and how it relates to the conflict and resolution. Then, pay attention to details or events that support or refute your idea. Be ready to rework your idea if the text does not support it.

Chapter Review

Directions: Read this story, and then answer the questions.

The Last Leaf

by O. Henry

Notes

1. In a little district west of Washington Square[1] the streets have run crazy and broken themselves into small strips called "places." These "places" make strange angles and curves. One street crosses itself a time or two. An artist once discovered a valuable possibility in this street. Suppose a collector with a bill for paints, paper and canvas should, in traversing this route, suddenly meet himself coming back, without a cent having been paid on account!

2. So, to quaint old Greenwich Village the art people soon came prowling, hunting for north windows and eighteenth-century gables and Dutch attics and low rents. Then they imported some pewter mugs and a chafing dish or two from Sixth Avenue, and became a "colony."

3. At the top of a squatty, three-story brick Sue and Johnsy had their studio. "Johnsy" was familiar for Joanna. One was from Maine; the other from California. They had met at the *table d'hot*e of an Eighth Street "Delmonico's,"[2] and found their tastes in art, chicory salad and bishop sleeves so congenial that the joint studio resulted.

4. That was in May. In November a cold, unseen stranger, whom the doctors called Pneumonia, stalked about the colony, touching one here and there with his icy fingers. Over on the east side this ravager strode boldly, smiting his victims by scores, but his feet trod slowly through the maze of the narrow and moss-grown "places."

5. Mr. Pneumonia was not what you would call a chivalric old gentleman. A mite of a little woman with blood thinned by California zephyrs[3] was hardly fair game for the red-fisted, short-breathed old duffer. But Johnsy he smote; and she lay, scarcely moving, on her painted iron bedstead, looking through the small Dutch window-panes at the blank side of the next brick house.

6. One morning the busy doctor invited Sue into the hallway with a shaggy, gray eyebrow.

7. "She has one chance in—let us say, ten," he said, as he shook down the mercury in his clinical thermometer. "And that chance is for her to want to live. This way people have of lining-up on the side of the undertaker makes the entire pharmacopeia[4] look silly. Your

1 Washington Square: a small public park in the center of New York City's Greenwich Village, a neighborhood that became a haven for artists in the early twentieth century, when the story takes place

2 *table d'hote* of an Eighth Street "Delmonico's": table set aside for guesthouse residents at an inexpensive Greenwich Village establishment (as opposed to the real Delmonico's, a famous and expensive New York City restaurant)

3 zephyrs: breezes

4 pharmacopeia: stock of medicines

little lady has made up her mind that she's not going to get well. Has she anything on her mind?"

8. "She—she wanted to paint the Bay of Naples some day," said Sue.

9. "Paint?—bosh! Has she anything on her mind worth thinking about twice—a man, for instance?"

10. "A man?" said Sue. "No, doctor; there is nothing of the kind."

11. "Well, it is the weakness, then," said the doctor. "I will do all that science, so far as it may filter through my efforts, can accomplish. But whenever my patient begins to count the carriages in her funeral procession I subtract 50 per cent from the curative power of medicines. If you will get her to ask one question about the new winter styles in cloak sleeves I will promise you a one-in-five chance for her, instead of one in ten."

12. After the doctor had gone Sue went into the workroom and cried a Japanese napkin to a pulp. Then she swaggered into Johnsy's room with her drawing board, whistling ragtime.[5]

13. Johnsy lay, scarcely making a ripple under the bedclothes, with her face toward the window. Sue stopped whistling, thinking she was asleep.

14. She arranged her board and began a pen-and-ink drawing to illustrate a magazine story. Young artists must pave their way to Art by drawing pictures for magazine stories that young authors write to pave their way to Literature.

15. As Sue was sketching a pair of elegant horseshow riding trousers and a monocle on the figure of the hero, an Idaho cowboy, she heard a low sound, several times repeated. She went quickly to the bedside.

16. Johnsy's eyes were open wide. She was looking out the window and counting—counting backward.

17. "Twelve," she said, and a little later "eleven;" and then "ten," and "nine;" and then "eight" and "seven," almost together.

18. Sue looked solicitously out the window. What was there to count? There was only a bare, dreary yard to be seen, and the blank side of the brick house twenty feet away. An old, old ivy vine, gnarled and decayed at the roots, climbed half way up the brick wall. The cold breath of autumn had stricken its leaves from the vine until its skeleton branches clung, almost bare, to the crumbling bricks.

19. "What is it, dear?" asked Sue.

20. "Six," said Johnsy, in almost a whisper. "They're falling faster now. Three days ago there were almost a hundred. It made my head ache to count them. But now it's easy. There goes another one. There are only five left now."

21. "Five what, dear. Tell your Sudie."

22. "Leaves. On the ivy vine. When the last one falls I must go, too. I've known that for three days. Didn't the doctor tell you?"

23. "Oh, I never heard of such nonsense," complained Sue, with magnificent scorn. "What have old ivy leaves to do with your getting well? And you used to love that vine so, you naughty girl. Don't be a

5 ragtime: a lively type of jazz music popular at the time of the story

Notes

goosey. Why, the doctor told me this morning that your chances for getting well real soon were—let's see exactly what he said—he said the chances were ten to one! Why, that's almost as good a chance as we have in New York when we ride on the streetcars or walk past a new building. Try to take some broth now, and let Sudie go back to her drawing, so she can sell the editor man with it, and buy port wine for her sick child, and pork chops for her greedy self."

24. "You needn't get any more wine," said Johnsy, keeping her eyes fixed out the window. "There goes another. No, I don't want any broth. That leaves just four. I want to see the last one fall before it gets dark. Then I'll go, too."

25. "Johnsy, dear," said Sue, bending over her, "will you promise me to keep your eyes closed, and not look out the window until I am done working? I must hand those drawings in by tomorrow. I need the light, or I would draw the shade down."

26. "Couldn't you draw in the other room?" asked Johnsy, coldly.

27. "I'd rather be here by you," said Sue. "Besides I don't want you to keep looking at those silly ivy leaves."

28. "Tell me as soon as you have finished," said Johnsy, closing her eyes, and lying white and still as a fallen statue, "because I want to see the last one fall. I'm tired of waiting. I'm tired of thinking. I want to turn loose my hold on everything, and go sailing down, down, just like one of those poor, tired leaves."

29. "Try to sleep," said Sue. "I must call Behrman up to be my model for the old hermit miner. I'll not be gone a minute. Don't try to move 'till I come back."

30. Old Behrman was a painter who lived on the ground floor beneath them. He was past sixty and had a Michelangelo's *Mose*s beard[6] curling down from the head of a satyr along the body of an imp. Behrman was a failure in art. Forty years he had wielded the brush without getting near enough to touch the hem of his Mistress's robe. He had been always about to paint a masterpiece, but had never yet begun it. For several years he had painted nothing except now and then a daub in the line of commerce or advertising. He earned a little by serving as a model to those young artists in the colony who could not pay the price of a professional. He drank gin to excess, and still talked of his coming masterpiece. For the rest he was a fierce little old man, who scoffed terribly at softness in any one, and who regarded himself as especial mastiff-in-waiting to protect the two young artists in the studio above.

31. Sue found Behrman smelling strongly of juniper berries[7] in his dimly lighted den below. In one corner was a blank canvas on an easel that had been waiting there for twenty-five years to receive the first line of the masterpiece. She told him of Johnsy's fancy, and how she feared she would, indeed, light and fragile as a leaf herself, float

Notes

6 Michelangelo's Moses beard: a long, curly beard, like the one on the famous statue of Moses by Renaissance artist Michelangelo

7 juniper berries: a key ingredient of gin

away when her slight hold upon the world grew weaker.

32. Old Behrman, with his red eyes, plainly streaming, shouted his contempt and derision for such idiotic imaginings.

33. "Vass!" he cried. "Is dere people in de world mit der foolishness to die because leafs dey drop off from a confounded vine? I haf not heard of such a thing. No, I will not bose as a model for your fool hermit-dunderhead. Vy do you allow dot silly pusiness to come in der prain of her? Ach, dot poor lettle Miss Johnsy."

34. "She is very ill and weak," said Sue, "and the fever has left her mind morbid and full of strange fancies. Very well, Mr. Behrman, if you do not care to pose for me, you needn't. But I think you are a horrid old—old flibbertigibbet."

35. "You are just like a woman!" yelled Behrman. "Who said I will not bose? Go on. I come mit you. For half an hour I haf peen trying to say dot I am ready to bose. Gott! dis is not any blace in which one so goot as Miss Yohnsy shall lie sick. Some day I vill baint a masterpiece, and ve shall all go away. Gott! yes."

36. Johnsy was sleeping when they went upstairs. Sue pulled the shade down to the window-sill, and motioned Behrman into the other room. In there they peered out the window fearfully at the ivy vine. Then they looked at each other for a moment without speaking. A persistent, cold rain was falling, mingled with snow. Behrman, in his old blue shirt, took his seat as the hermit-miner on an upturned kettle for a rock.

37. When Sue awoke from an hour's sleep the next morning she found Johnsy with dull, wide-open eyes staring at the drawn green shade.

38. "Pull it up; I want to see," she ordered, in a whisper.

39. Wearily Sue obeyed.

40. But, lo! after the beating rain and fierce gusts of wind that had endured through the livelong night, there yet stood out against the brick wall one ivy leaf. It was the last on the vine. Still dark green near its stem, but with its serrated edges tinted with the yellow of dissolution and decay, it hung bravely from a branch some twenty feet above the ground.

41. "It is the last one," said Johnsy. "I thought it would surely fall during the night. I heard the wind. It will fall today, and I shall die at the same time."

42. "Dear, dear!" said Sue, leaning her worn face down to the pillow, "think of me, if you won't think of yourself. What would I do?"

43. But Johnsy did not answer. The lonesomest thing in all the world is a soul when it is making ready to go on its mysterious, far journey. The fancy seemed to possess her more strongly as one by one the ties that bound her to friendship and to earth were loosed.

44. The day wore away, and even through the twilight they could see the lone ivy leaf clinging to its stem against the wall. And then, with the coming of the night the north wind was again loosed, while the rain still beat against the windows and pattered down from the low Dutch eaves.

Notes

Notes

45. When it was light enough Johnsy, the merciless, commanded that the shade be raised.

46. The ivy leaf was still there.

47. Johnsy lay for a long time looking at it. And then she called to Sue, who was stirring her chicken broth over the gas stove.

48. "I've been a bad girl, Sudie," said Johnsy. "Something has made that last leaf stay there to show me how wicked I was. It is a sin to want to die. You may bring me a little broth now, and some milk with a little port in it, and—no; bring me a hand-mirror first, and then pack some pillows about me, and I will sit up and watch you cook."

49. An hour later she said.

50. "Sudie, some day I hope to paint the Bay of Naples."

51. The doctor came in the afternoon, and Sue had an excuse to go into the hallway as he left.

52. "Even chances," said the doctor, taking Sue's thin, shaking hand in his. "With good nursing you'll win. And now I must see another case I have downstairs. Behrman, his name is—some kind of an artist, I believe. Pneumonia, too. He is an old, weak man, and the attack is acute. There is no hope for him; but he goes to the hospital today to be made more comfortable."

53. The next day the doctor said to Sue: "She's out of danger. You've won. Nutrition and care now—that's all."

54. And that afternoon Sue came to the bed where Johnsy lay, contentedly knitting a very blue and very useless woolen shoulder scarf, and put one arm around her, pillows and all.

55. "I have something to tell you, white mouse," she said. "Mr. Behrman died of pneumonia today in the hospital. He was ill only two days. The janitor found him on the morning of the first day in his room downstairs helpless with pain. His shoes and clothing were wet through and icy cold. They couldn't imagine where he had been on such a dreadful night. And then they found a lantern, still lighted, and a ladder that had been dragged from its place, and some scattered brushes, and a palette with green and yellow colors mixed on it, and—look out the window, dear, at the last ivy leaf on the wall. Didn't you wonder why it never fluttered or moved when the wind blew? Ah, darling, it's Behrman's masterpiece—he painted it there the night that the last leaf fell."

Questions 1–10: Choose the best answer or write your response on the lines.

1. The story opens—

Ⓐ with a frame narrative.

Ⓑ with a cliffhanger.

Ⓒ with a section of exposition.

Ⓓ *in medias res.*

2. What basic background information about the story's main characters and setting do you learn from the text or your inferences about it?

____

____

____

____

3. Which of these sentences from the opening paragraphs is the best example of foreshadowing?

Ⓐ These "places" make strange angles and curves.

Ⓑ Suppose a collector with a bill for paints, paper and canvas should, in traversing this route, suddenly meet himself coming back, without a cent having been paid on account!

Ⓒ In November a cold, unseen stranger, whom the doctors called Pneumonia, stalked about the colony, touching one here and there with his icy fingers.

Ⓓ One morning the busy doctor invited Sue into the hallway with a shaggy, gray eyebrow.

4. Explain what the sentence you chose in question 3 foreshadows.

____

____

____

5. Around what main conflict does the story's plot revolve?

Ⓐ the struggle to ensure that Johnsy survives her attack of pneumonia

Ⓑ the struggle to ensure that Johnsy paints the Bay of Naples

Ⓒ Behrman's struggle to paint a masterpiece before he dies

Ⓓ Sue and Johnsy's struggle to survive poverty in Greenwich Village

6. Cite and explain one complication that adds suspense to the conflict.

____

____

____

7. The climax of the story is expressed in—

Ⓐ the doctor's visit and diagnosis.

Ⓑ Behrman's conversation with Sue about Johnsy's illness.

Ⓒ the two days in which Johnsy waits for the last leaf to fall and it does not.

Ⓓ the revelation that Behrman painted the last leaf and contracted pneumonia while painting it.

8. Is the ending of the story comedic, tragic, mixed, or unresolved? Cite evidence to support your answer.

9. Citing evidence, explain why the story's ending is ironic.

10. Describe the chief effects of the story's ending.

Chapter 6 Author's Point of View & Tone (RL.11–12.6)

When it comes to literature, the term *point of view* has several meanings. *Narrative point of view* refers to the voice of the narrator, which can be first person, third person, and so on. *Author's point of view*—also known as tone—refers to the author's attitude toward the work and its intended audience. This chapter examines literature in which the tone expresses a difference between appearance and reality—a situation referred to as irony. The following topics will be addressed.

6.1 Irony
6.2 Satire
6.3 Sarcasm
6.4 Understatement

6.1 Irony

Review

Irony is a narrative device that highlights a difference between appearance and reality or between what is directly stated and what is meant. There are three basic types of irony.

Verbal irony occurs when a character *says* one thing but *means* just the opposite. This type of irony relies to some extent on tone and is always intentional. When you say "Another beautiful day for camping" upon waking up to a fifth straight day of rain, you are using verbal irony.

Situational irony occurs when an outcome is the opposite of what is expected. The irony, humorous or otherwise, is created by the difference between expectation and actual outcome. For example, in O. Henry's classic story "The Gift of the Magi," Della sells her hair so she can buy Jim a new watch chain. Jim, it turns out, has sold his watch to buy a beautiful comb for Della's hair. Despite their best intentions, neither one can use the other's gift.

Dramatic irony takes place when the reader or viewer is aware of circumstances of which the characters have no knowledge. For example, at the beginning of the play *Oedipus Rex* by Sophocles, Oedipus swears he will banish the person responsible for the plagues in his empire. The audience knows that Oedipus himself inadvertently caused those plagues. Dramatic irony is frequently used to create tension and suspense.

Key Terms

author's point of view: the writer's attitude toward the work.

dramatic irony: a literary technique in which the reader has more information about the events of a story than the characters do.

narrative point of view: the perspective of the narrator in a story or the speaker in a poem.

situational irony: a literary technique in which the outcome is the opposite of what is expected.

tone: the author's point of view on his or her work.

verbal irony: a statement by a character or author that in saying one thing, means just the opposite.

Check Understanding

Notice the irony in Emily Dickinson's brief poem "Much Madness Is Divinest Sense" on the next page.

from Romeo and Juliet (Act 1, Scene 5)

by William Shakespeare

JULIET. What's he that follows there, that would not dance?
NURSE. I know not.
JULIET. Go ask his name. —If he be married.
My grave is like to be my wedding bed.
NURSE. His name is Romeo, and a Montague;
The only son of your great enemy.
JULIET. My only love sprung from my only hate!
Too early seen unknown, and known too late!
Prodigious birth of love it is to me,
That I must love a loathed enemy.

Notes

Juliet's lament is not ironic; she is pointing out her bad luck by contrasting her feelings with the hate imposed upon her by the feud.

Activity 6.1 Highlight and comment on at least one example of irony. Share your findings with a partner.

Toolbox

As you reread a text—

- Be on the lookout for the unexpected. Pay close attention and take notes on any opposites, contradictions, unexpected outcomes, and unusual juxtapositions.
- Ask yourself what information you the reader have that a character or characters in the text may not know. The answer may lead you to a text's dramatic irony.

Try It

Directions: At the beginning of Kate Chopin's short story "The Story of an Hour," Louise Mallard, a young wife in frail health, receives the devastating news that her husband has been killed in an accident. After first breaking down in sobs, she retreats to her room, where she sits alone. Read the paragraphs excerpted from the end of the story and answer the questions that follow.

from The Story of an Hour

by Kate Chopin

Notes

1. . . . There would be no one to live for during those coming years; she would live for herself. There would be no powerful will bending hers in that blind persistence with which men and women believe they have a right to impose a private will upon a fellow-creature. A kind intention or a cruel intention made the act seem no less a crime as she looked upon it in that brief moment of illumination.

2. And yet she had loved him—sometimes. Often she had not. What did it matter! What could love, the unsolved mystery, count for in the face of this possession of self-assertion which she suddenly recognized as the strongest impulse of her being!

3. "Free! Body and soul free!" she kept whispering.

4. Josephine was kneeling before the closed door with her lips to the keyhold, imploring for admission. "Louise, open the door! I beg; open the door—you will make yourself ill. What are you doing, Louise? For heaven's sake open the door."

5. "Go away. I am not making myself ill." No; she was drinking in a very elixir of life through that open window.

6. Her fancy was running riot along those days ahead of her. Spring days, and summer days, and all sorts of days that would be her own. She breathed a quick prayer that life might be long. It was only yesterday she had thought with a shudder that life might be long.

7. She arose at length and opened the door to her sister's importunities. There was a feverish triumph in her eyes, and she carried herself unwittingly like a goddess of Victory. She clasped her sister's waist, and together they descended the stairs. Richards stood waiting for them at the bottom.

8. Some one was opening the front door with a latchkey. It was Brently Mallard who entered, a little travel-stained, composedly carrying his grip-sack and umbrella. He had been far from the scene of the accident, and did not even know there had been one. He stood amazed at Josephine's piercing cry; at Richards' quick motion to screen him from the view of his wife.

9. When the doctors came they said she had died of heart disease—of the joy that kills.

Notes

1. Which statement most accurately identifies the situational irony in "The Story of an Hour"?

Ⓐ A reversal makes it clear that Louise never actually loved her husband.

Ⓑ Louise realizes that she will now have to make some decisions for herself.

Ⓒ Louise's grief over her husband's death quickly gives way to relief and the anticipation of a long life of freedom.

Ⓓ Though she is at first shocked, Louise eventually gets over her husband's death entirely.

2. Write a brief description of the situational and dramatic irony in the story.

____

____

____

____

Question 1 asks you to identify the most accurate statement of the story's situational irony. Choice A is not correct because the story states that Louise did love her husband at times. While Choice B is true, it does not reflect the story's situational irony. Choice C is the best answer because the expected response from Louise would be grief, not relief and anticipation of a long life of freedom. Choice D seems to be true but there is not enough information to fully support it and in any case it is not an example of situational irony.

Question 2 asks you to write a brief description of the story's situational and dramatic irony. Here is a sample response:

An example of situational irony is the transformation of Louise's grief into a private celebration of freedom from her husband's control. This situational irony leads to the dramatic irony, in that the reader knows of Louise's true feelings while the other characters do not. In a sort of double ironic twist, the revelation that Mr. Mallard is alive leads to the "death" of Louise's freedom and to her actual death.

6.2 Satire

Review

If you have ever seen a political cartoon, then you are acquainted with satire. Broadly defined, **satire** is a criticism of a circumstance in society that the writer believes is in need of change. Although satire may employ humor, its intent is usually serious criticism. Besides irony, the satirist may employ several techniques, such as hyperbole, innuendo, and invective.

Hyperbole is an exaggeration or an overstatement in which an issue is made to appear larger or more important than it is. **Innuendo** is the use of hints and insinuations to attack someone indirectly. When all else fails, the satirical diatribe, or rant, using a technique called **invective**, can be highly effective in satire.

Key Terms

hyperbole: overstatement used to embellish a satirical point.

innuendo: language that creates an insinuation.

invective: strong, negatively charged language used against a particular target.

satire: criticism of a social issue or institution with intent to bring change.

Check Understanding

Satire sometimes relies on a surprise ending as in this poem by Dorothy Parker.

The Choice

by Dorothy Parker

He'd have given me rolling lands,
Houses of marble, and billowing farms,
Pearls, to trickle between my hands,
Smoldering rubies, to circle my arms.
You—you'd only a lilting song,
Only a melody, happy and high,
You were sudden and swift and strong—
Never a thought for another had I.

He'd have given me laces rare,
Dresses that glimmered with frosty sheen,
Shining ribbons to wrap my hair,
Horses to draw me, as fine as a queen.
You—you'd only to whistle low,
Gayly I followed wherever you led.
I took you, and I let him go—
Somebody ought to examine my head!

Notes

Classic dilemma: money or love. Of course, love wins the day.

Activity 6.2 Highlight and annotate lines that reveal the satire. Share with a partner.

Try It

Directions: Read "The Unknown Citizen" by W. H. Auden, then answer the question that follow.

The Unknown Citizen

by W. H. Auden

Notes

(To JS/07 M 378
This Marble Monument
Is Erected by the State)

He was found by the Bureau of Statistics to be
One against whom there was no official complaint,
And all the reports of his conduct agree
That, in the modern sense of the old-fashioned word, he was a saint,
For in everything he did he served the Greater Community.
Except for the war till the day he retired
He worked in a factory and never got fired,
But satisfied his employers, Fudge Motors Inc.
Yet he wasn't a scab or odd in his views,
For his union reports that he paid his dues,
(Our report of his union shows it was sound)
And our Social Psychology workers found
That he was popular with his mates and liked a drink.
The Press are convinced that he bought a paper every day
And that his reactions to advertisements were normal in every way.
Policies taken out in his name prove that he was fully insured,
And his Health-card shows he was once in hospital but left it cured.
Both Producers Research and High-Grade Living declare
He was fully sensible to the advantages of the Installment Plan
And had everything necessary to the Modern Man,
A phonograph, a radio, a car and a frigidaire.
Our researchers into Public Opinion are content
That he held the proper opinions for the time of year;
When there was peace, he was for peace: when there was war, he went.
He was married and added five children to the population,
Which our Eugenist says was the right number for a parent of his generation.
And our teachers report that he never interfered with their education.
Was he free? Was he happy? The question is absurd:
Had anything been wrong, we should certainly have heard.

Toolbox

Pay attention to hyperbole, innuendo, and irony. Such figures often reveal social criticism at the heart of the author's point of view.

3. Which statement best expresses the satire of the poem?

Ⓐ The unknown citizen is identified by a number.

Ⓑ The citizen is held up as a hero of the state.

Ⓒ The citizen had everything necessary to live a full life: "a phonograph, a radio, a car and a frigidaire."

Ⓓ The citizen never interfered with his education.

4. Using details from the poem, identify and explain the satire of the poem.

____

____

____

____

Question 3 asks you to identify the statement that best expresses the satire in the poem. Choices A, B, and D are accurate statements about the content of the poem, but by themselves they are not satirical. Choice C is satirical because the poet is pointing out the emptiness of a value system that equates "everything necessary to the Modern Man" to a few manufactured things.

Question 4 asks you to identify and explain its satire. There are many possible responses. Here is an example:

> The unknown citizen is held up as a hero of the state, as a saint. He is elevated to such a lofty station for doing nothing more than a series of mundane acts, such as buying into the installment plan and having a "normal" reaction to advertisements. By contrasting these mundane and materialistic acts to true heroism—selfless acts of courage, for example—the poet is questioning and satirizing the materialistic values of his society.

6.3 Sarcasm

Review

Sarcasm is a type of irony that is used to mock or insult. Though sarcasm often contains a vein of humor, it is typically intended to deliver a sting to its target. In literary sarcasm, no matter whether it is harsh or gentle, there is always an implicit put-down or insult. Sarcasm may seem like a compliment but upon closer examination, it reveals an insult.

Key Term

sarcasm: speech or text whose tone and content is intended as mockery.

For example, in Shakespeare's play *Julius Caesar*, Mark Antony, speaking at Caesar's funeral, repeatedly refers to Brutus as an "honorable man." Yet Mark Antony is well aware of that Brutus has murdered Caesar. He repeats the phrase, "an honorable man," to make it clear that Brutus is the exact opposite of an honorable man.

Check Understanding

Note the biting wit with which the title character takes down a young man who has made an insulting comment regarding his famously large nose.

from Cyrano de Bergerac

by Edmond Rostand

Notes

1. **The Viscount.** But wait! I'll treat him to . . . one of my quips!. . . See here!. . . (*He goes up to Cyrano, who is watching him, and with a conceited air*): Sir, your nose is . . . hmm . . . it is . . . very big!
2. **Cyrano** (*gravely*). Very!
3. **The Viscount** (*laughing*). Ha!
4. **Cyrano** (*imperturbably*). Is that all?. . .
5. **The Viscount.** What do you mean?
6. **Cyrano.** No, no, that's a little too short, young man! You might have said . . . . many things. . . . in different keys. For instance, listen: *Aggressive*: "I, Sir, had I such a nose, would at once have it amputated." *Descriptive*: "It is a rock!... a peak!!. . . . a headland!!! More than a headland, a whole peninsula!"—*Inquisitive*: "What may this oblong thing be used for? A writing-desk or a tool-chest?"—*Pleasant*: "Do you love birds so much that you feel bound to offer them so comfortable a resting place?" . . . That is about what you might have said, dear boy, if you had a sprinkling of letters and a bit of humor. Of humor, though, lamentable being, you never had an atom; and, as to letters, you never had but the four that spell the word Fool!—Some invention is requisite for extravagant jests before such an audience, but, even if you had it, you could not have uttered a quarter of the half of the beginning of what I said; for I may be willing to serve such sport myself, but I allow nobody to serve it to me.

Activity 6.3 Highlight at least one example of sarcasm and comment on its effect.

Toolbox

Read Between the Lines. Underline or highlight passages and add ideas and connections in the margins. By paying close attention to what is said as well as to what is not said, you will be more likely to grasp the author's purpose.

Try It

Directions: Oscar Wilde's greatest work, the play *The Importance of Being Earnest,* is famous for its sarcastic wit and witty critique of Victorian society. Read the following excerpt from the play. Then answer the questions that follow.

from The Importance of Being Earnest

by Oscar Wilde

In this scene, Jack and Algernon have just been scolded and rejected by Gwendolyn and Celia for not having the name Earnest.

	Notes
1. **JACK.** How can you sit there, calmly eating muffins when we are in this horrible trouble, I can't make out. You seem to me to be perfectly heartless.	
2. **ALGERNON.** Well, I can't eat muffins in an agitated manner. The butter would probably get on my cuffs. One should always eat muffins quite calmly. It is the only way to eat them.	
3. **JACK.** I say it's perfectly heartless your eating muffins at all under the circumstances.	
4. **ALGERNON.** When I am in trouble, eating is the only thing that consoles me. Indeed, when I am in really great trouble, as anyone who knows me intimately will tell you, I refuse everything except food and drink. At the present moment, I am eating muffins because I am unhappy. Besides, I am particularly fond of muffins.	
5. **JACK.** Well, that is no reason why you should eat them all in that greedy way. [*Takes muffins from* ALGERNON]	
6. **ALGERNON.** [*Offering tea-cake.*] I wish you would have tea-cake instead. I don't like tea-cake.	
7. **JACK.** Good heavens! I suppose a man may eat his own muffins in his own garden!	

5. Which of the following most accurately describes the author's tone and point of view in this excerpt?

Ⓐ Wilde uses a light tone to express his point of view that both characters are struggling mightily, though ineffectively, to deal with their horrible trouble.

Ⓑ Wilde uses sarcasm and a sense of the absurd to point out the fact that there is almost no actual difference between pastry items.

Ⓒ Wilde uses a playful tone to comment on a society that is obsessed with trivial concerns.

Ⓓ Wilde is humorously but pointedly commenting on the dangers of ignoring social conventions.

6. Write a paragraph explaining your answer to question 5.

____

____

____

____

____

Question 5 asks you to select the most accurate description of the author's tone and point of view in the excerpt. Choice A is incorrect because neither character shows the slightest interest in dealing with their so-called trouble. Choice B misses the mark because Wilde is mocking the young men, not the pastries. Choice C is correct. Having the two characters argue over the proper time, place, and method by which to eat muffins shows them as focused on trivial things. Choice D is incorrect because there is nothing in the excerpt to support it.

Question 6 asks you to write a paragraph explaining your answer to question 5. The following example shows one possible response.

> While Jack claims they are both in "horrible trouble," the argument that follows is about whether it is polite or decent of Algernon to eat muffins at this moment. The two get embroiled in a silly discussion that keeps them from focusing on the problem at hand—which itself is trivial. Wilde playfully uses their dialogue to expose his larger target, a society obsessed with trivialities instead of with real problems.

6.4 Understatement

Review

Understatement is a literary technique in which a serious situation is downplayed or made to appear insignificant. The opposite of **hyperbole**, which enlarges a point until it is out of proportion, understatement shrinks its point, leading the reader to think about what is not said.

Understatement is a versatile technique in that it can be used to highlight various human conditions and emotions such as modesty, sarcasm, or even love. Its aim is to emphasize a problem or situation by referring to it as much less severe than it is.

> **Key Terms**
>
> **hyperbole:** an exaggeration or overstatement.
>
> **understatement:** description of, or response to, a serious issue or event that deliberately undercuts its significance.

In J. D. Salinger's *A Catcher in the Rye,* the novel's youthful narrator chronicles a brief but turbulent period of his life. The narrative is peppered with comic understatements such as this one: "I have to have this little operation. It isn't very serious. I have this tiny little tumor on the brain."

Check Understanding

In the brief excerpt on the next page, note Shakespeare's use of understatement.

from Romeo and Juliet (Act 3, Scene 1)

by William Shakespeare

Notes

MERCUTIO. I am hurt.
A plague o' both your houses! I am sped.
. . . .
BENVOLIO. What, art thou hurt?
MERCUTIO. Ay, ay, a scratch, a scratch; marry, 'tis enough.
Where is my page? Go, villain, fetch a surgeon.
[*Exit Page.*]
ROMEO. Courage, man; the hurt cannot be much.
MERCUTIO. No, 'tis not so deep as a well, nor so wide as a church door; but 'tis enough, 'twill serve: ask for me to-morrow, and you shall find me a grave man. I am peppered, I warrant, for this world. . . .

Activity 6.4 Highlight and comment on any understatement in the passage.

Toolbox

Reading a passage aloud can help draw your attention to subtle changes in an author's tone. You can sometimes derive more meaning from what is not said than from what is.

Try It

Directions: Read the poem below and answer the questions that follow.

This Is Just to Say

by William Carlos Williams

Notes

I have eaten
the plums
that were in
the icebox

and which
you were probably
saving
for breakfast

Forgive me
they were delicious
so sweet
and so cold

7. "This Is Just to Say" is said to have started as a note from the poet to his wife. Given this, which statement do you think is the best interpretation of the author's purpose?

Ⓐ The speaker is deeply sorry for eating the plums because he knows his wife will be disappointed and perhaps even angry.

Ⓑ The speaker's words actually signify much larger issues of broken trust and a problematic marriage.

Ⓒ The speaker is making up for taking the plums by sharing with his wife the lovely, sensual experience of eating them.

Ⓓ The speaker is saying that he cannot really feel sorry about eating the plums because they were as delicious as he expected them to be.

8. Based on your answer to question 7, interpret the poem in your own words.

____

____

____

____

____

Question 7 asks for the strongest statement of the author's purpose in the poem. Choice A may or may not be true, but it is not clear from the poem, and it does not reflect the author's purpose. Choice B is incorrect because there is nothing in the poem to suggest a deep problem between the speaker and his wife. Choice C is correct because the poem reveals a desire to share a sensual experience. Choice D may or may not be true, but it is not a strong statement of the author's purpose.

Question 8 asks you to interpret the poem. Here is a sample answer:

> The speaker asks his wife for forgiveness, and then he goes on to describe his experience of eating the cold, sweet fruit. In this small moment and with simple, unadorned language, he shares with her a whole world of sensual pleasures that can come out of a seemingly ordinary experience.

Toolbox

Mine the Details. In a critical essay, don't feel that you have to retell the work you are interpreting. Assume that your reader is familiar enough with the work that a brief descriptive phrase will locate him or her in the text: "In the opening scene. . .", "In the parlor scene. . .", etc.

Strategies for Grasping Author's Point of View in Literary Texts

Use the following strategies to help you grasp an author's point of view and tone by distinguishing what is directly stated from what is actually meant, using satire, sarcasm, irony, or understatement.

- Be on the lookout for the unexpected. Pay close attention and take notes on any opposites, contradictions, unexpected outcomes, and unusual juxtapositions. These are often indicators of verbal, situational, or dramatic irony.
- Ask yourself what information you the reader might have that a character or characters in the text do not. The answer may lead you to a text's dramatic irony.
- Pay attention to satirical elements of hyperbole, innuendo, and irony to identify the social criticism at the heart of an author's point of view.
- The margin is a good place to add notes such as inferences and brief interpretations on figures of speech, literary devices, and author's point of view and tone.
- Once you have understood an author's use of irony, satire, sarcasm, or understatement, read through the work again to find added evidence to support your ideas.

Test-Taking Tips

- Preview the test or quiz before you write any answers. Get an idea of the test's scope and structure. This will help you more effectively budget your time.
- Read all the questions carefully and pay close attention to key words.
- Look for hints that reveal what is said and what is implied. This can help you locate clues you will need to understand the characters or themes and link them to the author's tone and purpose.
- Make a short outline before you begin a written response, making sure to address each part of the question.

Chapter Review

Directions: Read the story and answer the questions that follow.

Notes

The Necklace

by Guy de Maupassant

1. She was one of those pretty and charming girls born, as though fate had blundered over her, into a family of artisans. She had no marriage portion, no expectations, no means of getting known, understood, loved, and wedded by a man of wealth and distinction; and she let herself be married off to a little clerk in the Ministry of Education. Her tastes were simple because she had never been able to afford any other, but she was as unhappy as though she had married beneath her; for women have no caste or class, their beauty, grace, and charm serving them for birth or family, their natural delicacy, their instinctive elegance, their nimbleness of wit, are their only mark of rank, and put the slum girl on a level with the highest lady in the land.

2. She suffered endlessly, feeling herself born for every delicacy and luxury. She suffered from the poorness of her house, from its mean walls, worn chairs, and ugly curtains. All these things, of which other women of her class would not even have been aware, tormented and insulted her. The sight of the little Breton girl who came to do the work in her little house aroused heart-broken regrets and hopeless dreams in her mind. She imagined silent antechambers, heavy with Oriental tapestries, lit by torches in lofty bronze sockets, with two tall footmen in knee-breeches sleeping in large arm-chairs, overcome by the heavy warmth of the stove. She imagined vast saloons hung with antique silks, exquisite pieces of furniture supporting priceless ornaments, and small, charming, perfumed rooms, created just for little parties of intimate friends, men who were famous and sought after, whose homage roused every other woman's envious longings.

3. When she sat down for dinner at the round table covered with a three-days-old cloth, opposite her husband, who took the cover off the soup-tureen, exclaiming delightedly: "Aha! Scotch broth! What could be better?" she imagined delicate meals, gleaming silver, tapestries peopling the walls with folk of a past age and strange birds in faery forests; she imagined delicate food served in marvellous dishes, murmured gallantries, listened to with an inscrutable smile as one trifled with the rosy flesh of trout or wings of asparagus chicken.

4. She had no clothes, no jewels, nothing. And these were the only things she loved; she felt that she was made for them. She had longed so eagerly to charm, to be desired, to be wildly attractive and sought after.

5. She had a rich friend, an old school friend whom she refused to visit, because she suffered so keenly when she returned home. She would weep whole days, with grief, regret, despair, and misery.

6. One evening her husband came home with an exultant air, holding a large envelope in his hand.

7. "Here's something for you," he said.

8. Swiftly she tore the paper and drew out a printed card on which were these words:

9. "The Minister of Education and Madame Ramponneau request the pleasure of the company of Monsieur and Madame Loisel at the Ministry on the evening of Monday, January the 18th."

10. Instead of being delighted, as her husband hoped, she flung the invitation petulantly across the table, murmuring:

11. "What do you want me to do with this?"

12. "Why, darling, I thought you'd be pleased. You never go out, and this is a great occasion. I had tremendous trouble to get it. Every one wants one; it's very select, and very few go to the clerks. You'll see all the really big people there."

13. She looked at him out of furious eyes, and said impatiently: "And what do you suppose I am to wear at such an affair?"

14. He had not thought about it; he stammered:

15. "Why, the dress you go to the theatre in. It looks very nice, to me . . ."

16. He stopped, stupefied and utterly at a loss when he saw that his wife was beginning to cry. Two large tears ran slowly down from the corners of her eyes towards the corners of her mouth.

17. "What's the matter with you? What's the matter with you?" he faltered.

18. But with a violent effort she overcame her grief and replied in a calm voice, wiping her wet cheeks:

19. "Nothing. Only I haven't a dress and so I can't go to this party. Give your invitation to some friend of yours whose wife will be turned out better than I shall."

20. He was heart-broken.

21. "Look here, Mathilde," he persisted. "What would be the cost of a suitable dress, which you could use on other occasions as well, something very simple?"

22. She thought for several seconds, reckoning up prices and also wondering for how large a sum she could ask without bringing upon herself an immediate refusal and an exclamation of horror from the careful-minded clerk.

23. At last she replied with some hesitation:

24. "I don't know exactly, but I think I could do it on four hundred francs."

25. He grew slightly pale, for this was exactly the amount he had been saving for a gun, intending to get a little shooting next summer on the plain of Nanterre with some friends who went lark-shooting there on Sundays.

26. Nevertheless he said: "Very well. I'll give you four hundred francs. But try and get a really nice dress with the money."

27. The day of the party drew near, and Madame Loisel seemed sad,

Notes

uneasy and anxious. Her dress was ready, however. One evening her husband said to her:

28. "What's the matter with you? You've been very odd for the last three days."

29. "I'm utterly miserable at not having any jewels, not a single stone, to wear," she replied. "I shall look absolutely no one. I would almost rather not go to the party."

30. "Wear flowers," he said. "They're very smart at this time of the year. For ten francs you could get two or three gorgeous roses."

31. She was not convinced.

32. "No . . . there's nothing so humiliating as looking poor in the middle of a lot of rich women."

33. "How stupid you are!" exclaimed her husband. "Go and see Madame Forestier and ask her to lend you some jewels. You know her quite well enough for that."

34. She uttered a cry of delight.

35. "That's true. I never thought of it."

36. Next day she went to see her friend and told her her trouble.

37. Madame Forestier went to her dressing-table, took up a large box, brought it to Madame Loisel, opened it, and said:

38. "Choose, my dear."

39. First she saw some bracelets, then a pearl necklace, then a Venetian cross in gold and gems, of exquisite workmanship. She tried the effect of the jewels before the mirror, hesitating, unable to make up her mind to leave them, to give them up. She kept on asking:

40. "Haven't you anything else?"

41. "Yes. Look for yourself. I don't know what you would like best."

42. Suddenly she discovered, in a black satin case, a superb diamond necklace; her heart began to beat covetously. Her hands trembled as she lifted it. She fastened it round her neck, upon her high dress, and remained in ecstasy at sight of herself.

43. Then, with hesitation, she asked in anguish:

44. "Could you lend me this, just this alone?"

45. "Yes, of course."

46. She flung herself on her friend's breast, embraced her frenziedly, and went away with her treasure. The day of the party arrived. Madame Loisel was a success. She was the prettiest woman present, elegant, graceful, smiling, and quite above herself with happiness. All the men stared at her, inquired her name, and asked to be introduced to her. All the Under-Secretaries of State were eager to waltz with her. The Minister noticed her.

47. She danced madly, ecstatically, drunk with pleasure, with no thought for anything, in the triumph of her beauty, in the pride of her success, in a cloud of happiness made up of this universal homage and admiration, of the desires she had aroused, of the completeness of a victory so dear to her feminine heart.

48. She left about four o'clock in the morning. Since midnight her husband had been dozing in a deserted little room, in company with

Notes

three other men whose wives were having a good time. He threw over her shoulders the garments he had brought for them to go home in, modest everyday clothes, whose poverty clashed with the beauty of the ball-dress. She was conscious of this and was anxious to hurry away, so that she should not be noticed by the other women putting on their costly furs.

Notes

49. Loisel restrained her.

50. "Wait a little. You'll catch cold in the open. I'm going to fetch a cab."

51. But she did not listen to him and rapidly descended the staircase. When they were out in the street they could not find a cab; they began to look for one, shouting at the drivers whom they saw passing in the distance.

52. They walked down towards the Seine, desperate and shivering. At last they found on the quay one of those old nightprowling carriages which are only to be seen in Paris after dark, as though they were ashamed of their shabbiness in the daylight.

53. It brought them to their door in the Rue des Martyrs, and sadly they walked up to their own apartment. It was the end, for her. As for him, he was thinking that he must be at the office at ten.

54. She took off the garments in which she had wrapped her shoulders, so as to see herself in all her glory before the mirror. But suddenly she uttered a cry. The necklace was no longer round her neck!

55. "What's the matter with you?" asked her husband, already half undressed.

56. She turned towards him in the utmost distress.

57. "I . . . I . . . I've no longer got Madame Forestier's necklace. . . ."

58. He started with astonishment.

59. "What! . . . Impossible!"

60. They searched in the folds of her dress, in the folds of the coat, in the pockets, everywhere. They could not find it.

61. "Are you sure that you still had it on when you came away from the ball?" he asked.

62. "Yes, I touched it in the hall at the Ministry."

63. "But if you had lost it in the street, we should have heard it fall."

64. "Yes. Probably we should. Did you take the number of the cab?"

65. "No. You didn't notice it, did you?"

66. "No."

67. They stared at one another, dumbfounded. At last Loisel put on his clothes again.

68. "I'll go over all the ground we walked," he said, "and see if I can't find it."

69. And he went out. She remained in her evening clothes, lacking strength to get into bed, huddled on a chair, without volition or power of thought.

70. Her husband returned about seven. He had found nothing.

71. He went to the police station, to the newspapers, to offer a reward, to the cab companies, everywhere that a ray of hope impelled him.

72. She waited all day long, in the same state of bewilderment at this fearful catastrophe.

73. Loisel came home at night, his face lined and pale; he had discovered nothing.

74. "You must write to your friend," he said, "and tell her that you've broken the clasp of her necklace and are getting it mended. That will give us time to look about us."

75. She wrote at his dictation.

76. By the end of a week they had lost all hope.

77. Loisel, who had aged five years, declared:

78. "We must see about replacing the diamonds."

79. Next day they took the box which had held the necklace and went to the jewellers whose name was inside. He consulted his books.

80. "It was not I who sold this necklace, Madame; I must have merely supplied the clasp."

81. Then they went from jeweller to jeweller, searching for another necklace like the first, consulting their memories, both ill with remorse and anguish of mind.

82. In a shop at the Palais-Royal they found a string of diamonds which seemed to them exactly like the one they were looking for. It was worth forty thousand francs. They were allowed to have it for thirty-six thousand.

83. They begged the jeweller not to sell it for three days. And they arranged matters on the understanding that it would be taken back for thirty-four thousand francs, if the first one were found before the end of February.

84. Loisel possessed eighteen thousand francs left to him by his father. He intended to borrow the rest.

85. He did borrow it, getting a thousand from one man, five hundred from another, five louis here, three louis there. He gave notes of hand, entered into ruinous agreements, did business with usurers and the whole tribe of money-lenders. He mortgaged the whole remaining years of his existence, risked his signature without even knowing if he could honour it, and, appalled at the agonising face of the future, at the black misery about to fall upon him, at the prospect of every possible physical privation and moral torture, he went to get the new necklace and put down upon the jeweller's counter thirty-six thousand francs.

86. When Madame Loisel took back the necklace to Madame Forestier, the latter said to her in a chilly voice:

87. "You ought to have brought it back sooner; I might have needed it."

88. She did not, as her friend had feared, open the case. If she had noticed the substitution, what would she have thought? What would she have said? Would she not have taken her for a thief?

89. Madame Loisel came to know the ghastly life of abject poverty. From the very first she played her part heroically. This fearful debt must be paid off. She would pay it. The servant was dismissed. They changed their flat; they took a garret under the roof.

90. She came to know the heavy work of the house, the hateful duties of the kitchen. She washed the plates, wearing out her pink nails on the coarse pottery and the bottoms of pans. She washed the dirty

Notes

linen, the shirts and dish-cloths, and hung them out to dry on a string; every morning she took the dustbin down into the street and carried up the water, stopping on each landing to get her breath. And, clad like a poor woman, she went to the fruiterer, to the grocer, to the butcher, a basket on her arm, haggling, insulted, fighting for every wretched halfpenny of her money.

91. Every month notes had to be paid off, others renewed, time gained.

92. Her husband worked in the evenings at putting straight a merchant's accounts, and often at night he did copying at twopence-halfpenny a page.

93. And this life lasted ten years.

94. At the end of ten years everything was paid off, everything, the usurer's charges and the accumulation of superimposed interest.

95. Madame Loisel looked old now. She had become like all the other strong, hard, coarse women of poor households. Her hair was badly done, her skirts were awry, her hands were red. She spoke in a shrill voice, and the water slopped all over the floor when she scrubbed it. But sometimes, when her husband was at the office, she sat down by the window and thought of that evening long ago, of the ball at which she had been so beautiful and so much admired.

96. What would have happened if she had never lost those jewels. Who knows? Who knows? How strange life is, how fickle! How little is needed to ruin or to save!

97. One Sunday, as she had gone for a walk along the Champs-Elysees to freshen herself after the labours of the week, she caught sight suddenly of a woman who was taking a child out for a walk. It was Madame Forestier, still young, still beautiful, still attractive.

98. Madame Loisel was conscious of some emotion. Should she speak to her? Yes, certainly. And now that she had paid, she would tell her all. Why not?

99. She went up to her.

100. "Good morning, Jeanne."

101. The other did not recognise her, and was surprised at being thus familiarly addressed by a poor woman.

102. "But . . . Madame . . ." she stammered. "I don't know . . . you must be making a mistake."

103. "No . . . I am Mathilde Loisel."

104. Her friend uttered a cry.

105. "Oh! . . . my poor Mathilde, how you have changed! . . ."

106. "Yes, I've had some hard times since I saw you last; and many sorrows . . . and all on your account."

107. "On my account! . . . How was that?"

108. "You remember the diamond necklace you lent me for the ball at the Ministry?"

109. "Yes. Well?"

110. "Well, I lost it."

111. "How could you? Why, you brought it back."

112. "I brought you another one just like it. And for the last ten years we have been paying for it. You realise it wasn't easy for us; we had

Notes

no money. . . . Well, it's paid for at last, and I'm glad indeed."

113. Madame Forestier had halted.

114. "You say you bought a diamond necklace to replace mine?"

115. "Yes. You hadn't noticed it? They were very much alike."

116. And she smiled in proud and innocent happiness.

117. Madame Forestier, deeply moved, took her two hands.

118. "Oh, my poor Mathilde! But mine was imitation. It was worth at the very most five hundred francs! . . ."

Notes

Questions 1–7: Choose the best answer or write your response on the lines.

1. Which of the following shows an example of verbal irony in the story?

Ⓐ "Nothing. Only I haven't a dress and so I can't go to this party. Give your invitation to some friend of yours whose wife will be turned out better than I shall."

Ⓑ "Wear flowers," he said. "They're very smart at this time of the year. For ten francs you could get two or three gorgeous roses."

Ⓒ "Yes. Look for yourself. I don't know what you would like best."

Ⓓ "I brought you another one just like it. And for the last ten years we have been paying for it. You realise it wasn't easy for us; we had no money. . . . Well, it's paid for at last, and I'm glad indeed."

2. On the lines below, gives reasons to support your answer to question 1.

3. Describe the author's use of sarcasm in paragraph 2 of the story.

4. Explain how "The Necklace" might be described as a satire.

5. Use details from the story to back up your answer to question 4.

6. Which of the following offers the strongest statement of the situational irony in the story?

Ⓐ Mathilde's husband is innocent of wrongdoing, yet he suffers as greatly as she does as a result of her actions.

Ⓑ Mathilde spends the entire story trying to escape who she really is and in the end she finds out that such escape is not possible.

Ⓒ Mathilde tries to appear to have more money and social status than she actually does and her own actions bring on her financial ruin and even the loss of the status she once had.

Ⓓ Mathilde goes to the ministerial ball with her husband and ends up having a wonderful time even though she loses the borrowed necklace.

7. Explain an aspect of "The Necklace" that might be taken as dramatic irony.

Unit 1 Review Test

Questions 1–8: Read this shortened version of the story "The Piece of String." Then, for each of the multiple-choice questions that follow, select the best answer from the choices given.

from The Piece of String

by Guy de Maupassant

1. On all the roads about Goderville the peasants and their wives were coming toward the town, for it was market day. . . . On the square at Goderville there was a crowd, a medley of men and beasts. The sharp, shrill, high-pitched voices formed an incessant, uncivilized uproar, over which soared at times a roar of laughter from the powerful chest of a sturdy yokel, or the prolonged bellow of a cow. . . .

2. Master Hauchecorne, of Bréauté, had just arrived at Goderville, and was walking toward the square, when he saw a bit of string on the ground. Master Hauchecorne, economical like every true Norman,[1] thought that it was well to pick up everything that might be of use; and he stooped painfully, for he suffered with rheumatism. He took the piece of slender cord from the ground, and was about to roll it up carefully, when he saw Master Malandain, the harness-maker, standing in his doorway and looking at him. They had formerly had trouble on the subject of a halter, and had remained at odds, being both inclined to bear malice. Master Hauchecorne felt a sort of shame at being seen thus by his enemy, fumbling in the mud for a bit of string. He hurriedly concealed his treasure in his blouse, then in his breeches[2] pocket; then he pretended to look on the ground for something else, which he did not find; and finally he went on toward the market, his head thrust forward, bent double by his pains. . . .

3. At Jourdain's the common room[3] was full of customers, as the great yard was full of vehicles of every sort. . . .All the aristocracy of the plow ate there, the innkeeper and horse trader. . . .

4. Suddenly a drum rolled in the yard, and the public crier shouted in a jerky voice, making his pauses in the wrong places:

5. "The people of Goderville, and all those present at the market are informed that between—nine and ten o'clock this morning on the Beuzeville—road, a black leather wallet was lost, containing five—hundred francs, and business papers. The finder is requested to carry it to—the mayor's at once, or to Master Fortuné Huelbrèque of Manneville. A reward of twenty francs will be paid."

6. . . . They were finishing their coffee when the corporal of gendarmes[4] appeared in the doorway.

7. He inquired: "Is Master Hauchecorne of Bréauté here?"

1 Norman: a person of Normandy, a region in northwestern France
2 breeches: trousers reaching just below the knees
3 common room: room used by all the inn's patrons
4 gendarmes (zhän därm): French police

8. Master Hauchecorne, who was seated at the farther end of the table, answered: "Here I am."

9. And the corporal added: "Master Hauchecorne, will you be kind enough to go to the mayor's office with me? Monsieur[5] the mayor would like to speak to you."

10. The peasant, surprised and disturbed, . . . followed the brigadier.

11. The mayor was waiting for him, seated in his armchair. He was the local notary, a stout, solemn-faced man, given to pompous speeches.

12. "Master Hauchecorne," he said, "you were seen this morning, on the Beuzeville road, to pick up the wallet lost by Master Huelbrèque of Manneville."

13. The rustic, dumfounded, stared at the mayor, already alarmed by this suspicion which had fallen upon him, although he failed to understand it.

14. "I, I—I picked up that wallet?"

15. "Yes, you."

16. "On my word of honor, I didn't even so much as see it."

17. "You were seen."

18. "They saw me, me? Who was it saw me?"

19. "Monsieur Malandain, the harness-maker."

20. Thereupon the old man remembered and understood; and flushing with anger, he cried: "Ah! he saw me, did he, that sneak? He saw me pick up this string, look, m'sieu'[6] mayor."

21. And fumbling in the depths of his pocket, he produced the little piece of cord.

22. But the mayor was incredulous and shook his head.

23. "You won't make me believe, Master Hauchecorne, that Monsieur Malandain, who is a man deserving of credit, mistook this string for a wallet."

24. The peasant, in a rage, raised his hand, spit to one side to pledge his honor, and said: "It's God's own truth, the sacred truth, all the same, m'sieu' mayor. I say it again, by my soul and my salvation."

25. "After picking it up," rejoined the mayor, "you hunted a long while in the mud, to see if some piece of money hadn't fallen out."

26. The good man was suffocated with wrath and fear.

27. "If anyone can tell—if anyone can tell lies like that to ruin an honest man! If anyone can say—"

28. To no purpose did he protest; he was not believed.

29. He was confronted with Monsieur Malandain, who repeated and maintained his declaration. They insulted each other for a whole hour. At his own request, Master Hauchecorne was searched. They found nothing on him. At last the mayor, being sorely perplexed, discharged him, but warned him that he proposed to inform the prosecuting attorney's office and to ask for orders.

30. The news had spread. On leaving the mayor's office, the old man was surrounded and questioned with serious or bantering curiosity, in which, however, there was no trace of indignation. And he began to tell the story of the string. They did not believe him. They laughed. . . .

31. During the evening he made a circuit of the village of Bréauté, in order to tell everybody about it. He found none but incredulous listeners.

32. He was ill over it all night.

---

5 Monsieur: French title of respect, similar to *Mister* in English

6 m'sieu': Hauchecorne's clipped pronunciation of Monsieur

33. The next afternoon, about one o'clock, Marius Paumelle, a farmhand employed by Master Breton, a farmer of Ymauville, restored the wallet and its contents to Master Huelbrèque of Manneville.

34. The man claimed that he had found it on the road; but, being unable to read, had carried it home and given it to his employer.

35. The news soon became known in the neighborhood; Master Hauchecorne was informed of it. He started out again at once, and began to tell his story, now made complete by the dénouement. He was triumphant.

36. "What made me feel bad," he said, "wasn't so much the thing itself, you understand, but the lying. There's nothing hurts you so much as being blamed for lying."

37. . . . On Tuesday of the next week, he went to market at Goderville, impelled solely by the longing to tell his story. . . .

38. He accosted a farmer from Criquetot, who did not let him finish, but poked him in the pit of his stomach, and shouted in his face: "Go on, you old fox!" Then he turned on his heel.

39. Master Hauchecorne was speechless, and more and more disturbed. Why did he call him "old fox"?

40. When he was seated at the table in Jourdain's Inn, he set about explaining the affair once more.

41. A horse-trader from Montvilliers called out to him: "Nonsense, nonsense, you old dodger! I know all about your string!"

42. "But they've found the wallet!" faltered Hauchecorne.

43. "None of that, old boy; there's one who finds it, and there's one who carries it back. I don't know just how you did it, but I understand you."

44. The peasant was fairly stunned. He understood at last. He was accused of having sent the wallet back by a confederate, an accomplice.

45. He tried to protest. The whole table began to laugh.

46. He could not finish his dinner, but left the inn amid a chorus of jeers.

47. . . . Thereupon he began once more to tell of the adventure, making the story longer each day, adding each time new arguments, more forcible protestations, more solemn oaths, which he devised and prepared in his hours of solitude, his mind being wholly engrossed by the story of the string. The more complicated his defense and the more subtle his reasoning, the less he was believed.

48. "Those are a liar's reasons," people said behind his back.

49. He realized it: he gnawed his nails, and exhausted himself in vain efforts.

50. He grew perceptibly thinner.

51. Now the jokers asked him to tell the story of "The Piece of String" for their amusement, as a soldier who has seen service is asked to tell about his battles. His mind, attacked at its source, grew feebler.

52. Late in December he took to his bed.

53. In the first days of January he died, and in his delirium, of the death agony, he protested his innocence, repeating: "A little piece of string—a little piece of string—see, here it is, m'sieu' mayor."

1. How does the story open?

Ⓐ with a frame narrative

Ⓑ with a paragraph of exposition

Ⓒ with a flashback

Ⓓ *in medias res*

2. From the explicit details and implicit meanings, what can you infer is the setting of the story?

Ⓐ rural France

Ⓑ a Paris neighborhood

Ⓒ contemporary Normandy

Ⓓ the Québec frontier

3. What two chief character flaws does Hauchecorne display in this story?

Ⓐ He is greedy and dishonest.

Ⓑ He is overly proud and ambitious.

Ⓒ He worries too much and is too much of an intellectual.

Ⓓ He is overly thrifty and cares too much about his reputation.

4. On what conflict do the events of the story's plot center?

Ⓐ Hauchecorne's struggle with poverty

Ⓑ Hauchecorne's quarrel with Malandain

Ⓒ Hauchecorne's struggle to prove himself innocent

Ⓓ Hauchecorne's struggle, along with the other peasants', to sell goods at the market

5. Which of these statements from the story most clearly conveys a sarcastic tone?

Ⓐ On all the roads about Goderville the peasants and their wives were coming toward the town, for it was market day. (#1)

Ⓑ All the aristocracy of the plow ate there, the innkeeper and horse trader. (#3)

Ⓒ "You won't make me believe, Master Hauchecorne, that Monsieur Malandain, who is a man deserving of credit, mistook this string for a wallet." (#22)

Ⓓ He accosted a farmer from Criquetot, who did not let him finish, but poked him in the pit of his stomach, and shouted in his face: "Go on, you old fox!" (#37)

6. What motivates Hauchecorne to keep telling his story over and over?

Ⓐ He likes being the center of attention.

Ⓑ He wants to show his enemy Malandain in a bad light.

Ⓒ He wants others to recognize that he did not find and keep the wallet.

Ⓓ He wants to fool others with his lies.

7. What sort of resolution or ending does the story have?

Ⓐ tragic

Ⓑ comedic

Ⓒ unresolved

Ⓓ mixed

8. Which statement most accurately expresses the author's point of view with regard to the story's characters?

Ⓐ He considers them highly complex human beings whose motivations are often a mystery.

Ⓑ He considers them fairly flat and predictable and does not show them great sympathy.

Ⓒ He shows deep respect for his characters' struggles to survive.

Ⓓ He idealizes his characters as simple but noble folk who live close to the land.

Questions 9–16: Read this poem by Elinor Wylie. Then, for each of the multiple-choice questions that follow, select the best answer from the choices given.

Sanctuary

by Elinor Wylie

This is the bricklayer; hear the thud
Of his heavy load dumped down on stone.
His lustrous bricks are brighter than blood,
His smoking mortar[1] whiter than bone.

Set each sharp-edged, fire-bitten[2] brick
Straight by the plumb-line's[3] shivering length;
Make my marvelous wall so thick
Dead nor living may shake its strength.

Full as a crystal cup with drink
Is my cell with dreams, and quiet, and cool. . . .
Stop, old man! You must leave a chink;
How can I breathe? *You can't, you fool!*

1 mortar: mixture of sand, lime, and water used between bricks to bind them together

2 fire-bitten: made in a kiln, a small furnace or oven, usually with visible flames, in which clay is baked and dried into bricks

3 plumb-line: a piece of string with a lead weight at the bottom used to determine if something is vertical

9. Which statement gives the best objective summary of the explicit details of the poem?

Ⓐ The speaker describes a bricklayer who works hard and with great precision to make structures in which people live.

Ⓑ A bricklayer seeks revenge by building the speaker a "sanctuary" that is actually a tomb in which the speaker cannot breathe.

Ⓒ The speaker hires a bricklayer to build a sanctuary. The speaker realizes too late that the design is so secure that she cannot breathe.

Ⓓ The speaker is in love with a man who walls her off from others. She enjoys the experience at first but then feels stifled.

10. Consider the diction in the first two lines of the poem. What connotations do the words *thud* and *dumped* have?

Ⓐ Both words have positive connotations.

Ⓑ Both words have negative connotations.

Ⓒ *Thud* has positive connotations, but *dumped* has negative connotations.

Ⓓ *Thud* has negative connotations, but *dumped* has positive connotations.

11. What do the similes in lines 3 and 4 help capture?

Ⓐ the human spirit behind the bricklayer's actions

Ⓑ the foolishness of the speaker's ideas

Ⓒ the sense of relief that the speaker feels

Ⓓ the deadly finality of the bricklayer's actions

12. Which lines contain the clearest example of hyperbole used to emphasize the speaker's feelings?

Ⓐ lines 1–2

Ⓑ line 5–6

Ⓒ lines 7–8

Ⓓ lines 9–10

13. How is the tone in lines 9 and 10 unlike that of the rest of the poem?

Ⓐ It is peaceful and dreamy.

Ⓑ It is wise and clever.

Ⓒ It is scary and anxious.

Ⓓ It is harsh and bitter.

14. The identity of the speaker of the poem's last four words is one of its uncertainties. Which detail best supports the interpretation that the bricklayer speaks those words?

Ⓐ The poem opens "This is the bricklayer."

Ⓑ In lines 3–4, the bricklayer's bricks are described as "brighter than blood" and his mortar as "whiter than bone."

Ⓒ Line 6 uses the possessive form of the technical term *plumb-line.*

Ⓓ In lines 11–12, the speaker addresses the "old man," and the use of italics suggests that he is responding.

15. What do the poem's last two lines most clearly illustrate?

Ⓐ verbal irony

Ⓑ situational irony

Ⓒ dramatic irony

Ⓓ understatement

16. Which of these statements best expresses a main theme of the poem?

Ⓐ No one can ever really escape society.

Ⓑ Intellectuals in ivory towers do not understand the real-life problems of everyday people.

Ⓒ Shutting yourself off from the world is ultimately self-destructive.

Ⓓ Sometimes the person you think is helping you is actually harming you.

Questions 17–24: Read this excerpt from the opening scene of the drama *Pygmalion*. Then, for each of the multiple-choice questions that follow, select the best answer from the choices given.

from Pygmalion

by George Bernard Shaw

[*Covent Garden*[1] *at 11.15 p.m. Torrents of heavy summer rain. Cab whistles blowing frantically in all directions. Pedestrians running for shelter into the market and under the portico of St. Paul's Church, where there are already several people, among them a lady and her daughter in evening dress. They are all peering out gloomily at the rain, except one man with his back turned to the rest, who seems wholly preoccupied with a notebook in which he is writing busily.*] . . .

1. **The Bystander.** He ain't a tec.[2] He's a blooming busybody: that's what he is. I tell you, look at his boots.
2. **The Note Taker** [*turning on him genially*] And how are all your people down at Selsey?
3. **The Bystander** [*suspiciously*] Who told you my people come from Selsey?
4. **The Note Taker.** Never you mind. They did. [*To the girl*] How do you come to be up so far east? You were born in Lisson Grove.
5. **The Flower Girl**[3] [*appalled*] Oh, what harm is there in my leaving Lisson Grove? It wasn't fit for a pig to live in; and I had to pay four-and-six a week. [*In tears*] Oh, boo—hoo—oo—
6. **The Note Taker.** Live where you like; but stop that noise.
7. **The Gentleman** [*to the girl*] Come, come! he can't touch you: you have a right to live where you please. . . .
8. **The Flower Girl** [*subsiding into a brooding melancholy over her basket, and talking very low-spiritedly to herself*] I'm a good girl, I am.
9. **The Sarcastic Bystander** [*not attending to her*] Do you know where *I* come from?
10. **The Note Taker** [*promptly*] Hoxton.
11. [*Titterings. Popular interest in the note taker's performance increases.*]
12. **The Sarcastic One** [*amazed*] Well, who said I didn't? Bly me![4] You know everything, you do. . . . Tell HIM where he come from if you want to go fortune-telling.
13. **The Note Taker.** Cheltenham, Harrow, Cambridge,[5] and India.
14. **The Gentleman.** Quite right. [*Great laughter. Reaction in the note taker's favor.*

---

1 Covent Garden: area of central London with a large outdoor market, the Royal Opera House, and St. Paul's Church (a small church, not the large London cathedral also called St. Paul's)

2 tec: slang for a detective.

3 Flower Girl: young woman street vendor selling flowers.

4 Bly me: Shaw's spelling of *blimey*, a British exclamation of wonder

5 Harrow, Cambridge: Harrow is a prestigious British boys' school; Cambridge is one of Britain's two leading universities.

Exclamations of He knows all about it. Told him proper. Hear him tell the toff[6] *where he come from? etc.*]. May I ask, sir, do you do this for your living at a music hall?

15. **The Note Taker.** I've thought of that. Perhaps I shall some day.

16. [*The rain has stopped; and the persons on the outside of the crowd begin to drop off.*]

17. **The Flower Girl** [*resenting the reaction*] He's no gentleman, he ain't, to interfere with a poor girl.

18. **The Daughter** [*out of patience, pushing her way rudely to the front and displacing the gentleman, who politely retires to the other side of the pillar*] What on earth is Freddy doing? I shall get pneumonia if I stay in this draft any longer.

19. **The Note Taker** [*to himself, hastily making a note of her pronunciation of "monia"*] Earlscourt.

20. **The Daughter** [*violently*] Will you please keep your impertinent remarks to yourself?

21. **The Note Taker.** Did I say that out loud? I didn't mean to. I beg your pardon. Your mother's Epsom, unmistakably.

22. **The Mother** [*advancing between her daughter and the note taker*] How very curious! I was brought up in Largelady Park, near Epsom.

23. **The Note Taker** [*uproariously amused*] Ha! ha! What a devil of a name! . . .

24. **The Sarcastic Bystander.** I can tell where you come from. You come from Anwell. Go back there.

25. **The Note Taker** [*helpfully*] *H*anwell.[7]

26. **The Sarcastic Bystander** [*affecting great distinction of speech*] Thenk you, teacher. Haw haw! So long [*he touches his hat with mock respect and strolls off*]. . . .

27. [*All the rest have gone except the note taker, the gentleman, and the flower girl, who sits arranging her basket, and still pitying herself in murmurs. . . .*]

28. **The Gentleman** [*returning to his former place on the note taker's left*] How do you do it, if I may ask?

29. **The Note Taker.** Simply phonetics. The science of speech. That's my profession; also my hobby. Happy is the man who can make a living by his hobby! You can spot an Irishman or a Yorkshireman by his brogue. I can place any man within six miles. I can place him within two miles in London. Sometimes within two streets.

30. **The Flower Girl.** Ought to be ashamed of himself, unmanly coward!

31. **The Gentleman.** But is there a living in that?

32. **The Note Taker.** Oh yes. Quite a fat one. This is an age of upstarts. Men begin in Kentish Town with 80 pounds a year, and end in Park Lane with a hundred thousand. They want to drop Kentish Town; but they give themselves away every time they open their mouths. Now I can teach them—

---

6 toff: British slang for a fashionable, upper-class person

7 Hanwell: a well-known British mental asylum

33. **The Flower Girl.** Let him mind his own business and leave a poor girl—

34. **The Note Taker** [*explosively*] Woman: cease this detestable boohooing instantly; or else seek the shelter of some other place of worship.

35. **The Flower Girl** [*with feeble defiance*] I've a right to be here if I like, same as you.

36. **The Note Taker.** A woman who utters such depressing and disgusting sounds has no right to be anywhere—no right to live. Remember that you are a human being with a soul and the divine gift of articulate speech: that your native language is the language of Shakespeare and Milton and The Bible; and don't sit there crooning like a bilious pigeon.

37. **The Flower Girl** [*quite overwhelmed, and looking up at him in mingled wonder and deprecation without daring to raise her head*] Ah—ah—ah—ow—ow—oo!

38. **The Note Taker** [*whipping out his book*] Heavens! what a sound! [*He writes; then holds out the book and reads, reproducing her vowels exactly*] Ah—ah—ah—ow—ow—ow—oo!

39. **The Flower Girl** [*tickled by the performance, and laughing in spite of herself*] Garn!

40. **The Note Taker.** You see this creature with her curbstone English: the English that will keep her in the gutter to the end of her days. Well, sir, in three months I could pass that girl off as a duchess at an ambassador's garden party. I could even get her a place as lady's maid or shop assistant, which requires better English. That's the sort of thing I do for commercial millionaires. And on the profits of it I do genuine scientific work in phonetics, and a little as a poet on Miltonic lines.

41. **The Gentleman.** I am myself a student of Indian dialects; and—

42. **The Note Taker** [*eagerly*] Are you? Do you know Colonel Pickering, the author of *Spoken Sanskrit?*

43. **The Gentleman.** I am Colonel Pickering. Who are you?

44. **The Note Taker.** Henry Higgins, author of *Higgins's Universal Alphabet.*

45. **Pickering** [*with enthusiasm*] I came from India to meet you.

46. **Higgins.** I was going to India to meet you.

17. Reread the opening stage directions and the footnote that accompanies them. What does the textual evidence suggest has just happened as the scene opens?

Ⓐ The rain has just stopped.

Ⓑ St. Paul's Church has just let out.

Ⓒ The Covent Garden Market has just opened.

Ⓓ The Royal Opera House has just let out.

18. From the context, what do you conclude the word *blooming* means in the Bystander's first remarks (speech 1)?

Ⓐ just coming into flower; beginning

Ⓑ flowery; ornate

Ⓒ utter; total

Ⓓ shabby; unkempt

19. The Note Taker, Henry Higgins, is a round character who will turn out to be the play's protagonist. Which of these statements best describes him, based on his characterization in this scene?

Ⓐ He is smart and tactful.

Ⓑ He is clever and opinionated.

Ⓒ He is romantic and boastful.

Ⓓ He is knowledgeable but modest.

20. From the scene's explicit details as well as its implicit meanings, what motivation do you conclude Henry Higgins has for taking notes?

Ⓐ He is hunting for Colonel Pickering, author of *Spoken Sanskrit*.

Ⓑ He is looking for pupils for his speech-improvement business.

Ⓒ He is recording speech patterns for his study of phonetics.

Ⓓ He is practicing for an audition to be a performer at a British music hall.

21. Which word best describes the mood of this scene?

Ⓐ comical

Ⓑ gloomy

Ⓒ suspenseful

Ⓓ romantic

22. Which dialogue from the scene is the best example of verbal irony?

Ⓐ I'm a good girl, I am. (#8)

Ⓑ How very curious! I was brought up in Largelady Park, near Epsom. (#22)

Ⓒ Thenk you, teacher. Haw haw! (#26)

Ⓓ I was going to India to meet you. (#46)

23. Which dialogue from the scene most likely foreshadows something that will happen later in the play?

Ⓐ Oh, what harm is there in my leaving Lisson Grove? It wasn't fit for a pig to live in, and I had to pay four-and-six a week. (#5)

Ⓑ May I ask, sir, do you do this for your living at a music hall? (#14)

Ⓒ I shall get pneumonia if I stay in this draft any longer. (#18)

Ⓓ Well, sir, in three months I could pass that girl off as a duchess at an ambassador's garden party. (#40)

24. From the cultural context of this scene, which circumstance in society seems to be the main target of Shaw's satire in *Pygmalion?*

Ⓐ class distinctions

Ⓑ religious hypocrisy

Ⓒ the education system

Ⓓ the police

Text Analysis

Closely read this shortened version of the story "Like the Sun" and then write a text-based response of two to three paragraphs. In your response, identify a main theme that the author is trying to convey and analyze how the story's plot or characters help develop this theme. Use strong and thorough evidence from the text to support your analysis. Do not simply summarize the text. You may use the margins to take notes as you read and to plan your response.

Guidelines

Be sure to

- Clearly state the theme intended by the author.
- Accurately discuss the plot or characters in showing how one of these two elements helps develop the theme.
- Use strong and thorough evidence from the text to support your analysis.
- Organize your ideas in a cohesive and coherent manner.
- Maintain a formal style of writing.
- Follow the conventions of standard written English.

from Like the Sun

by R. K. Narayan

1. Truth, Sekhar reflected, is like the sun. I suppose no human being can ever look it straight in the face without blinking or being dazed. He realized that, morning till night, the essence of human relationships consisted in tempering truth so that it might not shock. This day he set apart as a unique day—at least one day in the year we must give and take absolute Truth whatever may happen. Otherwise life is not worth living. The day ahead seemed to him full of possibilities. He told no one of his experiment. It was a quiet resolve, a secret pact between him and eternity.

2. The very first test came while his wife served him his morning meal. He showed hesitation over a tidbit, which she had thought was her culinary masterpiece. She asked, "Why, isn't it good?" At other times he would have said, considering her feelings in the matter, "I feel full-up, that's all." But today he said, "It isn't good. I'm unable to swallow it." He saw her wince and said to himself, Can't be helped. Truth is like the sun.

3. His next trial was in the common room[1] when one of his colleagues came up and said, "Did you hear of the death of so and so? Don't you think it a pity?" "No," Sekhar answered. "He was such a fine man—" the other began. But Sekhar cut him short with: "Far from it. He always struck me as a mean and selfish brute."

4. During the last period when he was teaching geography for Third Form A[2], Sekhar received a note from the headmaster: "Please see me before you go home." Sekhar said to himself: It must be about these horrible test papers. A hundred papers in the boys' scrawls; he had shirked this work for weeks, feeling all the time as if a sword were hanging over his head.

1 common room: faculty lounge or meeting room

2 Third Form A: similar to a class of middle-school level in U.S. schools

5. . . . . The headmaster looked up at him in a very friendly manner and asked, "Are you free this evening? . . . . I've been learning and practicing secretly, and now I want . . . your opinion. I know it will be valuable."

6. Sekhar's taste in music was well known. He was one of the most dreaded music critics in the town. But he never anticipated his musical inclinations would lead him to this trial . . . .

7. At home the headmaster proved very ingratiating. He sat Sekhar on a red silk carpet, set before him several dishes of delicacies, and fussed over him as if he were a son-in-law of the house. He even said, "Well, you must listen with a free mind. Don't worry about these test papers." He added half humorously, "I will give you a week's time."

8. "Make it ten days, sir," Sekhar pleaded.

9. "All right, granted," the headmaster said generously. Sekhar felt really relieved now—he would attack them at the rate of ten a day and get rid of the nuisance.

10. The headmaster lighted incense sticks. "Just to create the right atmosphere," he explained. A drummer and a violinist, already seated on a Rangoon mat[3], were waiting for him. The headmaster sat down between them like a professional at a concert, cleared his throat, and began an *alapana*[4] and paused to ask, "Isn't it good *Kalyani*[5]?" Sekhar pretended not to have heard the question. The headmaster went on to sing a full song composed by Thyagaraja[6] and followed it with two more. All the time the headmaster was singing, Sekhar went on commenting within himself, He croaks like a dozen frogs. He is bellowing like a buffalo. Now he sounds like loose window shutters in a storm.

11. The incense sticks burned low. Sekhar's head throbbed with the medley of sounds that had assailed his eardrums for a couple of hours now. He felt half stupefied. The headmaster had gone nearly hoarse, when he paused to ask, "Shall I go on?" Sekhar replied, "Please don't, sir, I think this will do. . . ." Sekhar felt greatest pity for him. But he felt he could not help it. No judge delivering a sentence felt more pained and helpless. Sekhar noticed that the headmaster's wife peeped in from the kitchen, with eager curiosity. The drummer and the violinist put away their burdens with an air of relief. The headmaster removed his spectacles, mopped his brow, and asked, "Now, come out with your opinion."

12. "Can't I give it tomorrow, sir?" Sekhar asked tentatively.

13. "No. I want it immediately—your frank opinion. Was it good?"

14. "No, sir . . ." Sekhar replied.

15. "Oh! . . . . Is there any use continuing my lessons?"

16. "Absolutely none, sir . . ." Sekhar said with his voice trembling. He felt very unhappy that he could not speak more soothingly. Truth, he reflected, required as much strength to give as to receive.

17. All the way home he felt worried. He felt that his official life was not going to be smooth sailing hereafter. There were questions of increment and confirmation and so on, all depending upon the headmaster's goodwill . . . .

---

3 Rangoon mat: mat from Yangon, formerly called Rangoon, the city that served as capital of Myanmar when it was called Burma

4 alapana: traditional slow start of a performance of classical Indian music

5 Kalyani: type of classical Indian music

6 Thyagaraja: famous composer of classical Indian music; sometimes spelled Tyagaraja (1764–1848)

18. At home his wife served him with a sullen face. He knew she was still angry with him for his remark of the morning. Two casualties for today, Sekhar said to himself. If I practice it for a week, I don't think I shall have a single friend left.

19. He received a call from the headmaster in his classroom next day. He went up apprehensively.

20. "Your suggestion was useful. I have paid off the music master. No one would tell me the truth about my music all these days. Why such antics at my age! Thank you. By the way, what about those test papers?"

21. "You gave me ten days, sir, for correcting them."

22. "Oh, I've reconsidered it. I must positively have them here tomorrow . . . ." A hundred papers in a day! That meant all night's sitting up! "Give me a couple of days, sir..."

23. "No. I must have them tomorrow morning. And remember, every paper must be thoroughly scrutinized."

24. "Yes, sir," Sekhar said, feeling that sitting up all night with a hundred test papers was a small price to pay for the luxury of practicing Truth.

Unit 2 Reading Informational Texts

Unit Focus

The focus of this unit is on the close reading of informational texts. Chapters address central ideas, sequences of events, figurative language, and technical terms as well as the structure of expository and argumentative essays and author's point of view and purpose.

Chapter 7 Close Reading of Informational Texts
- Analyzing Explicit Details and Implicit Meanings
- Identifying and Interpreting Uncertainties
- Citing Strong and Thorough Textual Evidence
- Chapter Review—Practice Test

Chapter 8 Central Ideas
- Identifying Central Ideas
- Analyzing the Development of Ideas
- Providing an Objective Summary
- Chapter Review—Practice Test

Chapter 9 Complex Ideas & Events
- Analyzing a Complex Set of Ideas or Sequence of Events
- Explaining How Ideas and Events Interact and Develop
- Chapter Review—Practice Test

Chapter 10 The Language of Information
- Analyzing Figurative Language
- Analyzing the Connotation of Words
- Analyzing Technical Language
- Analyzing the Development of Key Words and Phrases
- Chapter Review—Practice Test

Chapter 11 Structure of Informational Texts
- Analyzing the Structure of Expository Texts
- Evaluating the Structure of Informational Texts
- Chapter Review—Practice Test

Chapter 12 Author's Point of View
- Determining Point of View and Purpose
- Analyzing Style and Content
- Chapter Review—Practice Test

Unit 2 Review Test

Chapter 7 Close Reading of Informational Texts (RI.11–12.1)

As with reading literature, close reading is a key skill for understanding informational texts. Taking time to focus your attention on an essay, memoir, or historical account, you begin to make it your own. By sharing the unique perspective you gain through close reading, you take part in the creative process. This chapter addresses the following three aspects of close reading.

7.1 Analyzing explicit details and implicit meanings
7.2 Identifying and interpreting uncertainties
7.3 Citing strong and thorough textual evidence

7.1 Analyzing Explicit Details and Implicit Meanings

Review

Close reading is the careful interpretation of a text. Reading a text closely does not consist of a single step; instead, it is a process. Generally, this process has three stages: 1) first reading, 2) rereading, 3) synthesizing.

In the *first reading*, focus on gaining the literal **explicit meaning** of the text. In informational texts, determine the main ideas and important details.

In *rereading*, focus on the **implicit meanings** or inferences that are suggested, but not directly stated. **Inferences** are based on what you bring to the text. When you infer, you start with a detail from the text and combine it with knowledge that you already have. Based on this combination, you make an educated guess about the text.

In *synthesizing*, you bring explicit details and implicit meanings together to form an interpretation of the text. In short, you identify patterns and make connections to interpret the text.

Key Terms

explicit detail: the actual text of a work. In the informational text below, "when Officer Fish Lips met Abdul in the police station" is an explicit detail.

implicit meaning: an inference or interpretation based on the explicit text.

inference: implicit meaning drawn from a text

Check Understanding

Read from the opening of Katherine Boo's *Behind the Beautiful Forevers* on the next page.

from Behind the Beautiful Forevers: Life, Death, and Hope in a Mumbai Undercity

by Katherine Boo

In her award-winning first full-length book of narrative nonfiction, Katherine Boo describes a present-day slum of Mumbai, India, and the people who live there.

1. . . . . Dawn came gusty, as it often did in January, the month of treed kites and head colds. Because his family lacked the floor space for all of its members to lie down, Abdul was asleep on the gritty maidan, which for years had passed as his bed. His mother stepped carefully over one of his younger brothers, and then another, bending low to Abdul's ear. "Wake up, fool!" she said exuberantly. "You think your work is dreaming?"

2. Superstitious, Zehrunisa had noticed that some of the family's most profitable days occurred after she had showered abuses on her eldest son. January's income being pivotal to the family's latest plan of escape from Annawadi, she had decided to make the curses routine.

3. Abdul rose with minimal whining, since the only whining his mother tolerated was her own. Besides, this was the gentle-going hour in which he hated Annawadi least. The pale sun lent the sewage lake a sparkling silver cast, and the parrots nesting at the far side of the lake could still be heard over the jets. Outside his neighbors' huts, some held together by duct tape and rope, damp rags were discreetly freshening bodies. Children in school-uniform neckties were hauling pots of water from the public taps. A languid line extended from an orange concrete block of public toilets. Even goats' eyes were heavy with sleep. It was the moment of the intimate and the familial, before the great pursuit of the small market niche got under way.

Notes

Abdul's family appears to be poor.

Activity 7.1 Reread the excerpt above. Highlight other details about the setting and draw inferences about them in the margin. Share your findings with a partner.

Toolbox

As you read a text, underline or highlight important ideas and add inferences or connections in the margin. These key ideas and notes will help trace the development of ideas.

Try It

Directions: Read the excerpt below and answer the questions.

from Nickel and Dimed: On (Not) Getting By in America

by Barbara Ehrenreich

Notes

In Nickel and Dimed, *reporter Barbara Ehrenreich chronicles her attempts to eke out a living while working in low-wage jobs in different cities in the United States.*

1. How did I do as a low-wage worker? If I may begin with a brief round of applause: I didn't do half bad at the work itself, and I claim this as a considerable achievement. You might think that unskilled jobs would be a snap for someone who holds a Ph.D. and whose normal line of work requires learning entirely new things every couple of weeks. Not so. The first thing I discovered is that no job, no matter how lowly, is truly "unskilled." Every one of the six jobs I entered into in the course of this project required concentration, and most demanded that I master new terms, new tools, and new skills—from placing orders on restaurant computers to wielding the backpack vacuum cleaner. None of these things came as easily to me as I would have liked; no one ever said, "Wow, you're fast!" or "Can you believe she just started?" Whatever my accomplishments in the rest of my life, in the low-wage work world I was a person of average ability—capable of learning the job and also capable of screwing up.

2. I did have my moments of glory. There were days at The Maids when I got my own tasks finished fast enough that I was able to lighten the load on others, and I feel good about that. There was my breakthrough at Wal-Mart, where I truly believe that, if I'd been able to keep my mouth shut, I would have progressed in a year or two to a wage of $7.50 or more an hour. And I'll bask for the rest of my life in the memory of that day at the Woodcrest when I fed the locked Alzheimer's ward all by myself, cleaned up afterward, and even managed to extract a few smiles from the vacant faces of my charges in the process.

1. What inference is best supported by the text?

Ⓐ Walmart pays its workers a lower wage than The Maids.

Ⓑ Many unskilled jobs require a two-week training period.

Ⓒ The narrator believes she was an exemplary low-wage worker.

Ⓓ The narrator found unskilled jobs to be surprisingly difficult.

2. Cite at least two details from the text that could be used to support your answer to question 1.

____

____

____

____

____

Question 1 asks you to select the inference that is best supported by the text. While Choice A may be true, the text offers no evidence to support it. Choice B may also be true, but again, the text contains no definitive evidence to support the claim. Choice C is not accurate because the text provides evidence that the narrator believes she was an average low-wage worker, not an exemplary one. Choice D is the best answer. Evidence in the text reveals that the narrator was surprised at how many new skills she had to learn at each job, which suggests she was surprised at their difficulty.

Question 2 asks you cite and explain two details from the text that could be used to support the inference you selected in question 1. Sample response:

> The narrator is surprised that the unskilled jobs do not come as easily to her as she expects. She declares, "The first thing I discovered is that no job, no matter how lowly, is truly 'unskilled.'" The narrator's use of the word "discovered" in the sentence suggests that she was surprised to find that she needed to learn new skills at her unskilled jobs. After the narrator explains the new tools and skills she had to learn at most jobs, she admits, "None of these things came as easily to me as I would have liked." This statement illustrates that the narrator found the jobs to be unexpectedly difficult for her.

7.2 Identifying and Interpreting Uncertainties

Review

Some implicit details, such as those noted in *Nickel and Dimed* above, are relatively easy to interpret, since the connection between detail and inference is fairly obvious. Ambiguous passages, however, may not be so easy to interpret. Different people could interpret them differently; indeed, the same reader may find new meaning in ambiguous passages after the passing of time. Figurative language, such as idioms, personification, similes, and metaphors are often open to interpretation. Some texts are deliberately ambiguous, challenging the reader to find meaning.

> **Key Terms**
>
> **ambiguity:** uncertainty or inexactness of meaning.
>
> **uncertainty:** part of a text in which meaning is not clear. Multiple interpretations can be based on such passages.

Check Understanding

Read the excerpt from Virginia Woolf's essay "A Room on One's Own" that starts on the next page.

from A Room of One's Own

by Virginia Woolf

"A Room of One's Own" is an extended essay based upon a series of lectures titled "Women and Fiction" delivered by Virginia Woolf in October 1929.

Notes

1. But, you may say, we asked you to speak about women and fiction—what, has that got to do with a room of one's own? I will try to explain. When you asked me to speak about women and fiction I sat down on the banks of a river and began to wonder what the words meant. They might mean simply a few remarks about . . . Jane Austen; a tribute to the Brontës . . . a respectful allusion to George Eliot; a reference to Mrs Gaskell and one would have done. But at second sight the words seemed not so simple. . . . . The title women and fiction might mean, and you may have meant it to mean, women and what they are like, or it might mean women and the fiction that they write; or it might mean women and the fiction that is written about them, or it might mean that somehow all three are inextricably mixed together and you want me to consider them in that light. But when I began to consider the subject in this last way, which seemed the most interesting, I soon saw that it had one fatal drawback. I should never be able to come to a conclusion. I should never be able to fulfill what is, I understand, the first duty of a lecturer to hand you after an hour's discourse a nugget of pure truth to wrap up between the pages of your notebooks and keep on the mantelpiece for ever. All I could do was to offer you an opinion upon one minor point—a woman must have money and a room of her own if she is to write fiction . . . .

The speaker is trying to come to terms with the assignment to speak about women and fiction.

2. Here then was I (call me Mary Beton, Mary Seton, Mary Carmichael or by any name you please—it is not a matter of any importance) sitting on the banks of a river a week or two ago in fine October weather, lost in thought. That collar I have spoken of, women and fiction, the need of coming to some conclusion on a subject that raises all sorts of prejudices and passions, bowed my head to the ground. To the right and left bushes of some sort, golden and crimson, glowed with the color, even it seemed burnt with the heat, of fire. On the further bank the willows wept in perpetual lamentation, their hair about their shoulders. The river reflected whatever it chose of sky and bridge and burning tree, and when the undergraduate had oared his boat through the reflections they closed again, completely, as if he had never been. There one might have sat the clock round lost in thought. Thought—to call it by a prouder name than it deserved—had let its line down into the stream. It swayed, minute after minute, hither and thither among the reflections and the weeds, letting the water lift it and sink it until—you know the little tug—the sudden conglomeration of an idea at the end of one's line: and then the cautious hauling of it in,

Why the list of names—to indicate that she is "any woman?"

Why the detail about bushes burnt in the heat—a reference to the Burning Bush—as if she is a sort of prophetess for women writers?

and the careful laying of it out? Alas, laid on the grass how small, how insignificant this thought of mine looked; the sort of fish that a good fisherman puts back into the water so that it may grow fatter and be one day worth cooking and eating. I will not trouble you with that thought now, though if you look carefully you may find it for yourselves in the course of what I am going to say.

Notes

Activity 7.2 Highlight uncertainties you see write brief interpretations of them in the margin. Compare your interpretations with a partner.

Toolbox

Interpreting Informational Texts. Informational texts present facts and details in different ways. An article may present its main ideas through subheads, call-outs, graphical elements, and an overview introduction. A nonfiction narrative, such as *Behind the Beautiful Forevers*, may present information through a narrator and exploit story elements commonly employed in fiction, such as characterization and conflict. A speech may open with an attention-getting anecdote followed by a main argument with its claims and warrants.

Each type of text requires a different interpretive ear. For example, for narrative nonfiction you may need to use interpretive skills you use while reading fiction; with a speech, you may need to employ skills used when dealing with arguments, such as watching for bias and matching claims with evidence and warrants.

Try It

Directions: Read the following paragraphs from "A Room of One's Own" and answer the questions that follow.

3. . . . . It is a curious fact that novelists have a way of making us believe that luncheon parties are invariably memorable for something very witty that was said, or for something very wise that was done. But they seldom spare a word for what was eaten. It is part of the novelist's convention not to mention soup and salmon and ducklings, as if soup and salmon and ducklings were of no importance whatsoever . . . .

4. . . . if things had been a little different from what they were, one would not have seen, presumably, a cat without a tail. The sight of that abrupt and truncated animal padding softly across the quadrangle changed by some fluke of the subconscious intelligence the emotional light for me. It was as if someone had let fall a shade. Perhaps the excellent hock was relinquishing its hold. Certainly, as I watched the Manx cat pause in the middle of the lawn as if it too questioned the universe, something seemed lacking, something seemed different. But what was lacking, what was different, I asked

Notes

myself, listening to the talk? And to answer that question I had to think myself out of the room, back into the past, before the war indeed, and to set before my eyes the model of another luncheon party held in rooms not very far distant from these; but different. Everything was different. Meanwhile the talk went on among the guests, who were many and young, some of this sex, some of that; it went on swimmingly, it went on agreeably, freely, amusingly. And as it went on I set it against the background of that other talk, and as I matched the two together I had no doubt that one was the descendant, the legitimate heir of the other. Nothing was changed; nothing was different save only here I listened with all my ears not entirely to what was being said, but to the murmur or current behind it. Yes, that was it—the change was there. Before the war at a luncheon party like this people would have said precisely the same things but they would have sounded different, because in those days they were accompanied by a sort of humming noise, not articulate, but musical, exciting, which changed the value of the words themselves. Could one set that humming noise to words? Perhaps with the help of the poets one could.

Notes

3. Identify a passage from the excerpt that is ambiguous, open to more than one possible interpretation. Write the passage on the lines below.

____

____

____

4. Write a brief interpretation of the passage you selected in question 3.

____

____

____

____

____

____

____

____

____

Question 3 asks you to identify a passage that is open to more than one possible interpretation. There are several possible answers. One is the sentence when the narrator discusses the humming noise that she believes pervaded pre-war luncheon party discussions.

> "Before the war at a luncheon party like this people would have said precisely the same things but they would have sounded different, because in those days they were accompanied by a sort of humming noise, not articulate, but musical, exciting, which changed the value of the words themselves. . ."

Question 4 asks you to interpret the passage you selected in question 3. Of course, your response will depend upon the passage you selected. You should be sure to cite specific details from the passage in your interpretation. Consider the response below, which is based on the response to question 3 above.

> The narrator explains that she believes people at a luncheon party before the war would have sounded different than during her time. She cites a humming noise as the reason for this difference, a humming sound "not articulate, but musical, exciting, which changed the value of the words themselves. . ." The narrator may be suggesting that people prior to the war were more hopeful or that their experiences and expectations imbued their words with more excitement than those of people after the war. The narrator may be experiencing nostalgia for a more poetic era.

7.3 Citing Strong and Thorough Textual Evidence

Review

The basis of any textual analysis is the **evidence** you use to support your analysis. Textual evidence can include direct quotations, paraphrases, or a combination of the two. Besides citing textual evidence, you must be prepared to explain how the evidence supports your interpretation.

Key Terms

evidence: direct quotation or paraphrase of a text used to support an interpretation.

paraphrase: a restatement of part of a text in your own words.

Check Understanding

Notice the use of textual evidence in the opening paragraph of this student draft essay on Virginia Woolf.

Virginia Woolf's Burning Bush

Virginia Woolf's evocative and descriptive writing style leaves much to the imagination of the reader and invites multiple interpretations. In the opening of "A Room on One's Own," for example, Woolf devotes time describing a river bank in "fine October weather." It is the setting for the narrator's contemplation of her assignment: to speak about women and fiction. But why does she take time to describe the surroundings in such detail? "To the right and left," she notes, "bushes of some sort, golden and crimson, glowed with the color, even it seemed burnt with the heat, of fire." Is she evoking a modern-day female prophet seeking wisdom from the burning bush? And what of the striking image of the willow tree swallowing the undergraduate?

> On the further bank the willows wept in perpetual lamentation, their hair about their shoulders. The river reflected whatever it chose of sky and bridge and burning tree, and when the undergraduate had oared his boat through the reflections they closed again, completely, as if he had never been.

Is the narrator imagining a future in which the dominant male writer has been swallowed up as if he had never been?

Activity 7.3 Underline two interpretive statements. Share your findings with a partner.

Toolbox

Assume your reader knows the work. In a critical essay, don't feel that you have to retell the work you are interpreting. Assume that your reader is familiar enough with the work that a brief descriptive phrase will locate him or her in the text: "In the opening paragraphs. . . ," "When the author discusses the budget crisis . . . ," etc.

Try It

Directions: Read these paragraphs from *Nickel and Dimed* and answer the questions that follow.

from Nickel and Dimed

by Barbara Ehrenreich

	Notes
1. . . . . I was baffled, initially, by what seemed like a certain lack of get-up-and-go on the part of my fellow workers. Why didn't they just leave for a better-paying job, as I did when I moved from the Hearthside to Jerry's? Part of the answer is that actual humans experience a little more "friction" than marbles do, and the poorer they are, the more constrained their mobility usually is. Low-wage people who don't have cars are often dependent on a relative who is willing to drop them off and pick them up again each day, sometimes on a route that includes the babysitter's house or the child care center. Change your place of work and you may be confronted with an impossible topographical problem to solve, or at least a reluctant driver to persuade. Some of my coworkers, in Minneapolis as well as Key West, rode bikes to work, and this clearly limited their geographical range. For those who do possess cars, there is still the problem of gas prices, not to mention the general hassle, which is of course far more onerous for the car-less, of getting around to fill out applications, to be interviewed, to take drug tests. I have mentioned, too, the general reluctance to exchange the devil you know for one that you don't know, even when the latter is tempting you with a better wage-benefit package. At each new job, you have to start all over, clueless and friendless.	

5. Cite two passages from the paragraph that could be used as evidence to show the difficulties low-wage job hunters face.

____

____

____

____

6. Explain how the citations you selected for question 5 support your view of the difficulties low-wage job hunters face.

____

____

____

____

Question 5 asks you to select two passages from the paragraph that could be used to show the difficulties low-wage job hunters face. Several passages could be used as evidence:

> "Low-wage people who don't have cars are often dependent on a relative who is willing to drop them off and pick them up again each day, sometimes on a route that includes the babysitter's house or the child care center."
>
> "For those who do possess cars, there is still the problem of gas prices, not to mention the general hassle, which is of course far more onerous for the car-less, of getting around to fill out applications, to be interviewed, to take drug tests."

Question 6 asks you to explain how the passages you selected in question 5 support your understanding of the difficulties faced by low-wage job hunters. Consider this response, which combines details and interpretation.

> Low-wage workers face several difficulties when searching for a job. Those who do not have their own transportation must rely on "a relative who is willing to drop them off and pick them up again each day." The route to work may also have to include "the babysitter's house or the child care center," and so involves a lengthier commute and the dependence of the low-wage worker on someone else's schedule. However, low-wage job hunters who own cars face their own challenges, including high gas prices. The job hunters must pay for the gas expended in driving to different places to pick up or hand in applications, interview for jobs, complete pre-employment screenings, and so on.

Strategies for Close Reading of Informational Text

Use the following strategies as you read closely, draw inferences, make connections, and cite explicit details and implicit meanings from text.

- Underline key ideas, such as details that support the text's main idea.
- Underline language that reveals the tone and attitude of the author.
- Add notes, such as inferences and brief interpretations, in the margin.
- Mark points in the text where matters are uncertain.
- Once you make an inference, watch for new information that confirms or changes your conclusion.

Test-Taking Tips

- Good informational texts rarely include unnecessary details. Think about the meaning of the details as you read. They often provide important information about the main idea, describe reasons for an argument or existing problem, or indicate an author's point of view.
- Make a short outline before you begin a written response, making sure to address each part of the question. Remember to use only those details that help explain your response.

Chapter Review

Read the excerpt and answer the questions that follow.

Notes

from Counting Coup: A True Story of Basketball and Honor on the Little Bighorn

by Larry Colton

In Counting Coup, *journalist Larry Colton tells the story of high school basketball player Sharon LaForge as she negotiates the realities of life on the Little Bighorn reservation.*

1. Hardin's opponent, the lady Eagles of Sidney, an agricultural town on the Yellowstone River five miles from the North Dakota border, has lost all five starters off last year's team that finished second at State. Despite this lack of experience, they're picked in the *Billings Gazette* coaches' poll to finish third in the conference, just ahead of the Lady Bulldogs, a ranking that rankles Coach Mac, who's always believed that the rest of the league doesn't respect her program. This adds more proof. Sharon hasn't seen the poll, a daily newspaper not part of her life.

2. Although the games in the Tip-Off Tournament, a preseason competition between teams in the Eastern Conference, won't count in league standings, Coach Mac considers tonight and tomorrow night's games crucial to her team's psyche. She worries that a bad start will disrupt its fragile chemistry. This is a team capable of going south in a hurry. With tip-off a minute away, she checks to make sure her bottle of Mylanta is next to the bench.

3. The starting five take the court. Tiffany, looking like she's strolling into Dandy Tom's Ice Cream Parlor down on Center Street, smiles and shakes hands with two opponents, both blondes, just like all the Sidney starters. Sharon glowers, her face pulled tighter than rawhide. She surveys an opponent's extended hand, hesitates, then shakes it, no smile, no pretense of chummy fraternization.

4. With the near capacity crowd on its feet Anita controls the opening tap, tipping it to a wide-open Sharon, who dribbles twice, then casts off from 15 feet. Swish. The season is four seconds old.

5. Against Hardin's full-court pressure, Sidney inbounds the ball, their panicked guards looking as if they've never seen a press before. Or an Indian. Sharon intercepts a crosscourt pass, then rifles the ball to Tiffany for an easy score. Five seconds later, Tiffany intercepts another lame pass and feeds it to Sharon, who drains a jumper from 17 feet. Six points in 18 seconds. Sidney still hasn't gotten the ball to midcourt. . . .

6. Midway through the first quarter, with Hardin cruising 13-3, Coach Mac pulls the starting five and inserts the second unit. She takes a deep breath. Her bench has looked relentlessly confused in practice, clueless as to where to be in the zone press . . . and in her fast-break, pressure-defense style of play, the zone press is everything. Stacie Greenwalt and Christina Chavez, the two sophomores I think should

Notes

be starting despite their inexperience, aren't even in uniform. Coach Mac wants them to play several games with the junior varsity before getting minutes with the varsity. The rule is that a player can play in a junior varsity and varsity game in the same day, but for no more than a total of four quarters. She worries that the three senior subs will pitch a fit if she leapfrogs the sophomores over them too soon.

7. "Relax!" she instructs as senior Geri Stewart turns it over.

8. It takes Sidney just 50 seconds to score seven straight points. The scrubeanies have flunked their first test.

9. "Horrible!" yells Coach Mac, waving the first team back into the game.

10. Coach Mac has always dreamed of that rare moment when everything comes together on the court—offensively, defensively, emotionally—that elusive circumstance when pure basketball synchronism happens and all five athletes enter a zone, everybody working in perfect union, a controlled frenzy. And for the next six minutes, that's exactly what she witnesses, something truly remarkable.

11. Sharon triggers it with a jump shot, then swipes a pass at midcourt and hits Anita with a look-left-dish-it-right pass for an easy two. Then she shanghaies another errant pass and fires a pass between two dazed defenders to Tiffany, who cashes in. Six points in 30 seconds. The crowd goes nuts.

12. Over the summer, Coach Mac decided to take the first string's two tallest starters, Tiffany, 5'10", and Anita, 5'9", and make them guards. It will be their job to hound the ball in the backcourt and use their quickness and long arms to pressure opponents into bad passes and turnovers. Now, just eight minutes into the season, the experiment is working. Six straight times the Sidney guards, confronted with a whirlwind of arms and elbows, turn it over, the Lady Bulldogs converting it into easy baskets, each score raising the crowd noise to a higher, more deafening level. After 14 unanswered points, the Sidney coach calls a timeout.

13. "Switch to a diamond zone," orders Coach Mac.

14. Sidney inbounds the ball and Sharon deflects it, diving sideways into the bleachers to save it. With a flick of the wrist, she flips it backward over her head as she crashes through the pep band. Tiffany gathers it in and drives the baseline, swooping beneath the basket like a giant bird of prey, releasing the ball softly over her head like an egg, kissing it off the backboard through the hoop.

15. It's bedlam in the stands, everybody standing and roaring, me included. I notice that Crows and whites, folks not likely to offer a glass of water to each other in a fire, are standing shoulder to shoulder, cheering themselves hoarse.

16. The Sidney coach frantically signals another timeout, but by now the run is up to 23, breathtaking in its energy and execution. Before Coach Mac finally calls off the attack dogs and puts the second string back in, the first unit has reeled off 26 unanswered points. Twenty-six.

17. At halftime Hardin leads 42-15, only three of Sidney's points coming against the first team. Coach Mac can't remember a better streak by any team she's ever seen. Who cares if Sharon cut practice?

Questions 1–6: Choose the best answer or write your response on the lines.

1. Which inference is best supported by the text?

   Ⓐ Sharon works the hardest on the basketball court.

   Ⓑ Hardin is the underdog team.

   Ⓒ The Lady Eagles of Sidney are the more experienced team.

   Ⓓ Whites and Indians in the area lead separate and segregated lives.

2. Using at least two passages from the text for support, explain your answer to question 1.

   ____

   ____

   ____

   ____

   ____

3. Which inference is best supported by the text?

   Ⓐ Coach Mac wants to get a better coaching job.

   Ⓑ Coach Mac favors Tiffany over the other players.

   Ⓒ Coach Mac finds coaching basketball stressful.

   Ⓓ Coach Mac believes everyone is against her.

4. Using at least two passages from the text for support, explain your answer to question 3.

   ____

   ____

   ____

   ____

   ____

5. What meaning, if any, can you draw from the detail that Sharon hesitates to shake the Sidney player's hand? Write your answer on the lines below.

6. Using evidence from the text, explain why Coach Mac is amazed by her team's performance.

Chapter 8 Central Ideas

(RI.11–12.2)

Unlike authors of fictional texts who frequently incorporate unexpected elements such as plot twists and surprise endings, authors of informational texts usually strive for clarity and directness expressed through central ideas and thesis statements. This chapter addresses the following aspects of reading informational texts.

- 8.1 Identifying central ideas
- 8.2 Analyzing the development of ideas
- 8.3 Providing an objective summary

8.1 Identifying Central Ideas

Review

An informational text will contain a number of ideas. The **central idea** is the most important concept expressed in the text.

A **secondary idea** is a minor concept used to support the central idea. For example, an article about establishing healthy habits may include a secondary idea noting that fast-food television commercials can trigger cravings and unhealthy eating habits.

Unlike fictional texts where the theme must generally be inferred, informational texts frequently state the central idea directly in a thesis statement. In a **thesis statement**, an author expresses an opinion or stance on a topic along with specific reasons and evidence in support of that stance.

Don't confuse the central idea with the topic. A **topic** is a broad subject, such as *health* or *pollution*. A central idea is specific and focused, such as *air pollution in American cities is creating health problems for many young children*.

Key Terms

central idea: a text's most vital concept. It is also called the main idea.

secondary idea: a minor concept briefly expressed in a text.

thesis statement: usually a single sentence explaining a stance on what is to be discussed in a text.

topic: the subject of a text.

Check Understanding

Read the excerpt on the next page, watching for the central idea.

from All Deliberate Speed

by Charles J. Ogletree, Jr.

1. On May 17, 1954, an otherwise uneventful Monday afternoon, fifteen months into Dwight D. Eisenhower's presidency, Chief Justice Earl Warren, speaking on behalf of a unanimous Supreme Court, issued a historic ruling that he and his colleagues hoped would irrevocably change the social fabric of the United States. "We conclude that in the field of public education the doctrine of 'separate-but-equal' has no place. Separate educational facilities are inherently unequal." Thurgood Marshall, who had passionately argued the case before the Court, joined a jubilant throng of other civil rights leaders in hailing this decision as the Court's most significant opinion of the twentieth century. The New *York Times* extolled the *Brown* decision as having "reaffirmed its faith and the underlying American faith in the equality of all men and all children before the law."

Notes

The Supreme Court's ruling is "historic" with the justices hoping the "social fabric" of America will change.

The ruling is against "separate but equal" facilities.

Activity 8.1 Reread the passage above. Highlight details you think are important. Write the central idea of the paragraph in the margin. Compare your findings with a partner.

Try It

Directions: Read two more paragraphs from *All Deliberate Speed* below and answer the questions that follow.

from All Deliberate Speed

by Charles J. Ogletree, Jr.

Notes

2. Having broadly proclaimed its support of desegregating public schools, the Supreme Court shortly thereafter issued its opinion—the opinion that legitimized much of the social upheaval that forms the central theme of this book. Fearful that southern segregationists, as well as the executive and legislative branches of state and federal governments, would both resist and impede this courageous decision, the Court offered a palliative[1] to those opposed to *Brown*'s directive. Speaking again with one voice, the Court concluded that, to achieve the goal of desegregation, the lower federal courts were to "enter such orders and decrees consistent with this opinion as are necessary and proper to admit to public schools on a racially nondiscriminatory basis *with all deliberate speed* the parties to these cases."

3. As Thurgood Marshall and other civil rights lawyers pondered the second decision, they tried to ascertain what the Court meant in adding the crucial phrase "all deliberate speed" to its opinion.

1 palliative: a gesture or action meant to pacify or lessen an ill without curing it.

It is reported that, after the lawyers read the decision, a staff member consulted a dictionary to confirm their worst fears—that the "all deliberate speed" language meant "slow" and that the apparent victory was compromised because resisters were allowed to end segregation on their own timetable. These three critical words would indeed turn out to be of great consequence, in that they ignore the urgency on which the *Brown* lawyers insisted. When asked to explain his view of "all deliberate speed," Thurgood Marshall frequently told anyone who would listen that the term meant S-L-O-W.

Notes

1. Identify two details in the passage that suggest the central idea and briefly explain your choices on the lines below.

____

____

____

____

____

2. State the central idea in your own words.

____

____

Question 1 asks you to identify details in the passage that suggest the central idea of the book. Here is a sample answer:

The court offering a "palliative to those opposed to *Brown's* directive," suggests that the Brown decision was not a complete victory for the supporters of civil rights and desegregation. This idea is followed up by the realization by Thurgood Marshall and other civil rights lawyers that the language "all deliberate speed" could be used by resistors of the law to "end segregation on their own timetable," that is very slowly.

Question 2 asks you to state the central idea in your own words. Here is a sample answer:

The Supreme Court's decision to add the language "with all deliberate speed" to their opinion undermined the civil rights victory and validated much of the resultant social upheaval.

8.2 Analyzing the Development of Ideas

Review

Authors have many choices in the manner in which they develop their ideas. For example, an author may choose the order of importance model. After introducing the main idea, she may list several supporting ideas or topics sequenced from least important to most important—saving the strongest idea for last to add punch to the conclusion.

Some topics lend themselves to other methods of development. For example, an author may develop an essay on the poetry of Emily Dickinson by contrasting two interpretive approaches, using the **point-by-point** or **whole-by-whole method.**

A cause and effect development model might work well in an essay on the influences of the ideas of Alain Locke on the arts during the Harlem Renaissance, with the cause—an idea or concept from the philosophical writings of Locke—linked to one or more effects—a poem, a jazz composition, or a novel.

Techniques borrowed from poetry and other forms can also be used to development ideas. For example, the repetition of an introductory phrase or a sentence structure can drive home a point or provide humor.

Finally, strategically placed **transitional word and phrases** can be used to signal the developmental logic of an essay. Review the chart below, which shows the purpose of some common transitional words and phrases.

Key Terms

point-by-point method: a comparison or contrast of one point of a topic with another

whole-by-whole method: a comparison or contrast of two things in which all facts of one side are presented followed by all the facts of the other sides.

transition: a word, phrase, or sentence used to connect one idea with another.

Purpose	Transition Word or Phrase
Cause	because, for this/that reason, on account of, since
Effect	as a result, for the reason that, because, as a result, since, due to the fact that
Comparison	similarly, in the same way, likewise, in the same manner, by the same token
Addition	also, in addition, moreover, furthermore, next, again, in the second place, another, to demonstrate
Contrast	however, on the other hand, nevertheless, in contrast, yet, on the contrary, conversely, but, nonetheless
Example	for example, for instance, to illustrate, specifically
Time Order	first, next, later, afterward, a few days later, at the same time, while, during, now, simultaneously, earlier, immediately, soon, subsequently, concurrently
Summary	to summarize, in summary, in sum, in short, in brief, finally

Check Understanding

Notice the techniques G. K. Chesterton uses to develop the main idea in the opening of "The Fallacy of Success."

from The Fallacy of Success

by G. K. Chesterton

1. There has appeared in our time a particular class of books and articles which I sincerely and solemnly think may be called the silliest ever known among men. They are much more wild than the wildest romances of chivalry and much more dull than the dullest religious tract. Moreover, the romances of chivalry were at least about chivalry; the religious tracts are about religion. But these things are about nothing; they are about what is called Success. On every bookstall, in every magazine, you may find works telling people how to succeed. They are books showing men how to succeed in everything; they are written by men who cannot even succeed in writing books. To begin with, of course, there is no such thing as Success. Or, if you like to put it so, there is nothing that is not successful. That a thing is successful merely means that it is; a millionaire is successful in being a millionaire and a donkey in being a donkey. Any live man has succeeded in living; any dead man may have succeeded in committing suicide. But, passing over the bad logic and bad philosophy in the phrase, we may take it, as these writers do, in the ordinary sense of success in obtaining money or worldly position. These writers profess to tell the ordinary man how he may succeed in his trade or speculation—how, if he is a builder, he may succeed as a builder; how, if he is a stockbroker, he may succeed as a stockbroker. They profess to show him how, if he is a grocer, he may become a sporting yachtsman; how, if he is a tenth-rate journalist, he may become a peer; and how, if he is a German Jew, he may become an Anglo-Saxon. This is a definite and business-like proposal, and I really think that the people who buy these books (if any people do buy them) have a moral, if not a legal, right to ask for their money back. Nobody would dare to publish a book about electricity which literally told one nothing about electricity; no one would dare to publish an article on botany which showed that the writer did not know which end of a plant grew in the earth. Yet our modern world is full of books about Success and successful people which literally contain no kind of idea, and scarcely any kind of verbal sense.

Notes

Repeated structure: "much more wild than ___" and "much more dull than ___" drives home contrasts.

Transition word "moreover" used to add another critique.

Repetition of "about ___" followed by "about nothing" creates humor.

Humor developed through repetition of "books" and "succeed" on both sides of the semicolon.

***Activity* 8.2** Reread the paragraph above. Highlight other examples of transitions and repetition used to develop and drive home the ideas in the passage. Comment on them in the margin and compare your notes with a partner.

Toolbox

If an author of a nonfiction work does not directly state the developmental structure, use transitions as clues. *Because, for this reason,* and *as a result* suggest a cause and effect development. *First of all, next,* and *finally* suggest a chronological development.

In some cases, an author will directly state the developmental structure. For example, in "Fenimore Cooper's Literary Offences," Mark Twain states early in the essay, "There are nineteen rules governing literary art in the domain of romantic fiction. . . . In *Deerslayer* Cooper violated eighteen of them." The numbered paragraphs that follow clearly show that the developmental structure is a list—albeit, a humorous list.

Try It

Directions: Read the paragraph and answer the questions that follow.

from The Spirit Catches You and You Fall Down: A Hmong Child, Her American Doctors, and the Collision of Two Cultures

by Anne Fadiman

Notes

1. In an intermediate French class at Merced College a few years ago, the students were assigned a five-minute oral report, to be delivered in French. The second student to stand up in front of the class was a young Hmong man. His chosen topic was a recipe for *la soupe de poissone*: Fish Soup. To prepare Fish Soup, he said, you must have a fish, and in order to have a fish, you have to go fishing. In order to go fishing, you need a hook, and in order to choose the right hook, you need to know whether the fish you are fishing for lives in fresh or salt water, how big it is, and what shape its mouth is. Continuing in this vein for forty-five minutes, the student filled the blackboard with a complexly branching tree of factors and options, a sort of piscatory[1] flow chart, written in French with an overlay of Hmong. He also told several anecdotes about his own fishing experiences. He concluded with a description of how to clean various kinds of fish, how to cut them up, and, finally, how to cook them in broths flavored with various herbs. When the class period ended, he told the other students that he hoped he had provided enough information, and he wished them good luck in preparing Fish Soup in the Hmong manner.

1 piscatory: of, or related to, fish.

3. What is the central idea?

4. Explain how the central idea is developed in the paragraph.

____

____

____

____

____

Question 3 asks you to identify the paragraph's central idea. The central idea is that a student gives a lengthy, tangential speech about making fish soup.

Question 4 asks you to explain how the central idea is developed in the paragraph. Here is a sample answer:

> The paragraph begins by introducing the Hmong student and his topic: making fish soup. The repeated phrase "in order to" illustrates the humorous progression from making fish soup to needing to catch a fish to choosing an appropriate hook to knowing what fish you want to catch, etc. The narrator uses the word "finally" in the second-to-last sentence to emphasize the numerous tangents the student had taken in demonstrating how to make fish soup.

8.3 Providing an Objective Summary

Review

When you **summarize** a nonfiction work, you provide a brief overview of its major ideas in your own words. You omit unimportant details and focus instead on central ideas and the key details that support these ideas.

An effective summary is **objective** and free of bias and does not include your own opinions.

As you read a text, underline key ideas and details. Then retell these ideas and details in a brief summary.

Key Terms

summarize: condensing a text's main ideas and events into shorter paragraphs, sentences, or phrases.

objective: not influenced by personal feelings or opinions.

Check Understanding

Notice the way one student underlines key details and jots down main ideas to prepare for writing a summary of the excerpt on the next page.

from All Things Considered
by G. K. Chesterton

1. It is perfectly obvious that in any decent occupation (such as bricklaying or writing books) there are only two ways (in any special sense) of succeeding. One is by doing very good work, the other is by cheating. Both are much too simple to require any literary explanation. If you are in for the high jump, either jump higher than any one else, or manage somehow to pretend that you have done so. If you want to succeed at whist, either be a good whist-player, or play with marked cards. You may want a book about jumping; you may want a book about whist; you may want a book about cheating at whist. But you cannot want a book about Success. Especially you cannot want a book about Success such as those which you can now find scattered by the hundred about the book-market. You may want to jump or to play cards; but you do not want to read wandering statements to the effect that jumping is jumping, or that games are won by winners.

Notes

Chesterton contends that success is achieved by doing good work or by cheating.

Activity 8.3 Reread the excerpt above. Highlight details you would include in a summary and write a brief summary on a separate sheet of paper.

Toolbox

Maintain objectivity. While a summary of Chesterton's paragraph above would not include the reader's opinions about self-help books, it should include Chesterton's opinions because they form key ideas in the text. To keep your the summary objective, introduce the author's statements with phrases such as, "Chesterton contends" or "Chesterton asserts," indicating to the reader that the opinions expressed are those of Chesterton, not those of the summary writer.

Try It

Directions: Read these paragraphs from a speech by Chief Joseph on a visit to Washington, D.C. in 1879. Then answer the questions that follow.

from A Speech on a Visit to Washington, D.C.
by Chief Joseph

1. At last I was granted permission to come to Washington and bring my friend Yellow Bull and our interpreter with me. I am glad I came. I have shaken hands with a good many friends, but there are some things I want to know which no one seems able to explain. I cannot understand how the Government sends a man out to fight us, as it did General Miles, and then breaks his word. Such a government has something wrong about it. I cannot understand why so many chiefs are allowed to talk so many different ways, and

Notes

promise so many different things. I have seen the Great Father Chief [President Hayes]; the Next Great Chief [Secretary of the Interior]; the Commissioner Chief; the Law Chief; and many other law chiefs [Congressmen] and they all say they are my friends, and that I shall have justice, but while all their mouths talk right I do not understand why nothing is done for my people. I have heard talk and talk but nothing is done. Good words do not last long unless they amount to something. Words do not pay for my dead people. They do not pay for my country now overrun by white men. They do not protect my father's grave. They do not pay for my horses and cattle. Good words do not give me back my children. Good words will not make good the promise of your war chief, General Miles. Good words will not give my people a home where they can live in peace and take care of themselves. I am tired of talk that comes to nothing. It makes my heart sick when I remember all the good words and all the broken promises. There has been too much talking by men who had no right to talk. Too many misinterpretations have been made; too many misunderstandings have come up between the white men and the Indians. If the white man wants to live in peace with the Indian he can live in peace. There need be no trouble. Treat all men alike. Give them the same laws. Give them all an even chance to live and grow. All men were made by the same Great Spirit Chief. They are all brothers. The earth is the mother of all people, and all people should have equal rights upon it. You might as well expect all rivers to run backward as that any man who was born a free man should be contented penned up and denied liberty to go where he pleases. If you tie a horse to a stake, do you expect he will grow fat? If you pen an Indian up on a small spot of earth and compel him to stay there, he will not be contented nor will he grow and prosper. I have asked some of the Great White Chiefs where they get their authority to say to the Indian that he shall stay in one place, while he sees white men going where they please. They cannot tell me.

Notes

5. State in your own words two key details that reveal Chief Joseph's attitude toward the United States government.

6. Write an objective summary of the paragraph. Then use your summary to infer the central idea of the passage.

____

____

____

____

____

____

Question 5 asks you to retell in your own words two key details from the passage that reveal Chief Joseph's attitude toward the United States government. Two key details are the following:

Chief Joseph cannot understand how so many "chiefs" of the white government can talk and promise but do nothing.

Chief Joseph asked government officials how they have the authority to restrict Indians to one place while white men are allowed to go where they please.

Question 6 asks you to provide a brief summary of the passage and tell what it reveals about the central idea. One possible response follows.

Chief Joseph expresses his anger at the way the U.S. government has treated Indians. He questions why so many government officials promise justice while taking no action to keep these promises. He explains that he is tired of all of the empty talk, the broken promises, and the misunderstandings. He asserts that Indians and white men can live in peace so long as all men are treated equally with the same laws and rights.

The central idea is that Chief Joseph wants the U.S. government to keep its promises and to treat Indians equally.

Strategies for Analyzing Central Ideas and Supporting Details

Use the following strategies as you analyze central ideas and supporting details in literary texts.

- Identify and underline the thesis statement and key details.
- Note ideas that build on one another.
- Synthesize important ideas and details and express them in your own words.
- Summarize main ideas and key details. Omit personal feelings and opinions as you summarize.

Test-Taking Tips

- Get in the habit of supporting your answers with evidence from the text. Try to use a wide range of evidence to support your analysis.
- Reread the question after you have completed a response to make sure you have addressed each part of it. If you discover an omission or weak part of your response, revise that section.
- Avoid overused words or phrases. Choose specific words over general and vague words.
- Leave time at the end to proofread your response.

Chapter Review

Read the excerpt from *The Immortal Life of Henrietta Lacks* and answer the questions that follow.

from The Immortal Life of Henrietta Lacks

by Rebecca Skloot

Notes

1. . . . . I first learned about HeLa cells and the woman behind them in 1988, thirty-seven years after her death, when I was sixteen and sitting in a community college biology class. My instructor, Donald Defler, a gnomish balding man, paced at the front of the lecture hall and flipped on an overhead projector. He pointed to two diagrams that appeared on the wall behind him. They were schematics of the cell reproduction cycle, but to me they just looked like a neon-colored mess of arrows, squares, and circles with words I didn't understand, like "MPF Triggering a Chain Reaction of Protein Activations."

2. I was a kid who'd failed freshman year at the regular public high school because she never showed up. I'd transferred to an alternative school that offered dream studies instead of biology, so I was taking Defler's class for high-school credit, which meant that I was sitting in a college lecture hall at sixteen with words like *mitosis* and *kinase inhibitors* flying around. I was completely lost.

3. "Do we have to memorize everything on those diagrams?" one student yelled.

4. Yes, Defler said, we had to memorize the diagrams, and yes, they'd be on the test, but that didn't matter right then. What he wanted us to understand was that cells are amazing things: There are about one hundred trillion of them in our bodies, each so small that several thousand could fit on the period at the end of this sentence. They make up all our tissues—muscle, bone, blood—which in turn make up our organs.

5. Under the microscope, a cell looks a lot like a fried egg: It has a white (the *cytoplasm*) that's full of water and proteins to keep it fed, and a yolk (the *nucleus*) that holds all the genetic information that makes you *you*. The cytoplasm buzzes like a New York City street. It's crammed full of molecules and vessels endlessly shuttling enzymes and sugars from one part of the cell to another, pumping water, nutrients, and oxygen in and out of the cell. All the while, little cytoplasmic factories work 24/7, cranking out sugars, fats, proteins, and energy to keep the whole thing running and feed the nucleus—the brains of the operation. Inside every nucleus within each cell in your body, there's an identical copy of your entire genome. That genome tells cells when to grow and divide and makes sure they do their jobs, whether that's controlling your heartbeat or helping your brain understand the words on this page.

6. Defler paced the front of the classroom telling us how mitosis—the process of cell division—makes it possible for embryos to grow into babies, and for our bodies to create new cells for healing wounds or replenishing blood we've lost. It was beautiful, he said, like a perfectly choreographed dance.

Notes

7. All it takes is one small mistake anywhere in the division process for cells to start growing out of control, he told us. Just *one* enzyme misfiring, just *one* wrong protein activation, and you could have cancer. Mitosis goes haywire, which is how it spreads. "We learned that by studying cancer cells in culture," Defler said. He grinned and spun to face the board, where he wrote two words in enormous print: HENRIETTA LACKS.

8. Henrietta died in 1951 from a vicious case of cervical cancer, he told us. But before she died, a surgeon took samples of her tumor and put them in a petri dish. Scientists had been trying to keep human cells alive in culture for decades, but they all eventually died. Henrietta's were different: they reproduced an entire generation every twenty-four hours, and they never stopped. They became the first immortal human cells ever grown in a laboratory.

9. "Henrietta's cells have now been living outside her body far longer than they ever lived inside it," Defler said. If we went to almost any cell culture lab in the world and opened its freezers, he told us, we'd probably find millions—if not billions—of Henrietta's cells in small vials on ice.

10. Her cells were part of research into the genes that cause cancer and those that suppress it; they helped develop drugs for treating herpes, leukemia, influenza, hemophilia, and Parkinson's disease; and they've been used to study lactose digestion, sexually transmitted diseases, appendicitis, human longevity, mosquito mating, and the negative cellular effects of working in sewers. Their chromosomes and proteins have been studied with such detail and precision that scientists know their every quirk. Like guinea pigs and mice, Henrietta's cells have become the standard laboratory workhorse.

11. "HeLa cells were one of the most important things that happened to medicine in the last hundred years," Defler said.

12. Then, matter-of-factly, almost as an afterthought, he said, "She was a black woman." He erased her name in one fast swipe and blew the chalk from his hands. Class was over.

13. As the other students filed out of the room, I sat thinking, *That's it? That's all we get? There has to be more to the story.*

14. I followed Defler to his office.

15. "Where was she from?" I asked. "Did she know how important her cells were? Did she have any children?"

16. "I wish I could tell you," he said, "but no one knows anything about her."

17. After class, I ran home and threw myself onto my bed with my biology textbook. I looked up "cell culture" in the index, and there she was, a small parenthetical:

> In culture, cancer cells can go on dividing indefinitely, if they have a continual supply of nutrients, and thus are said to be "immortal." A striking example is a cell line that has been reproducing in culture since 1951. (Cells of this line are called HeLa cells because their original source was a tumor removed from a woman named Henrietta Lacks.)

Notes

18. That was it. I looked up HeLa in my parents' encyclopedia, then my dictionary: No Henrietta.

19. As I graduated from high school and worked my way through college toward a biology degree, HeLa cells were omnipresent. I heard about them in histology, neurology, pathology; I used them in experiments on how neighboring cells communicate. But after Mr. Defler, no one mentioned Henrietta.

20. When I got my first computer in the mid-nineties and started using the Internet, I searched for information about her, but found only confused snippets: most sites said her name was Helen Lane; some said she died in the thirties; others said the forties, fifties, or even sixties. Some said ovarian cancer killed her, others said breast or cervical cancer.

21. Eventually I tracked down a few magazine articles about her from the seventies. *Ebony* quoted Henrietta's husband saying, "All I remember is that she had this disease, and right after she died they called me in the office wanting to get my permission to take a sample of some kind. I decided not to let them." *Jet* said the family was angry—angry that Henrietta's cells were being sold for twenty-five dollars a vial, and angry that articles had been published about the cells without their knowledge. It said, "Pounding in the back of their heads was a gnawing feeling that science and the press had taken advantage of them."

. . .

22. As I worked my way through graduate school studying writing, I became fixated on the idea of someday telling Henrietta's story. At one point I even called directory assistance in Baltimore looking for Henrietta's husband, David Lacks, but he wasn't listed. I had the idea that I'd write a book that was a biography of both the cells and the woman they came from—someone's daughter, wife, and mother.

23. I couldn't have imagined it then, but that phone call would mark the beginning of a decadelong adventure through scientific laboratories, hospitals, and mental institutions, with a cast of characters that would include Nobel laureates, grocery store clerks, convicted felons, and a professional con artist. While trying to make sense of the history of cell culture and the complicated ethical debate surrounding the use of human tissues in research, I'd be accused of conspiracy and slammed into a wall both physically and metaphorically, and I'd eventually find myself on the receiving end of something that looked a lot like an exorcism. I did eventually meet Deborah, who would turn out to be one of the strongest and most resilient women I'd ever known. We'd form a deep personal bond, and slowly, without realizing it, I'd become a character in her story, and she in mine.

Questions 1–7: Choose the best answer or write your response on the lines.

1. Which method of development is used throughout the selection?

   Ⓐ compare and contrast

   Ⓑ first-person narrative

   Ⓒ argument

   Ⓓ chronological

2. Cite three transitions that reveal the development method you selected in question 1.

3. How do paragraphs 9 and 10 contribute to the central idea of the passage?

   Ⓐ They tell a story about Henrietta Lacks' life.

   Ⓑ They explain how Henrietta Lacks' cells became important to science.

   Ⓒ They establish the relationship between the narrator and Henrietta Lacks.

   Ⓓ They explain the process of how cancer cells are formed.

4. Cite and explain two details that support your answer to question 3.

5. Placed in the context of the rest of the text, how does paragraph 17 develop the central idea? Support your answer with evidence from the text.

6. Cite and explain two details that develop the idea that the narrator's curiosity about Lacks is long-lasting.

7. Write an objective summary of the passage.

Chapter 9 Complex Ideas & Events (RI.11–12.3)

Not all topics are simple and straightforward, easily boiled down to a sound bite. Patient rereading may be needed to gain understanding of some complex text. This chapter addresses the following aspects of reading complex informational texts.

9.1 Analyzing a complex set of ideas or sequence of events

9.2 Explaining how ideas and events interact and develop

9.1 Analyzing a Complex Set of Ideas or Sequence of Events

Review

A nonfiction text may present a complex set of ideas or a sequence of events that is difficult to follow. One way to unpack such a text is to determine its logical structure.

Authors of persuasion frequently use the logic of argumentation in which a **claim** is upheld with **evidence** and counterclaims are negated with rebuttals.

In the premise/conclusion structure, the author presents a **premise** that the audience already accepts as true, applies the premise to a particular situation, and draws convincing conclusions about the situation.

In **sequential structure**, commonly used in instructions, a series of steps are presented, one following the other.

In **chronological structure**, used in narrative nonfiction and historical writing, events are presented the order in which they happened.

In **cause/effect structure**, a chain reaction of causes and effects are presented. This logical structure is used in scientific and historical writing.

To understand the logic of complex text, it often helps to outline the main points and the logical connections between them. Look for transitional words and phrases, such as *first, next, because, as a result, therefore,* and *consequently*. They will provided clues to the author's logic.

Key Terms

chronological structure: structure in which events are presented in the order in which they occurred.

claim: an opinion or belief at the heart of an argument.

evidence: facts, examples, reasons, or other details used to support a claim.

premise: a proposition or statement that is accepted as true.

sequential structure: structure in which steps are presented in order.

transitional words and phrases: words and phrases that show the relationships of ideas and details

Check Understanding

Study the logic behind the ideas in the shortened version of the Declaration of Independence that starts on the next page.

from The Declaration of Independence

by Thomas Jefferson

Even after the American Revolution had begun, many colonists hoped for reconciliation with Great Britain. At the Second Continental Congress in Philadelphia, supporters of independence decided that a document was needed to state the case clearly before putting the issue to a vote. Thomas Jefferson of Virginia was given the task of writing this Declaration of Independence. After the rest of the committee made some changes, it was submitted to Congress, who voted for independence on July 2, 1776, and approved the declaration two days later.

1. When in the Course of human events, it becomes necessary for one people to dissolve the political bands which have connected them with another, and to assume among the powers of the earth, the separate and equal station to which the Laws of Nature and of Nature's God entitle them, a decent respect to the opinions of mankind requires that they should declare the causes which impel them to the separation.

2. We hold these truths to be self-evident, that all men are created equal, that they are endowed by their Creator with certain unalienable Rights, that among these are Life, Liberty and the pursuit of Happiness.—That to secure these rights, Governments are instituted among Men, deriving their just powers from the consent of the governed.—That whenever any Form of Government becomes destructive of these ends, it is the Right of the People to alter or to abolish it, and to institute new Government. . . .

3. The history of the present King of Great Britain is a history of repeated injuries and usurpations, all having in direct object the establishment of an absolute Tyranny over these States. To prove this, let Facts be submitted to a candid[1] world.

4. He has refused his Assent to Laws, the most wholesome and necessary for the public good. . . .

5. He has made Judges dependent on his Will alone, for the tenure of their offices, and the amount and payment of their salaries. . . .

6. He has kept among us, in times of peace, Standing Armies without the Consent of our legislatures.

7. He has affected to render the Military independent of and superior to the Civil power.

8. He has combined with others to subject us to a jurisdiction foreign to our constitution, and unacknowledged by our laws, giving his Assent to their Acts of pretended Legislation:

9. For Quartering large bodies of armed troops among us;

10. For protecting them, by a mock Trial, from punishment for any

Notes

Paragraph 1 is an introduction explaining why independence is being declared.

Logical argument based on two premises:

Premise 1) All men are created equal. Premise 2) Governments are instituted to secure the rights of the people. Conclusion: If the government fails to secure the rights of the people, they are entitled to alter or abolish it.

Claim: The present King of Great Britain has abused the rights of the people in Britain's American colonies.

Support for Claim: A long list of examples provide evidence to prove that the king has abused the colonists' rights.

1 candid: impartial

Murders which they should commit on the Inhabitants of these States;

11. For cutting off our Trade with all parts of the world;

12. For imposing Taxes on us without our Consent;

13. For depriving us, in many cases, of the benefits of Trial by Jury. . . .

14. In every stage of these Oppressions We have Petitioned for Redress in the most humble terms: Our repeated Petitions have been answered only by repeated injury. A Prince whose character is thus marked by every act which may define a Tyrant is unfit to be the ruler of a free people. . . .

15. We, therefore, the Representatives of the united States of America, in General Congress, Assembled, appealing to the Supreme Judge of the world for the rectitude of our intentions, do, in the Name, and by Authority of the good People of these Colonies, solemnly publish and declare, That these United Colonies are, and of Right ought to be Free and Independent States; that they are Absolved from all Allegiance to the British Crown, and that all political connection between them and the State of Great Britain, is and ought to be totally dissolved; and that as Free and Independent States, they have full Power to levy War, conclude Peace, contract Alliances, establish Commerce, and to do all other Acts and Things which Independent States may of right do. And for the support of this Declaration, with a firm reliance on the protection of divine Providence, we mutually pledge to each other our Lives, our Fortunes and our sacred Honor.

Notes

Activity 9.1 Reread the excerpt. Highlight transitional words and phrases in paragraphs 14 and 15. What kind of logic do they indicate? Write your answers in the margin and compare your response with a partner.

Toolbox

As you read the text—

- Paraphrase, or restate, complex language to help you understand it.
- Underline or highlight portions of the text that best reveal the main points.
- Consider how the main points are connected, using transitional words and phrases in the text to help you understand the relationships.
- Make marginal notes tracing the author's logic by showing connections between main points, using numbers, labels, arrows, or even outline form, charts, or diagrams if you find them helpful.

Try It

Directions: Read the excerpt below and answer the questions.

from Address to Congress, November 1917

by Carrie Chapman Catt

As president of the National American Woman Suffrage Association, Carrie Chapman Catt was a leading figure in the fight to gain women the right to vote. The following excerpt is from an address she made to Congress on the issue. The Nineteenth Amendment to the U.S. Constitution, giving women the right to vote, finally passed in 1920.

1. Ours is a nation born of revolution, of rebellion against a system of government so securely entrenched in the customs and traditions of human society that in 1776 it seemed impregnable. From the beginning of things, nations had been ruled by kings and for kings, while the people served and paid the cost. The American Revolutionists boldly proclaimed the heresies:[1] "Taxation without representation is tyranny." "Governments derive their just powers from the consent of the governed." The colonists won, and the nation which was established as a result of their victory has held unfailingly that these two fundamental principles of democratic government are not only the spiritual source of our national existence but have been our chief historic pride and at all times the sheet anchor of our liberties.

2. Eighty years after the Revolution, Abraham Lincoln welded those two maxims into a new one: "Ours is a government of the people, by the people, and for the people." Fifty years more passed and the president of the United States, Woodrow Wilson,[2] in a mighty crisis of the nation, proclaimed to the world: "We are fighting for the things which we have always carried nearest to our hearts: for democracy, for the right of those who submit to authority to have a voice in their own government."

3. All the way between these immortal aphorisms[3] political leaders have declared unabated faith in their truth. Not one American has arisen to question their logic in the 141 years of our national existence. However stupidly our country may have evaded the logical application at times, it has never swerved from its devotion to the theory of democracy as expressed by those two axioms.[4] . . .

4. With such a history behind it, how can our nation escape the logic it has never failed to follow, when its last unenfranchised[5] class calls for the vote? Behold our Uncle Sam floating the banner with one hand, "Taxation without representation is tyranny," and with the

Notes

1 heresies: ideas contrary to established views of the time
2 Woodrow Wilson: president who urged the United States to enter World War I in order to safeguard and promote democracy
3 aphorisms: short, concise statements of principle
4 axioms: established principles
5 unenfranchised: not permitted to vote

other seizing the billions of dollars paid in taxes by women to whom he refuses "representation." Behold him again, welcoming the boys of twenty-one[7] and the newly made immigrant citizen to "a voice in their own government" while he denies that fundamental right of democracy to thousands of women public school teachers from whom many of these men learn all they know of citizenship and patriotism, to women college presidents, to women who preach in our pulpits, interpret law in our courts, preside over our hospitals, write books and magazines, and serve in every uplifting moral and social enterprise. Is there a single man who can justify such inequality of treatment, such outrageous discrimination? Not one. . . .

Notes

1. On which two premises does Catt base her argument that American women should be able to vote?

______

______

______

______

______

2. Which of these logical arguments does the final paragraph most clearly make?

Ⓐ As public school teachers, women clearly have given their consent to be governed.

Ⓑ As tax-paying citizens, women should be able to vote for their representation.

Ⓒ As older Americans, women have more right to vote than twenty-one-year-old males do.

Ⓓ As native-born Americans, women have more right to vote than recent immigrants do.

3. How do the details in the last paragraph about women college presidents, preachers, and the like tie in to the logic of Catt's argument?

______

______

______

______

Question 1 asks you to identify the two premises on which Catt bases her argument. Catt's two premises are the two founding principles of the American Revolution that she cites in her opening paragraph: "Taxation without representation is tyranny" and "Governments derive their just powers from the consent of the governed."

Question 2 asks you to identify which of four arguments the last paragraph most clearly makes. Choice A is incorrect. The paragraph mentions women's work as public school teachers, but not to illustrate that they have given their consent to be governed. Choices C and D are also incorrect. The paragraph points out the irony of twenty-one-year-old and newly naturalized male American citizens being able to vote while the women who taught them about citizenship cannot; it says nothing about the women being older or being native born. The correct answer is B. The last paragraph clearly mentions the taxes women pay and argues that their not being able to vote is wrong, since one of the two principles on which the nation is founded is "Taxation without representation is tyranny."

Question 3 asks you to explain how the women's careers mentioned in the last paragraph relate Catt's argument. The careers she mentions show the remarkable success of many American women. They stress her argument that women should vote by showing the absurdity of their not being allowed to vote when they participate so successfully in so many other areas of American life.

9.2 Explaining How Ideas and Events Interact and Develop

Review

Often you will get a better understanding of complex texts if you examine how individuals, ideas, or events interact and develop.

The Declaration of Independence, for example, opens with a reason for the declaration (decent respect to the opinions of mankind) followed by the establishment of two premises. As evidence, the history of injuries by the King is presented in a detailed list. Finally, in the "therefore" statement at the end, the declaration of independence from the British Crown is made.

Such an examination will prove especially valuable in texts that do not follow a clear-cut **linear** organization.

Key Terms

linear: moving in a straight line

organic: forming a fluid, flexible network or web of ideas and details

A personal essay, for example, may develop more **organically**, jumping from a description of a significant location to a narrative of a related event to lyrics of a favorite song, and so forth.

A descriptive essay may provide a web of images in order to develop a general impression or mood. In these and other cases, you may need to focus on how individuals, ideas, and events interact.

Read the text more than once and ask yourself questions about how individuals, events, and ideas are related. Here are examples of questions you might ask:

- How does this event relate to earlier events?
- How does this idea clarify, modify, or contradict other ideas in the text?
- How does the narrator change and develop in the course of the text?
- What impressions do the ideas, events, and descriptions convey?

Check Understanding

Consider the relationship of individuals, events, and ideas in the excerpt that starts on the next page.

from Born on a Blue Day: Inside the Extraordinary Mind of an Autistic Savant

by Daniel Tammet

1. I was born on January 31, 1979—a Wednesday. I know it was a Wednesday, because the date is blue in my mind and Wednesdays are always blue, like the number 9 or the sound of loud voices arguing. I like my birth date, because of the way I'm able to visualize most of the numbers in it as smooth and round shapes, similar to pebbles on a beach. That's because they are prime numbers: 31, 19, 197, 97, 79 and 1979 are all divisible only by themselves and 1. I can recognize every prime up to 9,973 by their "pebble-like" quality. It's just the way my brain works.

2. I have a rare condition known as savant syndrome, little known before its portrayal by actor Dustin Hoffman in the Oscar-winning 1988 film *Rain Man*. Like Hoffman's character, Raymond Babbitt, I have an almost obsessive need for order and routine which affects virtually every aspect of my life.

3. For example, I eat exactly 45 grams of porridge for breakfast each morning; I weigh the bowl with an electronic scale to make sure. Then I count the number of items of clothing I'm wearing before I leave my house. I get anxious if I can't drink my cups of tea at the same time each day. Whenever I become too stressed and I can't breathe properly, I close my eyes and count. Thinking of numbers helps me to become calm again.

4. Numbers are my friends, and they are always around me. Each one is unique and has its own personality. The number 11 is friendly and 5 is loud, whereas 4 is both shy and quiet—it's my favorite number, perhaps because it reminds me of myself. Some are big—23, 667, 1,179—while others are small: 6, 13, 581. Some are beautiful, like 333, and some are ugly, like 289. To me, every number is special.

5. No matter where I go or what I'm doing, numbers are never far from my thoughts. In an interview with talk show host David Letterman in New York, I told David he looked like the number 117—tall and lanky. Later outside, in the appropriately numerically named Times Square, I gazed up at the towering skyscrapers and felt surrounded by 9s—the number I most associate with feelings of immensity.

6. Scientists call my visual, emotional experience of numbers *synesthesia*, a rare neurological mixing of the senses, which most commonly results in the ability to see alphabetical letters and/or numbers in color. Mine is an unusual and complex type, through which I see numbers as shapes, colors, textures and motions. The number 1, for example, is a brilliant and bright white, like someone shining a flashlight into my eyes. Five is a clap of thunder or the sound of waves crashing against rocks. Thirty-seven is lumpy like porridge, while 89 reminds me of falling snow. . . .

Notes

Tammet explains what the day of the week and numbers of his birth date mean to him.

Tammet ties his condition to that of a movie character familiar to many of his readers.

Details in paragraph 3 help illustrate the obsessive need for order and routine.

Notes

7. Using my own synesthetic experiences since early childhood, I have grown up with the ability to handle and calculate huge numbers in my head without any conscious effort, just like the Raymond Babbitt character. In fact, this is a talent common to several other real-life savants (sometimes referred to as "lightning calculators"). . . .

8. My favorite kind of calculation is power multiplication, which means multiplying a number by itself a specified number of times. Multiplying a number by itself is called squaring; for example, the square of 72 is 72 × 72 = 5,184. Squares are always symmetrical shapes in my mind, which makes them especially beautiful to me. Multiplying the same number three times over is called cubing or "raising" to the third power. The cube, or third power, of 51 is equivalent to 51 × 51 × 51 = 132,651. I see each result of a power multiplication as a distinctive visual pattern in my head. . . .

9. When I divide one number by another, in my head I see a spiral rotating downwards in larger and larger loops, which seem to warp and curve. Different divisions produce different sizes of spirals with varying curves. From my mental imagery I'm able to calculate a sum like 13 ÷ 97 (0.1340206...) to almost a hundred decimal places.

10. I never write anything down when I'm calculating, because I've always been able to do the sums in my head, and it's much easier for me to visualize the answer using my synesthetic shapes than to try to follow the "carry the one" techniques taught in the textbooks we are given at school. When multiplying, I see the two numbers as distinct shapes. The image changes and a third shape emerges—the correct answer. The process takes a matter of seconds and happens spontaneously. It's like doing math without having to think. . . .

11. For as long as I can remember, I have experienced numbers in the visual, synesthetic way that I do. Numbers are my first language, one I often think and feel in. Emotions can be hard for me to understand or know how to react to, so I often use numbers to help me. If a friend says they feel sad or depressed, I picture myself sitting in the dark hollowness of number 6 to help me experience the same sort of feeling and understand it. If I read in an article that a person felt intimidated by something, I imagine myself standing next to the number 9. Whenever someone describes visiting a beautiful place, I recall my numerical landscapes and how happy they make me feel inside. By doing this, numbers help me get closer to understanding other people.

12. Sometimes people I meet for the first time remind me of a particular number and this helps me to be comfortable around them. . . . Some nights, when I'm having difficulty falling asleep, I imagine myself walking around my numerical landscapes. Then I feel safe and happy. I never feel lost, because the prime number shapes act as signposts.

Activity 9.2 Reread the excerpt above. Highlight additional examples of connected ideas and note their development in the margin. Compare your findings with a partner.

Toolbox

Read the text more than once. As you read—

- Underline or highlight details that show how individuals, events, and ideas interact and develop.
- Ask and answer questions to help you pinpoint related ideas and details.
- Make marginal notes about the relationships you find and the main points they help develop.

Try It

Directions: Read the excerpt below and answer the questions.

from Made in America: An Informal History of the English Language in the United States

by Bill Bryson

Notes

1. In 1885, a young man named George Eastman formed the Eastman Dry Plate and Film Company in Rochester, New York. It was rather a bold thing to do. Aged just thirty-one, Eastman was a junior clerk in a bank on a comfortable but modest salary of $15 a week. He had no background in business. But he was passionately devoted to photography and had become increasingly gripped with the conviction that anyone who could develop a simple, untechnical camera, as opposed to the cumbersome, outsized, fussily complex contrivances then on the market, stood to make a fortune.

2. Eastman worked tirelessly for three years to perfect his invention, supporting himself in the meantime by making dry plates for commercial photographers, and in June 1888 produced a camera that was positively dazzling in its simplicity: a plain black box just six and a half inches long by three and a quarter inches wide, with a button on the side and a key for advancing the film. Eastman called his device the Detective Camera. Detectives were all the thing—Sherlock Holmes was just taking off with American readers—and the name implied that it was so small and simple that it could be used unnoticed, as a detective might. . . .

3. In September 1888, Eastman changed the name of the camera to Kodak—an odd choice, since it was meaningless, and in 1888 no one gave meaningless names to products, especially successful products. Since British patent applications at the time demanded a full explanation of trade and brand names, we know how Eastman arrived at his inspired name. He crisply summarized his reasoning in his patent application: "First. It is short. Second. It is not capable of mispronunciation. Third. It does not resemble anything in the art and cannot be associated with anything in the art except the Kodak." Four years later the whole enterprise was renamed the

Eastman Kodak Company.

4. Despite the considerable expense involved—a Kodak camera sold for $25, and each roll of film cost $10, including developing—by 1895, over 100,000 Kodaks had been sold and Eastman was a seriously wealthy man. . . .

5. From the outset, Eastman developed three crucial strategies that have been the hallmarks of virtually every successful consumer goods company since. First, he went for the mass market, reasoning that it was better to make a little money each from a lot of people rather than a lot of money from a few. He also showed a tireless, obsessive dedication to making his products better and cheaper. In the 1890s, such an approach was widely perceived as insane. If you had a successful product you milked it for all it was worth. If competitors came along with something better, you bought them out or tried to squash them with lengthy patent fights or other bullying tactics. What you certainly did not do was create new products that made your existing lines obsolete. Eastman did. Throughout the late 1890s, Kodak introduced a series of increasingly cheaper, niftier cameras—the Bull's Eye model of 1896, which cost just $12, and the famous slimline Folding Pocket Kodak of 1898, before finally in 1900 producing his eureka model[1]: the little box Brownie, priced at just $1 and with film at 15 cents a reel (though with only six exposures per reel.)

6. Above all, what set Eastman apart was the breathtaking lavishness of his advertising. In 1899 alone he spent $750,000, an unheard-of sum, on advertising. Moreover, it was good advertising: crisp, catchy, reassuringly trustworthy. "You press the button—we do the rest" ran the company's first slogan, thus making a virtue of its shortcomings. Never mind that you couldn't load or unload the film yourself. Kodak would do it for you. In 1905, it followed with another class slogan: "If It Isn't an Eastman, It Isn't a Kodak."

7. Kodak's success did not escape other businessmen, who also began to see virtue in the idea of steady product refinement and improvement. AT&T and Westinghouse, among others, set up research laboratories with the idea of creating a stream of new products, even at the risk of displacing old ones. Above all, everyone everywhere began to advertise.

Notes

---

1 eureka model: the breakthrough model that would go on to make Eastman's fortune. Eureka! (Greek for "I have found it!"), was supposedly exclaimed by Archimedes when he discovered the concept of specific gravity. The word came to be exclaimed at other discoveries, including when prospectors discovered gold in California (where it became the state motto).

5. Which idea or event in paragraph 1 is developed later in the text?

Ⓐ Rochester, New York, became a center of business innovation.

Ⓑ George Eastman was a talented and passionate photographer.

Ⓒ George Eastman developed and sold a simple, untechnical camera.

Ⓓ Almost anyone who works hard can achieve the American dream of success.

6. Explain the connection that the author implies, in paragraphs 2 and 3, between the two early names that Eastman chose for his camera. What idea or quality of George Eastman does this connection help convey?

____

____

____

____

7. How do the details in the next-to-last paragraph further develop the idea you identified in question 6?

____

____

____

____

8. Which of these ideas from earlier in the passage does the last paragraph most clearly develop?

Ⓐ Product development is important to a company's success.

Ⓑ Buying out your competitors is the best way to succeed in business.

Ⓒ Low prices mean high sales.

Ⓓ Catchy names help businesses to succeed.

Question 5 asks you to explain which idea in the first paragraph is developed later in the text. Choice A is incorrect; the first paragraph says nothing about business innovations in Rochester, New York, other than Eastman's. Choice B is also incorrect; though the paragraph does mention Eastman's passion for photography, it says nothing about his talent. Choice D is also incorrect. The paragraph does not mention the American dream, and since later paragraphs describe only Eastman's success, they do not support the idea that almost any American who works hard can succeed. Choice C is the correct answer. The description of Eastman's camera in paragraph 2 and of later models in paragraph 5 illustrate his success in developing and marketing simpler, less technical cameras.

Question 6 asks you to explain the connection between the first and second names that Eastman chose for his product and the idea about Eastman that they help develop. Sample response:

In paragraph 2, the author indicates that Eastman first chose the name Detective Camera because it would take advantage of the popularity of Sherlock Holmes at the time. In paragraph 3, the details indicate that Eastman chose the name Kodak because it seemed simple, catchy, and memorable. In both cases, the author implies that Eastman understood the importance of choosing a good name to market his product successfully.

Question 7 asks you to explain the connection between the next-to-last paragraph and the idea about Eastman you identified in question 6. Sample response:

The next-to-last paragraph stresses Eastman's use of effective advertising slogans. It confirms the idea that Eastman was a creative pioneer of product marketing and advertising.

Question 8 asks you to identify an idea from earlier in the passage that the final paragraph most clearly develops. Choice B is clearly incorrect. An earlier paragraph mentions the practice of buying out competitors as a means of business success but only to contrast that practice with Eastman's methods. Choices C and D are also incorrect. The passage does show that Eastman saw low prices and catchy names as keys to business success, but neither of those two methods are discussed in the final paragraph. Choice A is the correct answer. The last paragraph mentions that other companies have followed Eastman's lead in setting up laboratories to develop new products.

Strategies for Analyzing Complex Text

Use the following strategies as you analyze text that contains a complex set of ideas or sequence of events.

- Read the text more than once and mentally paraphrase complex language if necessary.
- Use transitional words and phrases as clues to the relationships of ideas and details.
- Ask and answer questions to help you understand how ideas, and events are developed.
- Underline or highlight main points and related ideas and details.
- Make marginal notes about the logic behind the text and the relationships of ideas and details.

Test-Taking Tips

- Read the text more than once, tracing the author's logic or examining the development of individuals, ideas, and events.
- Ask questions and paraphrase difficult language, if necessary, to help you better understand the text.
- Make a simple outline or diagram to map out the logic behind the text or the relationships of ideas and details.

Chapter Review

Directions: Read this excerpt, and then answer the questions.

from Statement at His 1922 Trial

by Mohandas K. Gandhi

Notes

In 1922, the government in British-ruled India charged Indian nationalist Mohandas Gandhi with inciting violence and rebellion after protests he led against British rule resulted in rioting and death. The following excerpt is from the famous speech he made in court before being found guilty and sentenced to six years in prison.

1. Before I read this statement I would like to state that I entirely endorse the learned Advocate-General's[1] remarks in connection with my humble self. . . . I have no desire whatsoever to conceal from this court the fact that to preach disaffection[2] towards the existing system of Government has become almost a passion with me, and the Advocate-General is entirely in the right when he says that my preaching of disaffection did not commence with my connection with *Young India*[3] but that it commenced much earlier, and in the statement that I am about to read, it will be my painful duty to admit before this court that it commenced much earlier than the period stated by the Advocate-General. It is a painful duty with me but I have to discharge that duty knowing the responsibility that rests upon my shoulders, and I wish to endorse all the blame that the learned Advocate-General has thrown on my shoulders in connection with the Bombay occurrences, Madras occurrences and the Chauri Chaura[4] occurrences. Thinking over these things deeply and sleeping over them night after night, it is impossible for me to dissociate myself from the diabolical crimes of Chauri Chaura or the mad outrages of Bombay. He is quite right when he says that as a man of responsibility, a man having received a fair share of education, having had a fair share of experience of this world, I should have known the consequences of every one of my acts. I know them. I knew that I was playing with fire. I ran the risk and if I was set free I would still do the same. I have felt it this morning that I would have failed in my duty, if I did not say what I said here just now.

2. I wanted to avoid violence. Nonviolence is the first article of my faith. It is also the last article of my creed. But I had to make my choice. I had either to submit to a system which I considered had done an irreparable harm to my country, or incur the risk of the mad fury of my people bursting forth when they understood the truth

1 Advocate-General: government prosecutor
2 disaffection: loss of loyalty, especially toward a government
3 *Young India*: weekly newspaper put out by Gandhi that protested British rule
4 Bombay . . . Chauri Chaura: places in British India where protests led by Gandhi resulted in violence

Notes

from my lips. I know that my people have sometimes gone mad. I am deeply sorry for it and I am, therefore, here to submit not to a light penalty but to the highest penalty. I do not ask for mercy. I do not plead any extending act. I am here, therefore, to invite and cheerfully submit to the highest penalty that can be inflicted upon me for what in law is a deliberate crime, and what appears to me to be the highest duty of a citizen. The only course open to you, the Judge, is, as I am going to say in my statement, either to resign your post, or inflict on me the severest penalty if you believe that the system and law you are assisting to administer are good for the people. I do not except that kind of conversion. But by the time I have finished with my statement you will have a glimpse of what is raging within my breast to run this maddest risk which a sane man can run.

3. I owe it perhaps to the Indian public and to the public in England, to . . . explain why from a staunch loyalist and cooperator, I have become an uncompromising disaffectionist and non-cooperator. To the court too I should say why I plead guilty to the charge of promoting disaffection towards the Government established by law in India.

4. My public life began in 1893 in South Africa in troubled weather. My first contact with British authority in that country was not of a happy character. I discovered that as a man and an Indian, I had no rights. More correctly I discovered that I had no rights as a man because I was an Indian.

5. But I was not baffled. I thought that this treatment of Indians was an excrescence[5] upon a system that was intrinsically and mainly good. I gave the Government my voluntary and hearty cooperation, criticizing it freely where I felt it was faulty but never wishing its destruction.

6. Consequently when the existence of the Empire[6] was threatened in 1899 by the Boer challenge,[7] I offered my services to it, raised a volunteer ambulance corps and served at several actions that took place for the relief of Ladysmith.[8] Similarly in 1906, at the time of the Zulu[9] "revolt," I raised a stretcher bearer party and served till the end of the "rebellion." On both the occasions I received medals and was even mentioned in dispatches. For my work in South Africa I was given by Lord Hardinge a Kaisar-i-Hind gold medal.[10] When the war broke out in 1914 between England and Germany,[11] I raised a volunteer ambulance cars in London, consisting of the then resident

5 excrescence: abnormal outgrowth
6 Empire: the British Empire, of which India and South Africa were then parts
7 Boer challenge: rebellion of South Africans of Dutch descent against British rule
8 Ladysmith: city in South Africa
9 Zulu: one of the native peoples of South Africa
10 Lord Hardinge . . . medal: public-service medal awarded in India by the British crown, here represented by Charles Hardinge, viceroy (crown-appointed ruler) of India from 1910 to 1916
11 war . . . Germany: World War I

Indians in London, chiefly students. Its work was acknowledge by the authorities to be valuable. . . . In all these efforts at service, I was actuated by the belief that it was possible by such services to gain a status of full equality in the Empire for my countrymen.

Notes

7. The first shock came in the shape of the Rowlatt Act[12]—a law designed to rob the people of all real freedom. I felt called upon to lead an intensive agitation against it. Then followed the Punjab horrors beginning with the massacre at Jallianwala Bagh[13] and culminating in crawling orders, public flogging and other indescribable humiliations. I discovered too that the plighted word of the Prime Minister to the [Muslims] of India regarding the integrity of Turkey and the holy places of Islam was not likely to be fulfilled. But in spite of the forebodings and the grave warnings of friends, at the Amritsar Congress in 1919, I fought for cooperation and working of the Montagu–Chelmsford reforms[14], hoping that the Prime Minister would redeem his promise to the Indian [Muslims], that the Punjab wound would be healed, and that the reforms, inadequate and unsatisfactory though they were, marked a new era of hope in the life of India.

8. But all that hope was shattered. The Khilafat promise[15] was not to be redeemed. The Punjab crime was whitewashed and most culprits went not only unpunished but remained in service, and some continued to draw pensions from the Indian revenue and in some cases were even rewarded. I saw too that not only did the reforms not mark a change of heart, but they were only a method of further raining India of her wealth and of prolonging her servitude.

9. I came reluctantly to the conclusion that the British connection had made India more helpless than she ever was before, politically and economically. A disarmed India has no power of resistance against any aggressor if she wanted to engage in an armed conflict with him. . . . She has become so poor that she has little power of resisting famines. Before the British advent India spun and wove in her millions of cottages, just the supplement she needed for adding to her meager agricultural resources. This cottage industry, so vital for India's existence, has been ruined by incredibly heartless and inhuman processes as described by English witnesses. Little do town dwellers know how the semi-starved masses of India are slowly sinking to lifelessness. Little do they know that their miserable comfort represents the brokerage[16] they get for their

12 Rowlatt Act: repressive measures passed in Britain in 1919 in response to unrest in India

13 massacre at Jallianwala Bagh: 1919 incident in the Indian region of Punjab in which British troops fired on a crowd of Indians peacefully celebrating the Punjabi New Year, killing hundreds

14 Montague–Chelmsford reforms: efforts briefly introduced by the British government to address India's problems with British rule

15 Khilafat promise: Britain's promise to Muslims of the Khilafat movement, including those in India, that their holy sites and interests would be respected after the defeat of Turkey's Ottoman Empire in World War I

16 brokerage: commission; fees

Notes

work they do for the foreign exploiter, that the profits and the brokerage are sucked from the masses. Little do they realize that the government established by law in British India is carried on for this exploitation of the masses. No sophistry,[17] no jugglery in figures, can explain away the evidence that the skeletons in many villages present to the naked eye. I have no doubt whatsoever that both England and the town dweller of India will have to answer, if there is a God above, for this crime against humanity, which is perhaps unequalled in history. The law itself in this country has been used to serve the foreign exploiter. My unbiased examination of the Punjab Martial Law cases has led me to believe that at least ninety-five per cent of convictions were wholly bad. My experience of political cases in India leads me to the conclusion, in nine out of every ten, the condemned men were totally innocent. Their crime consisted in the love of their country. In ninety-nine cases out of hundred, justice has been denied to Indians as against Europeans in the courts of India. This is not an exaggerated picture. It is the experience of almost every Indian who has had anything to do with such cases. In my opinion, the administration of the law is thus prostituted, consciously or unconsciously, for the benefit of the exploiter.

10. . . . Section 124A, under which I am happily charged, is perhaps the prince among the political sections of the Indian Penal Code designed to suppress the liberty of the citizen. Affection cannot be manufactured or regulated by law. If one has no affection for a person or system, one should be free to give the fullest expression to his disaffection, so long as he does not contemplate, promote, or incite to violence. But the section under which I and [my colleague] are charged is one under which mere promotion of disaffection is a crime. I have studied some of the cases tried under it; I know that some of the most loved of India's patriots have been convicted under it. I consider it a privilege, therefore, to be charged under that section. I have endeavored to give in their briefest outline the reasons for my disaffection. I have no personal ill-will against any single administrator, much less can I have any disaffection towards the King's person. But I hold it to be a virtue to be disaffected towards a Government which in its totality has done more harm to India than any previous system. . . . Holding such a belief, I consider it to be a sin to have affection for the system. And it has been a precious privilege for me to be able to write what I have in the various articles tendered in evidence against me.

11. In fact, I believe that I have rendered a service to India and England by showing in non-cooperation the way out of the unnatural state in which both are living. In my opinion, non-cooperation with evil is as much a duty as is cooperation with good. But in the past,

17 sophistry: misleading arguments

Notes

non-cooperation has been deliberately expressed in violence to the evildoer. I am endeavoring to show to my countrymen that violent non-cooperation only multiples evil, and that as evil can only be sustained by violence, withdrawal of support of evil requires complete abstention from violence. Nonviolence implies voluntary submission to the penalty for non-cooperation with evil. I am here, therefore, to invite and submit cheerfully to the highest penalty that can be inflicted upon me for what in law is deliberate crime, and what appears to me to be the highest duty of a citizen. The only course open to you, the Judge and the assessors, is either to resign your posts and thus dissociate yourselves from evil, if you feel that the law you are called upon to administer is an evil, and that in reality I am innocent, or to inflict on me the severest penalty, if you believe that the system and the law you are assisting to administer are good for the people of this country, and that my activity is, therefore, injurious to the common weal.[18]

18 weal: welfare

Questions 1–9: Choose the best answer or write your response on the lines.

1. What admission does Gandhi make in the opening paragraph?

   Ⓐ He is the secret publisher of *Young India*.

   Ⓑ He is guilty of arson, even though it was not planned.

   Ⓒ He led the protests but was not aware they could result in violence.

   Ⓓ He is guilty as charged.

2. Based on the ideas and details in the rest of the speech, why do you think he makes this admission?

3. How do the first three sentences of paragraph 2 relate to events Gandhi mentions in paragraph 1?

4. In the logic of Gandhi's speech, what is the main role of paragraph 3?

Ⓐ It restates his earlier remarks in simpler language.

Ⓑ It tries to turn public opinion against British rule and the authority of the court in which he appears.

Ⓒ It provides specific support for a general statement made earlier in the speech.

Ⓓ It makes clear what he is going to explain and who he thinks his audience is.

5. The logic behind Gandhi's mention of his activities during the Boer "challenge" and the other events in paragraph 6 is—

Ⓐ to prove that he was a loyal subject whose disaffection with Britain did not come lightly.

Ⓑ to prove that he was once a warrior whose journey to nonviolence did not come lightly.

Ⓒ to prove that he is an international figure who lived in South Africa and Europe as well as India.

Ⓓ to prove that he received justice and equality in the British Empire only when he lived outside India.

6. The logic behind the events Gandhi traces in paragraph 7, beginning with the Rowlatt Act, is—

Ⓐ a chronological progression that shows his increasing disillusionment with British rule.

Ⓑ a sequential progression that shows the steps he has taken to fight British rule.

Ⓒ a chain reaction that shows how one event caused another, which in turn caused another.

Ⓓ an argument that begins with a premise his audience accepts as true and then shows how British rule in India relates to that premise.

7. Which of these transitions signal the logical conclusion that Gandhi has drawn about British rule in India?

Ⓐ Thinking over these things deeply (middle of paragraph 1).

Ⓑ But by the time I have finished with my statement (end of paragraph 2).

Ⓒ Consequently (start of paragraph 6).

Ⓓ I came reluctantly to the conclusion (start of paragraph 9).

8. How do the details in the last sentence relate to Gandhi's words to the judge in the opening paragraph?

____

____

____

9. Explain the logic behind Gandhi's "cheerfully submitting to the highest penalty" for breaking the law, as he states in the final paragraph?

Chapter 10 The Language of Information (RI.11–12.4)

As with writers of fiction and poetry, authors of informational texts can use figurative language and other language techniques to enliven their works. This chapter will focus on the following aspects of language that can be exploited in the craft of writing.

10.1 Analyzing figurative language
10.2 Analyzing the connotation of words
10.3 Analyzing technical language
10.4 Analyzing the development of key words and phrases

10.1 Analyzing Figurative Language

Review

Figurative language, such as metaphor, simile, personification, and hyperbole, goes beyond literal meaning of the words to achieve a specific effect. In nonfiction, figurative language can be used to clarify an abstract concept or to enliven descriptive passages.

A **metaphor** draws a comparison by stating that one thing *is* another, as in "time is a thief," or by implying a connection, as in "a sea of grief." A **simile**, on the other hand, uses connecting words or phrases, such as *like* or *as,* to draw the connection. Henry David Thoreau uses several similes in this description of Walden Pond:

> . . . as the sun arose, I saw [the pond] throwing off its nightly clothing of mist, and . . . its smooth reflecting surface was revealed, while the mists, like ghosts, were stealthily withdrawing in every direction into the woods, as at the breaking up of some nocturnal conventicle.

In **personification,** an inanimate object, a state of being, or an idea is given a human or animal trait. In the quotation above, the pond is described as if it were a person throwing off its night clothes.

Key Terms

hyperbole: exaggeration used for emphasis or effect.

metaphor: a figure of speech that implies rather than states a comparison between two unlike things.

personification: a figure of speech that gives human traits to objects or ideas.

simile: a figure of speech that literally compares two unlike things, usually using *like* or *as*.

Hyperbole is a form of broad exaggeration used to emphasize a point. Thoreau uses hyperbole (and other figures of speech) when describing a locomotive and its impact on the neighborhood:

> [W]hen I hear the iron horse make the hills echo with his snort like thunder, shaking the earth with his feet, and breathing fire and smoke from his nostrils (what kind of winged horse or fiery dragon they will put into the new Mythology I don't know), it seems as if the earth had got a race now worthy to inhabit it.

Toolbox

Identifying Figurative Language. Figures of speech are everywhere. In conversation ("He's as gentle as a lamb"), songs ("You Light Up My Life"), and advertising ("Life's a ride"). Keep a journal of examples from your daily life. You may be surprised by the number you collect.

Check Understanding

Notice the way one reader responds to the figurative language in the excerpt below.

from Seabiscuit: An American Legend

by Laura Hillenbrand

Thoroughbred racehorse Seabiscuit was wildly popular and became a symbol of hope during the Great Depression.

1. . . . . Immediately, the reporters infested everything. Smith swatted at them. They staked out the barn, constantly asking Smith to pull the horse out of his stall for photo sessions and even to let them sit on his back, as if he were a carnival pony. They stood by the rail in noisy clumps during morning workouts, snapping pictures and buzzing in Smith's ear. . . . The earth seemed to dip under Seabiscuit's hoof-falls, pulling the world toward him and everyone around him.

Notes

Metaphor: newspaper reporters become annoying insects.

Activity 10.1 Reread the excerpt above. Highlight and annotate other figures of speech. Share your findings with a partner.

Try It

Directions: Read the excerpt below and answer the questions that follow.

from The Devil's Highway: A True Story

by Luis Alberto Urrea

The Devil's Highway *is an account of what happened to a group of men who attempted to cross the border from Mexico into the desert of southern Arizona in May 2001.*

1. The day tormented them. Thirst. Pain. Men crawled under creosotes, under the shade of scraggly mesquites. It was a dull repetition of the entire walk. As rote as factory work. Their hours clanged by like machines. They were in the dirt like animals.

2. Six o'clock in the morning took ten hours to become seven o'clock.

3. A week later, it was eight o'clock.

4. The temperature screamed into the nineties before nine o'clock.

5. They waited. They couldn't even talk. They panted like dogs, groaned. Men put their hands to their chests, almost delicately, as if checking their own pulses. But they were barely awake. They were half in dreams and half in the day, and the day itself was a bad dream. Dry wings swished in the air around them. Voices coughing. Far above, the icy silver chips of airplanes cut the blue. Out of reach.

6. Ten o'clock.

7. "Just a little longer."

8. Their arms were too heavy to lift. They couldn't get their watches up to their eyes. The heat was heavy. The sunlight weighed a thousand pounds.

Notes

1. The author recreates the experience of a small group of travelers lost in the desert. Which choice below is an example of a simile from the excerpt?

   Ⓐ "the shade of scraggly mesquites"

   Ⓑ "hours clanged by like machines"

   Ⓒ "The temperature screamed into the nineties"

   Ⓓ "the icy silver chips of airplanes cut the blue"

2. Explain the reasoning behind your answer to question 1. Then identify a metaphor in the excerpt.

3. Cite and explain the author's use of hyperbole in the excerpt's final paragraph.

Question 1 asks you to select the option that contains a simile. Choice A, the phrase "the shade of scraggly mesquites," is not a figure of speech. Choice B is correct. Choice C is an example of personification, not simile. Choice D is a metaphor comparing airplanes to ice chips; it is not a simile because it does not use the words *like* or *as*.

Question 2 directs you to explain your reasoning for your answer to question 1 and to identify a metaphor in the excerpt. Here is a sample response:

> Choice B is the correct response because the phrase uses the word "like" to draw a comparison between the passing of time to the clanging of a machine. The phrase "the day itself was a bad dream" from paragraph 5 is an example of a metaphor.

Question 3 asks you to cite and explain the author's use of hyperbole in the final paragraph. Here is a possible response.

> The author uses hyperbole when he says, "the sunlight weighed a thousand pounds." Obviously, sunlight has no weight, but the author uses hyperbole here to make a point about how the travelers felt in the extreme heat.

10.2 Analyzing the Connotation of Words

Review

Close reading not only requires an understanding of the **denotation**, or dictionary definition, of a specific word, but also its connotation. The **connotation** of a word or phrase is its emotional overtone or implied meaning. For example, the words *inquisitive*, *probing*, and *nosy* have similar denotations—*curious*. But *nosy* carries a negative connotation while *inquisitive* and *probing* carry positive connotations.

Key Terms

denotation: the dictionary definition of a word.

connotation: the implied or subjective meaning of a word.

Check Understanding

Notice the connotation one reader notes in the excerpt below.

from Seabiscuit: An American Legend

by Laura Hillenbrand

1. A Thoroughbred racehorse is one of God's most impressive engines. Tipping the scales at up to 1,450 pounds, he can sustain speeds of forty miles per hour. Equipped with reflexes much faster than those of the most quick-wired man, he swoops over as much as twenty-eight feet of earth in a single stride, and corners on a dime. His body is a paradox of mass and lightness, crafted to slip through air with the ease of an arrow. His mind is impressed with a single command: *run*. He pursues speed with superlative courage, pushing beyond defeat, beyond exhaustion, sometimes beyond the structural limits of bone and sinew. In flight, he is nature's ultimate wedding of form and purpose.

2. To pilot a racehorse is to ride a half-ton catapult. It is without question one of the most formidable feats in sport. The extraordinary athleticism of the jockey is unparalleled: A study of the elements of athleticism conducted by Los Angeles exercise physiologists and physicians found that of all major sports competitors, jockeys may be, pound for pound, the best overall athletes. They have to be. To begin with, there are the demands on balance, coordination, and reflex. A horse's body is a constantly shifting topography, with a bobbing head and neck and roiling muscle over the shoulders, back, and rump. On a running horse, a jockey does not sit in the saddle, he crouches over it, leaning all of his weight on his toes, which rest on the thin metal bases of stirrups dangling about a foot from the horse's topline. When a horse is in full stride, the only parts of the jockey that are in continuous contact with the animal are the insides of the feet and ankles—everything else is balanced in midair.

Notes

An engine is a machine that converts energy into motion. The connotation is that a thoroughbred racehorse is fast.

***Activity* 10.2** Highlight and annotate at least two other words or phrases with connotative meanings in the descriptions above. Compare your findings with a partner.

Toolbox

Sometimes you can figure out the connotation of a word simply by considering the emotional response it evokes. Often, though, you will need to consider its context.

Try It

Directions: Read this excerpt from Edmund Morris's biography of Theodore Roosevelt, *Theodore Rex*, and answer the questions that follow.

from Theodore Rex

by Edmund Morris

Theodore Rex *is the story of Theodore Roosevelt's two terms as President of the United States.*

Notes

1. Walter Wellman, reporter, was strolling beside the Potomac one day early in 1902 when a horsewoman rode past at a sedate clip. Presently another rider followed, cantering to catch up with her. The stiff beard and haughty posture identified him as Senator Henry Cabot Lodge. Then came the noise of a big stallion moving at full gallop. Wellman stepped out of the way as it drummed by in a spray of gravel. The bespectacled rider was waving an old campaign hat and laughing with pleasure. "Ki-yi!" he screamed, galloping on. "Ki-yi!"

2. To Wellman and other Washington correspondents, Roosevelt's recreational antics were a welcome diversion from politics. The president was variously reported to have marched twenty miles through heavy rain (in Norfolk jacket, corduroy knickers, yellow leggings, and russet shoes), swum nude across a freezing river, and climbed with fingers and toes up the blast holes of a disused quarry. His habit of forcing luncheon guests to accompany him on afternoon treks did not endear him to those who would have preferred to remain behind with the wine and walnuts.

4. Which word provides the best synonym for "drummed" as it is used in paragraph 1?

Ⓐ cracked
Ⓑ battled
C thundered
D bounced

5. Write a brief explanation of how the riding styles of the first two riders described in paragraph 1 offer both contrast and context for the third rider, President Theodore Roosevelt. Then use paragraph 1 as context for your interpretation of the president's "antics" described in paragraph 2.

___

___

___

___

Question 4 asks you to select the closest synonym to the word *drummed*. Choice A, "cracked" is not supported by details in the paragraph. Choice B, "battled," implies some sort of dispute or conflict, which is not supported by the text. Choice C "thundered," is correct as it implies a loud rumbling similar to drumming. Choice D, "bounced," does not make sense given the other details of the text.

Question 5 Your answer to the first part of the item may vary but it should mention the more leisurely pace of the first two riders as compared to the vigor of the third rider.

> The movement of the first two horses are described with the words "sedate," and "cantering," which suggests a leisurely pace. The third rider, however, "drummed by" at a "full gallop," spraying gravel while laughing and screaming.

Your answer to the second part of the question should point out how the raucous behavior of the third rider matches the reputation of President Theodore Roosevelt.

> The description of the third rider is in keeping with the stories told about President Theodore Roosevelt, in which he faced obstacles with intense energy: trekking through heavy rain and climbing out of a quarry.

10.3 Analyzing Technical Language

Review

Some informational texts, such as articles in scientific and academic journals, will contain **technical terms** or **jargon** associated with the topic. Very often the definition will be provided in the text itself, perhaps in parentheses after its mention or in the next sentence. When a term you don't know is not defined in the text, you may have to use context clues and guess a meaning. If the unknown term is key to understanding the passage, consult a dictionary.

Key Terms

jargon: specialized words used by a profession or group that are difficult for outsiders to understand.

technical term: a word that refers to a particular process or activity.

Check Understanding

Notice how one reader uses the context to determine the meaning of a technical term.

1. . . . . the cause of cancer is not entirely a mystery. In fact, a decade ago many geneticists were confident that science was homing in on a final answer: cancer is the result of cumulative mutations that alter specific locations in a cell's DNA and thus change the particular proteins encoded by cancer-related genes at those spots. The mutations affect two kinds of cancer genes. The first are called tumor suppressors. They normally restrain cells' ability to divide, and mutations permanently disable the genes. The second variety, known as oncogenes, stimulate growth—in other words, cell division. Mutations lock oncogenes into an active state. Some researchers still take it as axiomatic that such growth-promoting changes to a small number of cancer genes are the initial event and root cause of every human cancer.

Notes

A "tumor suppressor" is a gene that restrains the formation of tumors.

source: Gibbs, W. Wayt. "Untangling the Roots of Cancer." *Scientific American Special Edition* June 2008.

Activity 10.3 Highlight another technical term and write its definition in the margin. Share your findings with a partner.

Toolbox

Check References. When possible, look up the definition of a technical term after working out the meaning through context clues. In addition to dictionaries, encyclopedias, and thesauruses, you may want to check specific references devoted to historical, biographical, scientific, or medical terms.

Try It

Directions: Read the excerpt below and answer the questions that follow.

from The Man Who Mistook His Wife for a Hat

by Oliver Sachs

Oliver Sachs is a professor of neurology and psychiatry at Columbia University and the author of many books about the human mind.

Notes

1. One always fears that a case is "unique," especially if it has such extraordinary features as those of Dr. P. It was, therefore, with a sense of great interest and delight, not unmixed with relief, that I found, quite by chance—looking through the periodical *Brain* for 1956—a detailed description of an almost comically similar case, similar (indeed identical) neuropsychologically[1] . . . , though the underlying pathology (an acute head injury) and all personal circumstances were wholly different. The authors speak of their case as "unique in the documented history of this disorder"—and evidently experienced, as I did, amazement at their own findings. . . . . (Only since the completion of this book have I found that there is, in fact, a rather extensive literature on visual agnosia in general, and prosopagnosia in particular. In particular I had the great pleasure recently of meeting Dr. Andrew Kertesz, who has himself published some extremely detailed studies of patients with such agnosias. . . . Dr. Kertesz mentioned to me a case known to him of a farmer who had developed prosopagnosia and in consequence could no longer distinguish (the faces of) his *cows,* and of another such patient, an attendant in a Natural History Museum, who mistook his own reflection for the diorama of an *ape.* As with Dr. P., and as with Macrae and Trolle's patient, it is especially the animate which is so absurdly misperceived. . . .

2. Their patient was a young man of 32, who, following a severe automobile accident, with unconsciousness for three weeks, . . . complained, exclusively, of an inability to recognize faces, even those of his wife and children." Not a single face was "familiar" to him, but there were three he could identify; these were workmates: one with an eye-blinking tic, one with a large mole on his cheek, and a third "because he was so tall and thin that no one else was like him." Each of these, Macrae and Trolle bring out, was "recognized solely by the single prominent feature mentioned." In general (like Dr. P.) he

1 neuropsychology: the study of the relationship between the brain and psychological problems

recognized familiars only by their voices.

Notes

3. He had difficulty even recognizing himself in a mirror, as Macrae and Trolle describe in detail: "In the early convalescent phase he frequently, especially when shaving, questioned whether the face gazing at him was really his own, and even though he knew it could physically be none other, on several occasions grimaced or stuck out his tongue "just to make sure." By carefully studying his face in the mirror he slowly began to recognize it, but "not in a flash" as in the past—he relied on the hair and facial outline, and on two small moles on his left cheek."

4. In general he could not recognize objects "at a glance," but would have to seek out, and guess from, one or two features—occasionally his guesses were absurdly wrong. In particular, the authors note, there was difficulty with the animate.

5. On the other hand, simple schematic objects—scissors, watch, key, etc.—presented no difficulties. Macrae and Trolle also note that: "His topographical memory was strange: the seeming paradox existed that he could find his way from home to hospital and around the hospital, but yet could not name streets en route [unlike Dr P., he also had some aphasia] or appear to visualize the topography."

6. It was also evident that visual memories of people, even from long before the accident, were severely impaired—there was memory of conduct, or perhaps a mannerism, but not of visual appearance or face. Similarly, it appeared, when he was questioned closely, that he no longer had visual images in his dreams. Thus, as with Dr. P., it was not just visual perception, but visual imagination and memory, the fundamental powers of visual representation, which were essentially damaged in this patient—at least those powers insofar as they pertained to the personal, the familiar, the concrete.

7. A final, humorous point. Where Dr. P. might mistake his wife for a hat, Macrae's patient, also unable to recognize his wife, needed her to identify herself by a visual marker, by ". . . a conspicuous article of clothing, such as a large hat."

6. Based on context clues in paragraph 1, what is the most likely definition of *agnosia*?

Ⓐ complete blindness

Ⓑ impairment of visual recognition

Ⓒ the part of the brain responsible for visual processing

Ⓓ brain damage

7. Based on the excerpt, distinguish between *agnosia* and *prosopagnosia*. Point out the context clues that led you to your answer.

Question 6 asks you to select the correct definition of agnosia. Choice A is incorrect because the text shows clearly that the patient in question is not completely blind. Choice B is correct because though the patient can see, he cannot always recognize what he is seeing. Choice C is incorrect because there is not evidence that agnosia is a physical part of the brain. Choice D is too general to be correct.

Question 7 asks you to state the difference between two technical terms mentioned in the passage: agnosia and prosopagnosia. Sample answer:

> The text mentions that Dr. Kertesz published papers on agnosias and, specifically, on prosopagnosia. It goes on to describe one of Kertesz's case studies, a man who has trouble recognizing first the faces of his cows and then those of his wife and others. Yet he has no problem recognizing inanimate objects. It seems that agnosias is a general term that means an inability to recognize things and that prosopagnosia is a more specific type of agnosia: the inability to recognize faces.

10.4 Analyzing the Development of Key Words and Phrases

Review

Reading informational text often means learning new vocabulary and **domain-specific terms**—words specific to a particular field of study or endeavor. For this type of material, you may need to trace a complex or evolving definition of a term.

> **Key Terms**
>
> **domain-specific terms:** words that are commonly used in a particular area of study or field of endeavor.

Check Understanding

Notice how one reader begins to track the criteria that define a global tsunami.

1. The catastrophic and highly destructive December 26, 2004 Sumatra tsunami is the third known global tsunami, which severely damaged coast regions of the Indian Ocean, including 12 countries: Indonesia, Thailand, Myanmar, India, Sri Lanka, Bangladesh, Maldives, Somalia, Kenya, Tanzani, and South Africa. This tsunami killed more than 230,000 people; injured almost 283,000 people from 60 countries; caused the deaths of nationals in 73 countries in the age of globalization and ecotourism; and left millions homeless and displaced. . . . The long-term psychosocial and intergenerational impact of the Indian Ocean tsunami is likely to be experienced for decades. In association with the 2004 Sumatra tsunami, the coastal areas of the Indian Ocean received the brunt of destruction and loss of life, with the most distant recorded death having occurred in Port Elizabeth (in the Republic of South Africa), about 8000 km from the earthquake epicenter.

Notes

What is a "global tsunami"?

- 12 countries hit

Source: *Tsunamis: Detection, Monitoring, and Early-Warning Technologies* by Antony Joseph

Activity 10.4 Highlight other criteria that define a global tsunami. Then write a complete definition on a separate sheet of paper. Compare your definition with that of a partner.

Toolbox

Paraphrase the Meaning. As you move through a text, you will often find that your understanding of a key word or phrase has changed. To check your evolving understanding, it can be helpful to take a moment to write down a paraphrase of the term or phrase.

Try It

Directions: Read the excerpt from the historical document below and answer the questions that follow.

from The Federalist, No. 10

by James Madison

Notes

1. Among the numerous advantages promised by a well constructed Union, none deserves to be more accurately developed than its tendency to break and control the violence of faction. . . .

2. By a faction, I understand a number of citizens, whether amounting to a majority or a minority of the whole, who are united and actuated by some common impulse of passion, or of interest, adversed to the rights of other citizens, or to the permanent and aggregate interests of the community. There are two methods of curing the mischiefs of faction: the one, by removing its causes; the other, by controlling its effects.

3. There are again two methods of removing the causes of faction: the one, by destroying the liberty which is essential to its existence; the other, by giving to every citizen the same opinions, the same passions, and the same interests.

4. It could never be more truly said than of the first remedy, that it was worse than the disease. Liberty is to faction what air is to fire, an aliment without which it instantly expires. But it could not be less folly to abolish liberty, which is essential to political life, because it nourishes faction, than it would be to wish the annihilation of air, which is essential to animal life, because it imparts to fire its destructive agency.

5. The second expedient is as impracticable as the first would be unwise. As long as the reason of man continues fallible, and he is at liberty to exercise it, different opinions will be formed. As long as the connection subsists between his reason and his self-love, his opinions and his passions will have a reciprocal influence on each other; and the former will be objects to which the latter will attach themselves. The diversity in the faculties of men, from which the rights of property originate, is not less an insuperable obstacle to a uniformity of interests. The protection of these faculties is the first object of government. From the protection of different and unequal faculties of acquiring property, the possession of different degrees

and kinds of property immediately results; and from the influence of these on the sentiments and views of the respective proprietors, ensues a division of the society into different interests and parties.

Notes

6. The latent causes of faction are thus sown in the nature of man; and we see them everywhere brought into different degrees of activity, according to the different circumstances of civil society. A zeal for different opinions concerning religion, concerning government, and many other points, as well of speculation as of practice; an attachment to different leaders ambitiously contending for pre-eminence and power; or to persons of other descriptions whose fortunes have been interesting to the human passions, have, in turn, divided mankind into parties, inflamed them with mutual animosity, and rendered them much more disposed to vex and oppress each other than to co-operate for their common good. So strong is this propensity of mankind to fall into mutual animosities, that where no substantial occasion presents itself, the most frivolous and fanciful distinctions have been sufficient to kindle their unfriendly passions and excite their most violent conflicts. But the most common and durable source of factions has been the various and unequal distribution of property. Those who hold and those who are without property have ever formed distinct interests in society. . . . The regulation of these various and interfering interests forms the principal task of modern legislation, and involves the spirit of party and faction in the necessary and ordinary operations of the government. . . .

8. Which of the following is the best paraphrase of the definition of *faction* in paragraph 2?

Ⓐ a group entitled by money and position and opposed to the rest of the community

Ⓑ a group of members of the newly formed American government

Ⓒ a minority group opposed to the ideals of the majority and the community at large

Ⓓ a group of any size bonded by common interests to the detriment of the rights of others

9. In "The Federalist, No 10," James Madison addresses the issue of factions. Briefly trace the ideas about factions presented in the excerpt from the essay.

____

____

____

____

____

____

____

____

Question 8 asks for the best paraphrase of the author's definition of the term *faction* in paragraph 2. Choice A is true in some cases, but it is not the author's definition. Choice B is not based on information in the passage. Choice C specifies that a faction must be a minority, but that idea is not backed up by the passage. Choice D correctly reflects the essential details of paragraph 2's definition.

Question 9 prompts you to trace the ideas about factions presented in the excerpt.

> Madison begins by stating that a well-constructed Union will "break and control the violence of factions," implying that factions are a threat to the Union. He then defines a faction: ". . . a number of citizens, whether amounting to a majority or a minority of the whole, who are united and actuated by some common impulse of passion" (paragraph 2).
>
> He suggests that there are two ways to stop the creation of factions: one is to destroy liberty, which is essential to the creation of factions; the other is to give all citizens the same passions and interests. The first way is rejected because the remedy is "worse than the disease" (paragraph 4). The second way is impractical because it is not possible to implement. This is because the causes of factions are "sown in the nature of man" (paragraph 6)" Different life experiences give rise to different passions and interests.

Strategies for Close Reading of Informational Text

Use the following strategies to identify and deepen your understanding of figures of speech, connotative meanings of words, technical language, and evolving definitions of key words and phrases.

- To locate similes in text, look for signal words such as *like* or *as*. For metaphors, pay attention to comparisons ("my heart is a pack animal weighed down by love").
- Look for both the literal and emotional quality of words to help you identify the author's intended meaning.
- Pay attention to context clues in the sentence or passage to help you identify the correct meaning of unfamiliar vocabulary and terms.
- Use reference texts when necessary to find definitions for technical language or jargon.

Test-Taking Tips

- When asked for a written response, make sure you use examples, details, and evidence from the text to support your ideas.
- Figurative language is common in informational texts as well as literary works. As you read, keep track of similes, metaphors, and hyperbole to make sure you understand the intended meaning.
- Avoid using flowery or overblown language in your written responses. In most cases, a straightforward approach works best.

Chapter Review

Read the essay and answer the questions that follow.

from Where I Lived, and What I Lived For

by Henry David Thoreau

Solitude

Notes

1. This is a delicious evening, when the whole body is one sense, and imbibes delight through every pore. I go and come with a strange liberty in Nature, a part of herself. As I walk along the stony shore of the pond in my shirt-sleeves, though it is cool as well as cloudy and windy, and I see nothing special to attract me, all the elements are unusually congenial to me. The bullfrogs trump to usher in the night, and the note of the whip-poor-will is borne on the rippling wind from over the water. Sympathy with the fluttering alder and poplar leaves almost takes away my breath; yet, like the lake, my serenity is rippled but not ruffled. These small waves raised by the evening wind are as remote from storm as the smooth reflecting surface. Though it is now dark, the wind still blows and roars in the wood, the waves still dash, and some creatures lull the rest with their notes. The repose is never complete. The wildest animals do not repose, but seek their prey now; the fox, and skunk, and rabbit, now roam the fields and woods without fear. They are Nature's watchmen—links which connect the days of animated life.

2. When I return to my house I find that visitors have been there and left their cards, either a bunch of flowers, or a wreath of evergreen, or a name in pencil on a yellow walnut leaf or a chip. They who come rarely to the woods take some little piece of the forest into their hands to play with by the way, which they leave, either intentionally or accidentally. One has peeled a willow wand, woven it into a ring, and dropped it on my table. I could always tell if visitors had called in my absence, either by the bended twigs or grass, or the print of their shoes, and generally of what sex or age or quality they were by some slight trace left, as a flower dropped, or a bunch of grass plucked and thrown away, even as far off as the railroad, half a mile distant, or by the lingering odor of a cigar or pipe. Nay, I was frequently notified of the passage of a traveler along the highway sixty rods off by the scent of his pipe.

3. There is commonly sufficient space about us. Our horizon is never quite at our elbows. The thick wood is not just at our door, nor the pond, but somewhat is always clearing, familiar and worn by us, appropriated and fenced in some way, and reclaimed from Nature. For what reason have I this vast range and circuit, some square miles of unfrequented forest, for my privacy, abandoned to me by men? My nearest neighbor is a mile distant, and no house is visible from

Notes

any place but the hill-tops within half a mile of my own. I have my horizon bounded by woods all to myself; a distant view of the railroad where it touches the pond on the one hand, and of the fence which skirts the woodland road on the other. But for the most part it is as solitary where I live as on the prairies. It is as much Asia or Africa as New England. I have, as it were, my own sun and moon and stars, and a little world all to myself. At night there was never a traveler passed my house, or knocked at my door, more than if I were the first or last man; unless it were in the spring, when at long intervals some came from the village to fish for pouts—they plainly fished much more in the Walden Pond of their own natures, and baited their hooks with darkness—but they soon retreated, usually with light baskets, and left "the world to darkness and to me," and the black kernel of the night was never profaned by any human neighborhood. I believe that men are generally still a little afraid of the dark, though the witches are all hung, and Christianity and candles have been introduced.

4. Yet I experienced sometimes that the most sweet and tender, the most innocent and encouraging society may be found in any natural object, even for the poor misanthrope and most melancholy man. There can be no very black melancholy to him who lives in the midst of Nature and has his senses still. There was never yet such a storm but it was Aeolian music to a healthy and innocent ear. Nothing can rightly compel a simple and brave man to a vulgar sadness. While I enjoy the friendship of the seasons I trust that nothing can make life a burden to me. The gentle rain which waters my beans and keeps me in the house today is not drear and melancholy, but good for me too. Though it prevents my hoeing them, it is of far more worth than my hoeing. If it should continue so long as to cause the seeds to rot in the ground and destroy the potatoes in the low lands, it would still be good for the grass on the uplands, and, being good for the grass, it would be good for me. Sometimes, when I compare myself with other men, it seems as if I were more favored by the gods than they, beyond any deserts that I am conscious of; as if I had a warrant and surety at their hands which my fellows have not, and were especially guided and guarded. I do not flatter myself, but if it be possible they flatter me. I have never felt lonesome, or in the least oppressed by a sense of solitude, but once, and that was a few weeks after I came to the woods, when, for an hour, I doubted if the near neighborhood of man was not essential to a serene and healthy life. To be alone was something unpleasant. But I was at the same time conscious of a slight insanity in my mood, and seemed to foresee my recovery. In the midst of a gentle rain while these thoughts prevailed, I was suddenly sensible of such sweet and beneficent society in Nature, in the very pattering of the drops, and in every sound and sight around my house, an infinite and unaccountable friendliness all at once like an atmosphere sustaining me, as made the fancied advantages of human neighborhood insignificant, and I have never thought of them since. Every little pine needle expanded and swelled with sympathy and befriended me. I was so distinctly made aware of the presence of something kindred to me, even in scenes which we are accustomed to call wild and dreary, and also that the nearest of blood to me and humanest was not a person nor a villager, that I thought no place could ever be strange to me again. . . .

5. Some of my pleasantest hours were during the long rain-storms in the spring or fall, which confined me to the house for the afternoon as well as the forenoon, soothed by their ceaseless roar and pelting; when an early twilight ushered in a long evening in which many thoughts had time to take root and unfold themselves. In those driving northeast rains which tried the village houses so, when the maids stood ready with mop and pail in front entries to keep the deluge out, I sat behind my door in my little house, which was all entry, and thoroughly enjoyed its protection. In one heavy thunder-shower the lightning struck a large pitch pine across the pond, making a very conspicuous and perfectly regular spiral groove from top to bottom, an inch or more deep, and four or five inches wide, as you would groove a walking-stick. I passed it again the other day, and was struck with awe on looking up and beholding that mark, now more distinct than ever, where a terrific and resistless bolt came down out of the harmless sky eight years ago. Men frequently say to me, "I should think you would feel lonesome down there, and want to be nearer to folks, rainy and snowy days and nights especially." I am tempted to reply to such—This whole earth which we inhabit is but a point in space. How far apart, think you, dwell the two most distant inhabitants of yonder star, the breadth of whose disk cannot be appreciated by our instruments? Why should I feel lonely? is not our planet in the Milky Way? This which you put seems to me not to be the most important question. What sort of space is that which separates a man from his fellows and makes him solitary? I have found that no exertion of the legs can bring two minds much nearer to one another. What do we want most to dwell near to? Not to many men surely, the depot, the post-office, the bar-room, the meeting-house, the school-house, the grocery, Beacon Hill, or the Five Points, where men most congregate, but to the perennial source of our life, whence in all our experience we have found that to issue, as the willow stands near the water and sends out its roots in that direction. This will vary with different natures, but this is the place where a wise man will dig his cellar. . . . I one evening overtook one of my townsmen, who has accumulated what is called "a handsome property"—though I never got a fair view of it—on the Walden road, driving a pair of cattle to market, who inquired of me how I could bring my mind to give up so many of the comforts of life. I answered that I was very sure I liked it passably well; I was not joking. And so

Notes

I went home to my bed, and left him to pick his way through the darkness and the mud to Brighton—or Bright-town—which place he would reach some time in the morning.

6. Any prospect of awakening or coming to life to a dead man makes indifferent all times and places. The place where that may occur is always the same, and indescribably pleasant to all our senses. For the most part we allow only outlying and transient circumstances to make our occasions. They are, in fact, the cause of our distraction. Nearest to all things is that power which fashions their being. Next to us the grandest laws are continually being executed. Next to us is not the workman whom we have hired, with whom we love so well to talk, but the workman whose work we are.

7. "How vast and profound is the influence of the subtle powers of Heaven and of Earth!"

8. "We seek to perceive them, and we do not see them; we seek to hear them, and we do not hear them; identified with the substance of things, they cannot be separated from them."

9. "They cause that in all the universe men purify and sanctify their hearts, and clothe themselves in their holiday garments to offer sacrifices and oblations to their ancestors. It is an ocean of subtle intelligences. They are everywhere, above us, on our left, on our right; they environ us on all sides."

10. We are the subjects of an experiment which is not a little interesting to me. Can we not do without the society of our gossips a little while under these circumstances—have our own thoughts to cheer us? Confucius says truly, "Virtue does not remain as an abandoned orphan; it must of necessity have neighbors."

11. With thinking we may be beside ourselves in a sane sense. By a conscious effort of the mind we can stand aloof from actions and their consequences; and all things, good and bad, go by us like a torrent. We are not wholly involved in Nature. I may be either the driftwood in the stream, or Indra in the sky looking down on it. I may be affected by a theatrical exhibition; on the other hand, I may not be affected by an actual event which appears to concern me much more. I only know myself as a human entity; the scene, so to speak, of thoughts and affections; and am sensible of a certain doubleness by which I can stand as remote from myself as from another. However intense my experience, I am conscious of the presence and criticism of a part of me, which, as it were, is not a part of me, but spectator, sharing no experience, but taking note of it, and that is no more I than it is you. When the play, it may be the tragedy, of life is over, the spectator goes his way. It was a kind of fiction, a work of the imagination only, so far as he was concerned. This doubleness may easily make us poor neighbors and friends sometimes.

12. I find it wholesome to be alone the greater part of the time. To be in company, even with the best, is soon wearisome and dissipating. I love to be alone. I never found the companion that was

Notes

so companionable as solitude. We are for the most part more lonely when we go abroad among men than when we stay in our chambers. A man thinking or working is always alone, let him be where he will. Solitude is not measured by the miles of space that intervene between a man and his fellows. The really diligent student in one of the crowded hives of Cambridge College is as solitary as a dervish in the desert. The farmer can work alone in the field or the woods all day, hoeing or chopping, and not feel lonesome, because he is employed; but when he comes home at night he cannot sit down in a room alone, at the mercy of his thoughts, but must be where he can "see the folks," and recreate, and, as he thinks, remunerate himself for his day's solitude; and hence he wonders how the student can sit alone in the house all night and most of the day without ennui and "the blues"; but he does not realize that the student, though in the house, is still at work in his field, and chopping in his woods, as the farmer in his, and in turn seeks the same recreation and society that the latter does, though it may be a more condensed form of it.

13. Society is commonly too cheap. We meet at very short intervals, not having had time to acquire any new value for each other. We meet at meals three times a day, and give each other a new taste of that old musty cheese that we are. We have had to agree on a certain set of rules, called etiquette and politeness, to make this frequent meeting tolerable and that we need not come to open war. We meet at the post-office, and at the sociable, and about the fireside every night; we live thick and are in each other's way, and stumble over one another, and I think that we thus lose some respect for one another. Certainly less frequency would suffice for all important and hearty communications. Consider the girls in a factory—never alone, hardly in their dreams. It would be better if there were but one inhabitant to a square mile, as where I live. The value of a man is not in his skin, that we should touch him.

Notes

Questions 1–7: Choose the best answer or write your response on the lines.

1. Which of the following quotes from the paragraph 1 contains a metaphor?

Ⓐ "As I walk along the stony shore of the pond in my shirt-sleeves, though it is cool as well as cloudy and windy, and I see nothing special to attract me"

Ⓑ "Sympathy with the fluttering alder and poplar leaves almost takes away my breath . . ."

Ⓒ "These small waves raised by the evening wind are as remote from storm as the smooth reflecting surface."

Ⓓ "They are Nature's watchmen—links which connect the days of animated life."

2. The idiom *beside oneself* means "almost out of one's senses from strong emotions." Consider Thoreau's use of *beside ourselves* in the first sentence of paragraph 11. Cite evidence from the text to describe how he uses the phrase.

3. Based on your reading of the passage, what does the author mean by the metaphor "a new taste of that old musty cheese that we are" in paragraph 13? Citing evidence from the text, write a short paragraph to explain your interpretation.

4. Reread paragraph 10. Which of the following most accurately paraphrases the figurative language of the final sentence as it relates to the passage?

Ⓐ A positive force does not remain positive without the support of other positive forces.

Ⓑ People need the company of others or else they stagnate.

Ⓒ People should spend more time alone because the gossip of others is distracting.

Ⓓ A distracted person is very likely to end up feeling lonely and unhappy.

5. What is the meaning of *ennui* as it is used in paragraph 12?

Ⓐ a kind of popular music

Ⓑ an artistic or educational pursuit

Ⓒ a feeling of distraction or boredom

Ⓓ a need for distraction and the company of others

6. What context clues in paragraph 12 support your answer to question 5?

7. In this essay, Thoreau focuses on the concept of solitude. Trace at least two benefits Thoreau sees in the practice of solitude. Cite passages from the text as support.

Chapter 11 Structure of Informational Texts (RI.11–12.5)

Authors have several options available when deciding how to structure and present information. They may use chronological structure when presenting history, for example. Or when presenting an argument, they may rely on a claim-and-support structure. In this chapter we will review these and other text structures and the transitions that typically accompany them.

11.1 Analyzing the Structure of Expository Texts

Review

When you analyze the structure of a text, you consider how the ideas and details relate to one another. Several kinds of structures are commonly used in exposition and argument. Some of these structures are listed and explained in the chart below.

As you review the chart, keep in mind that authors often combine different structures within a single text. For example, a history article may use chronological structure in one section but cause-and-effect structure in another.

Key Terms

structure: the organizational pattern an author uses to present and develop ideas.

exposition: nonfiction writing that explains or informs.

claim: an assertion made in an argumentative essay.

evidence: facts, statistics, examples, reasons, expert opinions, or other details used to support a general statement or a claim.

counterclaim: an opposing view or opinion.

Structure	Description
Chronological	Presents events in the order in which they happened. Historical writing often uses chronological structure.
Sequential	Presents actions step by step. "How-to" instructions often use sequential structure.
Spatial	Presents details using a visual organization—left to right, top to bottom, near to far, and so on. Descriptions often use spatial structure.
Topical or List	Presents a subject divided into parts or details. Outlines use topical structure.
Claim-and-Support	Presents a view or an opinion and then supports it with evidence. Editorials, persuasive speeches, and other forms of argument frequently use claim-and-support structure.

Structure	Description
Comparison-and-Contrast	Presents similarities and differences and is often used to discuss related topics or to clarify something unfamiliar by showing how it is like or unlike something familiar. **Pro-and-con structure** is a related structure in which advantages and disadvantages are listed.
Cause-and-Effect	Shows the results of one or more events or situations. It is often used in historical or scientific writing to help readers understand the reasons things happen. **Problem-and-solution structure** is a related structure that explains a problem and then shows how it has been or could be solved.
Degree-of-Importance	Presents items from most to least or least to most important. It is often used along with another structure; for instance, the subcategories or details in a text using topical structure may be organized by degree of importance.

Check Understanding

Analyze the structure in this excerpt from William Bartram's *Travels*.

from Travels

by William Bartram

In 1773, William Bartram began a two-year journey through what is now the southeastern United States. His Travels *describes the wonders of nature that he encountered there, many of them quite unfamiliar to readers of his day.*

1. . . . As I passed by Battle Lagoon, I began to tremble and keep a good look out, when suddenly a huge alligator rushed out of the reeds, and with a tremendous roar, came up and darted as swift as an arrow under my boat, emerging upright on my lee quarter,[1] with open jaws, and belching water and smoke that fell upon me like rain in a hurricane. I laid soundly about his head with my club and beat him off, and after plunging and darting about my boat, he went off on a straight line through the water, seemingly with the rapidity of lightning, and entered the cape of the lagoon. I now employed my time to the very best advantage in paddling close along shore, but could not forbear[2] looking now and then behind me, and presently perceived one of them coming up again. The water of the river hereabouts was shoal[3] and very clear; the monster came up with the usual roar and menaces, and passed close by the side of my boat, when I could distinctly see a young brood of alligators to the number of one hundred or more, following after her in a long train. They kept close together in a column without straggling off to the one side or the other; the young appeared to be of an equal size, about fifteen inches in length, almost black, with pale

Notes

The structure here is chronological:

1) An alligator rushed from the shore;

2) it went under the boat;

3) it surfaced with open jaws;

4) the author beat it off;

5) another alligator surfaced . . . .

1 lee quarter: the side of the boat away from the wind
2 forbear: refrain from
3 shoal: shallow

Notes

yellow traverse-waved clouds or blotches, much like rattlesnakes in color. I now lost sight of my enemy again.

2. Still keeping close along shore, on turning a point or projection of the river bank, at once I beheld a great number of hillocks[4] or small pyramids, resembling haycocks[5], ranged like an encampment along the banks. They stood fifteen or twenty yards distant from the water, on a high marsh, about four feet perpendicular about the water. I knew them to be the nests of the crocodile,[6] having had a description of them before, and now expected a furious and general attack, as I saw several large crocodiles swimming abreast of these buildings. These nests being so great a curiosity to me, I was determined at all events immediately to land and examine them. Accordingly I ran my bark[7] on shore at one of their landing places, which was a sort of nick, or little dock, from which ascended a sloping path or road up to the edge of the meadow, where their nests were. Most of them were deserted, and the great thick whitish eggshells lay broken and scattered upon the ground round about them.

The author uses cause-and-effect structure in explaining how curiosity (the cause) prompted him to take risky actions (the effects).

3. The nests or hillocks are of the form of an obtuse cone, four feet high and four or five feet in diameter at their bases; they are constructed with mud, grass and herbage. At first they lay a floor of this kind of tempered mortar on the ground, upon which they deposit a layer of eggs, and upon this a stratum of mortar seven or eight inches in thickness, and then another layer of eggs, and in this manner one stratum upon another, nearly to the top. I believe they commonly lay from one to two hundred eggs in a nest.

---

4 hillocks: small hills
5 haycocks: small cone-shaped haystacks
6 crocodile: used by Bartram as a synonym for alligator
7 bark: small boat

Activity 11.1 Reread the excerpt above. Identify the type of structure used in the highlighted text in paragraph 3. Add a note in the margin and share your findings with a partner.

Toolbox

As you read the text—

- underline or highlight portions of the text that best reveal the structure, and make notes about the structure in the margin.
- in your marginal notes or on the text itself, include labels to clarify the structure. For example, use numbers for the events or steps in chronological or sequential structures, and label causes and effects in cause-and-effect structures.

Try It

Directions: Read the excerpt below and answer the questions.

Notes

from Innumeracy: Mathematical Illiteracy and Its Consequences

by John Allen Paulos

1. Innumeracy, an inability to deal comfortably with the fundamental notions of number and chance, plagues far too many otherwise knowledgeable citizens. The same people who cringe when words such as "imply" and "infer" are confused react without a trace of embarrassment to even the most egregious of numerical solecisms.[1] I remember listening to someone at a party drone on about the difference between "continually" and "continuously." Later that evening we were watching the news, and the TV weathercaster announced that there was a 50 percent chance of rain for Saturday and a 50 percent chance for Sunday, and concluded that there was therefore a 100 percent chance of rain that weekend. The remark went right by the self-styled grammarian, and even after I explained the mistake to him, he wasn't nearly as indignant as he would have been had the weathercaster left a dangling participle. . . .

2. In a *Scientific American* column on innumeracy, the computer scientist Douglas Hofstadter cites the case of the Ideal Toy Company, which stated on the package of the original Rubik's cube[2] that there were more than three billion possible states the cube could attain. Calculations show that there are more than 4×10^{19} possible states, 4 with 19 zeroes after it. What the package says isn't wrong; there are more than three billion possible states. The understatement, however, is symptomatic of a pervasive innumeracy which ill suits a technologically based society. It's analogous to a sign at the entrance to the Lincoln Tunnel[3] stating: New York, population more than 6; or McDonald's proudly announcing that they've sold more than 120 hamburgers.

---

1 solecisms: mistakes

2 Rubik's cube: best-selling puzzle invented by Hungarian professor Ern Rubik, consisting of a cube on which the six faces are made up of smaller differently colored blocks (red, yellow, white, orange, green, and blue) attached to a rotating device in the center; the object of the puzzle is to rotate the blocks until each face of the cube is a single color.

3 Lincoln Tunnel: tunnel leading from New Jersey to New York City

1. Which best describes the overall structure used in the excerpt?

   Ⓐ chronological structure

   Ⓑ degree-of-importance structure

   Ⓒ cause-and-effect structure

   Ⓓ claim-and-support structure

2. Cite details from the text that support your answer to question 1.

   ____

   ____

   ____

   ____

3. What additional structure is used at the end of the paragraph 2?

   ____

   ____

   ____

Question 1 asks you to determine the overall structure of the excerpt from the choices given. Choices A and B are both incorrect. Although the excerpt does mention two events, no information is given about their chronology, and neither is presented as more important than the other. Choice C is also incorrect; the excerpt does not discuss causes and effects at all. Choice D is the correct answer. The excerpt opens with a claim about innumeracy and then gives two examples as evidence to support it.

Question 2 asks you to cite details from the text that support the structure you chose in question 1. A correct answer should cite the opening claim, "Innumeracy, an inability to deal comfortably with the fundamental notions of number and chance, plagues far too many otherwise knowledgeable citizens." It should then cite the two examples that support the claim: the example of the weathercaster's error with percentages compounded by the "self-styled grammarian's" failure to notice or appreciate it; and the vast mathematical understatement on the packaging of the original Rubik's cube.

Question 3 asks you to identify an additional structure used near the end of the excerpt. The analogies presented, which compare the understatement about the Rubik's cube's number of possible states to ridiculous understatements about New York City's population and McDonald's hamburger sales, are part of a comparison-and-contrast structure.

11.2 Evaluating the Structure of Informational Texts

Review

When you evaluate the structure of exposition or argument, consider how the structure helps make the author's points clear, convincing, and engaging.

Also pay attention to any chapter titles, section headings, subheadings, labels, and other **graphics aids** that help clarify the structure of text. These features are especially common in exposition, including "how-to" instructions and textbooks, and in writing that relies on a strong visual presentation, such as Web sites and magazine articles.

In examining the clarity of a text's structure, pay special attention to **transitional words and phrases** that clarify the relationships of ideas and details. The chart below shows some common structures and the transitions typically used in them.

Key Terms

transitional words and phrases: words and phrases that help clarify structure by showing the relationships of ideas and details.

graphic aids: visual features that help clarify structure and contents in a text.

Structure	Transitions Used
Chronological and sequential	first, secondly, then, the next step, meanwhile, later, finally, at last, after a few moments, the following day, on [day or date], in [month or year]
Spatial	above, below, on top of, under, to the right, on the left, in the middle, next to, behind, in front of
Topical or List	the [first, second, etc.] part, one type of, another kind of, many sorts of, may be divided into [two, three, four, etc.] categories, for instance, another example, in addition
Claim-and-Support	as these examples show, another reason, to demonstrate, therefore, moreover
Comparison-and-Contrast	similarly, just as . . . so too, in the same way, likewise, in contrast, but, yet, although, on the contrary, on the one hand, on the other hand, however
Cause-and-Effect	because, since, the main cause of, on account of, one effect is, consequently, as a result, for that reason
Degree-of-Importance	more importantly, of more significance, above all, most important of all

Check Understanding

Consider how transitional words and phrases and graphic aids help clarify the structure of this excerpt from Chapter III of H. L. Mencken's *American Language.*

from The American Language

by H. L. Mencken

III. The Beginnings of American

I. The First Loan-Words

1. The first Americanisms were probably words borrowed bodily from the Indian languages—words, in the main, indicating natural objects that had no counterparts in England. Thus, in Captain John Smith's "True Relation," published in 1608, one finds mention of a strange beast described variously as a *rahaugcum* and a *raugroughcum*. Four years later, in William Strachey's "Historie of Trevaile into Virginia Britannia," it became *aracoune*, "much like a badger," and by 1624 Smith had made it a *rarowcun* in his "Virginia." It was not until 1672 that it emerged as the *raccoon* we know today. Opossum has had much the same history. It first appeared in 1610 as *apossoun*, and two years later Smith made it *opassom* in his "Map of Virginia," at the same time describing the animal as having "an head like a swine, a taile like a rat, and is of the bigness of a cat." The word finally became *opossom* toward the end of the Seventeenth Century, and by 1763 the third *o* had changed to *u*.

Notes

The chapter title and subhead indicate the overall structure: chronological.

Activity 11.2 Reread the excerpt above. Highlight examples of transitional words or phrases. Identify the types of structure they signal in the margin. Share your findings with a partner.

Toolbox

As you read the text—

- underline or highlight transitional words and phrase that help make the structure clear, and make notes in the margin explaining what they show.
- underline, highlight, or circle any graphic aids that help make the structure clear, and make notes in the margin explaining what they show.
- make marginal notes evaluating the effectiveness of each structure in making the author's points clear, convincing, and/or engaging.

Try It

Directions: Read the excerpt below and answer the questions.

from The Particle Garden: Our Universe as Understood by Particle Physicists

by Gordon Kane

Notes

What Are We Made Of?

1. Particles, so tiny that one is less than insignificant, and in numbers large beyond counting, seed the garden that is our universe. A few ancient Greeks wondered what things were made of, and they guessed that the elaborate workings of nature depended on tiny elements. They coined the term "atoms" (*atomos*) meaning "uncuttable," and the name was given to the units now recognized [as] a nucleus fenced by whirling electrons. Most people, if pressed, would probably concede that Adam was made of molecules that were made of atoms. That's true, but not the whole story. We now know that Adam's atoms were made of particles called quarks [and] electrons, bound together by particles called gluons and protons. . . .

2. Astonishingly, physicists now believe that all things we can see, from the smallest to the largest, are made up of just three particles. One is the electron, the same electron that moves in wires when you use electricity. The other two are the "up quark" and the "down quark." Quarks are a lot like electrons. . . .

3. During the past half century we have discovered that there are even more particles beyond those that are the constituents of what we see. . . .

Leptons and More Quarks

4. The first to be found were neutrinos, ephemeral things that move forever, not bound by any force (so not bound into protons, nuclei, etc.), occasionally but rarely colliding with a quark or electron. In addition there are four more quarks, called the charm, strange, top, and bottom quarks. There are also two more particles, the muon and the tau, that are like the electron. Together the electron, the neutrinos, and the particles like the electron are called leptons. They are created naturally in cosmic ray collisions and by experimenters at particle accelerators.

5. While the leptons and quarks may be indivisible, they are more interesting than the Greek "atoms" because under certain conditions they can convert into other particles. The complete set of particle interactions includes some that allow one particle to make a transition into two or more other particles (with calculable probabilities). When a heavier particle converts into several lighter ones, the transition is called a "decay." The additional quarks and leptons do not occur in the things around us, because they are unstable. They exist only a very short time before they decay into

Notes

up quarks and down quarks and electrons and neutrinos. The muon is the longest lived of the additional quarks or leptons, and it lives only a millionth of a second before decaying into an electron and two neutrinos. . . .

6. The additional particles may seem very different from an electron, which exists permanently if left on its own, while a muon or a heavy quark decays in less than a millionth of a second. Nevertheless, it is appropriate to classify all of them as particles in the same sense, because each has a unique and unchanging set of properties that can be identified under all conditions. . . .

Antiparticles

7. There are additional particles in another sense too. In 1928 Paul Dirac proved that any theory that successfully integrated quantum theory and Einstein's special relativity (as the Standard Theory[1] does) required every particle to have a partner. Particles are represented in the theory by solutions to the theory's equations. Dirac showed that if the equations had a solution for a particle, then they also always had a solution for another particle with all charges opposite in sign, but otherwise identical. If an electron, with negative electric charge, a certain mass etc. existed, then another particle with the same mass etc. but positive electric charge must exist. The result holds for all particles. The partner was called an antiparticle. There are anti-up quarks, antigluons, etc.

1 Standard Theory: the Standard Model of particle physics that scientists in the field now accept, combining quantum theory with Albert Einstein's theory of relativity.

4. Which structure does the word *but* in the first paragraph signal?

Ⓐ pro-and-con structure

Ⓑ topical structure

Ⓒ comparison-and-contrast structure

Ⓓ sequential structure

5. How does the main heading "What Are We Made Of?" help make the structure in the first paragraph clear and the information more engaging?

____

____

____

6. Which of these words and phrases from paragraphs 4 and 5 signal transitions in a topical structure?

Ⓐ the first; In addition

Ⓑ neutrinos; the muon and the tau

Ⓒ but; while

Ⓓ when; because

7. How does the subheading "Antiparticles" reinforce the compare-and-contrast structure in the final paragraphs?

____

____

____

Question 4 asks you the kind of structure that a particular transitional word helps show. Choices A and D are incorrect. The transitional word *but* might signal a pro-and-con contrast and perhaps even a step in a sequence, but the paragraph does not discuss pros and cons or a sequence. Choice B is also incorrect. The paragraph does discuss a topic and some details that make it up, but the word *but* does not signal a topical structure. Choice C is the correct answer. The word *but* usually signals a contrast, and here it signals the contrast between what most people think and what science now knows about the smallest particles that make us up.

Question 5 asks you to explain how the main heading makes the structure of the text below it clear more engaging. In asking a question, the heading points to the two contrasting answers in the text that follows, making clearer the comparison-and-contrast structure. The question form of the heading also helps engage readers, asking them to read actively and look for an answer.

Question 6 asks you to identify transitional words and phrases that signal a topical structure. Choice B is incorrect; these choices are details in the topical structure, not transitional words and phrases that signal the structure. Though choices C and D do contain transitional words, the words do not signal the overall topical structure. Because, for example, shows a cause-and-effect structure in a particular sentence. Choice A is the correct answer.

Question 7 asks you to explain how the last subheading signals the comparison-and-contrast structure near the end of the excerpt. The text above the subheading discusses a variety of particles. The subheading "Antiparticles"—with the prefix *anti-*, meaning "against" or "the opposite of"—suggests that the last paragraph will discuss something that is the opposite of particles. In other words, it will present a contrast.

Strategies for Analyzing and Evaluating Structure

Use the following strategies as you analyze and evaluate the structure of exposition or argument.

- Underline, highlight, or circle ideas and details that help reveal the structure of the text, including transitional words and phrases and graphic aids such as headings and subheadings.
- Make notes in the margin about the structure of the text, including your evaluation of how the structure makes the text clear, convincing, and engaging.

Test-Taking Tips

- Preview informational text before you read it, scanning for graphic aids and transitional words and phrases that help show the structure of the text.
- Read the text, using the structure or structures to help you understand the relationships of the ideas and details it contains.
- Go back over the text, jotting down notes, if you need to evaluate how the structure helped make the text clear, convincing, and engaging.

Chapter Review

Read this excerpt from the chapter on Ascorbic Acid from *Napoleon's Buttons* by Peggy Le Couteur and Jay Burreson. Then answer the questions that follow.

from Napoleon's Buttons: 17 Molecules That Changed History

by Peggy Le Couteur and Jay Burreson

Notes

Ascorbic Acid

1. The Age of Discovery[1] was fueled by molecules of the spice trade, but it was the lack of another, quite different molecule that almost ended it. Over 90 percent of his crew didn't survive Magellan's[2] 1519–1522 circumnavigation of the world—in large part due to scurvy, a devastating disease caused by deficiency of the ascorbic acid molecule, dietary vitamin C.

2. Exhaustion and weakness, swelling of the arms and legs, softening of the gums, excessive bruising, hemorrhaging from the nose and mouth, foul breath, diarrhea, muscle pain, loss of teeth, lung and kidney problems—the list of symptoms of scurvy is long and horrible. Death generally results from an acute infection such as pneumonia or some other respiratory ailment or, even in young people, from heart failure. . . .

Scurvy at Sea

3. In the fourteenth and fifteenth centuries, as longer voyages were made possible by the development of more efficient sets of sails and fully rigged ships, scurvy became common at sea. Oar-propelled galleys, such as those used by the [ancient] Greeks and Romans, and the small sailing boats of [early] Arab traders had stayed fairly close to the coast. These vessels were not seaworthy enough to withstand the rough waters and huge swells of the open ocean. Consequently, they would seldom venture far from the coast, and supplies could be replenished every few days or weeks. Access to fresh food on a regular basis meant that scurvy was seldom a major problem. But in the fifteenth century, long ocean voyages in large sailing ships heralded not only the Age of Discovery but also reliance on preserved food. . . .

4. The standard sailor's fare was salted beef or pork and ship's biscuits known as hardtack, a mixture of flour and water without salt that was baked rock hard and used as a substitute for bread. Hardtack had the desirable characteristic of being relatively

1 Age of Discovery: the centuries in which European navigators sailed great distances to explore the world, establish trade routes, and claim overseas colonies

2 Magellan: Ferdinand Magellan, a Portuguese explorer who sailed for Spain and led the first European voyage around the world

immune to mildew. It was baked to such a degree of hardness that it remained edible for decades, but it was extremely difficult to bite into, especially for those whose gums were inflamed by the onset of scurvy. . . .

5. Scurvy's toll on the lives and health of sailors is recorded in the logs of early voyages. By the time the Portuguese explorer Vasco De Gama sailed around the southern tip of Africa in 1497, one hundred of his 160-member crew had died from scurvy. Reports exist of the discovery of ships adrift at sea with entire crews dead from the disease. It is estimated that for centuries scurvy was responsible for more death at sea than all other causes—more than the combined total of navy battles, piracy, shipwrecks, and other illnesses.

6. Astonishingly, preventives and remedies for scurvy during these years were known—but largely ignored. As early as the fifth century, the Chinese were growing fresh ginger in pots on board their ships. The idea that fresh fruit and vegetables could alleviate symptoms of scurvy was, no doubt, available to other countries in southeast Asia in contact with Chinese trading vessels. It would have been passed on to the Dutch and been reported by them to other Europeans as, by 1601, the first fleet of the English East India Company is known to have collected oranges and lemons at Madagascar on the way to the East. This small squadron of four ships was under the command of Captain James Lancaster, who carried bottled lemon juice with him on his flagship, the Dragon. Anyone [on the Dragon] who showed signs of scurvy was dosed with three teaspoons of lemon juice every morning. . . . Despite Lancaster's instructions and example, nearly a quarter of the total crew of this expedition died from scurvy—[but] not one of those deaths was on his flagship. . . .

Cook: Hundreds–Scurvy: Nil

7. James Cook of the British Royal Navy was the first ship's captain to ensure that his crews remained scurvy free. . . . A healthy, well-functioning crew was essential for Cook to accomplish what he did on his voyages. This fact was recognized by the Royal Society[3] when it awarded him its highest honor, the Copley gold medal, not for his navigational feats but for his demonstration that scurvy was not an inevitable companion on long ocean voyages. Cook's methods were simple. He insisted on maintaining cleanliness throughout the ship, especially in the tight confines of the seaman's quarters. All hands were required to wash their clothes regularly, to air and dry their bedding when the weather permitted, to fumigate between decks, and in general to live up to the meaning of the term shipshape. When it was not possible to obtain the fresh fruit and vegetables he

Notes

3 Royal Society: an organization founded in London in 1660 with the aim of promoting knowledge in the natural sciences

Notes

thought necessary for a balanced diet, he required that his men eat the sauerkraut that he had included in the ship's provisions. Cook touched land at every possible opportunity to replenish stores and gather local grasses [and other] plants from which he brewed teas.

8. The diet was not at all popular with the crew, accustomed as they were to the standard seaman's fare and reluctant to try anything new. But Cook was adamant. He and his officers also adhered to this diet, and it was by his example, authority, and determination that his regimen was followed. . . .

9. Success no doubt helped convince Cook's crew that their captain's strange obsession with what they ate was worthwhile. Cook never lost a single man to scurvy. . . . Thanks to vitamin C, the ascorbic acid molecule, Cook was able to compile an impressive list of accomplishments: the [European] discovery of the Hawaiian islands and the Great Barrier Reef, the first circumnavigation of New Zealand, the first charting of the coast of the Pacific Northwest, and [the] first crossing of the Antarctic Circle.

Questions 1–9: Choose the best answer or write your response on the lines.

1. What overall structure do the subheadings "Scurvy at Sea" and "Cook: Hundreds–Scurvy: Nil" indicate?

   Ⓐ pro-and-con structure

   Ⓑ problem-and-solution structure

   Ⓒ sequential structure

   Ⓓ claim-and-support structure

2. Explain how the subheadings reflect the structure you identified in question 1.

3. How does the structure that you identified in question 1 help make the text more engaging?

4. Explain how the first two paragraphs of the excerpt reflect cause-and-effect structure.

____

____

____

5. Identify two transitional words or phrases that point to the cause-and-effect structure of the first two paragraphs. Write them on the line below.

____

6. Explain how the third paragraph of the excerpt uses both comparison-and-contrast and cause-and-effect structures.

____

____

____

7. Which transitional word or phrase in the third paragraph most clearly points to its comparison-and-contrast structure?

   Ⓐ In the fourteenth and fifteenth centuries

   Ⓑ such as

   Ⓒ consequently

   Ⓓ But

8. Which of these paragraphs from the excerpt most clearly uses chronological structure?

   Ⓐ paragraph 1   C paragraph 6

   Ⓑ paragraph 4   D paragraph 9

9. How does the claim-and-support structure at the very end of the passage make clear and convincing the claim that Captain Cook "was able to compile an impressive list of accomplishments"?

____

____

____

Chapter 12 Author's Point of View (RI.11–12.6)

Point of view and purpose are closely related. The purpose is the reason for writing; the point of view is the attitude toward the subject and the audience. The following topics will be addressed in this chapter.

12.1 Determining point of view and purpose
12.2 Analyzing style and content

12.1 Determining Point of View and Purpose

Review

An author's **point of view** is his or her overall stance or perspective on a subject. It reflects the author's beliefs, attitudes, and experiences.

An author may explicitly state his or her point of view. Usually, however, you will have to make inferences based on details in the work and your prior knowledge and experience. In considering an author's point of view, pay attention not only to precise meanings, or **denotations**, of words and phrases, but also to their emotional associations, or **connotations**. In using your prior knowledge, be sure to consider any information you have about the author.

Closely tied to the author's point of view is the author's **purpose** in writing. There are three main purposes of writing: to inform (or explain), to persuade, and to entertain. The main purpose of a news article, for example, is to inform readers about events; the main purpose of an editorial is to persuade readers to think or act in a certain way. An author may have more than one purpose. For instance, an author may write an amusing personal narrative not only to entertain but also to explain a situation or to persuade readers to follow a particular path in life.

Key Terms

author's point of view: the author's overall stance or perspective on a subject.

inference: logical guess based on details in a work as well as the reader's prior knowledge or experience.

denotation: the precise dictionary definition of a word or phrase.

connotation: an emotional association of a word or phrase.

author's purpose: the author's main reason for writing a work.

Check Understanding

Think about the author's point of view and purpose as you read the excerpt on the next page.

from A Description of New England

by John Smith

Captain John Smith led the settlement of Jamestown, the first successful English colony in the New World. A few years later, a group of English merchants paid him to explore the coast of New England, where they hoped to strike it rich. In 1616, after his return to England, Smith published A Description of New England, *a popular pamphlet from which the following passage comes.*

1. . . . Here nature and liberty affords us that freely, which in England we want,[1] or it costeth us dearly. What pleasure can be more, than (being tired with any occasion a-shore in planting vines, fruits, or herbs, in contriving their own grounds, to the pleasure of their own minds, their fields, gardens, orchards, buildings, ships, and other works, &c.) to recreate[2] themselves before their own doors, in their own boats upon the sea, where man, woman and child, with a small hook and line, by angling,[3] may take diverse sorts of excellent fish, at their pleasures? And is it not pretty sport, to pull up two pence, six pence, and twelve pence, as fast as you can haul and veer a line?[4] He is a very bad fisher [who] cannot kill in one day with his hook and line, one, two, or three hundred cods: which dressed and dried, if they be sold there for ten shillings the hundred, though in England they will give more than twenty; may not both the servant, the master, and merchant, be well content with this gain? If a man work but three days in seven, he may get more then he can spend, unless he be excessive. Now that carpenter, mason, gardener, tailor, smith, sailor, forgers,[5] or what other, may they not make this a pretty recreation though they fish but an hour in a day, to take more than they eat in a week: or? if they will not eat it, because there is so much better choice; yet sell it, or change it, with the fishermen, or merchants, for any thing they want. And what sport doth yield a more pleasing content, and less hurt or charge than angling with a hook, and crossing the sweet air from isle to isle, over the silent streams of a calm sea? Wherein the most curious may find pleasure, profit, and content.

1 want: lack
2 recreate: verb form of recreation
3 angling: fishing
4 haul and veer a line: pull a fishing line through the water
5 forgers: metal workers

Notes

The background information suggests that the author would want to promote settlement of New England.

Words with positive connotations: *liberty, freely, pleasure*

Activity 12.1 Reread the passage. Highlight and annotate details that provide evidence of John Smith's purpose. Then write his purpose in the margin. Compare your findings with a partner.

Toolbox

As you read a text—

- Underline or highlight details that suggest the author's point of view and purpose, and make inferences about them in the margin. If the author directly states his or her point of view, underline or highlight the sentence that states it.
- Look for information about the author that sometimes appears before or after the main body of the text. Be sure to consider that information, as well as other relevant information from your prior experience and knowledge, in making inferences about the author's point of view and purpose.

Try It

Directions: Read the excerpt below and answer the questions.

from Latitude

by Dava Sobel

Dava Sobel, once a science reporter for The New York Times, *has contributed science articles to* The New Yorker, Audubon, *and many other magazines.* Longitude, *her first book, was a surprise international bestseller and won her awards from the National Science Board, the Worshipful Company of Clockmakers, and several other organizations on both sides of the Atlantic.*

1. Any sailor worth his salt can gauge his latitude well enough by the length of the day, or by the height of the sun or known guide stars above the horizon. Christopher Columbus followed a straight path across the Atlantic when he "sailed the parallel"[1] on his 1492 journey, and the technique would doubtless have carried him to the Indies had not the Americas intervened.

2. The measurement of longitude meridians, in comparison, is tempered by time. To learn one's longitude at sea, one needs to know what time it is aboard ship and also the time at the home port or another place of known longitude—at that very same moment. The two clocks enable the navigator to convert the hour difference into a geographical separation. Since the Earth takes twenty-four hours to complete one full revolution of three hundred sixty degrees, one hour marks one twenty-fourth of a spin, or fifteen degrees. And so each hour's time difference between the ship and the starting point marks a progress of fifteen degrees longitude to the east or west. Every day at sea, when the navigator resets his ship's clock to local noon when the sun reaches its highest point in the sky and then consults the home-port clock, every hour's discrepancy between

Notes

1 parallel: any of the imaginary lines of latitude that circle the globe

them translates into another fifteen degrees of longitude. . . .

3. [But] precise knowledge of the hour in two different places at once—a longitude prerequisite so easily accessible today from any pair of cheap wristwatches—was utterly unattainable up to and including the era of pendulum clocks.[2] On the deck of a rolling ship, such clocks would slow down, or speed up, or stop running altogether. Normal changes in temperature encountered en route from a cold country of origin to a tropical trade zone thinned or thickened a clock's lubricating oil and made its metal parts expand or contrast with equally disastrous results. A rise or fall in barometric pressure, or the subtle variations in the Earth's gravity from one latitude to another, could also cause a clock to gain or lose time.

4. . . . The search for a solution to the longitude problem assumed legendary proportions, on a par with discovering the Fountain of Youth, the secret of perpetual motion, or the formula for transforming lead into gold. The governments of the great maritime nations—including Spain, the Netherlands, and certain city-states of Italy—periodically roiled the fervor by offering jackpot purses for a workable method. The British Parliament, in its famed Longitude Act of 1714, set the highest bounty of all, naming a prize equal to a king's ransom (several million dollars in today's currency) for a "Practicable and Useful" means of determining longitude.

5. English clockmaker John Harrison, a mechanical genius who pioneered the science of portable precision timekeeping, devoted his life to this quest. He accomplished what Newton[3] had feared was impossible: He invented a clock that would carry the true time from the home port, like an eternal flame, to any remote corner of the world.

6. Harrison, a man of simple birth and high intelligence, crossed swords with the leading lights of his day. He made a special enemy of the Reverent Nevil Maskelyne, the fifth astronomer royal, who contested his claim to the coveted prize money, and whose tactics at certain junctures can only be described as foul play.

7. With no formal education or apprenticeship to any watchmaker, Harrison nevertheless constructed a series of virtually friction-free clocks that required no lubrication and no cleaning, that were made from materials impervious to rust, and that kept their moving parts perfectly balanced in relation to one another, regardless of how the world pitched or tossed them about. He did away with the pendulum, and he combined different metals inside his works[4] in such a way that when one component expanded or contracted with changes in temperature, the other counteracted the change and kept the clock's rate constant.

Notes

2 pendulum clocks: clocks that keep time through the movement of a freely swinging weight called a pendulum

3 Newton: Sir Isaac Newton (1642-1727), one of England's greatest scientists

4 works: the inner parts of a clock

1. Which statement best expresses the author's point of view in this text?

   Ⓐ She thinks very little of Christopher Columbus's achievements as an explorer.

   Ⓑ She thinks very highly of John Harrison's achievement as the inventor of a practical means of determining longitude at sea.

   Ⓒ She deeply admires Sir Isaac Newton and other scientists associated with English royalty.

   Ⓓ She disapproves of formal education and apprenticeships.

2. Cite at least three details from the text that support your answer to question 1. Include and explain at least one detail that involves the connotation of a word or phrase.

   ____

   ____

   ____

   ____

   ____

3. Which statement best expresses the author's main purpose in this text?

   Ⓐ to entertain readers with an exciting adventure of seafaring in earlier times

   Ⓑ to inform readers about John Harrison's invention

   Ⓒ to explain the steps readers should take to use John Harrison's invention if they go sailing

   Ⓓ to persuade readers that John Harrison did not deserve the treatment he received from Nevil Maskelyne and others.

4. How does the background information about the author, which appears in italics before the main body of the excerpt, help you determine the author's purpose?

   ____

   ____

   ____

Question 1 asks you to determine the author's point of view best supported by the text. Choice A is not correct because, while Sobel does point out the relative ease of Columbus's sailing along one parallel of latitude, she nowhere indicates that she does not admire other aspects of his achievements as an explorer. Choice C may be true, but the text offers no evidence to support it, and Sobel's criticism of Nevil Maskelyne, "fifth astronomer royal," shows at least one case in which she does not approve of a scientist associated with English royalty. Choice D is not correct because even though Sobel is amazed that Harrison achieved what he did without formal education or an apprenticeship, it does not follow that she disapproves of either. Choice B is the best answer. Evidence in the text reveals that Sobel deeply admires Harrison's achievement.

Question 2 asks you to cite at least three details from the text that support the author's point of view you selected in question 1, including at least one that involves connotations. Sobel's description of Harrison in the fifth paragraph as a "mechanical genius" and her comparison of his invention to an "eternal flame" are examples of details with positive connotations. Other details you might cite are those in the third paragraph, which show the difficulty of determining longitude at sea in the era of pendulum clocks, and those in the last paragraph, which give an extensive description of Harrison's achievement.

Question 3 asks you to determine the author's main purpose for writing the text. Choice A is incorrect because even though the text is fairly entertaining, the author is not writing an adventure tale, and entertaining the reader is not her main purpose. Choice C is also incorrect; while the author does explain how Harrison's invention works, she does not provide clear instructions for using it. Choice D states an opinion the author holds, but persuading readers to share that opinion is not her main purpose. Choice C is the best answer: The text contains a great deal of information about Harrison's invention.

Question 4 asks how the background information on the author helps determine the author's purpose. The background information stresses the author's credentials as a science writer. Such a writer would most likely aim to provide information about a scientific achievement, such as Harrison's invention.

12.2 Analyzing Style and Content

Review

In effective **rhetoric**, style and content contribute to the power, persuasiveness, and beauty of the text.

In analyzing **style**, two important elements to consider are the author's **diction**, or word choice, and the **syntax**, word arrangement. Good writers choose words that suit their subject, audience, and purpose. As for syntax, they consider the structure, length, and variety of their sentences. Repeating ideas and putting related or contrasting ideas in **parallel structures** makes them more memorable. Using sentences of different lengths and types, including commands and **rhetorical questions**, makes writing more lively and engaging.

In analyzing the **content** of effective rhetoric, consider not only its subject but also on its purpose. Good writing that aims to persuade, for example, usually contains examples and logical reasoning to support claims and refute counterclaims. In addition, it usually includes strong appeals to the audience's emotions.

Key Terms

content: the ideas and details that a work contains.

diction: the author's word choice.

parallel structures: similar grammatical structures used to express related or contrasting ideas.

rhetoric: language used to achieve an effect.

rhetorical question: a question asked for effect and not because an answer is expected

style: the manner in which ideas are expressed.

syntax: the arrangement of words in sentences.

Check Understanding

Notice how style and content combine in the excerpt below.

from Speech to the Second Virginia Convention

by Patrick Henry

In 1775, Patrick Henry and several other prominent Virginians gathered to discuss Britain's military buildup in America. At the time, the first shots of what would become the American Revolution had already been fired in Boston, to the north. Here are the final paragraphs of Henry's famous speech.

1. . . . They tell us, sir, that we are weak—unable to cope with so formidable an adversary. But when shall we be stronger? Will it be the next week, or the next year? Will it be when we are totally disarmed, and when a British guard shall be stationed in every house? Shall we gather strength by irresolution and inaction? Shall we acquire the means of effectual resistance by lying supinely on our backs and hugging the delusive phantom of hope, until our enemies shall have bound us hand and foot?

2. Sir, we are not weak if we make a proper use of those means which the God of nature has placed in our power. Three millions of people armed in the holy cause of liberty, and in such a country as that which we possess, are invincible by any force which our enemy can send against us. Besides, sir, we shall not fight our battles alone. There is a just God who presides over the destinies of nations, and who will raise up friends to fight our battles for us. The battle, sir, is not to the strong alone; it is to the vigilant, the active, the brave. Besides, sir, we have no election.[1] If we were base[2] enough to desire it, it is now too late to retire from the contest. There is no retreat but in submission and slavery! Our chains are forged! Their clanking may be heard on the plains of Boston! The war is inevitable—and let it come! I repeat it, sir, let it come!

3. It is in vain, sir, to extenuate[3] the matter. Gentlemen may cry, Peace, Peace—but there is no peace. The war is actually begun! The next gale that sweeps from the north will bring to our ears the clash of resounding arms! Our brethren are already in the field! Why stand we here idle? What is it that gentlemen wish? What would they have? Is life so dear, or peace so sweet, as to be purchased at the price of chains and slavery? Forbid it, Almighty God! I know not what course others may take; but as for me, give me liberty or give me death!

Notes

Rhetorical questions instead of statements; he makes it seem that the answers are obvious.

Elevated vocabulary (*effectual, supinely, delusive*) creates vivid imagery.

Appeals to emotions, tapping into religious faith, love of country, and love of freedom.

1 election: choice
2 base: low
3 extenuate: lessen the seriousness of; make excuses for

***Activity* 12.2** Reread the text above. Highlight other examples of effective diction and syntax and briefly explain them in the margin. Share your findings with a partner.

Toolbox

As you read a text—

Underline or highlight words, phrases, and sentences that illustrate the diction and syntax that are part of the author's style, and make notes in the margin explaining what they illustrate. Be sure to include rhetorical questions and parallel structures if they appear.

Highlight and annotate details of the content that reflect the author's subject and purpose. For example, if the author's purpose is to persuade, underline examples, logical reasons, and emotional appeals, and explain how they help support a claim or refute a counterclaim.

Try It

Directions: Read the excerpt below and answer the questions.

from Statement of Defense at His 1964 Trial

by Nelson Mandela

From 1948 to 1994, South Africa was ruled by a white government under a policy of apartheid, or racial separation, that gave few rights to the nation's nonwhite majority. Nelson Mandela was among the black South Africans who fought apartheid. His opposition led to his arrest in 1962 for crimes against the state punishable by death. At his trial in 1964, he made a famous statement of defense from which the following excerpt comes. He was found guilty but not put to death; instead he received a life sentence that ended with his release from prison in 1990.

1. . . . South Africa is the richest country in Africa, and could be one of the richest countries in the world. But it is a land of extremes and remarkable contrasts. The whites enjoy what may well be the highest standard of living in the world, whilst Africans live in poverty and misery. Forty per cent of the Africans live in hopelessly overcrowded and, in some cases, drought-stricken Reserves, where soil erosion and the overworking of the soil makes it impossible for them to live properly off the land. Thirty per cent are laborers, labor tenants, and squatters on white farms and work and live under conditions similar to those of the serfs of the Middle Ages. The other 30 per cent live in towns where they have developed economic and social habits which bring them closer in many respects to white standards. Yet most Africans, even in this group, are impoverished by low incomes and high cost of living. . . .

Notes

Notes

2. The Government often answers its critics by saying that [nonwhite] Africans in South Africa are economically better off than the inhabitants of the other countries in Africa. I do not know whether this statement is true and doubt whether any comparison can be made without having regard to the cost-of-living index in such countries. But even if it is true, as far as the African people are concerned it is irrelevant. Our complaint is not that we are poor by comparison with people in other countries, but that we are poor by comparison with the white people in our own country, and that we are prevented by legislation from altering this imbalance.

3. The lack of human dignity experienced by Africans is the direct result of the policy of white supremacy. White supremacy implies black inferiority. Legislation designed to preserve white supremacy entrenches this notion. Menial tasks in South Africa are invariably performed by Africans. When anything has to be carried or cleaned the white man will look around for an African to do it for him, whether the African is employed by him or not. Because of this sort of attitude, whites tend to regard Africans as a separate breed. They do not look upon them as people with families of their own; they do not realize that they have emotions—that they fall in love like white people do; that they want to be with their wives and children like white people want to be with theirs; that they want to earn enough money to support their families properly, to feed and clothe them and send them to school. And what 'house-boy' or 'garden-boy' or laborer can ever hope to do this? . . .

4. Africans want to be paid a living wage. Africans want to perform work which they are capable of doing, and not work which the Government declares them to be capable of. Africans want to be allowed to live where they obtain work, and not be endorsed out of an area because they were not born there. . . . Above all, we want equal political rights, because without them, our disabilities will be permanent. . . .

5. During my lifetime I have dedicated myself to this struggle of the African people. I have fought against white domination, and I have fought against black domination. I have cherished the ideal of a democratic and free society in which all persons live together in harmony and with equal opportunities. It is an ideal which I hope to live for and to achieve. But if needs be, it is an ideal for which I am prepared to die.

5. Which words best describe Mandela's overall diction in the excerpt?

Ⓐ simple and childlike

Ⓑ eloquent and detailed

Ⓒ highly imaginative and poetic

Ⓓ highly informal

6. In which paragraph does Mandela use logical reasoning to refute a counterclaim to his argument against apartheid?

   Ⓐ the first paragraph

   Ⓑ the second paragraph

   Ⓒ the third paragraph

   Ⓓ the last paragraph

7. Which of these sentences from the excerpt is the best example of parallel structure used to make contrasting ideas more powerful and memorable?

   Ⓐ The whites enjoy what may well be the highest standard of living in the world, whilst Africans live in poverty and misery.

   Ⓑ The lack of human dignity experienced by Africans is the direct result of the policy of white supremacy.

   Ⓒ They do not look upon them as people with families of their own; they do not realize that they have emotions.

   Ⓓ And what 'house-boy' or 'garden-boy' or laborer can ever hope to do this?

8. To which of the audience's emotions do the last two sentences in the excerpt most strongly appeal?

   Ⓐ fear of punishment

   Ⓑ faith in God

   Ⓒ sense of justice and fair play

   Ⓓ admiration of courage and commitment

Question 5 asks you to select the best description of Mandela's overall diction. Choice D is clearly wrong. The selection contains no slang or conversational English and does not seek to create intimacy with the audience. Choices A and C are also not well supported by the text. Although Mandela's diction is not highly complex, there is nothing childlike about the words he uses or the ideas they express; and while he is occasionally poetic (as in the final paragraph), most of the excerpt provides facts and opinions, with little reliance on the imagination. Choice B is clearly the best answer. Mandela uses language effectively to communicate his views on the plight of black South Africans under apartheid and provides many factual details to support his opinions.

Question 6 asks you to identify the paragraph in which Mandela uses logical reasoning to refute a counterclaim to his argument. Choices A, C, and D are incorrect—the first, third, and last paragraphs do not contain any claims that counter Mandel's argument against apartheid. Choice B is the correct answer. The second paragraph restates the white South African government's claim that life under apartheid is economically better for nonwhites than it would be if they lived in another nation in Africa. This claim aims to counter criticisms of apartheid by Mandela and others. In the rest of the paragraph, however, Mandela logically questions the government's claim and then goes on to show why it is not relevant.

Question 7 asks you to identify a sentence from the text that uses parallel structure to express contrasting ideas. The sentence in Choice B does not illustrate parallel structure. The sentence in Choice C does illustrate parallel structure, but the parallel ideas are similar, not contrasting. The sentence in Choice D is a rhetorical question. It does also contain parallel structure in listing the three menial jobs, but again, these parallel terms are similar, not contrasting. Choice A is the correct answer. It uses parallel structure to contrast the lives of whites and nonwhites in South Africa under apartheid.

Question 8 asks you to identify the emotional appeal made in the last two sentences of the excerpt. Choice A is incorrect. The sentences express a lack of fear, even of the ultimate punishment of death, and do not suggest that the audience will face punishment. Choice B is incorrect. Though faith in God may well sustain the courage that the sentences express, it is not mentioned in the sentences. Choice C is incorrect. Earlier details in the excerpt do appeal to the audience's sense of justice and fair play, but these sentences do not. Choice D is the correct answer. Mandela expresses strong convictions and bravely indicates that he is willing to die for them, thus appealing to the audience's admiration for such principles and courage.

Strategies for Author's Point of View and Purpose

Use the following strategies as you determine the author's point of view and purpose and analyze the style and content of text.

- Underline ideas and details that help reveal the author's point of view or purpose.
- Underline elements of style or syntax that help the author effectively convey his or her point of view or achieve his or her purpose.
- Add notes in the margin, such as inferences and explanations of the text you underlined.

Test-Taking Tips

- Read informational text twice, once for content and once for style. In each reading, think about what the details suggest about the author's point of view and purpose.
- As you read, list on a chart the details from the text that you might use to support your statements about it. Then use those details in your written response, making sure to supply enough details to support your statements.
- Make sure you have addressed all parts of the test question in your response.

Chapter Review

Read this excerpt from Frederick Douglass's *My Bondage and My Freedom* and then answer the questions that follow.

from My Bondage and My Freedom

by Frederick Douglass

Born a slave, Frederick Douglass had several masters before finally escaping to freedom in 1836. He then became a leader in the movement to abolish slavery. Known for his brilliant oratory, Douglass also produced three autobiographical accounts of his life. My Bondage and My Freedom, *from which this excerpt is taken, was first published in the decade before the Civil War, when slavery was still legal in many parts of the United States.*

1. I lived in the family of Master Hugh [Auld], at Baltimore, seven years, during which time—as the almanac makers say of the weather—my condition was variable. The most interesting feature of my history here was my learning to read and write, under somewhat marked disadvantages. In attaining this knowledge, I was compelled to resort to indirections[1] by no means congenial to my nature and which were really humiliating to me. My mistress, who [had] begun to teach me, was suddenly checked in her benevolent design by the strong advice of her husband. . . .

2. It is easy to see that, in entering upon the duties of a slaveholder, some little experience is needed. Nature has done almost nothing to prepare men and women to be either slaves or slaveholders. Nothing but rigid training, long persisted in, can perfect the character of the one or the other. One cannot easily forget to love freedom; and it is as hard to cease to respect that natural love in our fellow creatures. On entering upon the career of a slaveholding mistress, Mrs. Auld was singularly deficient; nature, which fits nobody for such an office, had done less for her than any lady I had known. It was no easy matter to induce her to think and to feel that the curly-headed boy, who stood by her side, and even leaned on her lap; who was loved by [her son] little Tommy, and who loved little Tommy in turn; sustained[2] to her only the relation of a chattel.[3] I was more than that, and she felt me to be more than that. I could talk and sing; I could laugh and weep; I could reason and remember; I could love and hate. I was human, and she, dear lady, knew and felt me to be so. How could she, then, treat me as a brute, without a mighty struggle with all the noble powers of her own soul? That struggle came, and the will and power of the husband was victorious. Her noble soul was overthrown; but he that overthrew it did not himself escape the consequences. He, not less

Notes

1 indirections: deceitful roundabout means
2 sustained: existed
3 chattel: item of property

than the other parties, was injured in his domestic peace by the fall.

3. When I went into their family, it was the abode of happiness and content. The mistress of the house was a model of affection and tenderness. Her fervent piety and watchful uprightness made it impossible to see her without thinking and feeling—"that woman is a Christian." There was no sorrow nor suffering for which she had not a tear, and there was no innocent joy for which she had not a smile. She had bread for the hungry, clothes for the naked, and comfort for every mourner that came within her reach. Slavery soon proved its ability to divest her of these excellent qualities, and her home of its early happiness. Conscience cannot stand much violence. Once thoroughly broken down, who is he that can repair the damage? It may be broken toward the slave on Sunday, and toward the master on Monday. It cannot endure such shocks. It must stand entire, or it does not stand at all. If my condition waxed[4] bad, that of the family waxed not better. The first step in the wrong direction was the violence done to nature and to conscience in arresting the benevolence that would have enlightened my young mind. In ceasing to instruct me, she must justify herself to herself; and, once consenting to take sides in such a debate, she was riveted to her position. One needs very little knowledge of moral philosophy to see where my mistress now landed. She finally became even more violent in her opposition to my learning to read than was her husband himself. She was not satisfied with simply doing well as he had commanded her, but seemed resolved to better his instruction. Nothing appeared to make my poor mistress—after her turning toward the downward path—more angry than seeing me seated in some nook or corner, quietly reading a book or a newspaper. I have had her rush at me, with the utmost fury, and snatch from my hand such newspaper or book, with something of the wrath and consternation which a traitor might be supposed to feel on being discovered in a plot by some dangerous spy. . . .

4. All this, however, was entirely too late. The first, and never to be retraced, step had been taken. In teaching me the alphabet, in the days of her simplicity and kindness, my mistress had given me the "itch," and now no ordinary precaution could prevent me from taking the "ell."[5]

5. Seized with a determination to learn to read at any cost, I hit upon many expedients to accomplish the desired end. The plea[6] which I mainly adopted, and the one by which I was most successful, was that of using my young white playmates, with whom I met in the streets, as teachers. . . . I am strongly temped to give the names of two or three of those little boys, as a slight testimonial of the gratitude and affection I bear them, but prudence forbids; not that it would injure me, but it might possibly embarrass them, for it is almost an unpardonable offense to do any thing, directly or indirectly, to promote a slave's freedom in a slave state.

Notes

4 waxed: gradually grew
5 ell: former measure equal to forty-five inches
6 plea: ploy

Questions 1–10: Choose the best answer or write your response on the lines.

1. Which statement best expresses the author's point of view in this text?

   Ⓐ As a former slave, he has little sympathy for slaveholders.

   Ⓑ He thinks that slavery is harmful to both slaves and slaveholders.

   Ⓒ He thinks that tricking his owners is clever and amusing.

   Ⓓ He feels superior to his white playmates who could not read.

2. Cite two details that help convey the author's point of view that you identified in question 1.

3. List two words or phrases with negative connotations that help convey the author's point of view that you identified in question 1.

4. Which statement best expresses the author's main purpose in this text?

   Ⓐ to entertain readers with an amusing incident from his childhood

   Ⓑ to inform readers about the psychology of slaveholders

   Ⓒ to persuade readers about the value of getting an education

   Ⓓ to persuade readers about the evils of slavery

5. How does the background information about the author, which appears in italics before the main body of the excerpt, help you determine the author's purpose for question 4?

6. Which words best describe the diction in the excerpt?

Ⓐ simple and childlike

Ⓑ formal and eloquent

Ⓒ strident and exaggerated

Ⓓ highly informal

7. Cite three examples of diction that support your answer to question 6.

____

____

____

____

8. Cite two examples of parallel structure that help make the rhetoric in the excerpt more effective.

____

____

____

____

9. To which of his reader's emotions does the author most strongly appeal in the second paragraph?

Ⓐ love of nature

Ⓑ nostalgia for childhood

Ⓒ sense of common humanity

Ⓓ admiration of courage

10. Explain in your own words the examples and logical reasoning that the author supplies to persuade readers to accept the opening statement of the second paragraph.

____

____

____

____

Unit 2 Review Test

Questions 1–8: Read the excerpt below. Then, for each of the multiple-choice questions that follow, select the best answer from the choices given.

from The American Crisis, Volume 1

by Thomas Paine

December 23, 1776

1. These are the times that try men's souls. The summer soldier and the sunshine patriot will, in this crisis, shrink from the service of their country; but he that stands it now, deserves the love and thanks of man and woman. Tyranny, like hell, is not easily conquered; yet we have this consolation with us, that the harder the conflict, the more glorious the triumph. What we obtain too cheap, we esteem too lightly: it is dearness only that gives every thing its value. Heaven knows how to put a proper price upon its goods; and it would be strange indeed if so celestial an article as FREEDOM should not be highly rated. Britain, with an army to enforce her tyranny, has declared that she has a right (not only to TAX) but "to BIND us in ALL CASES WHATSOEVER,"[1] and if being bound in that manner, is not slavery, then is there not such a thing as slavery upon earth. Even the expression is impious; for so unlimited a power can belong only to God.

2. . . . . Not a man lives on the continent but fully believes that a separation must some time or other finally take place, and a generous parent should have said, "If there must be trouble, let it be in my day, that my child may have peace;" and this single reflection, well applied, is sufficient to awaken every man to duty. Not a place upon earth might be so happy as America. Her situation is remote from all the wrangling world, and she has nothing to do but to trade with them. A man can distinguish himself between temper and principle, and I am as confident, as I am that God governs the world, that America will never be happy till she gets clear of foreign dominion. Wars, without ceasing, will break out till that period arrives, and the continent must in the end be conqueror; for though the flame of liberty may sometimes cease to shine, the coal can never expire.

3. America did not, nor does not want force; but she wanted a proper application of that force. Wisdom is not the purchase of a day, and it is no wonder that we should err at the first setting off. From an excess of tenderness, we were unwilling to raise an army, and trusted our cause to the temporary defense of a well-meaning militia. A summer's experience has now taught us better; yet with those troops, while they were collected, we were able to set bounds to the progress of the enemy, and, thank God! they are again assembling.

4. . . . I turn with the warm ardor of a friend to those who have nobly stood, and are yet determined to stand the matter out: I call not upon a few, but upon all: not on

---

1 "BIND us in ALL CASES WHATSOEVER": quotation from the British Declaratory Act of 1766, which stipulated that Britain had the right to force the American colonists to comply with any law the British Parliament passed

this state or that state, but on every state: up and help us; lay your shoulders to the wheel; better have too much force than too little, when so great an object is at stake. Let it be told to the future world, that in the depth of winter, when nothing but hope and virtue could survive, that the city and the country, alarmed at one common danger, came forth to meet and to repulse it. Say not, that thousands are gone, turn out your tens of thousands. . . . My own line of reasoning is to myself as straight and clear as a ray of light. Not all the treasures of the world, so far as I believe, could have induced me to support an offensive war, for I think it murder; but if a thief breaks into my house, burns and destroys my property, and kills or threatens to kill me, or those that are in it, and to "bind me in all cases whatsoever" to his absolute will, am I to suffer it? What signifies it to me, whether he who does it is a king or a common man; my countryman or not my countryman; whether it be done by an individual villain, or an army of them?. . .

5. There are cases which cannot be overdone by language, and this is one. There are persons, too, who see not the full extent of the evil which threatens them; they solace themselves with hopes that the enemy, if he succeed, will be merciful. It is the madness of folly, to expect mercy from those who have refused to do justice; and even mercy, where conquest is the object, is only a trick of war; the cunning of the fox is as murderous as the violence of the wolf, and we ought to guard equally against both. Howe's[2] first object is, partly by threats and partly by promises, to terrify or seduce the people to deliver up their arms and receive mercy. . . . Howe is mercifully inviting you to barbarous destruction, and men must be either rogues or fools that will not see it. I dwell not upon the vapors of imagination; I bring reason to your ears, and, in language as plain as A, B, C, hold up truth to your eyes.

6. I thank God that I fear not. I see no real cause for fear. I know our situation well, and can see the way out of it. While our army was collected, Howe dared not risk a battle; and it is no credit to him that he decamped from the White Plains, and waited a mean opportunity to ravage the defenseless Jerseys;[3] but it is great credit to us, that, with a handful of men, we sustained an orderly retreat for near an hundred miles, brought off our ammunition, all our field pieces, the greatest part of our stores, and had four rivers to pass. None can say that our retreat was precipitate, for we were near three weeks in performing it, that the country might have time to come in. Twice we marched back to meet the enemy, and remained out till dark. The sign of fear was not seen in our camp, and had not some of the cowardly and disaffected inhabitants spread false alarms through the country, the Jerseys had never[4] been ravaged. Once more we are again collected and collecting; our new army at both ends of the continent is recruiting fast, and we shall be able to open the next campaign with sixty thousand men, well armed and clothed. This is our situation, and who will may know it. By perseverance and fortitude we have the prospect of a glorious issue; by cowardice and submission, the sad choice of a variety of evils—a ravaged country—a depopulated city—habitations without safety, and slavery without hope. . . .

---

2 Howe's: referring to General William Howe, commander of the British forces during the American Revolution

3 White Plains . . . Jerseys: Howe's troops had driven out Washington's forces in the village of White Plains north of New York City in October and then chased them across New Jersey into Pennsylvania.

4 had never: would have never

1. What is Paine's main purpose in writing?

Ⓐ to persuade American colonists to support the American Revolution

Ⓑ to explore successful military strategies to win the war against Britain

Ⓒ to defend the American Revolution to the rest of the world

Ⓓ to tell future generations what it was like to live through the American Revolution

2. In paragraph 1, what evidence does the author provide to persuade readers that Britain's rule of the American colonies is tyrannical?

Ⓐ the description of the summer soldier and sunshine patriot

Ⓑ the indication that Britain is making the colonists pay taxes

Ⓒ the quotation about Britain's law binding the colonists "in all cases whatsoever"

Ⓓ the view that unlimited power can belong only to God

3. How does paragraph 2 further develop the ideas in the paragraph before it?

Ⓐ It stresses the importance of developing America's natural resources independently.

Ⓑ It explains the similarity between an independent America and a child gaining independence from its parents.

Ⓒ It shows how all the people and nations of the world are interconnected.

Ⓓ It explains how wonderful America would be if it were free from foreign influence.

4. In paragraph 3, what do the context clues suggest is the meaning of the word *militia*?

Ⓐ a professional standing army

Ⓑ a temporary citizen army

Ⓒ a group of citizens submitting a petition to their government

Ⓓ muskets and other long-barreled firearms

5. In paragraph 4, what logical reasoning does Paine provide to support the idea of fighting the British?

Ⓐ He argues that many colonists have already died fighting, and it would be wrong for them to have died in vain.

Ⓑ He argues that all thirteen colonies, or states, must support independence in order for the fight to be justified.

Ⓒ He argues that the Revolution, like any war not motivated by greed, is a just war.

Ⓓ He argues that Britain's king and troops have behaved like thieves and must be stopped like thieves.

6. How does Paine refute the counterclaim that all will be well if the colonists just give up their arms and throw themselves on the mercy of the British?

Ⓐ He says that British proposals that the colonists give up their arms are a trick.

Ⓑ He says that the colonists need their weapons to defend themselves in the wilderness.

Ⓒ He says that the recent retreats of colonial troops are just temporary setbacks.

Ⓓ He says that the war is not one of aggression but of self-defense.

7. Consider the diction in paragraph 6. What do the connotations of the words *decamped* and *defenseless* suggest about General Howe?

   Ⓐ He is a clever trickster.

   Ⓑ He is a sneaky bully.

   Ⓒ He is deceitful liar.

   Ⓓ He is a frightening enemy.

8. Which of these sentences or clauses from the excerpt uses parallel structure to make contrasting ideas more powerful and memorable?

   Ⓐ Tyranny, like hell, is not easily conquered. . . .

   Ⓑ Her situation is remote from all the wrangling world, and she has nothing to do but to trade with them.

   Ⓒ . . . though the flame of liberty may sometimes cease to shine, the coal can never expire.

   Ⓓ . . . our new army at both ends of the continent is recruiting fast, and we shall be able to open the next campaign with sixty thousand men, well armed and clothed.

Questions 9–16: Read this abridged chapter from *Prairyerth* by William Least Heat-Moon. Then, for each of the multiple-choice questions that follow, select the best answer from the choices given.

from Prairyerth

by William Least Heat-Moon

Under Old Nell's Skirt

1. . . . Yesterday I walked down a ridge to get out of the November wind while I ate a sandwich, and I came upon a house foundation on a slope bereft of anything but grasses and knee-high plants. It was absolutely exposed, an oddity here, since most of the houses sit in the shelter of wooded vales.[1] This one faced east—or it would have, had it still been there—and the only relief from the prevailing winds that the builder had sought was to set the back of the house to them. There was the foundation, some broken boards, a few rusting things, and, thirty feet away, a storm cellar, its door torn off, and that was all except for a rock road of two ruts. The cave, as people here call tornado cellars, was of rough-cut native stone with an arched roof, wooden shelves, and a packed-earth floor with Mason jar[2] fragments glinting blue in the sunlight; one had been so broken that twin pieces at my feet said:

SON MA

The shards seemed to be lost voices locked in silica[3] and calling still. . . .

2. Was there a connection between this cave and that house absent but for its foundation? The site, sloping southwest, seemed placed to catch a cyclone in a county in the heart of the notorious Tornado Alley of the Middle West, a belt that

1 vales: valleys

2 Mason jar: a wide-mouthed glass jar with a screw top, used for preserving foods in home canning

3 silica: here, glass

can average 250 tornadoes a year, more than anywhere else in the world. A hundred and sixty miles from here, Codell, Kansas, got thumped by a tornado every twentieth of May for three successive years, and five months ago a twister "touched down," mashed down really, a mile north of Saffordville at the small conglomeration of houses and trailers called Toledo. . . . Riding out a tornado in a mobile home is like stepping into combine blades:[4] trailers can become airborne chambers full of flying knives of aluminum and glass. No: if there is a dread in the county, it is not of dark skies but of the opposite, of clear skies, days and days of clear skies, of a drought nobody escapes, not even the shopkeepers. That any one person will suffer losses from a tornado, however deadly, goes much against the odds, and many residents reach high school before they first see a twister; yet, nobody who lives his full span in the county dies without a tornado story.

3. Tornado: a Spanish past participle meaning turned, from a verb meaning to turn, alter, transform, repeat, *and* to restore. Meteorologists speak of the reasons why the Midlands of the United States suffer so many tornadoes: a range of high mountains west of a great expanse of sun-heated plains at a much lower altitude, where dry and cold northern air can meet warm and moist southern air from a large body of water to combine with a circulation pattern mixing things up: that is to say, the jet stream from Arctic Canada crosses the Rockies to meet a front from the Gulf of Mexico over the Great Plains in the center of which sits Kansas, where, since 1950, people have sighted seventeen hundred tornadoes. It is a place of such potential celestial violence that the meteorologists at the National Severe Storms Forecast Center in Kansas City, Missouri, are sometimes called the Keepers of the Gates of Hell. Countians[5] who have smelled the fulminous, cyclonic sky up close, who have felt the ground shake and heard the earth itself roar and have taken to a storm cellar that soon filled with a loathsome greenish air, find the image apt. The Keepers of the Gates of Hell have, in recent years, become adept at forecasting tornadoes, and they might even be able to suggest cures for them if only they could study them up close. Years ago a fellow proposed sending scientists into the eye of a tornado in an army tank until he considered the problem of transporting the machine to a funnel that usually lasts only minutes, and someone else suggested flying into a cyclone, whereupon a weather research pilot said, yes, it was feasible if the aviator would first practice by flying into mountains. . . .

4. I know here a grandfather, a man as bald as if a cyclone wind had taken his scalp—something witnesses claim has happened elsewhere—who calls twisters Old Nell, and he threatens to set crying children outside the back door for her to carry off. People who have seen Old Nell close, up under her skirt, talk about her colors: pastel-pink, black, blue, gray, and a survivor said this: *All at once a big hole opened in the sky with a mass of cherry-red, a yellow tinge in the center,* and another said: *a funnel with beautiful electric-blue light,* and a third person: *It was glowing like it was illuminated from the inside.* The witnesses speak of shapes: a formless black mass, a cone, cylinder, tube, ribbon, pendant, thrashing hose, dangling lariat, writhing snake, elephant trunk. They tell of ponds being vacuumed dry, eyes of geese sucked out, chickens clean-plucked . . . , a wife killed after being jerked through a car window, a child carried two miles and set down with only scratches, a Cottonwood Falls mother (fearful of wind) cured of chronic headaches when a

4 combine blades: the blades of a farm machine used to harvest grain

5 Countians: inhabitants of Chase County, Kansas, the county William Least Heat-Moon is writing about

twister passed harmlessly within a few feet of her house, and, just south of Chase, a woman blown out of her living room window and dropped unhurt sixty feet away and falling unbroken beside her phonograph record of "Stormy Weather."[6]

5. . . . Yesterday: in the sun the broken words on the Mason jar glinted and, against the foundation, the wind whacked dry grasses and seed pods, *tap-tap-tap, rasp-rasp,* and a yellow light lay over the November slope, and Ma and son: did they one afternoon come out of the cave to see what I see, an unhoused foundation, some twisted fence wire, and a sky turning golden in all innocence?

---

6 "Stormy Weather": popular song most famous in the renditions by Billie Holliday and Lena Horne

9. In the structure of the text, what function does the chapter title "Under Old Nell's Skirt" serve?
   Ⓐ It clarifies a key idea in the text that follows.
   Ⓑ It emphasizes the most important idea in the text that follows.
   Ⓒ It piques the reader's curiosity about the text that follows.
   Ⓓ It sums up the main idea of the text that follows.

10. Which statement provides the best objective summary of the information in paragraph 1?
    Ⓐ Yesterday the author found something unexpected and thought-provoking when he walked down a ridge to escape the November wind.
    Ⓑ Yesterday the author came upon a destroyed house that had been unwisely built in a much more exposed location than people usually choose in this part of the country.
    Ⓒ Yesterday the author came upon a storm cellar with its door torn off and its dirt floor littered by fragments of broken Mason jars, including two pieces that said "son" and "Ma."
    Ⓓ Yesterday the author came upon the foundation of a house and a nearby storm cellar containing fragments of broken Mason jars.

11. In paragraph 2, what does the simile about mobile homes stress about tornadoes?
    Ⓐ They are strong and dangerous.
    Ⓑ They are surprisingly beautiful.
    Ⓒ They form suddenly and touch down unexpectedly.
    Ⓓ They last only a short time.

12. In paragraph 3, what does the context suggest is the meaning of the technical term *jet stream?*
    Ⓐ a weather plane that flies into storms to learn more about them
    Ⓑ a river turned into a gushing spout of water by the action of a tornado
    Ⓒ a tropical storm
    Ⓓ a high-speed band of wind moving across the Earth

13. Which of these transitional phrases in paragraph 3 signals a cause-and-effect structure?
    Ⓐ reasons why
    Ⓑ that is to say
    Ⓒ in the center of which
    Ⓓ since 1950

14. Which of these structures does paragraph 4 primarily use?

Ⓐ chronological structure

Ⓑ topical or list structure

Ⓒ spatial structure

Ⓓ comparison-and-contrast structure

15. In calling twisters Old Nell, what type of figurative language is the grandfather in paragraph 4 using?

Ⓐ hyperbole

Ⓑ metaphor

Ⓒ personification

Ⓓ simile

16. How does the final paragraph of the passage develop ideas from earlier paragraphs?

Ⓐ It shows the effects of the November wind that the author is trying to escape in paragraph 1 by providing a "tornado story" like the ones mentioned at the end of paragraph 2.

Ⓑ It answers the question that opens paragraph 2 by speculating about a "Ma" and "son" whose lives were shattered like the Mason jar in paragraph 1.

Ⓒ It gives further details about riding out a tornado in a mobile home, which is first described toward the end of paragraph 2.

Ⓓ It gives the etymology, or word history, of the term *Mason jar* just as paragraph 3 gives the etymology of the term *tornado.*

Questions 17–24: Read this speech by Mark Twain. Then, for each of the multiple-choice questions that follow, select the best answer from the choices given.

Mark Twain's First Appearance

by Mark Twain

1. *On October 5, 1906, Mr. Clemens,[1] following a musical recital by his daughter in Norfolk, Connecticut, addressed her audience on the subject of stage-fright. He thanked the people for making things as easy as possible for his daughter's American debut as a contralto,[2] and then told of his first experience before the public.*

2. My heart goes out in sympathy to anyone who is making his first appearance before an audience of human beings. By a direct process of memory I go back forty years, less one month—for I'm older than I look.

3. I recall the occasion of my first appearance. San Francisco knew me then only as a reporter, and I was to make my bow to San Francisco as a lecturer. I knew that nothing short of compulsion would get me to the theatre. So I bound myself by a hard-and-fast contract so that I could not escape. I got to the theatre forty-five minutes before the hour set for the lecture. My knees were shaking so that I didn't know whether I could stand up. If there is an awful, horrible malady in the world, it is stage-fright-and seasickness. They are a pair. I had stage-fright then for the first and last time. I was only seasick once, too. It was on a little ship on which there were two hundred other passengers. I—was—sick. I was so sick that there wasn't any left for those other two hundred passengers.

---

1 Mr. Clemens: Mark Twain's real name was Samuel Clemens

2 contralto: the lowest female singing voice

4. It was dark and lonely behind the scenes in that theatre, and I peeked through the little peekholes they have in theatre curtains and looked into the big auditorium. That was dark and empty, too. By-and-by it lighted up, and the audience began to arrive.

5. I had got a number of friends of mine, stalwart men, to sprinkle themselves through the audience armed with big clubs. Every time I said anything they could possibly guess I intended to be funny they were to pound those clubs on the floor. Then there was a kind lady in a box up there, also a good friend of mine, the wife of the Governor. She was to watch me intently, and whenever I glanced toward her she was going to deliver a gubernatorial laugh that would lead the whole audience into applause.

6. At last I began. I had the manuscript tucked under a United States flag in front of me where I could get at it in case of need. But I managed to get started without it. I walked up and down—I was young in those days and needed the exercise—and talked and talked.

7. Right in the middle of the speech I had placed a gem. I had put in a moving, pathetic part which was to get at the hearts and souls of my hearers. When I delivered it they did just what I hoped and expected. They sat silent and awed. I had touched them. Then I happened to glance up at the box where the Governor's wife was—you know what happened.

8. Well, after the first agonizing five minutes, my stage-fright left me, never to return. I know if I was going to be hanged I could get up and make a good showing, and I intend to. But I shall never forget my feelings before the agony left me, and I got up here to thank you for her for helping my daughter, by your kindness, to live through her first appearance. And I want to thank you for your appreciation of her singing, which is, by-the-way, hereditary.

17. What do the background information in paragraph 1 and the speech itself suggest is the author's main purpose for making the speech?

Ⓐ to use humor to help his daughter relax before her upcoming performance

Ⓑ to explain the causes and effects of stage-fright

Ⓒ to add to the evening's entertainment and thank the audience for attending his daughter's performance

Ⓓ to recapture an era that no longer exists and express nostalgia for the experiences he remembers from that time

18. How is the speech organized?

Ⓐ chronologically

Ⓑ sequentially

Ⓒ logically

Ⓓ organically

19. Which sentence best states the central idea of the speech?

Ⓐ Mark Twain's daughter is a talented performer, just like her father.

Ⓑ Stage-fright is awful but can be overcome.

Ⓒ The most famous people frequently suffer from stage-fright.

Ⓓ Packing an audience with your friends can sometimes backfire.

20. From the details in the selection, what can you infer about Mark Twain's situation at the time he made his first speech?

Ⓐ He was a complete unknown in California.

Ⓑ He was reasonably well known in California even though this was his first speech.

Ⓒ He was intimidated by his meetings with the governor's wife and other important people.

Ⓓ He had not yet acquired the sense of humor for which he became famous.

21. In paragraph 7, Twain never explicitly says what the governor's wife does. What is his implicit meaning when he says "you know what happened"?

Ⓐ The governor's wife laughs at a highly inappropriate time during his speech.

Ⓑ The governor's wife sobs loudly at a highly inappropriate time during his speech.

Ⓒ The governor's wife signals all Twain's "stalwart" friends to pound their clubs at a highly inappropriate time during his speech.

Ⓓ The governor's wife is so sad that she forgets to laugh when she is supposed to.

22. What ambiguity or uncertainty does Twain's speech contain?

Ⓐ We cannot be certain when Twain's attack of stage-fright took place.

Ⓑ We cannot be certain where Twain's attack of stage-fright took place.

Ⓒ We cannot be certain how Twain felt when he had his attack of stage-fright.

Ⓓ We cannot be certain why Twain never suffered another attack of stage-fright.

23. Which of these quotations from the speech is the best example of hyperbole?

Ⓐ "By a direct process of memory I go back forty years, less one month—for I'm older than I look." (paragraph 2)

Ⓑ "So I bound myself by a hard-and-fast contract so that I could not escape." (paragraph 3)

Ⓒ "I walked up and down—I was a young man in those days and needed the exercise. . . ." (paragraph 6)

Ⓓ "I know if I was going to be hanged I could get up and make a good showing, and I intend to." (paragraph 7)

24. To which of the audience's emotions do the final sentences of paragraphs 2, 6, and 8 most clearly appeal?

Ⓐ the audience's anger

Ⓑ the audience's sympathy

Ⓒ the audience's gratitude

Ⓓ the audience's sense of humor

Text Analysis

Closely read this shortened version of an 1897 magazine article by the famous American naturalist John Muir and then write a text-based response of two to three paragraphs. In your response, identify the author's main purpose and analyze how his diction or logical arguments help him achieve that purpose. Use strong and thorough evidence from the text to support your analysis. Do not simply summarize the text. You may use the margins to take notes as you read and to plan your response.

Guidelines

Be sure to—

- Clearly state the main purpose of the author.
- Analyze how the author's diction or logical arguments help him achieve his purpose.
- Use strong and thorough evidence from the text to support your analysis.
- Organize your ideas in a cohesive and coherent manner.
- Maintain a formal style of writing.
- Follow the conventions of standard written English.

from The American Forests

by John Muir

1. The forests of America, however slighted by man, must have been a great delight to God; for they were the best he ever planted. The whole continent was a garden, and from the beginning it seemed to be favored above all the other wild parks and gardens of the globe. . . . The Indians with stone axes could do them no more harm than could gnawing beavers and browsing moose. Even the fires of the Indians and the fierce shattering lightning seemed to work together only for good in clearing spots here and there for smooth garden prairies, and openings for sunflowers seeking the light. But when the steel axe of the white man rang out in the startled air their doom was sealed.

2. . . . . In the settlement and civilization of the country, bread more than timber or beauty was wanted; and in the blindness of hunger, the early settlers, claiming Heaven as their guide, regarded God's trees as only a larger kind of pernicious weeds, extremely hard to get rid of. . . . After the Atlantic coast from Maine to Georgia had been mostly cleared and scorched into melancholy ruins, the overflowing multitude of bread and money seekers poured over the Alleghenies into the fertile Middle West, spreading ruthless devastation ever wider and farther over the rich valley of the Mississippi and the vast shadowy pine region about the Great Lakes. Thence still westward the invading horde of destroyers called settlers made its fiery way over the broad Rocky Mountains, felling and burning more fiercely than ever, until at last it has reached the wild side of the continent, and entered the last of the great aboriginal forests on the shores of the Pacific.

3. . . . . Every other civilized nation in the world has been compelled to care for its forests, and so must we if waste and destruction are not to go on to the bitter end. . . . In Switzerland, after many laws like our own had been found wanting,[1] the

1 wanting: lacking

Swiss forest school was established in 1865, and soon after the Federal Forest Law was enacted. . . . In India systematic forest management was begun about forty years ago, under difficulties—presented by the character of the country, the prevalence of running fires, opposition from lumbermen, settlers, etc.—not unlike those which confront us now. Of the total area of government forests, perhaps 70,000,000 acres, 55,000,000 acres have been brought under the control of the forestry department. . . .

4. So far our government has done nothing effective with its forests, though the best in the world, but is like a rich and foolish spendthrift who has inherited a magnificent estate in perfect order, and then has left his rich fields and meadows, forests and parks, to be sold and plundered and wasted at will. . . . It is not yet too late, though it is high time, for the government to begin a rational administration of its forests. About seventy million acres it still owns—enough for all the country, if wisely used. These residual forests are generally on mountain slopes, just where they are doing the most good, and where their removal would be followed by the greatest number of evils; the lands they cover are too rocky and high for agriculture, and can never be made as valuable for any other crop as for the present crop of trees. It has been shown over and over again that if these mountains were to be stripped of their trees and underbrush, and kept bare and sodless[2] by hordes of sheep and the innumerable fires the shepherds set, besides those of the millmen,[3] prospectors, shake-makers,[4] and all sorts of adventurers, both lowlands and mountains would speedily become little better than deserts, compared with their present beneficent fertility. . . .

5. In their natural condition, or under wise management, keeping out destructive sheep, preventing fires, selecting the trees that should be cut for lumber, and preserving the young ones and the shrubs and sod of herbaceous vegetation, these forests would be a never failing fountain of wealth and beauty. The cool shades of the forest give rise to moist beds and currents of air, and the sod of grasses and the various flowering plants and shrubs thus fostered, together with the network and sponge of tree roots, absorb and hold back the rain and the waters from melting snow, compelling them to ooze and percolate and flow gently through the soil in streams that never dry. All the pine needles and rootlets and blades of grass, and the fallen decaying trunks of trees, are dams, storing the bounty of the clouds and dispensing it in perennial life-giving streams, instead of allowing it to gather suddenly and rush headlong in short-lived devastating floods. Everybody on the dry side of the continent is beginning to find this out, and, in view of the waste going on, is growing more and more anxious for government protection. . . .

6. All sorts of local laws and regulations have been tried and found wanting, and the costly lessons of our own experience, as well as that of every civilized nation, show conclusively that the fate of the remnant of our forests is in the hands of the federal government, and that if the remnant is to be saved at all, it must be saved quickly.

7. Any fool can destroy trees. They cannot run away; and if they could, they would still be destroyed—chased and hunted down as long as fun or a dollar could be got out of their bark hides, branching horns, or magnificent bole backbones. Few

2 sodless: grassless

3 millmen: those who own, operate, or work in lumber mills

4 shake-makers: those who make shingles out of wood

that fell trees plant them; nor would planting avail[5] much towards getting back anything like the noble primeval[6] forests. During a man's life only saplings can be grown, in the place of the old trees—tens of centuries old—that have been destroyed. It took more than three thousand years to make some of the trees in these Western woods—trees that are still standing in perfect strength and beauty, waving and singing in the mighty forests of the Sierra.[7] Through all the wonderful, eventful centuries since Christ's time—and long before that—God has cared for these trees, saved them from drought, disease, avalanches, and a thousand straining, leveling tempests and floods; but he cannot save them from fools—only Uncle Sam can do that.

---

5 avail: be of use

6 primeval: from or related to the earliest age

7 Sierra: California mountain chain

Unit 3 Writing to Sources

Unit Focus

The focus of this unit is developing the skills and confidence needed to respond to writing prompts such as those that appear on writing assessments and exit exams. Special attention is given to the writing of argumentative, informational, and literary essays.

Chapter 13 **Characteristics of Good Writing**

- Development
- Organization
- Evidence
- Language and Style
- Conventions
- Chapter Review—Practice Test

Chapter 14 **Writing Arguments**

- Writing a Claim
- Supporting a Claim
- Using Counterclaims
- Using Evidence from Sources
- Writing an Argumentative Essay
- Chapter Review—Practice Test

Chapter 15 **Writing Informational Texts**

- Writing a Thesis Statement
- Supporting a Thesis Statement
- Using and Citing Sources
- Writing an Informational Essay from Sources
- Chapter Review—Practice Test

Chapter 16 **Writing About Literature**

- Elements of Literary Analysis
- Using Evidence from Sources
- Writing a Literary Analysis
- Chapter Review—Practice Test

Chapter 13 Characteristics of Good Writing (W.11–12.4)

Whether you are reporting on research or narrating your life story, good writing shares some common characteristics. Good writing is well developed, has a cohesive organization, contains strong evidence, employs precise language and a formal style, and uses standard grammar, spelling, and punctuation. Your writing will be evaluated on these qualities. Look for these elements on writing rubrics.

13.1 Development
13.2 Organization
13.3 Evidence
13.4 Language and Style
13.5 Conventions

13.1 Development

Review

Well-developed writing focuses in on a **main idea**. This central idea is then expanded with interesting details, relevant facts, and carefully chosen evidence. Good writing also has a clear **purpose** appropriate to the task and to the audience. Common writing purposes include informing, explaining, narrating a real or imagined story, and presenting an argument to persuade others.

Your purpose for writing will dictate the type of development you will use. For example, when writing an essay on worker dog breeds, you might use a general to specific development. In a narrative essay on a memorable event, on the other hand, you might use narrative development, including exposition, characterization, rising action, turning point, and resolution.

While a narrative essay may include dialogue and other narrative techniques, an informational essay relies on supporting details, such as examples and facts. Such details must be **sufficient** and **relevant**. That is, there must be enough details to answer the main questions readers may have about the topic, and the details must relate to the main idea.

Key Terms

writing purpose: the reason for writing. Common writing purposes are to inform, explain, persuade, or entertain.

audience: the people whom authors expect will read their texts. In other words, the intended readership of a text.

relevant details: details that relate to the topic discussed in a text.

sufficient details: details that are enough to answer the main questions readers may have about the topic discussed.

Check Understanding

Directions: Read the following selection. Then answer the questions that follow.

Notes

1. Back in October of 2006, when Netflix announced its million-dollar prize contest, the competition seemed to be a neat idea, but not necessarily a big one. The movie rental company declared it would pay $1 million to the contestant who could improve its web site's movie recommendation system by 10% or more. The contest presented an intriguing problem—and a lucrative one for the winner. For Netflix, it was a shrewd ploy that promised to pay off in improved service and publicity.

2. But the Netflix contest, which lasted nearly three years, turned out to have a significance that extended well beyond movie recommendations and money. The competition became a model of Internet-era collaboration and innovation, attracting entries from thousands of teams around the world. The leading teams added members as they sought help to improve their results and climb up the Netflix leaderboard. Team members were often located in different countries, communicating by email and sharing work on the web with people they never met face to face.

3. This kind of Internet-enabled cooperative work—known as crowdsourcing—has become a hot topic . . . . The Netflix contest is widely cited as proof of its potential.

Source: "The Contest That Shaped Careers and Inspired Research Papers" by Steve Lohr. Published in *Chance*, Vol 23, No 1, Winter 2010.

1. What is the main purpose of the selection?

____

____

2. Which statement from the passage best expresses the main idea of the selection?

Ⓐ . . . when Netflix announced its million-dollar prize contest, the competition seemed to be a neat idea . . .

Ⓑ The contest presented an intriguing problem—and a lucrative one for the winner.

Ⓒ The competition became a model of Internet-era collaboration and innovation . . .

Ⓓ This kind of Internet-enabled cooperative work—known as crowdsourcing—has become a hot topic in industry and academia.

3. Identify one detail that supports the main idea.

____

____

Question 1: The purpose of the passage is to describe one of the main effects of the Netflix competition.

Question 2 asks you to select the statement that best expresses the main idea of the passage. Choices A, B, and D are details; the best answer is C.

Question 3: There are several details that support the main idea. Sample answers:

"The leading teams added members as they sought help to improve their results . . . ."

"Team members were often located in different countries, communicating by email and sharing work on the web with people they never met face to face."

Try It

Directions: Read the passage below and answer the questions that follow.

from What Is the Right Amount of Group Work in School?

by Shannon Doyne

Notes

1. Solitude is out of fashion. Our companies, our schools and our culture are in thrall to an idea I call the New Groupthink, which holds that creativity and achievement come from an oddly gregarious place. Most of us now work in teams, in offices without walls, for managers who prize people skills above all. Lone geniuses are out. Collaboration is in.

2. But there's a problem with this view. Research strongly suggests that people are more creative when they enjoy privacy and freedom from interruption. And the most spectacularly creative people in many fields are often introverted, according to studies by the psychologists Mihaly Csikszentmihalyi and Gregory Feist. They're extroverted enough to exchange and advance ideas, but see themselves as independent and individualistic. They're not joiners by nature. . . .

3. Culturally, we're often so dazzled by charisma that we overlook the quiet part of the creative process. Consider Apple. In the wake of Steve Jobs's death, we've seen a profusion of myths about the company's success. Most focus on Mr. Jobs's supernatural magnetism and tend to ignore the other crucial figure in Apple's creation: a kindly, introverted engineering wizard, Steve Wozniak, who toiled alone on a beloved invention, the personal computer. . . .

4. Our schools have . . . been transformed by the New Groupthink. Today, elementary school classrooms are commonly arranged in pods of desks, the better to foster group learning. Even subjects like math and creative writing are often taught as committee projects. . . .

5. [I]t's one thing to associate with a group in which each member works autonomously on his piece of the puzzle; it's another to be corralled into endless meetings or conference calls conducted in offices that afford no respite from the noise and gaze of co-workers. Studies show that open-plan offices make workers hostile, insecure and distracted. They're also more likely to suffer from high blood pressure, stress, the flu and exhaustion. And people whose work is interrupted make 50 percent more mistakes and take twice as long to finish it.

6. Many introverts seem to know this instinctively, and resist being herded together. Backbone Entertainment, a video game development company in Emeryville, Calif., initially used an open-plan office, but found that its game developers, many of whom were introverts, were unhappy. "It was one big warehouse space, with just tables, no walls, and everyone could see each other," recalled Mike Mika, the former creative director. "We switched over to cubicles and were worried about it—you'd think in a creative environment that people would hate that. But it turns out they prefer having nooks and crannies they can hide away in and just be away from everybody."

7. Privacy also makes us productive. In a fascinating study known as the Coding War Games, consultants Tom DeMarco and Timothy Lister compared the work of more than 600 computer programmers at 92 companies. They found that people from the same companies performed at roughly the same level—but that there was an enormous performance gap between organizations. What distinguished programmers at the top-performing companies wasn't greater experience or better pay. It was how much privacy, personal workspace and freedom from interruption they enjoyed. Sixty-two percent of the best performers said their workspace was sufficiently private compared with only 19 percent of the worst performers. Seventy-six percent of the worst programmers but only 38 percent of the best said that they were often interrupted needlessly. . . .

8. My point is not that man is an island. Life is meaningless without love, trust and friendship.

9. And I'm not suggesting that we abolish teamwork. Indeed, recent studies suggest that influential academic work is increasingly conducted by teams rather than by individuals. (Although teams whose members collaborate remotely, from separate universities, appear to be the most influential of all.) The problems we face in science, economics and many other fields are more complex than ever before, and we'll need to stand on one another's shoulders if we can possibly hope to solve them.

10. But even if the problems are different, human nature remains the same. And most humans have two contradictory impulses: we love and need one another, yet we crave privacy and autonomy.

Notes

1. Use the text above as a source of information for a paragraph of your own. Write the main idea statement for your paragraph.

2. Go back to the passage and underline three details you can use to support your main idea.

3. Write a paragraph that will be read by your classmates. Be sure to include your main idea statement and relevant, sufficient details. Put the information in your own words. Do not merely copy sentences from the passage.

13.2 Organization

Review

Most essays are organized using an introduction, a body, and a conclusion. The introduction and conclusion are one paragraph in length, and the body is several paragraphs.

Organize your writing to fit your purpose. Present details in a logical order so that the reader can follow the train of thought. **Transitional** words and phrases help the reader understand how ideas fit together cohesively, resulting in clear, unified writing.

The chart below shows several organization types and the purposes and transitions commonly associated with them.

Key Terms

transition: a word, phrase, or sentence that connects one idea to the next within a paragraph or essay.

Organization	Use when your purpose is to	Transitional phrases
Chronological time order	explain events (narrative writing) explain steps in a process (expository writing)	first, next, later, afterward, a few days later, at the same time
Order of Importance least to most important or most to least important	explain reasons (argumentative or persuasive writing) explain procedures or rules (expository writing)	first, another reason, however, on the other hand, finally
Cause and Effect explain the causes first and then the results	describe the relationship between causes and results (expository writing)	as a result, for the reason that, because, since, due to the fact that
Comparison and Contrast group all similarities and all differences together or explain how each element is the same or different	show how things are alike and/or different (expository writing)	similarly, in the same way, on the other hand, but, conversely

Check Understanding

Directions: Read the passage below and answer the questions that follow.

from All Deliberate Speed

by Charles J. Ogletree Jr.

Notes

1. *All Deliberate Speed* offers my personal reflections on the historic civil rights decision *Brown v. Board of Education*, issued by the U.S. Supreme Court on May 17, 1954. I have three goals in mind. First, I want to explain why the *Brown* decision, coming at a time of great racial inequality in America, marked a critical effort by the Supreme Court to send to the country a strong message: that legalized racial inequality in America would no longer be tolerated. The Court's decision, stemming from a careful examination of our history of slavery and Jim Crow segregation, held that disparities in public education opportunities that were based on the race of America's children had to end. The Court sent this message to all the stakeholders in America, including Congress, the president, and the general public. At the same time, its decision, though unanimous, contained a critical compromise, which I argue undermined the broad purposes of the campaign to end racial segregation immediately and comprehensively. While ordering the end of segregation, given its corrosive effects on black children, the Court removed much of the force of its decision by allowing proponents of segregation to end it not immediately but with "all deliberate speed." Those three words form the title of this book and reflect, in my view, the slow and ultimately unsuccessful effort to eliminate segregated education.

2. This compromise left the decision flawed from the beginning. Over the past fifty years, the attempt to integrate the public education system and to achieve full racial equality in other areas has been resisted and openly defied, by policy makers and the public, to the detriment of the laudable aim of achieving racial equality in America.

3. My second goal is to discuss the important work of lawyers who started the legal fight for racial integration decades before the *Brown* decision, the obstacles they faced and overcame, and the disappointment they eventually experienced, as they saw a critical decision weakened not only by the legislative and executive branches of our government but also by the same Court, as its membership changed and as conservatives narrowed and, in the end, turned their back on the mandate articulated in *Brown*. . . .

4. Finally, I want to bring into this story my personal reflections on *Brown* over the past fifty years . . . . This book tells how I, like millions of other African-Americans born during or after *Brown*, have experienced its celebration, condemnation, and evisceration.

1. Underline the main idea in the passage.

2. How are the main points organized? Refer to the chart on the previous page for organizational structures.

____

____

3. Circle three transitional words or phrases that help the reader make connections between the ideas.

Question 1 asks you to underline the main idea. The main idea is best expressed in these sentences:

> "While ordering the end of segregation, given its corrosive effects on black children, the Court removed much of the force of its decision by allowing proponents of segregation to end it not immediately but with "all deliberate speed." Those three words form the title of this book and reflect, in my view, the slow and ultimately unsuccessful effort to eliminate segregated education."

Question 2 asks you to identify the organizational structures. Possible answers: cause and effect and order of importance.

Question 3 directs you to circle three transitional words. There are several possibilities: *First* (paragraph 1), *My second goal* (paragraph 3), and *Finally* (paragraph 4).

Try It

Directions: Read the following editorial. Then respond to the question that follows.

Dying to Play
by Kevin Cook

Kevin Cook is an award-winning author of several books, including The Last Headbangers: NFL Football in the Rowdy, Reckless '70s: The Era That Created Modern Sports.

1. The beating goes on. This past Saturday [September 8, 2012] a Tulane University football player, Devon Walker, collided with a teammate while making a tackle. Walker, who is 21, broke his neck. Fans gasped. Doctors performed C.P.R. He may or may not walk again.

2. The incident was an urgent reminder of a problem that even the National Football League seems finally ready to acknowledge: all that on-field headbanging is taking a serious toll.

3. Just three days earlier, the N.F.L. said that it would donate $30 million to the National Institutes of Health to support research on brain injuries and other serious medical conditions prominent in athletes—an announcement that came hours before the Giants and Cowboys kicked off the 2012–13 season in a festive, nationally televised event that drew more than 20 million viewers.

Notes

Notes

(For comparison, that rivals the number of Americans who tuned in to Bill Clinton's speech at the Democratic National Convention the same night.)

4. Earlier that day, the journal *Neurology* carried the results of a study of 3,439 retired pro football players. It reported that veterans of N.F.L. combat are more likely than the rest of us to die from brain diseases including Alzheimer's, Parkinson's and amyotrophic lateral sclerosis, known as Lou Gehrig's disease. Not 50 percent more likely, or twice as likely, but three to four times more likely.

5. America's ready for some football, but the human brain may never be.

6. More than 3,000 former players have sued the N.F.L., charging that the league failed to inform them of the dangers they faced, to protect them against concussions and to provide health care. Those men played in the years when nobody talked about getting "concussed." You got your bell rung, your clock cleaned. You got nuked or blown up. You got your head handed to you. And unless you liked being called frilly names, you got back on the field as soon as you could locate it.

7. We know more about concussions today, but not how to prevent them. No helmet can offer much help, since the injury occurs when a fast-moving body suddenly stops or changes direction. The brain keeps moving until it collides with the inside of the skull, causing damage that can lead to chronic traumatic encephalopathy, or C.T.E.

8. Sports science's next frontier may be discovering why some brains are so vulnerable to concussions while others seem resistant. Meanwhile, it is heartbreaking when football heroes wind up in wheelchairs or worse. John Mackey, the pioneering president of the N.F.L. Players' Association, was found to have frontal temporal dementia in his early 60s. Former Bears safety Dave Duerson was 50 years old when he committed suicide, shooting himself in the chest so that his brain could be studied. (It showed signs of C.T.E.) Junior Seau, a 12-time Pro Bowler for the Chargers, was 43 when he shot himself in the chest last spring.

9. Fans may wonder whether they should support such a sport. Many parents face a more practical question: Should our kid play football? When the Raiders' Phil Villapiano, one of the hardest hitters in N.F.L. history, watched his son Mike get his bell rung in a high school game, they had a father-son talk about it. Mike dreamed of playing college football, maybe even making the N.F.L. They both felt he wouldn't get there by sitting on the sidelines, waiting for a doctor to send him back in. Father and son agreed: Mike kept his mouth shut and his options open. He stayed in the game and led his team to a state championship.

10. I'm not about to second-guess the Villapianos, whose fortitude I admire. But no family should face such a choice.

11. The N.F.L. now uses simple written or computerized cognitive

tests to assess concussions. Before each season, players are shown a page featuring 20 words and asked to write down as many as they remember when the page is taken away. The same with 20 simple pictures: Draw as many as you can remember. Later, after an on-field hammering rings their mental bells, the pros take the same test. Match your baseline results or sit out.

12. Some players cheat. They purposely give wrong answers on the preseason baseline test in hopes of passing the test when they're concussed. But no screening plan is foolproof, and this one has the virtue of simplicity. Every college and high school football program should use such a test until we find something better. Above all, though, football needs a culture change: parents, coaches and fans must never pressure an injured player to "get back in the game" before it's clear that he's of sound mind and body.

13. How should we view last week's donation from the N.F.L. to the N.I.H.? Cynics will no doubt see the pledge as a cheap public relations move. Given that $30 million represents four and a half minutes of commercial time during the Super Bowl, the league's donation might seem paltry.

14. But it's a start.

Notes

Source: *The New York Times*, September 11, 2012.

1. The editorial points to several cause and effect relationships. Identify two such relationships, citing brief passage from the text as support.

Relationship 1:

Relationship 2:

13.3 Evidence

Review

Often a prompt will ask you to develop your essay by providing **textual evidence**. Textual evidence includes direct quotations as well as paraphrases of specific information found in the reading. Gather evidence by reading texts closely and drawing information from them.

Key Terms

textual evidence: a direct quotation or paraphrase of a text used to support an interpretation.

paraphrase: a restatement of part of a text in your own words.

Check Understanding

Directions: Read the following passage and answer the questions that follow.

1. It's no secret that most Americans aren't exactly the healthiest eaters. Decades of research has shown the connection between poor diet and health. Eating too much meat and other animal products is associated with various forms of chronic illness, including heart disease, stroke, diabetes, and cancer. Every health organization recognizes that eating a mostly whole foods, plant-based diet is optimum for good health. Yet Americans continue to eat all the wrong foods. According to federal data, Americans eat more than the recommended amounts of meat, oils, added sweeteners, and refined grains, while our diets are falling short on health-promoting foods such as whole grains, fruits, and vegetables. The good news is that in recent years, meat consumption is declining. But we still have a long way to go toward consuming an optimum diet to prevent chronic diseases.

Liquid Candy

2. Of particular concern is America's love affair with sweetened soft drinks. Americans drink more than twice as much soda today as they did in 1971. One-half of the U.S. population consumes sugar drinks on any given day, and 25% consumes at least 200 calories (more than one 12-oz can of cola). Males drink more than females and teen boys consume the most. An incredible 70 percent of boys aged 12–19 drink sweetened drinks every day and adolescents (ages 12–19) consume a whopping 273 calories per day from beverages. The science is clear that excess consumption of soft drinks contributes to obesity and type 2 diabetes, among other health problems, and is associated with overall poor diet.

Notes

Source: "Nutrition, Obesity, & Processed Food," *Food Safety Fact Sheet*, May 2012.

1. Underline the main idea of the passage.

2. Cite at least two examples of textual evidence used to support the main idea.

____

____

____

Question 1 asks you to underline the main idea of the selection. The following sentences from paragraph 1 best express the main idea of the passage:

> "Every health organization recognizes that eating a mostly whole foods, plant-based diet is optimum for good health. Yet Americans continue to eat all the wrong foods."

Question 2 directs you to cite two examples of textual evidence. Your response may differ. The following are some examples of textual evidence.

> "According to federal data, Americans eat more than the recommended amounts of meat, oils, added sweeteners, and refined grains, while our diets are falling short on health-promoting foods such as whole grains, fruits, and vegetables."

> "Americans drink more than twice as much soda today as they did in 1971."

Toolbox

Use quotation marks to set off direct quotations from the text. For example, a direct quotation from the article on the previous page might be written like this:

> The writer states that Americans "drink more than twice as much soda today as they did in 1971."

If you are paraphrasing information, do not use quotation marks but put the information in your own words. A paraphrase of this same text might be written like this:

> The writer asserts that we drink more than two times as much soda as we did in 1971.

The following sentence starters show some ways to introduce textual evidence:

> The writer explains . . .
>
> X states, ". . ."
>
> Based upon his actions, Character X reveals . . .
>
> Another example of X is . . .
>
> In the first paragraph, the writer states . . .

Once you have cited textual evidence, you need to explain how it relates to your main idea. The following are examples of ways to begin a sentence explaining textual evidence:

> This shows that . . .
>
> Based upon this evidence, . . .
>
> The writer clearly shows that . . .
>
> This evidence supports the idea that . . .

Try It

Directions: Read the following passage and follow the directions below.

Reducing Obesity in America Calls for Tough Policies and a "Sugar Tax"

by Shirley L. Smith

Notes

1. Policymakers say aggressive action is needed to stem the growth of the obesity epidemic in the United States, which is crippling the nation's health-care system, pushing thousands of Americans into an early grave each year and jeopardizing the lives of millions of children, many of whom are overweight or obese before they enter kindergarten.

2. "One in five U.S. children, aged 2 to 5 years, is overweight or obese," said Sohyun Park, Ph.D., an epidemiologist at the Centers for Disease Control and Prevention (CDC) Division of Nutrition, Physical Activity and Obesity.

3. Studies indicate that overweight children are more likely to become overweight teenagers, who have a 70 percent chance of becoming overweight or obese adults.

4. "The U.S. health-care system is going to fold with the burden of chronic disease management if we don't take aggressive action to reduce obesity the same way we took aggressive action to reduce the tobacco problem," said Ann Ferris, Ph.D., a professor of medicine at the University of Connecticut Health Center and director of the Center for Public Health and Health Policy.

5. Ferris is conducting a three-year intervention study, funded by the U.S. Department of Agriculture, of sugar-sweetened beverages, which are one of the main culprits behind the U.S. obesity epidemic. The goal of the study is to reduce consumption of sugar-sweetened beverages among low-income preschoolers, who have a higher prevalence of consumption and a higher obesity rate than children from higher-income families; although Ferris said the gap is narrowing.

6. Ferris and other researchers say the obesity epidemic is being driven by changes in the food market and the environment.

7. "In the 1960s, when I was growing up, there were one or two children in my classroom who was very overweight," Ferris recalled, noting that her class had 60 students.

8. Sheanell Giraud, a kindergarten teacher at Rodney B. Cox Elementary School in Dade City, Florida, said she has 19 students in her class, and five are overweight. The school recently instituted a policy banning vending machines, and limiting snacks to fruits and vegetables, she said. "Students are not allowed to have soda, and teachers are encouraged not to use sweets as a reward in classes," Giraud added.

Notes

9. Many schools, local governments and hospitals around the country have implemented similar policies to reduce obesity by banning the serving and sale of sugary drinks, which are high in calories and have little or no nutritional value, said Roberta Friedman, director of public policy at Yale University's Rudd Center for Food Policy and Obesity.

10. Additionally, several state and local governments have proposed implementing an excise tax on sugar-sweetened beverages, a measure the Rudd Center endorses. "One of the government's roles is to protect the public's health, and given that we have clear evidence that the consumption of sugar-sweetened beverages is having a detrimental effect on people, the government should step in with policies to reduce consumption," Friedman said.

11. Ferris, who supports the tax initiative, said, "There is very good data that show that as you increased the cost of cigarettes, the purchase of cigarettes went down."

12. If a tax is high enough, Friedman contends that it would discourage the purchase and consumption of sugar-sweetened drinks as well. "A 10 percent price increase in the cost of a soda, according to the economic modeling we have done, would result in a 10 to 12 percent reduction in consumption," she said.

13. Last year, about 17 states tried passing a tax on sugar-sweetened beverages, but Friedman said none succeeded. About 15 states are currently considering the measure, she said.

14. A tax on sugar-sweetened beverages would have the added benefit of generating revenues to fund obesity prevention programs and offset some of the obesity-related, health-care costs, Friedman said.

15. The CDC estimates that medical costs associated with obesity are $147 billion annually. "Half of these costs are paid for with taxpayer dollars through Medicaid and Medicare," according to a Rudd Center report.

16. Governments can also help reduce obesity, researchers say, by providing supermarkets and farmers' markets with incentives to offer healthier foods and establish their businesses in low-income areas. They say low-income families are more susceptible to obesity, because healthy foods like fruits and vegetables are more expensive and less accessible than high-fat, processed foods like fast food and sugar-sweetened beverages. Opportunities for physical activity are also more difficult in low-income neighborhoods, because recreational facilities and sidewalks are usually nonexistent or unsafe.

17. "When you are in an environment that makes it so hard to eat well and to exercise, because you have limited choices, it's really hard. What do you do with your child, there is no place outside for them to play, so they watch TV," Ferris said.

18. Another problem is that parents are oftentimes confused about what's healthy, because many sugar-sweetened beverages are promoted as "natural" or being good for you. "In our low-income households, the young children are not getting soda, because the

moms know that soda is bad for them, but they are giving the kids sugar-sweetened beverages, because they think they are equivalent to juice and they can't tell the difference, but sugar-sweetened beverages are fake juices. They are mostly just sugar and water," Ferris explained.

Notes

19. Given the drastic rise in poverty in America, which is the highest it's been in 51 years according to the 2009 U.S. Census, Ferris said it is crucial that policymakers address the needs of low-income families and involve them in the decision-making process.

20. These initiatives will only be effective, however, if parents do their part. "If the nutritional habits are not good in the family, then the child will adopt that eating pattern." said Dr. Robert Mendelson, a pediatrician and spokesperson for the American Academy of Pediatrics. Parents need to instill good nutritional habits in their children at an early age, he said. "It is much easier to prevent obesity than to treat it."

21. The CDC recommends that parents, child caregivers and schools limit access to sugar-sweetened drinks, and replace them with fat-free or low-fat milk, water and a limited amount of 100 percent fruit juices. Although these juices contain natural sugar and lots of calories, Park said, unlike drinks with added sugar, they contain important nutrients.

22. Additionally, the CDC advises parents to encourage their children to live physically active lives and reduce television viewing to less than two hours a day, because children are influenced by commercials that promote unhealthy foods and beverages.

1. Write a paragraph describing steps that are planned or that are being taken to reduce obesity rates. Support your ideas using evidence from the passage.

Toolbox

Annotating a Source Text. Reading a text to learn new ideas is different from reading for pleasure. Your goal is to gain information so that you can develop an argument, explain a topic, or analyze a work of literature. Annotating is an important skill to use as you read a text critically. Think of annotating as a way of talking back to the text as you read. Annotate a text by

- underlining the main ideas and supporting details.
- marking key terms or unfamiliar words you want to look up later.
- writing questions and marking confusing parts with a question mark so you can return to them later.
- drawing arrows to show relationships between ideas.

When reading and annotating fiction, think like a writer of literature. Look for the elements that create meaning, including plot, characterization, symbolism, and theme. Annotate literature by

- underlining words and phrases that describe the characters.
- underlining repeated ideas (motifs) and themes.
- starring important scenes or dialogue.
- identifying symbols.
- writing personal connections to the text.

13.4 Language and Style

Review

Good writing uses language that is precise, clear, and forceful. In informational writing, use a formal writing style, avoiding slang and personal pronouns unless used in source material. Varying sentence length and structure will do much to draw your reader in. When possible, use **active voice** over **passive voice** and specific nouns over general.

Although figures of speech, such as similes and metaphors, may be especially purposeful in poetry and fiction, figurative language can also be used in informative writing to add punch and interest and to help the reader understand complex ideas.

Other techniques borrowed from poetry, such as repetition, alliteration, and imagery, can breathe life into what otherwise might be a dry presentation of facts.

Key Terms

active voice: when the subject is performing the action described by the verb, as in "The dog chased the squirrel."

passive voice: when the object of the action is made the subject of the sentence, as in "The squirrel was chased by the dog."

Check Understanding

Notice the use of figurative language and repetition in the excerpt below.

from The Worst Hard Time: The Untold Story of Those Who Survived the Great American Dust Bowl

by Timothy Egan

1. On those days when the wind stops blowing across the face of the southern plains, the land falls into a silence that scares people in the way that a big house can haunt after the lights go out and no one else is there. It scares them because the land is too much, too empty, claustrophobic in its immensity. It scares them because they feel lost, with nothing to cling to, disoriented. Not a tree, anywhere. Not a slice of shade. Not a river dancing away, life in its blood. Not a bump of high ground to break the horizon, give some perspective, spell the monotone of flatness. It scares them because they wonder what is next. It scared Coronado, looking for cities of gold in 1541. It scared the Anglo traders who cut a trail from Independence to Santa Fe, after they dared let go of the lifeline of the Cimarron River in hopes of shaving a few days off a seven-week trek. It even scared some of the Comanche as they chased bison over the grass. It scared the Germans from Russia and the Scots-Irish from Alabama—the Last Chancers, exiled twice over, looking to build a hovel from overturned sod, even if that dirt house was crawling with centipedes and snakes, and leaked mud on the children when thunderheads broke.

2. It still scares people driving cars named Expedition and Outlander. It scares them because of the forced intimacy with a place that gives nothing back to a stranger, a place where the land and its weather—

Notes

Simile compares silence of the land to a big house

Repetition of "not a" drives home the bleakness.

Personification of river, again, driving home the lack of life.

probably the most violent and extreme on earth—demand only one thing: humility.

3. Throughout the Great Plains, a visitor passes more nothing than something. Or so it seems. An hour goes by on the same straight line and then up pops a town on a map—Twitty, Texas, or Inavale, Nebraska. The town has slipped away, dying at some point without funeral or proper burial.

4. In other places, scraps of life are frozen in death at mid stride, as Lot's wife was petrified to salt while fleeing to higher ground. Here is a wood-framed shack buried by sand, with only the roof joists still visible. In the distance is a copse of skeletal trees, the bones of orchards dried to a brittleness like charcoal. And is that a schoolhouse, with just the chimney and two walls still standing? Then you see fence posts, the nubs sticking out of sterile brown earth. Once, the posts enclosed an idea that something could come from a shank of the southern plains to make life better than it was in a place that an Ehrlich, an O'Leary, or a Montoya had left. The fence posts rose six feet or more out of the ground. They are buried now but for the nubs that poke through layers of dust.

Notes

1. Highlight at least one use of figurative language and explain its effect.

____

____

____

____

2. Identify one example of repetition and explain its effect.

____

____

____

____

Question 1 asks you to identify and explain an example of figurative language. Your answer may vary. Here is a sample answer:

> In paragraph 4, Egan describes abandoned places as "scraps of life . . . frozen in death at mid stride, as Lot's wife was petrified to salt while fleeing to higher ground." The metaphoric language paints a vivid picture of the transformation of the human and natural world from living to dead in a short time.

Question 2 asks you to identify an example of repetition and explain its effect. Your answer may vary. Here is a sample answer:

> In paragraph 2, the author repeats the phrase "a place." The effect of the repetition is to drive home the power of the natural forces at work in the Great Plains.

Try It

Directions: Describe a public place you visit often, such as a store, a library, a park, etc. Do not name the location. See if a partner can guess it from the description alone. Use formal language and figures of speech, repetition, and imagery as it seems appropriate to you.

____

____

____

____

____

____

____

____

13.5 Conventions

Review

You may not be overly concerned about using correct **grammar**, spelling, and **punctuation** when sending a text or email to a friend.

However, these things do matter to employers and professors. Incorrect spelling, lack of capital letters and punctuation, or using wrong forms of words confuses your message. Mistakes also imply that you don't know the rules of formal English, or that you don't care enough to proofread your writing.

Be sure to check your work for grammar, spelling, and punctuation errors.

Key Terms

grammar: the rules of a language, such as subject/verb agreement and pronoun usage.

punctuation: the proper placement of commas, periods, and other punctuation marks.

Toolbox

Spell-Check. If you take a writing assessment on a computer, you will likely have access to spell-check. However, spell-check does not replace your own proofreading. The computer will not catch all of your errors, especially errors in which you spell a word "rite" but misuse it.

Try It

Directions: Edit the following passage for mistakes in grammar, spelling, and punctuation by rewriting it correctly on the lines below. Compare your corrections with a partner.

1. In architecture, romanticism took the form of a return to medieval styles and was known as the Gothic Revival. The trend was especially strong in England. Where it began in the mid-eighteenth century. The Gothic Revival was inspired by literary romantics which found drama and mystery in the Middle Ages.

2. Probably the writer Horace Walpole was an early figure of the most importance in the movement. In the mid-1800s he acquired a country estate, Strawberry Hill, which he soon began converting into a sort of Gothic castle. Actually its basic design was sort of neoclassical, but it had such medieval details as pointed arches and gargoyles.

3. Soon castlelike homes sprang up all over England the most unique was Fonthill Abbey, built for a rich and eccentric author named William Beckford. He urged his builder to work with such haste that the central tower collapsed soon after it was built. The whole building was in ruins in a few years.

4. In truth, remains that were left from broken-down buildings were all that some people wanted. Several firms specialized in the "built ruin," a crumbling fantasy of walls and towers that could lend a picturesque air to any estate, however new.

Chapter 14 Writing Arguments (W.11–12.1)

The purpose of an argumentative essay is to present an assertion and provide strong, relevant, and logical evidence to back up that assertion. Argumentative writing differs from persuasive writing in its dependence on appeals to reason rather than to the character of the writer or the emotions of the reader. Strong argumentative writing also addresses and refutes opposing views fairly and honestly. This chapter addresses the following aspects of argumentative writing.

14.1 Writing a Claim

Review

Every argumentative essay begins with a claim. A **claim** is your assertion, or the main point you want readers to accept. It is more than just an opinion or a personal preference. It is a precise, arguable statement resulting from research, one that you can support with accurate, objective information. Here is an example of a specific, significant, and arguable claim:

> Because recent studies have shown that playing football can cause long-term brain damage, players under the age of twelve should not be allowed to play.

Key Terms

arguable: uncertain; capable of being argued.

claim: an arguable statement.

Some people will agree; some will disagree and respond with evidence that supports their position. It's even possible that some may agree that football can cause long-term damage, but disagree that preventing young children from playing is the best solution.

Toolbox

In an argumentative essay, the claim almost always appears in the first paragraph. Often it is the last sentence of the paragraph. Most claims serve one of the following purposes:

- to clarify a definition
- to explain a cause or effect
- to make a judgment
- to advocate an action

The claim in the sample paragraph above advocates an action: prohibiting children under the age of twelve from playing football.

Check Understanding

Directions: Read the following excerpt from a speech by Theodore Roosevelt and complete the activity that follows.

from Conservation as a National Duty

by Theodore Roosevelt

From a speech delivered on May 13, 1908, to a White House conference of governors organized by Gifford Pinchot, chief of the U.S. Forest Service.

1. Governors of the several States; and Gentlemen:

2. I welcome you to this Conference at the White House. You have come hither at my request, so that we may join together to consider the question of the conservation and use of the great fundamental sources of wealth of this Nation. . . .

3. We are coming to recognize as never before the right of the Nation to guard its own future in the essential matter of natural resources. In the past we have admitted the right of the individual to injure the future of the Republic for his own present profit. In fact there has been a good deal of a demand for unrestricted individualism, for the right of the individual to injure the future of all of us for his own temporary and immediate profit. The time has come for a change. As a people we have the right and the duty . . . to protect ourselves and our children against the wasteful development of our natural resources, whether that waste is caused by the actual destruction of such resources or by making them impossible of development hereafter.

Notes

1. Underline a claim in the paragraph that is arguable.

2. Explain how the claim you underlined is arguable.

___

___

___

Question 1 asks you to identify an arguable claim in the passage. Sample response:

"As a people we have the right and the duty . . . to protect ourselves and our children against the wasteful development of our natural resources."

Question 2 asks you to explain how the claim you underlined is arguable. Here is a sample response:

Some could argue that private ownership of a resource gives the owner the absolute right to exploit that resource for personal gain.

Try It

Directions: Read the excerpt below from Thoreau's *Walden* and complete the activity that follows.

from Where I Lived, and What I Lived For

by Henry David Thoreau

Thoreau's "Where I Lived, and What I Lived For" is one chapter from his famous work, Walden*—an extended reflection on simple living in a natural setting.* Walden *was published in 1854.*

Notes

1. . . . . We must learn to reawaken and keep ourselves awake, not by mechanical aids, but by an infinite expectation of the dawn, which does not forsake us in our soundest sleep. I know of no more encouraging fact than the unquestionable ability of man to elevate his life by a conscious endeavor. It is something to be able to paint a particular picture, or to carve a statue, and so to make a few objects beautiful; but it is far more glorious to carve and paint the very atmosphere and medium through which we look, which morally we can do. To affect the quality of the day, that is the highest of arts. Every man is tasked to make his life, even in its details, worthy of the contemplation of his most elevated and critical hour. . . .

2. I went to the woods because I wished to live deliberately, to front only the essential facts of life, and see if I could not learn what it had to teach, and not, when I came to die, discover that I had not lived. I did not wish to live what was not life, living is so dear; nor did I wish to practice resignation, unless it was quite necessary. I wanted to live deep and suck out all the marrow of life, to live so sturdily and Spartan-like as to put to rout all that was not life, to cut a broad swath and shave close, to drive life into a corner, and reduce it to its lowest terms, and, if it proved to be mean, why then to get the whole and genuine meanness of it, and publish its meanness to the world; or if it were sublime, to know it by experience, and be able to give a true account of it in my next excursion.

1. Write a claim based on the information presented in the passage. Share your claim with a partner and discuss the differences between your claims, if any.

____

____

____

____

14.2 Supporting a Claim

Review

To convince your readers of your point of view, your claim requires the support of evidence and reasons. **Evidence** includes facts and informed judgments. **Reasons** include logical conclusions based on the evidence.

Support is strong if it comes from a reliable source and is stated precisely. In general, more recent information from a reliable source is stronger than older information.

Key Terms

evidence: facts and informed judgments used to support an argument.

reasons: logical conclusions based on evidence or ideas that are used to support an argument.

Check Understanding

Directions: Imagine that you are writing a letter to your principal, arguing that high school classes should include more group work. Each box includes a pair of similar sentences that might be used in the letter. In the Explanation box, tell which sentence provides the best support and explain why.

A. Students involved in group work learn valuable skills.	B. Students who participate in group work often develop stronger communication skills and better problem-solving abilities.
1. Explanation:	

C. I think students would be more motivated if they were allowed to collaborate on projects more frequently.	D. A survey of high school students shows that 70 percent of them would feel more motivated to complete assignments on time if they were part of a group working together.
2. Explanation:	

E. Through working together, both advanced and less advanced students gain a deeper understanding of concepts.	F. Students learn more when they work together.
3. Explanation:	

Question 1: directs you to identify the sentence with the stronger support for the claim and to explain your choice. Here is a sample response:

> *Sentence B offers stronger support for the claim because it is more specific; it identifies skills developed through group work activities.*

Question 2: Sample response:

Sentence D is the correct choice because it cites statistical evidence that 70 percent of high school students would feel more motivated to complete group assignments.

Question 3: Sample response:

Both sentences make a similar point, but sentence E uses precise phrases and gives a specific reason: group work facilitates student understanding.

Try It

Directions: Read the following passage from Theodore Roosevelt's speech. Then complete the activity that follows.

from Conservation as a National Duty

by Theodore Roosevelt

Notes

1. We have become great in a material sense because of the lavish use of our resources, and we have just reason to be proud of our growth. But the time has come to inquire seriously what will happen when our forests are gone, when the coal, the iron, the oil, and the gas are exhausted, when the soils shall have been still further impoverished and washed into the streams, polluting the rivers, denuding the fields, and obstructing navigation. These questions do not relate only to the next century or to the next generation. One distinguishing characteristic of really civilized men is foresight; we have to, as a nation, exercise foresight for this nation in the future; and if we do not exercise that foresight, dark will be the future! [Applause] We should exercise foresight now, as the ordinarily prudent man exercises foresight in conserving and wisely using the property which contains the assurance of well-being for himself and his children. We want to see a man own his farm rather than rent it, because we want to see it an object to him to transfer it in better order to his children. We want to see him exercise forethought for the next generation. We need to exercise it in some fashion ourselves as a nation for the next generation.

1. Select one of the claims below and circle it. On the lines below, cite evidence from the passage you could use to support that claim. Share and discuss your response with a partner.

A. If we do not exercise foresight, our future will be dark.

B. These questions do not relate only to the next century or to the next generation.

____

____

____

____

14.3 Using Counterclaims

Review

A **counterclaim** is an assertion that opposes your claim. If your claim is truly arguable, there will be other opinions or positions that contradict it.

For the claim that more group work should be assigned in school, a counterclaim might read as follows:

> Too much group work can lead to the lack of original thinking on the part of students who just "get by."

Including one or two counterclaims and then refuting them with strong **rebuttals** will strengthen your position. Readers will view you as unbiased and knowledgeable.

Key Terms

counterclaim: a point of view disagreeing with part of an argument.

rebuttal: an argument that disproves or weakens a counterclaim.

Check Understanding

Directions: For each claim listed below, write a counterclaim.

1. Making the school year longer will help students perform better on standardized tests.

   Counterclaim: ____________________

   ____

   ____

   ____

2. People should be able to use pseudonyms or aliases as online identities instead of their real names.

   Counterclaim: ____________________

   ____

   ____

   ____

Questions 1: Sample counterclaim:

> Students will perform better on standardized tests if more special services, such as one-on-one tutoring, are provided.

Question 2: Sample counterclaim:

> People should be required to use their legal name online, but they should also have the option of displaying an additional nickname or other alias.

Toolbox

Rebuttals. A weak counterclaim might be easy to refute, but its refutation will not strengthen your argument much. However, if you use evidence and facts to refute a strong counterclaim, that refutation will strengthen your position.

Try It

Directions: Read the following excerpt and answer the questions that follow.

from Remarks at Conservation Conference

by Barack Obama

From a speech delivered to a conference on conservation, March 2, 1212.

Notes

1. . . . . Now, I have to say that this is a pretty diverse group. . . . We've got hunters and fishermen; we've got farmers and ranchers; we've got conservationists; we've got small business owners; we've got local government leaders; we've got tribal leaders. . . . But you're all here for the same reason. Each of you has a deep appreciation for the incredible natural resources, . . . we've been blessed with as a nation. And you're working hard every day to make sure those resources are around for my daughters and your children and hopefully their children to enjoy.

2. Doing that takes creativity. The great Aldo Leopold once said that conservation is "a positive exercise of skill and insight, not merely a negative exercise of abstinence and caution." It's not just about doing nothing; it's about doing something affirmative . . . . And you also know that effective conservation is about more than just protecting our environment—it's about strengthening our economy. When we put in place new common-sense rules to reduce air pollution, . . . , it was to prevent our kids from breathing in dangerous chemicals. That's something we should all be able to agree on. But it will also create new jobs, building and installing all sorts of pollution control technology.

1. Underline one claim made by President Obama in the passage.

2. Write a counterclaim based on the claim you underlined. Compare counterclaims with a partner.

____

____

____

____

14.4 Using Evidence from Sources

Review

Argumentative writing is always based on evidence. The evidence could be the result of original research or experimentation. Most often, the evidence you use will be in **sources** that record the research of established experts.

When assigned an argumentative essay outside testing situations, you will need to conduct your own research. Avoid making snap judgments about an issue or short-circuiting your thinking on a topic. Read as much as possible from multiple perspectives on an issue before forming a position or writing a claim.

Key Terms

source: a text, graphic, or other work referred to in an argument or informational essay.

Toolbox

Citations. A citation is a note that identifies the source of information. There are many acceptable ways to cite sources. This workbook uses the Modern Language Association (MLA) format. According to MLA, any information, statistic, or idea that is not common knowledge and that is not your own must be cited in parentheses by including—

- the writer's last name and page number (Gonzolas 178)
- if the writer is not listed, the first word of the title is noted in parentheses ("Dangers" 178)
- If the source has no page numbers, they are omitted from the citation. ("Dangers")

For example, consider this paraphrased sentence:

> While companies producing software, movies, and music cry for piracy laws, no one seems to agree on a clear definition of the word "piracy" (Johns 6).

The citation indicates that the information came from page 6 of a book by an author whose last name is Johns. The author's full name (Adrian Johns), the book title (*Piracy: The Intellectual Property Wars from Gutenberg to Gates*), and other information about the book should appear on a page of sources entitled *Works Cited* at the end of a report.

Check Understanding

Directions: Read Source 1 and Source 2 on the next two pages. Then answer the questions.

Source 1

from High School Sports Participation and Educational Attainment

by Dr. Douglas Hartmann

Notes

1. . . . . [T]he crucial point for a general audience is that periodic updates, reviews, reappraisals and re-evaluations . . . have, over the years, consistently and invariably yielded evidence concluding that there is a significant baseline correlation between high school sports participation and higher rates of academic achievement and aspiration for individual students. This strong, positive relationship . . . appears to hold for a whole range of educational outcomes ranging from good grades and better test scores to higher graduation rates and college aspirations as well as the avoidance of negative trajectories such as dropouts . . . or, in a more complicated case, delinquency . . . The relationship between high school sports participation and scholastic achievement is, in the words of one such research team . . . , a "fact, well established" . . . .

2. Here it is also worth pointing out that educational attainment is far from the only pro-social activity, attitude, or outcome associated with high school sports participation. Developmental theorists, for example, have long talked about the character-building and socializing impacts of sport, based upon a correlation between skills and habits required for success in the classroom, sports arena, and daily life . . . . Recent psychological and social psychological research appears to confirm a relationship between sports participation and both mental health and self-esteem . . . , and in recent years economists have found that sports participation is associated with higher post-school wages and income. . . . At the same time, all of the empirical evidence that demonstrates a strong statistical correlation between sports participation and educational attainment does not mean that sports automatically and inevitably contributes to academic achievement at either an individual or institutional (i.e., school) level. Correlation, in short, does not necessarily indicate causation. In fact, scholars and other experts believe that the relationship between sports participation and academic achievement—or any other type of positive social outcome, for that matter—is far more complicated, multifaceted, and contingent and less direct than this.

Source: Hartmann, Dr. Douglas. *High School Sports Participation and Educational Attainment: Recognizing, Assessing, and Utilizing the Relationship.* LA84 Foundation: University of Minnesota, 2008. Web. 23 January 2014.

Source 2

Notes

from The Case Against High-School Sports

by Amanda Ripley

1. Every year, thousands of teenagers move to the United States from all over the world, for all kinds of reasons. They observe everything in their new country with fresh eyes, including basic features of American life that most of us never stop to consider.

2. One element of our education system consistently surprises them: "Sports are a big deal here," says Jenny, who moved to America from South Korea with her family in 2011. Shawnee High, her public school in southern New Jersey, fields teams in 18 sports over the course of the school year, including golf and bowling. Its campus has lush grass fields, six tennis courts, and an athletic Hall of Fame. "They have days when teams dress up in Hawaiian clothes or pajamas just because—'We're the soccer team!,'" Jenny says. (To protect the privacy of Jenny and other students in this story, only their first names are used.)

3. By contrast, in South Korea, whose 15-year-olds rank fourth in the world (behind Shanghai, Singapore, and Hong Kong) on a test of critical thinking in math, Jenny's classmates played pickup soccer on a dirt field at lunchtime. They brought badminton rackets from home and pretended there was a net. If they made it into the newspaper, it was usually for their academic accomplishments.

4. Sports are embedded in American schools in a way they are not almost anywhere else. Yet this difference hardly ever comes up in domestic debates about America's international mediocrity in education. (The U.S. ranks 31st on the same international math test.) The challenges we do talk about are real ones, from undertrained teachers to entrenched poverty. But what to make of this other glaring reality, and the signal it sends to children, parents, and teachers about the very purpose of school?

5. Even in eighth grade, American kids spend more than twice the time Korean kids spend playing sports, according to a 2010 study published in the *Journal of Advanced Academics*. In countries with more holistic, less hard-driving education systems than Korea's, like Finland and Germany, many kids play club sports in their local towns—outside of school. Most schools do not staff, manage, transport, insure, or glorify sports teams, because, well, why would they?

6. As states and districts continue to slash education budgets, as more kids play on traveling teams outside of school, and as the globalized economy demands that children learn higher-order skills so they can compete down the line, it's worth reevaluating the American sporting tradition. . . .

Source: Ripley, Amanda. "The Case Against High-School Sports" *theatlantic.com*. *The Atlantic*. September 18, 2013. Web. 23 January 2014. Copyright 2013. *The Atlantic.com* as published in *The Atlantic Online*. Distributed by Tribune Content Agency.

1. Write a claim based on the topic of high school sports covered in the two sources above. Make sure you can support your claim using information from one or both of the sources.

____

____

2. Identify two pieces of evidence from one of the sources above that you could use to support your claim in question 1. Write them below, along with a citation inside parentheses for each.

____

____

____

____

____

____

Question 1 asks you to write a claim based on the topic of high school sports. Here is a sample answer:

> High school sports are an important part of the educational experience in America. They should be supported because participation in sports has pro-social as well as academic benefits.

Question 2 directs you to identify two pieces of evidence you could use to support your claim. Here is a sample answer based on the above claim:

> ". . . there is a significant baseline correlation between high school sports participation and higher rates of academic achievement and aspiration for individual students" (Hartman, paragraph 1).
>
> "Developmental theorists, for example, have long talked about the character-building and socializing impacts of sport, based upon a correlation between skills and habits required for success in the classroom, sports arena, and daily life . . . ." (Hartman, paragraph 2).

Try It

Directions: Read Source 3 on the next page and reread Source 1 on page 252 and Source 2 on page 253. Then write an evidence-based paragraph on the topic of high school sports and academics. Support your claim with specific and relevant evidence from at least two of the source documents. Include one counterclaim. Write your paragraph on the lines provided on page 256 or on a separate sheet of paper. Share and discuss your paragraph with a partner and offer constructive comments on your partner's paragraph.

Be sure to—

- Use clear and precise language.
- Use a formal style.
- Include specific and relevant evidence from the source documents.
- Include one counterclaim.

Source 3

from What Do International Tests Really Show About U.S. Student Performance?

by Martin Carnoy and Richard Rothstein

Notes

1. Because social class inequality is greater in the United States than in any of the countries with which we can reasonably be compared, the relative performance of U.S. adolescents is better than it appears when countries' national average performance is conventionally compared.
   - Because in every country, students at the bottom of the social class distribution perform worse than students higher in that distribution, U.S. average performance appears to be relatively low partly because we have so many more test takers from the bottom of the social class distribution.
   - A sampling error in the U.S. administration of the most recent international (PISA) test resulted in students from the most disadvantaged schools being over-represented in the overall U.S. test-taker sample. This error further depressed the reported average U.S. test score.
   - If U.S. adolescents had a social class distribution that was similar to the distribution in countries to which the United States is frequently compared, average reading scores in the United States would be higher than average reading scores in the similar post-industrial countries we examined (France, Germany, and the United Kingdom), and average math scores in the United States would be about the same as average math scores in similar post-industrial countries.
   - A re-estimated U.S. average PISA score that adjusted for a student population in the United States that is more disadvantaged than populations in otherwise similar post-industrial countries, and for the over-sampling of students from the most-disadvantaged schools in a recent U.S. international assessment sample, finds that the U.S. average score in both reading and mathematics would be higher than official reports indicate (in the case of mathematics, substantially higher).
   - Disadvantaged and lower-middle-class U.S. students perform better (and in most cases, substantially better) than comparable students in similar post-industrial countries in reading. In math, disadvantaged and lower-middle-class U.S. students perform about the same as comparable students in similar post-industrial countries.

Source: Carnoy, Martin and Richard Rothstein. "What Do International Tests Really Show About U.S. Student Performance?" *epi.org*. Economic Policy Institute, January 29, 2013. Web. 29 January 2014.

Write your evidence-based paragraph here or on a separate sheet of paper.

14.5 Writing an Argumentative Essay

Review

Research: Avoid making snap judgments about an issue or short-circuiting your thinking on a topic. Read as much as possible from multiple perspectives on an issue before forming a position or writing a claim.

Write a claim: Write an arguable claim based on evidence from the research.

Counterclaim: Write a strong counterclaim and use evidence to compose a strong rebuttal.

Organize your argument: Decide on the order you plan to present your evidence and the placement of the counterclaim and rebuttal.

Write the argument: Clarify relationships among claims, counterclaims, reasons, and evidence with transitions.

Edit and proofread your argument.

Check Understanding

Directions: Edit the paragraph below for mistakes in grammar, spelling, and punctuation. Rewrite it correctly on the lines on the next page.

1. On weekends, families used to go out together to restaurants movie theaters and sporting events. Thanks to wireless Internet mega-size televisions, and lifelike video games, more americans are staying in. Trend forecasters called this behavior "cocooning." Streaming movies to a tablet cumputer and to watch sporting events in high definition is more convenint than sitting in a crowded theater or stadium. Why drive over to a friends house to hang out when you can Facebook them or play online video games together. "I think were looking for protection." Faith Popcorn, a trend forecaster explains, "Almost like the Jetsons we want to walk around in a little bubble. We are moving toward that.

The activity asks you to correct the errors in the paragraph. Check your paragraph against the corrected paragraph below.

On weekends, families used to go out together to restaurants, movie theaters, and sporting events. Thanks to wireless Internet, mega-size televisions, and lifelike video games, more Americans are staying in. Trend forecasters call this behavior "cocooning." Streaming movies to a tablet computer and watching sporting events in high-definition are more convenient than sitting in a crowded theater or stadium. Why drive over to a friend's house to hang out when you can Facebook them or play online video games together? "I think we're looking for protection," Faith Popcorn, a trend forecaster, explains. "Almost like the Jetsons, we want to walk around in a little bubble. We are moving toward that."

Toolbox

Steps in Writing an Argumentative Essay

Step 1: Understand the prompt.

Step 2: Gather evidence from sources.

Step 3: Write a claim and a counterclaim based on evidence.

Step 4: Organize your evidence and your counterclaim.

Step 5: Write your essay.

Step 6: Revise your essay (if there is time).

Step 7: Edit and proofread your essay.

Chapter Review

Directions: Closely read each of the six source documents provided in this chapter and write an evidence-based argument on the topic below. Write your argument on separate sheets of paper. Use page 262 to plan your response.

Topic

High school sports have a dominant place in American culture. At the same time, students are falling behind the world academically. Is the emphasis on sports having a negative effect on American high school students?

Your Task

Carefully read each of the six source documents provided. Then write a well-developed argument regarding the effects of sports on American high school students. Address at least one counterclaim. Support your ideas with specific and relevant evidence from at least four of the source documents.

Guidelines

Be sure to—

- Establish your claim regarding the effect of sports on American high school students.
- Address at least one counterclaim.
- Use specific, relevant, and sufficient evidence from at least four of the sources to develop your argument.
- Identify the source that you reference by source document number and paragraph number(s) (for example: Source 1, paragraph 4).
- Organize your ideas in a logical manner.
- Maintain a formal writing style and objective tone.
- Follow the conventions of standard written English.

Texts

Source 1 (on page 252): from *High School Sports Participation and Educational Attainment* by Dr. Douglas Hartmann

Source 2 (on page 253): *from* "The Case Against High-School Sports" by Amanda Ripley

Source 3 (on page 255): *from* "What Do International Tests Really Show about U.S. Student Performance?" by Martin Carnoy and Richard Rothstein

Source 4 (on page 259): *from* "The Case for High School Activities"

Source 5 (on page 260): Two Graphs: "Mean Grade Point Average by Gender" and "Mean Number of Absences by Gender"

Source 6 (on page 261): Graph: "Mean Cumulative GPA in Core Subjects"

Source 4

from The Case for High School Activities

Notes

1. Results of a 1987 survey of individuals at the executive vice-president level or above in 75 Fortune 500 companies indicated that 95 percent of those corporate executives participated in sports during high school. In addition, 54 percent were involved in student government, 43 percent in the National Honor Society, 37 percent in music, 35 percent in scouts and 18 percent in the school's publication.

2. The American College Testing Service compared the value of four factors in predicting success after high school. "Success" was defined as self-satisfaction and participation in a variety of community activities two years after college. The one yardstick that could be used to predict later success in life was achievement in school activities. Not useful as predictors were high grades in high school, high grades in college or high ACT scores.

3. The College Entrance Examination Board's Scholastic Aptitude Test (SAT) was examined in much the same way. It was found that having a high SAT score did not necessarily indicate success in a chosen career. The best predictor of later success, the study showed, was a person's independent, self-sustained ventures. Teens who were active in school activities, had hobbies or jobs, were found to be most likely to succeed at their chosen profession and make creative contributions to their community.

Source: "The Case for High School Activities." *nchsaa.org. The National Federation of State High School Associations*: 14–15. N.d., Web. 3 February 2014.

Source 5

The two graphs below are from a study of 19,543 high school students from the largest school district in Colorado.

Notes

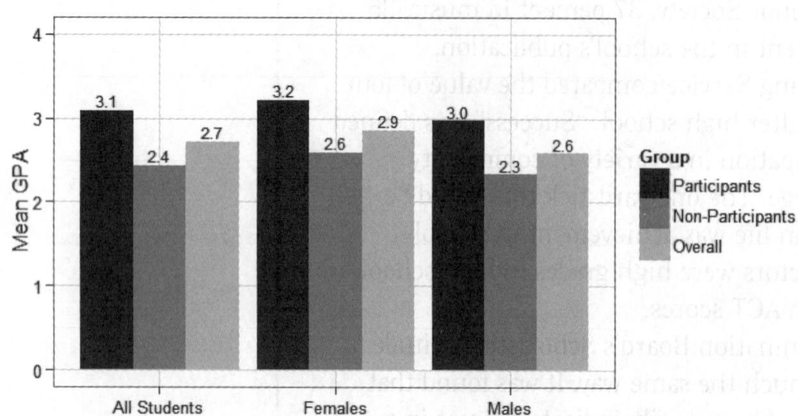

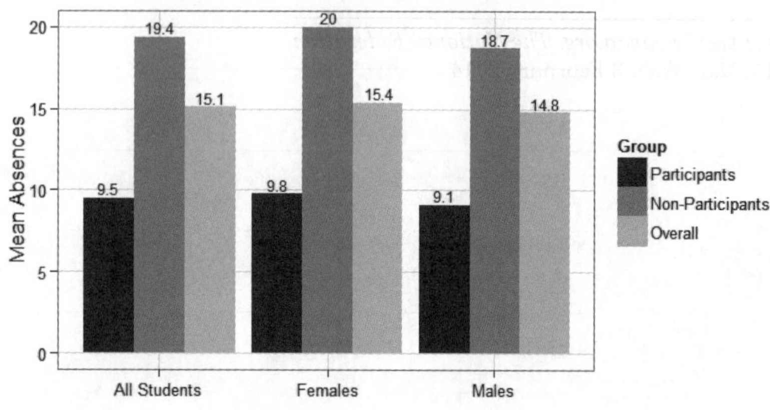

Source: "The Effects of Student Activity Participation, Gender, Ethnicity, and Socio-Economic Level on High School Grade Point Average and Attendance" by Dr. Kevin J. McCarthy, University of Colorado at Boulder, 2000

Source 6

The graph below is based on a study published in 2001 of 449 high school students in a private school in north central Texas.

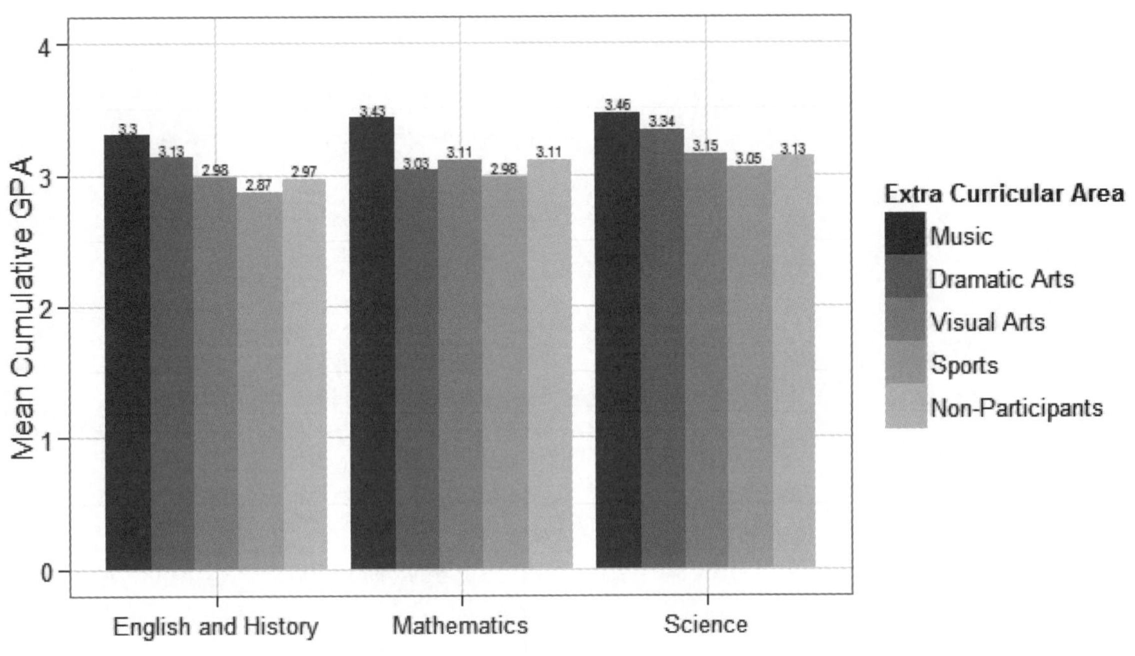

Source: "A study of the Effect of School-Sponsored, Extra-Curricular Activities on High School Students' Cumulative Grade Point Average, SAT Score, ACT Score, and Core Curriculum Subject Grade Point Average," by Janet Young Miranda, University of North Texas, 2001.

Notes

Planning Page

Chapter 15 Writing Informational Texts (W.11–12.2)

The purpose of an informational text is to explain or to provide information about a topic. When you explain how a bill becomes a law or analyze the causes of the Civil War, you are using informational writing. You will often be asked to write an informational text during testing. This chapter will address the following aspects of informational writing:

15.1 Writing a thesis statement
15.2 Supporting a thesis statement
15.3 Using and citing sources
15.4 Writing an informative essay from sources

15.1 Writing a Thesis Statement

Review

After you have jotted down some notes for an informational essay, including ideas you have acquired from research or sources, you should have enough information to write a thesis statement. A **thesis statement** establishes the central idea and purpose of your piece of writing. Once you have composed a precise thesis statement—even if it is only a draft—it will help you select and organize relevant supporting details from the information you have gathered.

Be direct when writing a thesis statement. Avoid empty phrases such as "My main idea is . . ." or "In this essay I will . . . ." A clear and direct thesis statement will communicate your main idea and purpose and set the **scope** of your writing.

Key Terms

thesis statement: the main idea or purpose of a piece of informational writing. The thesis statement is typically found in the first paragraph.

scope: the extent of the subject matter that something deals with.

Check Understanding

Directions: Select the statement below that is most precise and label it "good." Rewrite the other two statements to make them more precise.

Thesis Statement	Revision
1. After reading this paper, you will know the steps you have to take to plan a vacation somewhere.	
2. A number of successful television series feature strong female lead characters.	
3. Businesses and farms must meet a set of specific standards defined by the USDA to earn an organic certification.	

Statement 1 is wooden and wordy. There is no need for the introductory clause "After reading this paper, ..." The statement also lacks detail and focus. A better statement might read as follows:

Use the following steps to plan a vacation to Ireland.

Statement 2 is vague and lacks focus. Supplying details will help:

The successful television series "Bones," "The Good Wife," and "Rizzoli and Isles" feature strong female lead characters.

Statement 3 is good as is.

Toolbox

The Purpose of Informational Writing. Clearly, the purpose of informational writing is to inform, but more specifically, informational writing should increase the reader's knowledge of a subject.

Try It

Directions: Read the definitions of friendship listed below. Find two or three that strike a special chord in you and synthesize them with your own experience to develop a unique statement. Then write a thesis statement for an informational essay that deals with some aspect of the topic of friendship.

1. Wishing to be friends is quick work, but friendship is a slow ripening fruit. (Aristotle)
2. Friendship improves happiness, and abates misery, by doubling our joys, and dividing our grief. (Marcus Tullius Cicero)
3. I don't need a friend who changes when I change and who nods when I nod; my shadow does that much better. (Plutarch)
4. Anybody can sympathize with the sufferings of a friend, but it requires a very fine nature to sympathize with a friend's success. (Oscar Wilde)
5. Friendship is born at that moment when one person says to another: "What! You too? I thought I was the only one." (C. S. Lewis)
6. The friend who holds your hand and says the wrong thing is made of dearer stuff than the one who stays away. (Barbara Kingsolver)
7. Lots of people want to ride with you in the limo, but what you want is someone who will take the bus with you when the limo breaks down. (Oprah Winfrey)
8. A "Facebook Friend" is someone who is added to your network on a social media website. A "Facebook Friend" may or may not be someone . . . you have ever met or interacted with. (Bradley S. Shear, from *Shear on Social Media Law*, www.shearsocialmedia.com.)

Notes

Thesis Statement:

____

____

____

____

15.2 Supporting a Thesis Statement

Review

An informational article or essay lives or dies on the quality of its details. Without specific and relevant details, your writing will be vague and lack interest.

Select different types of supporting details, such as **facts**, **statistics**, extended definitions, concrete details, quotations, and **anecdotes**. If all your supporting details are statistics, for example, your paper will be dry and hard to follow. If available, incorporate relevant anecdotes and firsthand statements to reveal the lived experience represented by the data.

The organization and presentation of the details will depend on the type of article you are writing. For example, an article on the history of Facebook might be organized chronologically, starting with the beginnings of the company and ending with current news events. An article about the difference between Facebook friends and real friends might use a compare and contrast structure.

Key Terms

anecdote: a short and interesting story about a real person.

fact: a piece of information that is indisputable.

statistics: facts and data from a study.

Check Understanding

Directions: Cross out sentences that would not be effective supporting details for the thesis statement. In the margin, write notes explaining why.

Thesis Statement

Research shows that having friends and a network of social support leads to health benefits.

Possible Supporting Details

1. In 1989, David Spiegel, MD, a professor of psychiatry at Stanford University, published a landmark paper in *Lancet*. It showed that women with breast cancer who participated in a support group lived twice as long as those who didn't. They also had much less pain.
2. [S]tudies have shown that people with fewer friends tend to die sooner after having a heart attack than people with a strong social network.
3. Research has . . . shown that teens are likely to become friends with people who are similar to them—particularly in terms of race, ethnicity, and gender.

Notes

4. Our findings show that the effects of high school classes on the formation of teens' new friendships are surprisingly strong. For example, teens are more likely to make a friend in shared courses than if they are in the same extracurricular activities . . . .
5. "People with social support have fewer cardiovascular problems and immune problems, and lower levels of cortisol—a stress hormone," says Tasha R. Howe, PhD, associate professor of psychology at Humboldt State University.
6. Patricia Greenfield, a UCLA developmental psychologist, has seen a decline in intimate friendships between young people as a result of their use of social media. Instead, many young people now derive personal support and affirmation from "likes" and feedback to their postings.
7. The findings suggest that teenage peer pressure has a distinct effect on brain signals involving risk and reward, helping to explain why young people are more likely to misbehave and take risks when their friends are watching.

Notes

Answer: This activity asks you to cross out details that fail to support the thesis. You should have crossed out details 3, 4, 6, and 7. Details 3 and 4 are off-topic; they refer to how and with whom teenagers form friendships. Detail 6 is unrelated to the thesis, since it discusses the decline of intimate friendships between young people, and detail 7 discusses the relationship between taking risks and peer pressure.

Toolbox

Maintaining Purpose. When choosing supporting details, remember the focus of informative writing is to convey ideas, not to argue with evidence.

Try It

1. Write two details you might use to support the general topic below.

There are some surprising hidden benefits to friendship.

2. List three possible sources of information (or types of information) on the topic of the benefits of friendship you could use to find supporting details. Tell where you could locate each one. Share your list with a partner.

____

____

____

____

____

____

15.3 Using and Citing Sources

Review

Whether you quote the exact words or paraphrase a source, you are required by law to give credit to any author whose ideas or words you use. Failure to give credit is called **plagiarism**, a serious offense. In informational writing, each use of another author's words or ideas must be indicated with a **citation** within the paper, usually in parentheses immediately following the quotation or paraphrase. (See the Toolbox below for citation formats.) The citation is then keyed to a list of your sources at the end of the paper, if required.

Key Terms

plagiarism: using another's work without giving credit.

citation: a note in a text identifying the source of information.

Just as it is good practice to vary the length and type of sentences in your writing, it is also good practice to vary the way you introduce borrowed material. Here are three strategies to add variety to your writing.

Use a quotation to complete a sentence you start.

> According to research on teen friendship formation, teens are more likely to "make a friend in a shared class than if they are in the same extracurricular activities, have parents with similar levels of education or even if they have a friend in common" (Frank, paragraph 3).

Include information about the source in an introductory clause followed by a paraphrase.

> According to the report "Teens, Friends and Bad Decisions," the presence of friends can influence teenagers to take risks they would otherwise avoid (Parker-Pope, paragraph 2).

Break a quotation into two parts joined by information about the source.

> "[M]any young people," the report confirms, "derive personal support and affirmation from 'likes' and feedback to their postings" (Dakin, paragraph 7).

Toolbox

Citation Formats. A citation is a note in a text that identifies the source of the information. There are many acceptable ways to cite sources. For research reports, for example, you may be required to use the Modern Language Association (MLA) format. In testing situations, you may be asked to follow a specific format outlined in the prompt. Be sure to read the prompt closely and follow the directions for citing sources. In this workbook, follow these instructions:

- Article with author: Author's last name and the paragraph number. (Gonzolas, paragraph 5)
- Article without author: The first word of the title followed by paragraph number. ("Diet," paragraph 3)

For example, consider this quoted sentence:

"[M]any young people," the report confirms, "derive personal support and affirmation from 'likes' and feedback to their postings" (Dakin, paragraph 7).

The citation indicates that the information came from paragraph 7 of an article by Dakin. The full title ("Diet, Nutrition, and the Prevention of Chronic Diseases") and other information about the book would appear on a page of sources entitled *Works Cited* at the end of a report.

Note: Unless otherwise directed, there is usually no requirement to include a *Works Cited* page in testing situations.

Check Understanding

Directions: Read the text and follow the directions.

Source 1

from Social Media Affecting Teens' Concept of Friendship, Intimacy

by Pauline Dakin

Notes

1. Social media is affecting the way kids look at friendship and intimacy, according to researchers.
2. The typical teenager has 300 Facebook friends and 79 Twitter followers, the Pew Internet and American Life project found in its report, *Teens, Social Media, and Privacy*. . . .
3. The research contributes to an emerging picture of how teens' ideas about friendship and intimacy have been influenced by their immersion in the on-line world, says Patricia Greenfield, a UCLA developmental psychologist and the director of the Children's Digital Media Center at Los Angeles.
4. In her own research, Greenfield has found that young people feel socially supported by having large networks of on-line friends, and these are not necessarily friends they ever see face-to-face.
5. "We found in our study that people, college students, are not

getting a sense of social support from being on the phone. They're getting social support through bigger networks and having a sense that their audience is large."

6. The result is a decline in intimate friendships, Greenfield says. Instead, many young people now derive personal support and affirmation from "likes" and feedback to their postings.

7. "The whole idea behind intimacy is self-disclosure. Now they're doing self-disclosure to an audience of hundreds."

8. Other research at UCLA shows teens' increasingly preferred mode of communication with their friends, texting, makes them feel less connected and bonded than face-to-face communication.

9. Graduate student Lauren Sherman studied various forms of communication between pairs of friends. She found the closer the experience was to in-person conversation, the more emotionally connected the friends felt. For example, video chat rated higher than a phone call, but the phone created a closer connection than texting.

10. "I don't think digital communication in itself is a bad thing," said Sherman, "but if we're losing out on opportunities to connect with people as well as we can, that's a problem."

11. Studies have estimated teens typically send more than 3,000 texts a month.

12. Greenfield says that indicates kids are opting for efficiency of connection over intimacy.

Notes

Source: "Social Media Affecting Teens' Concept of Friendship, Intimacy" by Pauline Dakin. CBC News. http://www.cbc.ca/news/health/social-media-affecting-teens-concepts-of-friendship-intimacy-1.2543158.

1. Write a sentence that uses a direct quotation from the source. Include a citation.

____

____

____

2. Write a sentence that paraphrases information from the source. Include a citation.

____

____

____

Question 1: Sample response:

"Greenfield has found that young people feel socially supported by having large networks of on-line friends, and these are not necessarily friends they ever see face-to-face" (Dakin, paragraph 4).

Question 2: Sample response:

According to Greenfield, teenagers appear to avoid intimacy in favor of online forms of communication (Dakin, paragraph 12).

Toolbox

Quotation. If you repeat a statement word for word from a source, enclose the words in quotation marks and cite your source in parentheses. If you introduce the quotation with the author's name, include only the page number (or paragraph or line number) in the citation. For example:

> Researcher Patricia Greenfield notes that the "whole idea behind intimacy is self-disclosure. Now [young people are] doing self-disclosure to an audience of hundreds" (paragraph 7).

Paraphrase. If you put information in your own words, you still must cite your source in parentheses. Do not use quotation marks around your paraphrase. Failing to cite paraphrases is plagiarism.

Try It

Directions: Read the text and follow the directions.

Source 2

from Health Benefits of Friendship

by Chris Woolston

Notes

1. Humans have always relied on friendship. We never would have made it out of the Stone Age without cooperation and companionship. Nowadays, we may not need our immediate circle to help gather food or fend off predators, but friends can still be absolute lifesavers. Many studies over the years have found that people generally live longer, happier, healthier lives if they have a strong network of support from friends and family. . . .

Friendship and the Heart

2. Good friendships seem to be especially helpful for the heart. . . . A two-year study of more than 500 women with suspected coronary artery disease showed similar results. Women who reported the lowest levels of social support were twice as likely to die during the study. The women who enjoyed close support were not only more likely to be alive after two years, they also had lower rates of high blood pressure and diabetes and were less likely to have excessive abdominal fat.

3. How do friendships manage to affect the heart? As reported in the *Journal of the National Medical Association* in 2009, friendships and other types of social support can help relieve stress, a well-known contributor to heart disease. . . . The research is still preliminary, but some studies have found that people who enjoy close support from friends and family generally have fewer inflammatory chemicals in their blood. . . .

Good and Bad Friendships

4. . . . . Clearly, not all types of friendship are good for your health. A 2008 study published in *Hormones and Behavior* found that friends who talk excessively about problems—researchers called it "co-ruminating," evoking cows endlessly chewing their cud—can actually ramp up each other's stress levels. . . .

5. . . . . Looking at reports from more than 4,700 people over 20 years, . . . researchers found that both happiness and unhappiness spread from one friend to another. Having a happy friend who lived less than a mile away increased the chances of finding personal happiness by 25 percent. Being surrounded by unhappy friends, on the other hand, could drag a person down. In short, the most helpful—and healthful—friends are happy, encouraging, and supportive within reason. They're also willing to ask for help once in a while. As reported in *Current Opinion in Psychiatry*, giving support to a friend may be as good for a person's health and well-being as receiving it. That's the great thing about friendship—it works both ways.

Notes

Source: Chris Woolston, "Health Benefits of Friendship," published on healthday.com http://consumer.healthday.com/encyclopedia/emotional-health-17/psychology-and-mental-health-news-566/health-benefits-of-friendship-648397.html

1. Write a paragraph incorporating one quotation and one paraphrase from the source. Include citations.

15.4 Writing an Informative Essay from Sources

Review

In a testing situation, you will be presented with a prompt and one or more source documents. Your first task should be to read and thoroughly understand the prompt. Next read the source documents, which you can think of as research.

> **Key Terms**
>
> **prompt:** the directions for writing an essay.

You may want to follow the writing process outlined below or another that works well for you.

Set your purpose: Review the prompt and restate the directions as a purpose statement.

Research: Avoid making snap judgments or short-circuiting your thinking about a topic. Read all the source documents before limiting your focus and writing a thesis statement.

Limit your focus: Choose specific aspects of the topic you will focus on in your paper.

Write a draft thesis statement: Write a thesis statement based on your limited focus.

Select and organize supporting details: Create a brief outline, in which you plan the details to include in your introduction and those that you will use to illustrate the ideas, concepts, connections, and distinctions of your topic. If appropriate, include heads and graphics.

Write the essay: Clarify relationships among topics and details with appropriate transitions.

Edit and proofread your essay.

Check Understanding

Directions: Read the prompt below. Underline key words that tell you what to do. Then write a purpose statement on the lines provided.

Prompt: Experts claim that most teenagers need to sleep for 8 to 10 hours a night. According to researchers, however, many teenagers get fewer than 7 hours a night. Write an informational essay on the effects of insufficient sleep on teenagers.

My purpose is to—

____

____

____

____

Sample answer: My purpose is to write an informational essay on how lack of sleep affects teenagers.

Try It

Directions: Read each passage. Then decide which transition word or phrase best fits in the blank and completes the idea. Compare your answers with a partner.

1. If you want to tell people the truth, make them laugh, _____ they'll kill you. (Oscar Wilde)

Ⓐ though
Ⓑ because
Ⓒ indeed
Ⓓ otherwise

2. To call woman the weaker sex is a libel; it is man's injustice to woman. If by strength is meant brute strength, then, _____, is woman less brute than man. If by strength is meant moral power, _____ woman is immeasurably man's superior. (Mahatma Gandhi)

Ⓐ because / however
Ⓑ though / though
Ⓒ indeed / then
Ⓓ moreover / however

3. Everything starts somewhere, _____ many physicists disagree. But people have always been dimly aware of the problem with the start of things. They wonder how the snowplough driver gets to work, or how the makers of dictionaries look up the spelling of words. (Terry Pratchett)

Ⓐ though
Ⓑ and
Ⓒ indeed
Ⓓ instead

4. Read the passage. On each numbered blank, write the letter of the transition that best fits the corresponding numbered blank in the excerpt.

_____ **1.**
_____ **2.**
_____ **3.**
_____ **4.**

a) but
b) luckily
c) moreover
d) currently

Almost two years ago I asked the question, "Do Solar Storms Threaten Life as We Know It?" The answer then and even more so now could very well be a scary "yes" . . . .

___(1)___, while one is not inevitable, should there be a solar strike capable of causing widespread blackouts and crippling disruptions of satellite and radio communications, it's likely there would be little advance notice, and ___(2)___ there is virtually no capability to shield much of the planet and virtually no planning on the books to recover from the potentially disastrous consequences.

The solar flare that erupted from the sun on Valentine's Day—the strongest solar eruption in four or five years—was a loud and clear wake-up call to the potentially dire threat of solar storms. . . .

___(3)___, the only disruptive consequences were interruptions in radio communications in the western Pacific Ocean and parts of Asia, which caused airlines to reroute some polar flights to avoid radio outages. ___(4)___ experts say that more potent solar storms . . . have the potential to wreak long-lasting havoc on electric power supply and communications infrastructure around the globe.

Chapter Review

Directions: Closely read each of the six source documents provided in this chapter and write a source-based informational essay on the topic below. Write your article on separate sheets of paper.

Topic

Friendship is ambiguous. On the one hand, friendship is valued as one of life's great pleasures. On the other hand, problems with friends can be a source of stress and disappointment. What is the meaning of friendship in this era of Facebook and other digital communication formats?

Your Task

Carefully read each of the six source documents provided. Five are nonfiction; one, the excerpt from *Roomies,* is fictional. Then write a well-developed informational essay. Support your ideas with specific and relevant evidence from at least four of the source documents.

Guidelines

Be sure to—

- introduce your topic with a clear and direct thesis statement.
- use specific and relevant details from at least four of the sources.
- identify the source that you reference by source document number and paragraph number(s) (for example: Source 1, paragraph 4).
- organize your ideas in a logical manner.
- maintain a formal writing style and objective tone.
- follow the conventions of standard written English.

Texts

Source 1 (on page 268): "Social Media Affecting Teens' Concept of Friendship, Intimacy" by Pauline Dakin

Source 2 (on page 270): "Health Benefits of Friendship" by Chris Woolston

Source 3 (on page 275): *from* "R U friends 4 Real?" by Amy Novotney

Source 4 (on page 276): from *The Meaning of Friendship* by Mark Vernon

Source 5 (on page 277): from *Roomies* by Sara Zarr and Tara Altebrando

Source 6 (on page 279): *from* "Grown Women Don't Need a 'Best Friend' " by Alice Robb

Source 3

from R U Friends 4 Real?

by Amy Novotney

Notes

1. . . . Today's two-hour telephone calls with friends are often now conducted via marathon text messaging or Facebook sessions. And that cultural shift has psychologists asking lots of questions: What happens to adolescent friendships when so much interpersonal communication is via text? Or when fights between best friends explode via Facebook for all to see? . . .

2. So far, the answers to those questions are mixed. Margarita Azmitia, PhD, a psychology professor at the University of California, Santa Cruz, who studies adolescent friendships, is among those who contend that these technologies have only changed some of the ways teens interact. Today's youth still count the friends they see and talk to every day among their closest, she says.

3. "The [qualities] teens value in friendships, like loyalty and trust, remain the same," Azmitia says. "Technology has just changed some of the ways kids can be friends with each other."

4. Other psychologists, however, say today's ways of communicating can change the message, and wonder what effect that has on adolescent friendships, and even teens' social development. For example, instead of learning how to handle the give and take of conversation—one of our most basic human attributes and a connection we all crave—teens instead are crafting and often constantly editing witty text responses, says Massachusetts Institute of Technology social psychologist Sherry Turkle, PhD.

5. "We're losing our sense of the human voice and what it means—the inflections, hesitations and the proof that someone isn't just giving you stock answers," says Turkle, whose book *Alone Together* (2011) is based on 15 years of research and observation of children and adult interactions with technology. "That's a radical thing to do to our relationships."

Outcasts Reaching Out

6. One of social networking's greatest benefits is its ability to bring meaningful friendships to people who might otherwise be shunned as outcasts. . . . In one study, published in *School Psychology Review*, educational psychologist Beth Doll, PhD, of the University of Nebraska–Lincoln, found that friendless adolescents are more likely to be unemployed, aggressive or have poor mental health as adults.

7. But thanks to text messaging and the Internet, socially anxious teens who might have been left out now have a voice. In a 2010 study with 626 children and teens, researchers at the Queensland University of Technology in Australia found that lonely adolescents reported using the Internet to make new friends, and that they communicated online significantly more frequently about personal and intimate topics than those who did not report loneliness.

Source: "R U Friends 4 Real?" by Amy Novotney, *Monitor on Psychology*, Feb. 2012, Vol. 43, No. 2, page 62 in print edition. (http://www.apa.org/monitor/2012/02/friends.aspx).

Source 4

from The Meaning of Friendship

by Mark Vernon

Notes

1. What exactly is friendship? What is its nature, its rules, its promise? How can one differentiate between its many forms? How does it compare to, and mix with, the connections shared between lovers and within families? . . .

2. These questions are trickier to answer than it might first seem because friendship is hugely diverse. . . . Aristotle, whose writing on friendship still sets the philosophical agenda to this day, found as much 2,500 years ago. Friendship, he proposed, is at the very least a relationship of goodwill between individuals who reciprocate that goodwill. A reasonable starter for ten.[1] However, as soon as he tried to expand it, the definition seemed to unravel.

3. He looked around him and saw three broad groupings of relationships people called friendship. The first group are friends primarily because they are useful to each other—like the friendship between an employee and a boss, or a doctor and a patient, or a politician and an ally; they share goodwill because they get something out of the relationship. The second group are friends primarily because some pleasure is enjoyed by being together; it may be the football, the shopping, the gossip . . ., but the friendship thrives insofar, and possibly only insofar, as the thing that gives the pleasure continues to exist between them. Aristotle noted that these first two groups are therefore like each other because if you take the utility or the pleasure away, then the chances are the friendship will fade.

4. This, though, is not true of the third group. These are people who love each other because of who they are in themselves. It may be their depth of character, their innate goodness, their intensity of passion or their simple *joie de vivre,* but once established on such a basis these friendships are ones that tend to last. . . .

5. That there are better or higher friendships–different people may call them soul friends, close or old friends, or best friends–as opposed to instrumental and casual friendships, or mere friendliness, is surely right. But to say that great friendship is defined solely by its goodwill seems to miss its essence. Goodwill exists in these best kinds of friendship, but, unlike the lesser types, best friendship–arguably the quintessential sort–is based on something far more profound. In other words, a definitional approach to friendship has its limits.

6. This ambiguity as to what friendship is reflects, then, the ambiguity that appears to be part and parcel of friendship in life. Try listing some of the friends you have . . . whoever you might at some time think of as a friend. A look at such a list puts your friends

1 Reasonable starter for ten: the opening question of a British popular game show called "University Challenge." Each team has to answer the "starter" question worth 10 points.

in front of you, as it were, and highlights the vast differences. For example, the friendship with your partner will in certain key respects be unlike that of your oldest friend, though you may be very close to both. . . .

7. As you continue further down the list to the friends who are in many ways little more than acquaintances, . . . it is obvious that friendship stretches from a love you could scarcely do without to an affection that you'd barely miss if it ended. . . .

8. Personally, I think that Aristotle is on to something in his belief that the closest kind of friendship is only possible with a handful of individuals. . . . He actually went so far as to express a fear of having too many friends, "polyphilia" as it might be called. There is an expression attributed to Aristotle that captures the concern: "Oh my friends, there is no friend." . . . [He] was not worrying about the loneliness of the modern individual, . . . but rather the dangers of knowing so many people, you really know no one. One of the things I think the philosophy of friendship tells us is that life produces personal relationships of many types, but out of these connections good friendship may or may not grow.

Notes

Source 5

from Roomies

by Sara Zarr and Tara Altebrando

Lauren, the narrator of the passage below, and Elizabeth (Ebb) find out that they will be college roommates in the fall. They exchange emails and texts as they negotiate new and old friendships during their last summer at home.

1. There are three unanswered e-mails from Zoe in my in-box at the end of the day. I'm scared to read the most recent one because I know I'm in trouble for not replying. The message preview shows me the first line. **Did you get my last two e-mails? Or my texts? Are you dead? Because if you are it would be nice**—I can imagine the rest. Something in me won't click on the message. . . .

2. Dad appears in the doorway of my room, . . . [and] crooks his finger at me to beckon me into the hall. . . .

3. "What?" I ask.

4. "Nothing." He puts his arms around me for a hug. "How are you doing? I feel like we haven't talked in ages."

5. "We haven't."

6. . . . . Dad releases the hug and takes my hand, pulling me into the living room, where Mom lies on the couch with her eyes closed.

7. "I'm taking Lauren out for gelato. Want us to bring you anything?"

8. Mom moves her head about a quarter of an inch back and forth in a no, then lifts one index finger. We know from experience it means "See you later, have fun, don't talk to me anymore because I am getting some precious rest."

Notes

Notes

9. We walk up the hill to Marco Polo, where Dad gets spumoni and I get half mocha chip and half cinnamon. And we sit at an outside table . . . and talk. It's not like we have this deep father-daughter discussion or anything; he shares what's going on at work and I talk about what I still need to wrap up before moving across the Bay.

10. And I ask, "When you were in college, were you friends with your roommate?"

11. He shrugs. "Not particularly. Well, wait. There was one, sophomore year. Dale Greenwald. He was a good guy."

12. "Are you in touch anymore?"

13. "Oh, gosh. Haven't heard from Dale since graduation."

14. . . . . "Did you guys, like, agree about everything?"

15. He laughs. "No. He was more into the Grateful Dead than any thinking person should be."

16. "I don't mean about that stuff. I mean important stuff. "The meaning of life. Ethics and morals and sh . . . stuff."

17. "To be honest, it's hard to remember. We got along. I don't remember us fighting about anything." He stretches his legs out in front of him. . . . "Ethics and morals, huh? Do you have some deep thoughts about that?"

18. I shrug. . . . "Not really. Just kind of wondering what it would be like to live with someone who thinks about things in a totally different way than you do, you know? I've never exactly had a roommate who was capable of opinions much stronger than favorite color, or thoughts more profound than fairness in toy sharing."

19. "True, that."

20. Also I wonder about Dale Greenwald, and how he and my dad never talk. Is that the destiny of all friendships, no matter how good they are? To die out or fade away? To end? "Maybe if you'd had e-mail and stuff when you were in school you'd still be friends with Dale. I bet if you went on Facebook you'd find him in about two minutes."

21. Dad grimaces. "That could be fun for nostalgia purposes. But I've got your mom, and one or two good buddies. A person doesn't need much more than that. As you get older you tighten up that circle pretty well, I think."

22. One or two good buddies. And hopefully a partner or spouse. Zoe, whose self esteem sometimes seems governed by how many friends and followers she has online, wouldn't like that. But then maybe it doesn't matter that much how Zoe and I are different, or how Ebb and I may be.

23. "Zoe is my Dale, I guess."

24. He laughs. "Zoe is *not* your Dale, Hon. Zoe is your Thelma."

25. "Who?"

26. "*Thelma and Louise*?[1] Don't tell me Mom and I haven't made you watch that yet.

27. Great movie. The ending, though. . . I'm not saying that should be

---

1 *Thelma and Louise*: A movie about two female best friends who take a two-day road trip that ends dramatically and tragically.

a model of friendship for you. I only mean—"

28. I interrupt him before he goes on a whole big tangent. "Okay, maybe Zoe isn't my Dale. But I think I'm probably going to be friends with my roommate this fall and then she'll be my Dale. That's totally depressing."

29. "Forget about Dale," Dad says. "Live in the present. Take care of the relationships in front of you now. Most friendships have a natural life, and when they've lived that out, you'll know."

30. "It's still depressing."

31. He lifts his spoon to me in acquiescence as the L train rattles down the hill.

Notes

Source 6

from Grown Women Don't Need a 'Best Friend'

by Alice Robb

Notes

1. . . . . Data on "best-friendship" is hard to come by; it's only recently that friendship has become a serious topic of inquiry for sociologists, who traditionally focused more on romantic and familial ties. And, as Jan Yager, a sociologist who has been studying friendship since the 1970s, points out, many friendship studies fail to distinguish among degrees of friendship, conflating casual acquaintances and best friends in a single category. Yager's own research can offer some statistics: For her 1980 doctoral dissertation, "Friendship Patterns Among Young Urban Single Women," Yager interviewed 27 single women who lived alone on a single block of Manhattan's Upper East Side. Nearly all of them—24—had at least one "close friend," but just five could name one "best friend." . . .

2. [Anxieties] about best-friendship are regularly being aired. . . . In a 2011 book, *MWF Seeking BFF*, Rachel Bertsche documents what sounds like an exhausting quest to fill her need for a new best friend after following her boyfriend to Chicago. Some best friends, according to *The Daily Mail*, get couples counseling when they hit a rough patch. . . .

3. Sociologists confirm that women often do maintain more intense friendships than men. "Women have 'face-to-face' relationships where they confide in each other," said Rebecca Adams, a gerontological sociologist at the University of North Carolina at Greensboro and author of several books on friendship, including *Placing Friendship in Context*. "Men tend to have more 'side-by-side' relationships where they do activities together. They tend not to talk about things that reveal their weaknesses. That makes men

less worthy candidates for close friendship. Men tend to open up and confide more to women than to other men."

4. If "best friendship"—even just rhetorically—is on the rise, what does it mean? Psychologists across the board agree that relying on one person to fulfill all your emotional needs is unhealthy. . . . Labeling one friend as "the best" seems to combine the pressure and commitment of a monogamous relationship with few of the benefits. . . .

5. Having one all-consuming best friend may be more appropriate for children . . . than for adults. But psychologists have begun to re-examine the assumption that it's A-OK even for kids to have a best friend. . . . "I don't think it's particularly healthy for a child to rely on one friend," Timber Lake Camp director Jay Jacobs told *The New York Times* in 2010. "If something goes awry, it can be devastating. It also limits a child's ability to explore other options in the world." Last year, the headmaster of a London prep school told parents to discourage their children from seeking "best friends." He explained his stance to *The Daily Telegraph*: "It is much easier if they share friendships and have a wide range of good friends rather than obsessing too much about who their best friend is."

Notes

Chapter 16 Writing About Literature (W.11–12.9)

When you write a summary of a story, you briefly state the main idea and the important details. An analysis goes deeper by interpreting some aspects of it, such as characterization, figurative language, or plot. This chapter will focus on the following aspects of writing about literature.

16.1 Elements of literary analysis
16.2 Using evidence from sources
16.3 Writing a literary analysis

16.1 Elements of Literary Analysis

Review

A literary analysis requires you to study and write about specific elements of a work of literature. The chart below explains some commonly used literary devices found in stories and poems and how you might be asked to write about them in an essay.

Definitions of literary elements	A prompt may ask you to . . .
Author Point of View: The author's attitude toward the characters, events, etc.	• describe who (or what) is being satirized in the story.
Characterization: The manner in which characters are described and developed in a story	• trace the manner in which characters are introduced and developed. • analyze how character choices develop the plot and theme.
Narrative Point of View: The perspective from which a story is told	• explain how the narrative point of view impacts the reader's understanding of events and characters.
Plot: The events of the story	• describe how events build upon each other and reach a conclusion.
Structure: In fiction, the order in which events are presented. In poetry, the arrangement of lines, rhymes, etc.	• explain how the author's choices of where to begin or end a story supports the overall structure. • analyze how a comedic or tragic resolution impacts the reader.
Setting: Where and when the events of a story take place	• analyze how the setting influences the plot and the characters' choices.
Language: Word choice and figurative language	• analyze the impact of words and phrases on meaning and tone.
Theme: The message or central idea of a piece of literature	• describe how two or more themes interact and build upon each other.

Toolbox

The Three Types of Irony

Verbal irony is the difference between what is said and what is meant, often resulting in sarcasm. Example: "I'm really looking forward to going to the dentist today."

Dramatic irony is when the audience or reader knows something a character doesn't know. Example: Thinking Juliet is dead, Romeo kills himself. The audience knows, however, that Juliet is merely asleep.

Situational irony is the difference between what is expected and what actually happens. Example: In "Gift of the Magi," a husband pawns his pocket watch to buy combs for his wife's hair only to discover that she has cut her hair to buy him a watch chain.

As you read a work of literature, take notes about anything that strikes you. For example, underline words that describe characters or explain their feelings or motivations. Flag figurative language, unusual words, or changes of direction in the plot and comment about them in the margin. Use your notes to help you analyze the text.

Check Understanding

Directions: Read the following excerpt from Nathaniel Hawthorne's "The Minister's Black Veil." Then answer the questions that follow.

from The Minister's Black Veil

A Parable[1]

by Nathaniel Hawthorne

1. The sexton[2] stood in the porch of Milford meeting-house pulling lustily at the bell-rope. The old people of the village came stooping along the street. Children with bright faces tripped merrily beside their parents or mimicked a graver gait in the conscious dignity of their Sunday clothes. Spruce bachelors looked sidelong at the pretty maidens, and fancied that the Sabbath sunshine made them prettier than on week-days. When the throng had mostly streamed into

Notes

1 Another clergyman in New England, Mr. Joseph Moody, of York, Maine, who died about eighty years since, made himself remarkable by the same eccentricity that is here related of the Reverend Mr. Hooper. In his case, however, the symbol had a different import. In early life he had accidentally killed a beloved friend, and from that day till the hour of his own death he hid his face from men. [Hawthorne's note]

2 sexton: a church caretaker who is often in charge of ringing the bell and digging graves.

Notes

the porch, the sexton began to toll the bell, keeping his eye on the Reverend Mr. Hooper's door. The first glimpse of the clergyman's figure was the signal for the bell to cease its summons.

2. "But what has good Parson Hooper got upon his face?" cried the sexton, in astonishment.

3. All within hearing immediately turned about and beheld the semblance of Mr. Hooper pacing slowly his meditative way toward the meeting-house. With one accord they started, expressing more wonder than if some strange minister were coming to dust the cushions of Mr. Hooper's pulpit.

4. "Are you sure it is our parson?" inquired Goodman Gray of the sexton.

5. "Of a certainty it is good Mr. Hooper," replied the sexton. . . .

6. The cause of so much amazement may appear sufficiently slight. Mr. Hooper, a gentlemanly person of about thirty, though still a bachelor, was dressed with due clerical neatness, as if a careful wife had starched his band and brushed the weekly dust from his Sunday's garb. There was but one thing remarkable in his appearance. Swathed about his forehead and hanging down over his face, so low as to be shaken by his breath, Mr. Hooper had on a black veil. On a nearer view it seemed to consist of two folds of crape, which entirely concealed his features except the mouth and chin, but probably did not intercept his sight further than to give a darkened aspect to all living and inanimate things. With this gloomy shade before him, good Mr. Hooper walked onward at a slow and quiet pace, stooping somewhat and looking on the ground, as is customary with abstracted men, yet nodding kindly to those of his parishioners who still waited on the meeting-house steps. But so wonder-struck were they that his greeting hardly met with a return.

7. "I can't really feel as if good Mr. Hooper's face was behind that piece of crape," said the sexton.

8. "I don't like it," muttered an old woman as she hobbled into the meeting-house. "He has changed himself into something awful only by hiding his face."

9. "Our parson has gone mad!" cried Goodman Gray, following him across the threshold.

1. How does the author characterize Mr. Hooper? Point to details in the text.

____

____

____

____

2. How do the parishioners react to Mr. Hooper's wearing a veil?

____

____

____

____

____

Question 1 asks you how the author characterizes Mr. Hooper. Responses will vary. Here is a sample response:

> Mr. Hooper is characterized as "a gentlemanly person of about thirty" who is well dressed, "as if a careful wife had starched his band and brushed the weekly dust from his Sunday's garb." Except for the veil he wears, which causes consternation among his congregation, he is drawn as a sympathetic person who nods kindly to his parishioners (paragraph 6).

Question 2 asks you to explain how the parishioners react when they see Mr. Hooper wearing a black veil. Here is a sample response:

> The parishioners appear shocked when they see Mr. Hooper wearing the black veil. Several parishioners have no idea how to respond when Mr. Hooper nods to them. An old woman states that the minister "has changed himself into something awful only by hiding his face." Another parishioner even suggests that Mr. Hooper has descended into insanity. In short, the parishioners are shocked by the sight of the black veil on Mr. Hooper's face.

Try It

Directions: Read the excerpt from Hawthorne's "The Minister's Black Veil" and answer the questions that follow.

from The Minister's Black Veil

by Nathaniel Hawthorne

Notes

1. Mr. Hooper had the reputation of a good preacher, but not an energetic one: he strove to win his people heavenward by mild, persuasive influences rather than to drive them thither by the thunders of the word. The sermon which he now delivered was marked by the same characteristics of style and manner as the general series of his pulpit oratory, but there was something either in the sentiment of the discourse itself or in the imagination of the auditors which made it greatly the most powerful effort that they had ever heard from their pastor's lips. It was tinged rather more darkly than usual with the gentle gloom of Mr. Hooper's temperament. The subject had reference to secret sin and those sad mysteries which we hide from our nearest and dearest, and would fain conceal from our own consciousness, even forgetting that the Omniscient can detect them. . . .

2. At the close of the services the people hurried out with indecorous confusion, eager to communicate their pent-up amazement, and conscious of lighter spirits the moment they lost sight of the black

veil. Some gathered in little circles, huddled closely together, with their mouths all whispering in the center; some went homeward alone, wrapped in silent meditation; some talked loudly and profaned the Sabbath-day with ostentatious laughter. A few shook their sagacious heads, intimating that they could penetrate the mystery, while one or two affirmed that there was no mystery at all, but only that Mr. Hooper's eyes were so weakened by the midnight lamp as to require a shade.

3. After a brief interval forth came good Mr. Hooper also, in the rear of his flock. Turning his veiled face from one group to another, he paid due reverence to the hoary heads, saluted the middle-aged with kind dignity as their friend and spiritual guide, greeted the young with mingled authority and love, and laid his hands on the little children's heads to bless them. Such was always his custom on the Sabbath-day. Strange and bewildered looks repaid him for his courtesy. None, as on former occasions, aspired to the honor of walking by their pastor's side. Old Squire Saunders—doubtless by an accidental lapse of memory—neglected to invite Mr. Hooper to his table, where the good clergyman had been wont to bless the food almost every Sunday since his settlement. He returned, therefore, to the parsonage, and at the moment of closing the door was observed to look back upon the people, all of whom had their eyes fixed upon the minister. A sad smile gleamed faintly from beneath the black veil and flickered about his mouth, glimmering as he disappeared.

Notes

1. Cite at least one instance when a parishioner treats Mr. Hooper differently than usual.

____

____

____

2. Why does the minister smile sadly before he enters the parsonage? Share your response with a partner and discuss the smile's meaning.

____

____

____

____

____

____

16.2 Using Evidence from Sources

Review

Before you write an essay, you will be asked to read a selection of literature, such as an excerpt from a play or novel, or a short story or a poem. Watch for important details in the writing; underline key sentences that describe the characters and reveal the theme of the work.

If you are taking a writing assessment, you may be asked short answer or multiple-choice questions. You may be directed to identify or define key words or phrases, to write a brief summary, or to identify the theme. Answering these questions correctly will help you accurately interpret the literature.

> **Toolbox**
>
> **Draw Evidence from a Literary Text.** Writers indicate the key idea in their texts through the details they choose to include. If you can't support an idea with details from the text, then it probably isn't one of the text's themes or key ideas.

Check Understanding

Directions: Read the excerpt from William Faulkner's "A Rose for Emily" and answer the questions that follow.

Passage 1

from A Rose for Emily

by William Faulkner

In this scene, a group of aldermen of Jefferson meet with Miss Emily Grierson seeking back taxes. She believes that she is exempt from paying taxes based on an arrangement with a previous mayor, Colonel Sartoris.

1. . . . . They rose when she entered—a small, fat woman in black, with a thin gold chain descending to her waist and vanishing into her belt, leaning on an ebony cane with a tarnished gold head. Her skeleton was small and spare; perhaps that was why what would have been merely plumpness in another was obesity in her. She looked bloated, like a body long submerged in motionless water, and of that pallid hue. Her eyes, lost in the fatty ridges of her face, looked like two small pieces of coal pressed into a lump of dough as they moved from one face to another while the visitors stated their errand.

2. She did not ask them to sit. She just stood in the door and listened quietly until the spokesman came to a stumbling halt. Then they could hear the invisible watch ticking at the end of the gold chain.

3. Her voice was dry and cold. "I have no taxes in Jefferson. Colonel

Notes

Notes

Sartoris explained it to me. Perhaps one of you can gain access to the city records and satisfy yourselves."

4. "But we have. We are the city authorities, Miss Emily. Didn't you get a notice from the sheriff, signed by him?"

5. "I received a paper, yes," Miss Emily said. "Perhaps he considers himself the sheriff . . . I have no taxes in Jefferson."

6. "But there is nothing on the books to show that, you see. We must go by the—"

7. "See Colonel Sartoris. I have no taxes in Jefferson."

8. "But, Miss Emily—"

9. "See Colonel Sartoris." (Colonel Sartoris had been dead almost ten years.) "I have no taxes in Jefferson. Tobe!" The Negro appeared. "Show these gentlemen out."

1. In the second paragraph, the sound of the watch ticking emphasizes the men's feeling of—

Ⓐ composure. Ⓒ distrust.

Ⓑ self-assurance. Ⓓ discomfort.

2. Explain your answer to question 1 using evidence from the passage.

____

____

____

____

____

Question 1 asks you to identify what is emphasized by the narrator's description of the watch ticking. Choices A and B are incorrect. The men do not feel composed or self-assured—the spokesman has just come to a "stumbling halt" in his explanation of the reason for their visit. Choice C is incorrect because the passage does not provide any evidence that the men distrust Emily. The ticking watch serves to emphasize the men's feelings of growing discomfort. Choice D is correct.

Question 2 asks you to explain your answer to question 1 using evidence from the passage. Answers will vary. Here is a sample response:

> The gentlemen are experiencing discomfort. Their spokesman has just come "to a stumbling halt," suggesting that he feels unsure of himself in the face of Emily's stare. The silence in which they can hear the watch ticking serves to underscore the awkwardness of the situation. Emily's "dry and cold" response and their subsequent failed attempts to persuade her to pay taxes only accentuate their discomfort.

Try It

Directions: Read the excerpt below and answer the questions that follow.

Passage 2

from A Rose for Emily

by William Faulkner

Notes

1. . . . . When her father died, it got about that the house was all that was left to her; and in a way, people were glad. At last they could pity Miss Emily. Being left alone, and a pauper, she had become humanized. Now she too would know the old thrill and the old despair of a penny more or less.

2. The day after his death all the ladies prepared to call at the house and offer condolence and aid, as is our custom. Miss Emily met them at the door, dressed as usual and with no trace of grief on her face. She told them that her father was not dead. She did that for three days, with the ministers calling on her, and the doctors, trying to persuade her to let them dispose of the body. Just as they were about to resort to law and force, she broke down, and they buried her father quickly.

3. We did not say she was crazy then. We believed she had to do that. We remembered all the young men her father had driven away, and we knew that with nothing left, she would have to cling to that which had robbed her, as people will.

1. Explain the meaning of the narrator's statement "we knew that with nothing left, she would have to cling to that which had robbed her."

____

____

____

2. Compare and contrast how the townspeople feel about Emily and how Emily feels about them. Use evidence from the text to support your answer and then compare your answer with a partner.

____

____

____

____

____

____

____

16.3 Writing a Literary Analysis

Review

In a testing situation, you will be presented with a prompt and a piece of literature. The prompt will direct you to analyze one or more specific elements of the text, such as its theme, the development of its characters, or the author's point of view, and to use evidence from the text to support your analysis. The process can be broken down into the following manageable tasks.

Step 1—Understand the prompt: The directions for writing an essay are called the *prompt*. The verbs in a prompt tell you what to do. Here is an example:

> "A Rose for Emily" is told from the perspective of the townspeople of Jefferson. Analyze how this point of view influences the structure of the story. Include specific evidence from the text to support your ideas.

Key Terms

citation: a reference to the source of borrowed material, usually inside parentheses after the borrowed text.

literary present tense: the practice of referring to events in creative works in present tense even when the events are presented in past tense in the work itself.

Step 2—Take notes: As you read and reread the literature, underline important passages and write notes in the margin. For the prompt above, you would highlight details that reveal the narrative point of view and compose some initial thoughts on how the point of view influences the structure of the story.

Step 3—Write a thesis statement: After gathering notes, write a thesis statement. The thesis statement should clearly state the central idea of your analysis. It will guide your writing, so make sure it addresses the prompt and your notes.

Step 4—Organize your ideas: Next, think about how you will organize your analysis, keeping in mind the main parts of any essay: introduction, body, and conclusion. The introduction should include the title and author of the text as well as your thesis statement. In the body, develop your interpretation by selecting and citing the most significant and relevant details. Devote at least one paragraph to each main aspect of your analysis. The conclusion of the essay brings the writing together in a satisfying way.

Step 5—Write the essay: Include appropriate transitions so that the writing flows logically. Also remember to use **literary present tense** when writing about literature.

Step 6—Revise your essay: After you write a draft, revise it to make the content more specific, the ideas more clear, and the writing more smooth. Also make sure you have documented **citations** according to the style indicated in the prompt.

Toolbox

Narrative Point of View. Three main narrative points of view:

First-person point of view: a character in the story narrates the events. When referring to him- or herself, the narrator uses the pronouns "I," "me," "my," and (rarely) "we" (first-person plural).

Third-person limited point of view: a narrator outside the story relates the events from the limited perspective of a main character.

Third-person omniscient point of view: an outside narrator who has access to multiple characters' thoughts.

Check Understanding

Directions: Read the excerpt from William Faulkner's "A Rose for Emily" and answer the questions that follow.

Passage 3

	Notes

from A Rose for Emily

by William Faulkner

1. . . . . When she had first begun to be seen with Homer Barron, we had said, "She will marry him." Then we said, "She will persuade him yet," because Homer himself had remarked—he liked men, and it was known that he drank with the younger men in the Elks' Club—that he was not a marrying man. Later we said, "Poor Emily" behind the jalousies[1] as they passed on Sunday afternoon in the glittering buggy, Miss Emily with her head high and Homer Barron with his hat cocked and a cigar in his teeth, reins and whip in a yellow glove.

2. Then some of the ladies began to say that it was a disgrace to the town and a bad example to the young people. The men did not want to interfere, but at last the ladies forced the Baptist minister—Miss Emily's people were Episcopal—to call upon her. He would never divulge what happened during that interview, but he refused to go back again. The next Sunday they again drove about the streets, and the following day the minister's wife wrote to Miss Emily's relations in Alabama.

3. So she had blood-kin under her roof again and we sat back to watch developments. At first nothing happened. Then we were sure that they were to be married. We learned that Miss Emily had been to the jeweler's and ordered a man's toilet set in silver, with the letters H. B. on each piece. Two days later we learned that she had bought a complete outfit of men's clothing, including a nightshirt, and we said, "They are married." We were really glad. We were glad because the two female cousins were even more Grierson than Miss Emily had ever been.

---

1 jalousies: slatted window coverings

1. What is the point of view used in the passage?

   Ⓐ first person

   Ⓑ second person

   Ⓒ third-person limited

   Ⓓ third-person omniscient

2. From whose perspective is the story told?

____

____

____

____

Question 1 asks you to identify the point of view used in the passage. The passage features pronouns such as "she," "him," and "they." But the narrator, through the use of the pronouns "we" and "us," appears to be one of the townspeople reporting the news about Emily Grierson as it comes to light. Choice A, first person, is correct.

Question 2 asks you to explain from whose perspective the story is told. Answers will vary. Here is a sample response:

> The narrator is not named in the passage, but he or she appears to be a member of the community. The narrator uses the pronoun "we" often to indicate how the townspeople as a collective felt about Emily: "we sat back to watch developments." Like most of the people of Jefferson, the narrator is keenly interested in gossip and town events.

Toolbox

Organizing a Literary Analysis. A literary analysis may be organized several different ways. Here are three examples.

Comparison/Contrast: When dealing with more than one selection, describe the similarities of the texts and/or the differences between them.

Chronological Order: Use this structure when writing a summary, a plot analysis. Organize examples from the start of the story to the conclusion.

Order of Importance: Use this structure when writing about word choice or theme. Organize examples in order of importance (usually from least to most important).

Test-Taking Tips

Revision Tips. Check the content of your essay by asking yourself the following questions:

- Does my essay have a clear thesis or central idea?
- Does each part of my essay support my thesis?
- Does my writing provide enough evidence to support my conclusions?
- Is my supporting evidence relevant and specific?
- Is the style and tone of my writing appropriate for the audience and purpose?

Try It

Directions: Read the excerpt from William Faulkner's "A Rose for Emily" and answer the questions that follow.

Passage 4

from A Rose for Emily

by William Faulkner

	Notes
1. . . . . So we were not surprised when Homer Barron—the streets had been finished some time since—was gone. We were a little disappointed that there was not a public blowing-off, but we believed that he had gone on to prepare for Miss Emily's coming, or to give her a chance to get rid of the cousins. (By that time it was a cabal, and we were all Miss Emily's allies to help circumvent the cousins.) Sure enough, after another week they departed. And, as we had expected all along, within three days Homer Barron was back in town. A neighbor saw the Negro man admit him at the kitchen door at dusk one evening.	
2. And that was the last we saw of Homer Barron. And of Miss Emily for some time. The Negro man went in and out with the market basket, but the front door remained closed. Now and then we would see her at a window for a moment, as the men did that night when they sprinkled the lime, but for almost six months she did not appear on the streets. Then we knew that this was to be expected too; as if that quality of her father which had thwarted her woman's life so many times had been too virulent and too furious to die.	
3. When we next saw Miss Emily, she had grown fat and her hair was turning gray. During the next few years it grew grayer and grayer until it attained an even pepper-and-salt iron-gray, when it ceased turning. Up to the day of her death at seventy-four it was still that vigorous iron-gray, like the hair of an active man.	

Prompt: Write a paragraph describing how the narrator portrays the passage of time in this excerpt. Support your ideas using evidence from the passage. Share your response with a partner.

Chapter Review

Directions: Closely read the last section of "A Rose for Emily" (Passage 5 on page 295) and write a literary analysis on the topic below. Write your essay on separate paper. Feel free to read and refer to the other passages from "A Rose for Emily" included in this chapter.

Topic

An author's choice of narrative point of view is vital to the story. The point of view is a window through which readers see a story's events; it can evoke surprise, generate amusement, or create suspense. Focusing on the last section of the story below, analyze the narrative point of view in "A Rose for Emily" and the effect it has on the story.

Your Task

Carefully read the last section of "A Rose for Emily" (Passage 5 on page 295). Then write a well-developed literary essay analyzing how the point of view influences the story. Support your ideas with specific and relevant evidence from the excerpts. Feel free to read and refer to the other passages from "A Rose for Emily" included in this chapter.

Guidelines

Be sure to—

- establish your thesis regarding how the point of view influences the story.
- use specific, relevant, and sufficient evidence to develop your ideas.
- organize your ideas in a logical manner.
- maintain a formal writing style and objective tone.
- follow the conventions of standard written English.
- identify each passage that you reference by passage number and paragraph number(s). (For example: Passage 5, paragraph 4.)

Planning Notes

Passage 5

Notes

from A Rose for Emily

by William Faulkner

1. The Negro met the first of the ladies at the front door and let them in, with their hushed, sibilant voices and their quick, curious glances, and then he disappeared. He walked right through the house and out the back and was not seen again.

2. The two female cousins came at once. They held the funeral on the second day, with the town coming to look at Miss Emily beneath a mass of bought flowers, with the crayon face of her father musing profoundly above the bier and the ladies sibilant and macabre; and the very old men—some in their brushed Confederate uniforms—on the porch and the lawn, talking of Miss Emily as if she had been a contemporary of theirs, believing that they had danced with her and courted her perhaps, confusing time with its mathematical progression, as the old do, to whom all the past is not a diminishing road but, instead, a huge meadow which no winter ever quite touches, divided from them now by the narrow bottle-neck of the most recent decade of years.

3. Already we knew that there was one room in that region above stairs which no one had seen in forty years, and which would have to be forced. They waited until Miss Emily was decently in the ground before they opened it.

4. The violence of breaking down the door seemed to fill this room with pervading dust. A thin, acrid pall as of the tomb seemed to lie everywhere upon this room decked and furnished as for a bridal: upon the valance curtains of faded rose color, upon the rose-shaded lights, upon the dressing table, upon the delicate array of crystal and the man's toilet things backed with tarnished silver, silver so tarnished that the monogram was obscured. Among them lay a collar and tie, as if they had just been removed, which, lifted, left upon the surface a pale crescent in the dust. Upon a chair hung the suit, carefully folded; beneath it the two mute shoes and the discarded socks.

5. The man himself lay in the bed.

6. For a long while we just stood there, looking down at the profound and fleshless grin. The body had apparently once lain in the attitude of an embrace, but now the long sleep that outlasts love, that conquers even the grimace of love, had cuckolded him. What was left of him, rotted beneath what was left of the nightshirt, had become inextricable from the bed in which he lay; and upon him and upon the pillow beside him lay that even coating of the patient and biding dust.

7. Then we noticed that in the second pillow was the indentation of a head. One of us lifted something from it, and leaning forward, that faint and invisible dust dry and acrid in the nostrils, we saw a long strand of iron-gray hair.

Practice Test 1

Part I

Reading Comprehension

Questions 1–24: The story, poem, and nonfiction passage below are each followed by several multiple-choice questions. Read each selection closely. Then, for each question, select the best answer from the choices given. You may use the margins to take notes as you read.

Selection 1

The Far and the Near

by Thomas Wolfe

1. On the outskirts of a little town upon a rise of land that swept back from the railway there was a tidy little cottage of white boards, trimmed vividly with green blinds. To one side of the house there was a garden neatly patterned with plots of growing vegetables, and an arbor for the grapes which ripened late in August. Before the house there were three mighty oaks which sheltered it in their clean and massive shade in summer, and to the other side there was a border of gay flowers. The whole place had an air of tidiness, thrift, and modest comfort.

2. Every day, a few minutes after two o'clock in the afternoon, the limited express[1] between two cities passed this spot. At that moment the great train, having halted for a breathing space at the town nearby, was beginning to lengthen evenly into its stroke, but it had not yet reached the full drive of its terrific speed. It swung into view deliberately, swept past with a powerful swaying motion of the engine, a low smooth rumble of its heavy cars upon pressed steel, and then it vanished in the cut.[2] For a moment the progress of the engine could be marked by heavy bellowing puffs of smoke that burst at spaced intervals above the edges of the meadow grass, and finally nothing could be heard but the solid clacking tempo of the wheels receding into the drowsy stillness of the afternoon.

3. Every day for more than twenty years, as the train had approached this house, the engineer had blown on the whistle, and every day, as soon as she heard this signal, a woman had appeared on the back porch of the little house and waved to him. At first she had a small child clinging to her skirts, and now this child had grown to full womanhood, and every day she, too, came with her mother to the porch and waved.

4. The engineer had grown old and gray in service. He had driven his great train, loaded with its weight of lives, across the land ten thousand times. His own children had grown up, and married, and four times he had seen before him on the tracks the ghastly dot of tragedy converging like a cannon ball to its eclipse of horror at the boiler head[3]—a light spring wagon filled with children, with its clustered row of

1 limited express: rapid train making few stops between major cities

2 cut: dug-out passage or roadway, in this case for the train

3 boiler head: front section of a steam locomotive

small stunned faces; a cheap automobile stalled up the tracks, set with the wooden figures of people paralyzed with fear; a battered hobo walking by the rail, too deaf and old to hear the whistle's warning; and a form flung past his window with a scream—all this he had seen and known. He had known all the grief, the joy, the peril and the labor such a man could know; he had grown seamed and weathered in his loyal service, and now, schooled by the qualities of faith and courage and humbleness that attended his labor, he had grown old, and had the grandeur and the wisdom these men have.

5. But no matter what peril or tragedy he had known, the vision of the little house and the women waving to him with a brave free motion of the arm had become fixed in the mind of the engineer as something beautiful and enduring, something beyond all change and ruin, and something that would always be the same, no matter what mishap, grief or error might break the iron schedule of his days.

6. The sight of this little house and these two women gave him the most extraordinary happiness he had ever known. He had seen them in a thousand lights, a hundred weathers. He had seen them through the harsh light of wintry gray across the brown and frosted stubble of the earth, and he had seen them again in the green luring sorcery of April.

7. He felt for them and for the little house in which they lived such tenderness as a man might feel for his own children, and at length the picture of their lives was carved so sharply in his heart that he felt that he knew their lives completely, to every hour and moment of the day, and he resolved that one day, when his years of service should be ended, he would go and find these people and speak at last with them whose lives had been so wrought into his own.

8. That day came. At last the engineer stepped from a train onto the station platform of the town where these two women lived. His years upon the rail had ended. He was a pensioned servant of his company, with no more work to do. The engineer walked slowly through the station and out into the streets of the town. Everything was as strange to him as if he had never seen this town before. As he walked on, his sense of bewilderment and confusion grew. Could this be the town he had passed ten thousand times? Were these the same houses he had seen so often from the high windows of his cab?[4] It was all as unfamiliar, as disquieting as a city in a dream, and the perplexity of his spirit increased as he went on.

9. Presently the houses thinned into the straggling outposts of the town, and the street faded into a country road—the one on which the women lived. And the man plodded on slowly in the heat and dust. At length he stood before the house he sought. He knew at once that he had found the proper place. He saw the lordly oaks before the house, the flower beds, the garden and the arbor, and farther off, the glint of rails.

10. Yes, this was the house he sought, the place he had passed so many times, the destination he had longed for with such happiness. But now that he had found it, now that he was here, why did his hand falter on the gate; why had the town, the road, the earth, the very entrance to this place he loved turned unfamiliar as the landscape of some ugly dream? Why did he now feel this sense of confusion, doubt and hopelessness? At length he entered by the gate, walked slowly up the path and in a moment more had mounted three short steps that led up to the porch, and was knocking at the door. Presently he heard steps in the hall, the door was opened, and a woman stood facing him.

11. And instantly, with a sense of bitter loss and grief, he was sorry he had come. He

---

4 cab: part of a locomotive in which the engineer sits

knew at once that the woman who stood there looking at him with a mistrustful eye was the same woman who had waved to him so many thousand times. But her face was harsh and pinched and meager; the flesh sagged wearily in sallow folds, and the small eyes peered at him with timid suspicion and uneasy doubt. All the brave freedom, the warmth and the affection that he had read into her gesture, vanished in the moment that he saw her and heard her unfriendly tongue.

12. And now his own voice sounded unreal and ghastly to him as he tried to explain his presence, to tell her who he was and the reason he had come. But he faltered on, fighting stubbornly against the horror of regret, confusion, disbelief that surged up in his spirit, drowning all his former joy and making his act of hope and tenderness seem shameful to him.

13. At length the woman invited him almost unwillingly into the house, and called her daughter in a harsh shrill voice. Then, for a brief agony of time, the man sat in an ugly little parlor, and he tried to talk while the two women stared at him with a dull, bewildered hostility, a sullen, timorous restraint.

14. And finally, stammering a crude farewell, he departed. He walked away down the path and then along the road toward town, and suddenly he knew that he was an old man. His heart, which had been brave and confident when it looked along the familiar vista of the rails, was now sick with doubt and horror as it saw the strange and unsuspected visage of an earth which had always been within a stone's throw of him, and which he had never seen or known. And he knew that all the magic of that bright lost way, the vista of that shining line, the imagined corner of that small good universe of hope's desire, could never be got again.

1. What is the main purpose of the story's first paragraph?

   Ⓐ to provide exposition about the story's setting

   Ⓑ to pique readers' curiosity by opening *in medias res*

   Ⓒ foreshadow the ending of the story

   Ⓓ introduce the narrator to readers

2. In the first paragraph, what does the author's choice of language serve to emphasize about the cottage?

   Ⓐ its majestic grandeur

   Ⓑ its isolated location

   Ⓒ its cozy, attractive appearance

   Ⓓ its mystery

3. What impression of the woman and her daughter do we get when they are introduced in the third paragraph?

   Ⓐ They are bored and boring.

   Ⓑ They are friendly and cheerful.

   Ⓒ They are tired and hard-working.

   Ⓓ They are idealistic and noble.

4. In the fourth paragraph, what do the explicit details and their implications suggest about the engineer's attitude toward his job?

   Ⓐ He enjoys the variety his job provides and wishes he could continue working forever.

   Ⓑ He dislikes most things about his job and cannot wait to retire.

   Ⓒ He is overworked, and his exhaustion has led to accidents.

   Ⓓ He is a dedicated worker who takes his responsibilities very seriously.

5. In the fourth paragraph, to what does the figurative phrase "the ghastly dot of tragedy converging like a cannon ball to its eclipse of horror at the boiler head" refer?

Ⓐ fate

Ⓑ the smoke coming out of the train

Ⓒ a train accident

Ⓓ the disappointment the engineer will experience later

6. In the fifth paragraph, what tone does the author convey in describing the significance the cottage has for the engineer?

Ⓐ an informal, intimate tone

Ⓑ a lyrical, lofty tone

Ⓒ a clever, witty tone

Ⓓ a charming, whimsical tone

7. Which of these quotations from the story best reveals the irony of the engineer's visit to the cottage?

Ⓐ All the brave freedom, the warmth and the affection that he had read into her gesture, vanished in the moment that he saw her and hear her unfriendly tongue.

Ⓑ And now his own voice sounded unreal and ghastly to him as he tried to explain his presence, to tell her who he was and the reason he had come.

Ⓒ And finally, stammering a crude farewell, he departed.

Ⓓ He walked away down the path and then along the road toward town, and suddenly he knew that he was an old man.

8. What chief flaw in the engineer leads to the tragic resolution of the story?

Ⓐ lack of respect for the privacy of others

Ⓑ failure to appreciate his own family

Ⓒ excessive faith in hopes and dreams

Ⓓ excessive devotion to duty

9. Which of these sayings best expresses one of the main themes of the story?

Ⓐ Don't judge a book by its cover.

Ⓑ People in glass houses shouldn't throw stones.

Ⓒ A bird in the hand is worth two in the bush.

Ⓓ Beauty is in the eyes of the beholder.

10. What additional theme do the story's last two sentences most clearly convey?

Ⓐ The human heart is often a mystery.

Ⓑ Life's disappointments can be devastating.

Ⓒ We all hope for a brighter future.

Ⓓ It is hard to retire from a job you love.

Selection 2

A Winter Night

by Sara Teasdale

My window-pane is starred with frost,
The world is bitter cold tonight,
The moon is cruel, and the wind
Is like a two-edged sword to smite.[1]

God pity all the homeless ones,
The beggars pacing to and fro,
God pity all the poor tonight
Who walk the lamp-lit streets of snow.

My room is like a bit of June,
Warm and close-curtained fold on fold,
But somewhere, like a homeless child,
My heart is crying in the cold.

---

1 smite: strike

11. What does the simile in line 4 stress about the wind?

Ⓐ its sudden, biting strength

Ⓑ its icy chill

Ⓒ its random nature

Ⓓ its persistence over a long period of time

12. How does the structural relationship between the second and third stanzas help convey the poem's meaning?

Ⓐ In the cause-and-effect relationship of the two stanzas, stanza 2 explains the cause of the sorrow that the speaker expresses in stanza 3.

Ⓑ In the problem-and-solution relationship of the two stanzas, stanza 2 describes the problem of homelessness and stanza 3 offers a way to solve it.

Ⓒ In the chronological relationship of the two stanzas, stanza 2 recounts an event and stanza 3 tells what happened next.

Ⓓ In the comparison-and-contrast relationship of the two stanzas, stanza 2 describes the plight of people out in the night and stanza 3 shows how the speaker is like and unlike them.

13. Which of these sentences provides the best objective summary of the poem?

Ⓐ The speaker has sympathy for the homeless who suffer on a cold, windy night, for she too suffers, even though her room is warm.

Ⓑ The speaker foolishly thinks that she suffers like homeless people on a cold, windy night, even though she is safe and warm indoors.

Ⓒ On a windy winter night, it is safer to be in a warm room like the speaker than to be out in the cold like homeless people are.

Ⓓ Everyone needs shelter from the cold, whether it is physical or spiritual.

14. What tone do the commands in lines 5–8 and the figurative language in lines 11–12 help convey?

Ⓐ an angry tone

Ⓑ a nostalgic tone

Ⓒ an anguished tone

Ⓓ a mysterious tone

15. Although you can draw several inferences from the poem's details, what one thing does the text leave most uncertain?

Ⓐ the time of year that the poem describes

Ⓑ the speaker's attitude toward homeless people

Ⓒ the speaker's feelings in the third stanza

Ⓓ the reason for the speaker's unhappiness

16. Which statement best analyzes the impact of the poem's structure?

Ⓐ By describing how she feels about others in stanzas 1 and 2, the speaker makes readers more sympathetic to her own plight in stanza 3.

Ⓑ By describing a harsh setting in stanza 1 and the people suffering in it in stanza 2, the speaker helps readers understand her own suffering in stanza 3.

Ⓒ By opening with a stanza about a harsh winter night, the speaker helps readers accept the need to show understanding and sympathy for others in stanzas 2 and 3.

Ⓓ By describing a cold night in stanza 1 and the people out in it in stanza 2, the speaker helps us understand the contrasting contentment she feels in stanza 3.

Selection 3

The Gettysburg Address

by Abraham Lincoln

The Battle of Gettysburg took place near Gettysburg, Pennsylvania, in July of 1863. Although it ended in a Union victory and marked the turning point of the American Civil War, it was also a very costly battle in terms of deaths and injuries. On November 19, 1863, President Abraham Lincoln attended the dedication of the battlefield cemetery and spoke these famous words.

1. Four score[1] and seven years ago, our fathers brought forth upon this continent a new nation: conceived in liberty, and dedicated to the proposition that all men are created equal.

2. Now we are engaged in a great civil war, testing whether that nation, or any nation so conceived and so dedicated, can long endure. We are met on a great battlefield of that war. We have come to dedicate a portion of that field as a final resting place for those who here gave their lives that this nation might live. It is altogether fitting and proper that we should do this.

3. But, in a larger sense, we cannot dedicate—we cannot consecrate—we cannot hallow this ground. The brave men, living and dead, who struggled here have consecrated it, far above our poor power to add or detract. The world will little note, nor long remember, what we say here, but it can never forget what they did here. It is for us the living, rather, to be dedicated here to the unfinished work which they who fought here have thus far so nobly advanced. It is rather for us to be here dedicated to the great task remaining before us—that from these honored dead we take increased devotion to that cause for which they gave the last full measure of devotion—that we here highly resolve that these dead shall not have died in vain—that this nation, under God, shall have a new birth of freedom—and that government of the people, by the people, for the people, shall not perish from this earth.

1 score: twenty years

17. What overall structure does the speech use?

Ⓐ chronological (past, present, future)

Ⓑ sequential (first, second, third)

Ⓒ argumentative (claim supported by evidence)

Ⓓ spatial (foreground to background)

18. Which of these sentences or clauses further develops the main idea expressed in Lincoln's opening paragraph?

Ⓐ We are met on a great battlefield of that war.

Ⓑ The brave men, living and dead, who struggled here have consecrated it, far above our poor power to add or detract.

Ⓒ It is for us the living, rather, to be dedicated here to the unfinished work which they who fought here have thus far so nobly advanced.

Ⓓ . . . and that government of the people, by the people, for the people, shall not perish from this earth.

19. Which words further refine the meaning of the word *dedicate* at the start of the third paragraph?

Ⓐ *consecrate* and *hallow*

Ⓑ *add* and *detract*

Ⓒ *poor* and *power*

Ⓓ *living* and *dead*

20. From the details in the speech, what inference can be drawn about Lincoln's meaning when he refers to "unfinished work" in the last paragraph?

Ⓐ He means the digging of the final graves in the cemetery.

Ⓑ He means the additional speeches that need to be given at the ceremony.

Ⓒ He means the American Civil War, which still must be fought and won.

Ⓓ He means the jobs and families the soldiers left behind when they went off to war.

21. What does Lincoln's figurative language mean when he speaks of the honored dead giving their "last full measure of devotion"?

Ⓐ He means that their sacrifice cannot be measured.

Ⓑ He means that their lives were full.

Ⓒ He means that the ceremony honoring them is accompanied by music.

Ⓓ He means that they died showing their devotion to the nation.

22. What is the main effect of Lincoln's frequent use of parallel structure as a rhetorical device?

Ⓐ It helps make causes and effects clearer.

Ⓑ It helps display his eloquent vocabulary.

Ⓒ It interrupts the steady rhythm of his words, which would otherwise grow monotonous.

Ⓓ It helps make his words more powerful and memorable.

23. What are Lincoln's two chief purposes in making the speech?

Ⓐ to honor the dead and to pay tribute to America's founding fathers

Ⓑ to honor the dead and to encourage continued support of the war

Ⓒ to pay tribute to America's founding fathers and to show how their principles still apply

Ⓓ to explain the principles on which America was founded and to show how those principles still apply

24. Which two ideas or values are central to Lincoln's message?

Ⓐ the patriotic self-sacrifice of the soldiers and the democratic values for which they fought

Ⓑ the bravery of the soldiers and the security of the nation

Ⓒ the memorable courage of the soldiers and Lincoln's humble opinion that no words could do them justice

Ⓓ the courage of America's founding fathers and the democratic values they helped establish

Part II

Writing from Sources: Argument

Directions: Closely read each of the five source documents provided on pages 305 through 310 and write a source-based argument on the topic below. You may write notes in the margin as you read. Write your argument on separate paper.

Topic

Should companies be allowed to advertise prescription drugs directly to consumers?

Your Task

Carefully read each of the six source documents provided. Then write a well-developed argument, asserting a claim on the topic of the advertisement of prescription drugs. Address at least one counterclaim. Support your ideas with specific and relevant evidence from at least four of the source documents.

Guidelines

Be sure to—

- Establish your claim on the advertisement of prescription drugs to consumers.
- Evaluate the sources to identify any possible biases.
- Address at least one counterclaim.
- Use specific, relevant, and sufficient evidence from at least four of the sources to develop your argument.
- Identify the source that you reference by source document number and paragraph number(s) (for example: Source 1, paragraph 4).
- Organize your ideas in a logical manner.
- Maintain a formal writing style and objective tone.
- Follow the conventions of standard written English.

Texts

Source 1 (p. 305)	*from* Testimony to the US Senate Special Committee on Aging" presented by The American College of Physicians
Source 2 (p. 306)	from *Annals of Family Medicine,* editorial by Kurt C. Stange, MD, PhD
Source 3 (p. 307)	*from* "Maybe It's Time for Drug Companies to Drop TV Ads" by John LaMattina
Source 4 (p. 308)	*from* "Direct to Consumer Prescription Drug Advertising Builds Bridges Between Patients and Physicians" by Alan F. Holmer, JD, Director of Inspire Pharmaceuticals Inc.
Source 5 (pp. 309–310)	*from* "Direct-to-Consumer Pharmaceutical Advertising: Therapeutic or Toxic?" by C. Lee Ventola, MS

Source 1

from Testimony to the US Senate Special Committee on Aging

by The American College of Physicians

1. Since 1998, ACP has been opposed to the practice of DTC [Direct to Consumer] advertising, which often leaves our patients confused and misinformed about medications. It undermines the patient-physician relationship and impedes the practice of medicine by challenging the individual physician's medical judgment . . . .

2. Consider the toenail ad, my personal favorite. While I am trying to tell a senior that it is not life-threatening; that there really aren't little creatures with horns, legs, and arms under their toenails, living in sofas and chairs; that the drug is quite expensive; and that the risks of toxicity are significant and that it may not work, I lose valuable time that could have been directed at the underlying reason they have those toenails—their diabetes, their vascular disease, their cholesterol, their overall health . . . .

3. ACP would prefer to see Congress ban DTC advertising because it does not constitute appropriate patient education.

Source: Statement of the American College of Physicians to the Senate Special Committee on Aging for the Record of The Hearing on the Impact of Direct-to-Consumer Advertising on Seniors' Health and Health Care Costs. September 29, 2005.

Source 2

from Editorial, *Annals of Family Medicine*

by Kurt C. Stange, MD, PhD

1. It is time to ban direct-to-consumer (DTC) advertising of prescription drugs. The current US system of pharmaceutical company self-monitoring and Food and Drug Administration oversight is not working. Moreover, it cannot realistically be expected to work. A ban is needed to protect the public's health and the quality of healthcare . . . .

2. DTC ads manipulate the patient's agenda and steal precious time away from an evidence-based primary care clinician agenda that is attempting to promote healthy behavior, screen for early-stage treatable disease, and address mental health.

3. . . . . Discussing why the advertised drug is not the best option for a particular patient may mean that a mammogram is not ordered, an important health behavior is not discussed, a family matter is not brought up . . . The clinician is put in the role of gatekeeper for the advertised commodity rather than a gateway for prioritizing health care based on the concerns of patients and the science-based recommendations for preventative, chronic disease, mental health, and family care . . . .

4. Only a ban will work. The impossibility of regulating complex overt and covert multichannel messages with both rational and emotional appeals, the power imbalance between the public good and the commercial imperative, the difficulty of anticipating ads' unintended consequences, and the availability of less-biased sources of information and motivation all argue for totally proscribing DTC ads.

Source: Kurt C. Stange, "Time to Ban Direct-to-Consumer Prescription Drug Marketing," *Annals of Family Medicine*, 2007 5:101–104.

Source 3

from Maybe It's Time for Drug Companies to Drop TV Ads

by John LaMattina

1. . . . while I was a part of big pharma, I was sympathetic towards these ads. The justification for direct-to-consumer advertising has been focused on patient education. The stated goal has been to provide patients with information about new medicines and treatments for diseases that were previously untreatable. Furthermore, it is believed that advertising encourages patients to open a dialogue with their doctors about medical conditions and illnesses – communication that might not have previously existed. . . .

2. But the negatives that have evolved from TV ads are starting to outweigh the intended benefits. First of all, many consumers find the commercials offensive, pointing specifically to ads for erectile dysfunction. As a result, the FDA requires that, in terms of content and placement, television advertisements should be targeted to avoid audiences that are not age-appropriate for the messages involved. I am not sure that this is the type of aura that the industry wants around its image. Second, the intent and implication of these ads has come under particular scrutiny recently. A few years ago, Pfizer used Dr. Robert Jarvik, the inventor of the artificial heart, as a Lipitor spokesperson. Dr. Jarvik was, in fact, a Lipitor user. But critics attacked Pfizer for using Dr. Jarvik as an advocate for Lipitor, because it was felt that consumers would mistakenly believe that Dr. Jarvik is a cardiologist. . . . Did the negative publicity that arose from this incident justify having the TV ad? Probably not.

3. Another issue with these ads is the litany of side-effects that a manufacturer must disclose in order to comply with FDA advertising guidelines. After listening to all of the potential toleration issues that one may get from the drug, it is a wonder that anyone would want to try it. . . .

4. Finally, people believe that companies spend billions of dollars on the TV ads, money that could be better spent on R&D. In fact, some have the mistaken belief that more money is spent on direct-to-consumer advertising than on R&D. For the record, according to Nielsen TV, ad spending by the pharmaceutical industry was $2.4 billion in 2011. The amount spent by the industry on R&D was at least 30 times that amount. Nevertheless, this misconception only serves to continue the negative view that the public has to these ads.

5. If the pharmaceutical industry is really concerned about being better valued by the public, it might do well to drop TV ads completely. However well-intended they are, the negatives have always outweighed the benefits. If the members of the Pharmaceutical Research and Manufacturers Association agreed to halt TV ads, my guess is that the public's response would be overwhelmingly positive. My sense is that they wouldn't miss the commercials either.

Source: John LaMattina, "Maybe It's Time for Drug Companies to Drop TV Ads," *Forbes*, February 15, 2012.

Source 4

from Direct to Consumer Prescription Drug Advertising Builds Bridges Between Patients and Physicians

Alan F. Holmer, JD, Director of Inspire Pharmaceuticals Inc.

1. Direct-to-consumer (DTC) advertising is an excellent way to meet the growing demand for medical information, empowering consumers by educating them about health conditions and possible treatments. By so doing, it can play an important role in improving public health...
2. Direct-to-consumer advertising that encourages millions of Americans to consult their physicians can help to improve public health because a number of leading diseases are under diagnosed and under-treated...
3. Direct-to-consumer advertising is a highly effective way to communicate the availability of treatments to the public. In 1992, the first DTC consumer television advertisement for a nicotine patch aired during the Super Bowl. According to the American Association of Advertising Agencies (AAAA), the public response was so great that, within weeks, demand for the patches exceeded the supply. The product had been available for months, but people who might have been interested in quitting smoking were simply not aware of it.
4. Advertising promoted widespread awareness overnight, prompted patient-physician conversations, and may have helped many people to stop smoking.
5. Pharmaceutical companies have both a right and a responsibility to inform people about their products under the supervision of the FDA, which regulates prescription drug advertising. Companies are committed to responsible advertising that enhances the patient-physician relationship and encourages the appropriate use of prescription drugs under a physician's supervision. While such advertising prompts more people to seek professional help, it does not dictate the outcome of the physician visit or the kind of help patients eventually receive.
6. Direct-to-consumer advertising merely motivates patients to learn more about medical conditions and treatment options and to consult their physicians.

Source: Alan F. Holmer, JD, "Direct-to-Consumer Prescription Drug Advertising Builds Bridges Between Patients and Physicians," *The Journal of American Medical Associations*, January 27, 1999, Vol. 281, No 4.

Source 5

from Direct-to-Consumer Pharmaceutical Advertising: Therapeutic or Toxic?

by C. Lee Ventola, MS

Arguments in Support of Direct-to-Consumer Drug Ads

1. **Informs, educates, and empowers patients.** Proponents claim that DTCPA educates patients and allows them to take charge of their health. In the U.S., it is thought that informing consumers will benefit the drive for health care reform. . . .
2. **Encourages patients to contact a clinician.** A common claim is that DTCPA prompts patients to consult a health care provider to seek medical advice. A 2004 FDA consumer survey found that exposure to DTCPA prompted 27% of Americans to make an appointment with their doctor to talk about a condition they had not previously discussed. . . .
3. **Strengthens a patient's relationship with a clinician.** Studies generally agree that participation of an informed patient in clinical decision-making benefits the patient-clinician relationship. One research study of print DTCPA suggested that DTC ads reinforced the patient-clinician relationship: 83% of the ads focused on physician–patient communication, 76% explicitly promoted dialogue with health care providers, and 54% clearly placed the doctor in control. . . .
4. **Encourages patient compliance.** The data consistently show that small, but statistically significant, improvements in adherence occur among patients exposed to DTCPA. This increased compliance is believed to be due to drug ads serving as a reminder about a patient's medical conditions and prescriptions. . . . .
5. **Reduces underdiagnosis and undertreatment of conditions.** DTCPA has been credited with decreasing the under-diagnosis and undertreatment of medical conditions. Drug ads enhance patient perceptions about conditions that could be medically treatable and encourage dialogue with health care providers. . . .
6. **Removes the stigma associated with certain diseases.** Consumer drug advertising for health problems that could be embarrassing to a patient, such as depression . . . , can reduce the stigma associated with these conditions. . . .
7. **Encourages product competition and lower prices.** DTCPA is often assumed to be a major driver of rising pharmaceutical costs; however, economic theory and evidence suggest that pharmaceutical prices are instead largely influenced by consumer, physician, and payer perceptions of product value rather than advertising costs. Consumer drug ads may spur manufacturer price increases because of demand, but the evidence for this is mixed. . . .

Arguments Opposing Direct-to-Consumer Ads

8. **Misinforms patients.** Although DTC advertising may educate patients, it also has the ability to misinform them. A common complaint is that DTCPA omits important information. For example, in one study, 82% of DTCPA ads made some factual claims and rational arguments for use of the advertised drug; however, only 26% of the ads described risk factors or causes of the condition, and only 25% mentioned prevalence. . . .

9. **Overemphasizes drug benefits.** Opponents to DTCPA warn that ads for drugs overemphasize potential benefits. In support of this view, content analytic studies have found that most DTC ads emphasize drug benefits over risks. A 2007 study in the *Journal of Health Communication* also found that the average DTC television commercial devotes more time to benefits than to risks. . . .
10. **Promotes new drugs before safety profiles are fully known.** New drugs have been associated with previously unknown serious adverse events after they have been introduced to the market and a substantial amount of use has occurred. This is particularly true for "first-in-class" drugs. Clinical trials required for FDA approval are typically not designed to detect rare adverse effects, and current methods of postmarketing surveillance often fail to connect adverse events that have a high rate of background prevalence with the use of a particular drug. . . .
11. **Manufactures disease and encourages drug over-utilization.** DTCPA has been criticized as contributing to the "medicalization" of natural conditions, cosmetic issues, or trivial ailments, resulting in an overmedicated society. For this reason, some commentators have even referred to DTCPA as a threat to public health. . . .
12. **Leads to inappropriate prescribing.** If a patient's request for an advertised drug is clinically inappropriate and the health care provider is unable or unwilling to correct the patient's perception that it is a good choice, this situation may lead to unnecessary or harmful prescribing. An additional problem mentioned by critics is that patients may withhold information to fit a particular profile that they saw in DTC ads in an attempt to get the doctor to prescribe a drug . . . .
13. **Strains relationships with health care providers.** DTCPA is often criticized for its potential impact on the patient-clinician relationship. Drug ads can have an influence in diminishing a patient's trust in their health care provider's clinical decisions. Clinicians may also find themselves challenged with increased work and frustration when a patient questions their clinical authority with a piece of "evidence" obtained from an advertisement or Web site. . . .
14. **Wastes appointment time.** Supporters of DTCPA argue that doctors should act as learned intermediaries and should educate consumers about prescription drug indications, benefits, and alternatives. However, many physicians oppose DTCPA because they feel it is difficult and time-consuming to have to convince patients that a requested drug is inappropriate. . . .
15. **Is not rigorously regulated.** Some critics argue that FDA regulations concerning DTCPA are too relaxed. They complain that FDA rules don't prevent DTCPA violations, because drug manufacturers are held liable only after a violation has been identified. Because drug companies are not required to obtain clearance for DTCPA prior to dissemination ("pre-clearance"), a misleading advertisement could complete its run by the time the DDMAC issues a letter. The FDA can request that a DTC ad be amended in response to a violation; however, critics say that this won't make consumers forget the misleading information they saw in the original ad. . . .
16. **Increases costs.** Another common complaint is that manufacturers often use DTCPA to promote expensive "me-too" or "copycat" drugs that might not offer any significant benefits over older and cheaper medications. . . .

Source: C. Lee Ventola, MS, "Direct-to-Consumer Pharmaceutical Advertising: Therapeutic or Toxic?" *Pharmacy and Therapeutics*, Oct 2011; 36(10): 669–674, 681–684.

Part III

Text Analysis

Closely read the story on pages 312–314 by Norwegian author Bjørnstjerne Bjørnson. Then write a text-based response of two to three paragraphs. In your response identify a main theme and analyze how the story's plot or characters help develop this theme. Use strong and thorough evidence from the text to support your analysis. Do not simply summarize the text. You may use the margins to take notes as you read and to plan your response.

Guidelines

Be sure to—

- clearly state the theme intended by the author.
- accurately discuss how the plot or characters develops the theme.
- use strong and thorough evidence from the text to support your analysis.
- identify citations by paragraph number(s) (for example: paragraph 4)
- organize your ideas in a cohesive and coherent manner.
- maintain a formal style of writing.
- follow the conventions of standard written English.

Planning Notes

The Father

by Bjørnstjerne Bjørnson

translated from the Norwegian by Rasmus B. Anderson

1. The man whose story is here to be told was the wealthiest and most influential person in his parish; his name was Thord Överaas. He appeared in the priest's study one day, tall and earnest.

2. "I have gotten a son," said he, "and I wish to present him for baptism."

3. "What shall his name be?"

4. "Finn—after my father."

5. "And the sponsors?"

6. They were mentioned, and proved to be the best men and women of Thord's relations in the parish.

7. "Is there anything else?" inquired the priest, and looked up.

8. The peasant hesitated a little.

9. "I should like very much to have him baptized by himself," said he, finally.

10. "That is to say on a weekday?"

11. "Next Saturday, at twelve o'clock noon."

12. "Is there anything else?" inquired the priest,

13. "There is nothing else;" and the peasant twirled his cap, as though he were about to go.

14. Then the priest rose. "There is yet this, however," said he, and walking toward Thord, he took him by the hand and looked gravely into his eyes: "God grant that the child may become a blessing to you!"

15. One day sixteen years later, Thord stood once more in the priest's study.

16. "Really, you carry your age astonishingly well, Thord," said the priest; for he saw no change whatever in the man.

17. "That is because I have no troubles," replied Thord. To this the priest said nothing, but after a while he asked: "What is your pleasure this evening?"

18. "I have come this evening about that son of mine who is to be confirmed tomorrow."

19. "He is a bright boy."

20. "I did not wish to pay the priest until I heard what number the boy would have when he takes his place in the church tomorrow."

21. "He will stand number one."

22. "So I have heard; and here are ten dollars for the priest."

23. "Is there anything else I can do for you?" inquired the priest, fixing his eyes on Thord.

24. "There is nothing else."

25. Thord went out.

26. Eight years more rolled by, and then one day a noise was heard outside of the priest's study, for many men were approaching, and at their head was Thord, who entered first.

27. The priest looked up and recognized him.

28. "You come well attended this evening, Thord," said he.

29. "I am here to request that the banns[1] may be published for my son: he is about to

1 banns: marriage proclamations announced in church in the weeks leading up to a wedding

marry Karen Storliden, daughter of Gudmund, who stands here beside me."

30. "Why, that is the richest girl in the parish."

31. "So they say," replied the peasant, stroking back his hair with one hand.

32. The priest sat a while as if in deep thought, then entered the names in his book, without making any comments, and the men wrote their signatures underneath. Thord laid three dollars on the table.

33. "One is all I am to have," said the priest.

34. "I know that very well; but he is my only child; I want to do it handsomely."

35. The priest took the money.

36. "This is now the third time, Thord, that you have come here on your son's account."

37. "But now I am through with him," said Thord, and folding up his pocketbook he said farewell and walked away.

38. The men slowly followed him.

39. A fortnight[2] later, the father and son were rowing across the lake, one calm, still day, to Storliden to make arrangements for the wedding.

40. "This thwart[3] is not secure," said the son, and stood up to straighten the seat on which he was sitting.

41. At the same moment the board he was standing on slipped from under him; he threw out his arms, uttered a shriek, and fell overboard.

42. "Take hold of the oar!" shouted the father, springing to his feet, and holding out the oar.

43. But when the son had made a couple of efforts he grew stiff.

44. "Wait a moment!" cried the father, and began to row toward his son.

45. Then the son rolled over on his back, gave his father one long look, and sank.

46. Thord could scarcely believe it; he held the boat still, and stared at the spot where his son had gone down, as though he must surely come to the surface again. There rose some bubbles, then some more, and finally one large one that burst; and the lake lay there as smooth and bright as a mirror again.

47. For three days and three nights people saw the father rowing round and round the spot, without taking either food or sleep; he was dragging the lake for the body of his son. And toward morning of the third day he found it, and carried it in his arms up over the hills to his gard.[4]

48. It might have been about a year from that day, when the priest, late one autumn evening, heard someone in the passage outside of the door, carefully trying to find the latch. The priest opened the door, and in walked a tall, thin man, with bowed form and white hair. The priest looked long at him before he recognized him. It was Thord.

49. "Are you out walking so late?" said the priest, and stood still in front of him.

50. "Ah, yes! it is late," said Thord, and took a seat.

51. The priest sat down also, as though waiting. A long, long silence followed. At last Thord said, "I have something with me that I should like to give to the poor; I want it to be invested as a legacy in my son's name."

52. He rose, laid some money on the table, and sat down again. The priest counted it.

53. "It is a great deal of money," said he.

---

2 fortnight: two weeks

3 thwart: seat across a small boat where the oarsman sits

4 gard: Norwegian farm

54. "It is half the price of my gard. I sold it today."

55. The priest sat long in silence. At last he asked, but gently, "What do you propose to do now, Thord?"

56. "Something better."

57. They sat there for a while, Thord with downcast eyes, the priest with his eyes fixed on Thord. Presently the priest said, slowly and softly, "I think your son has at last brought you a true blessing."

58. "Yes, I think so myself," said Thord, looking up, while two big tears coursed slowly down his cheeks.

Practice Test 2

Part I

Reading Comprehension

Questions 1–24: The selections on pages 315–321 are each followed by several multiple-choice questions. Read each selection closely. Then, for each question, select the best answer from the choices given. You may use the margins to take notes as you read.

Selection 1

from Jane Eyre

by Charlotte Brontë

Chapter 1

1. There was no possibility of taking a walk that day. We had been wandering, indeed, in the leafless shrubbery an hour in the morning; but since dinner (Mrs. Reed, when there was no company, dined early) the cold winter wind had brought with it clouds so somber, and a rain so penetrating, that further outdoor exercise was now out of the question.

2. I was glad of it: I never liked long walks, especially on chilly afternoons: dreadful to me was the coming home in the raw twilight, with nipped fingers and toes, and a heart saddened by the chidings of Bessie, the nurse,[1] and humbled by the consciousness of my physical inferiority to Eliza, John, and Georgiana Reed.

3. The said Eliza, John, and Georgiana were now clustered round their mama in the drawing-room: she lay reclined on a sofa by the fireside, and with her darlings about her (for the time neither quarreling nor crying) looked perfectly happy. Me, she had dispensed from joining the group; saying, "She regretted to be under the necessity of keeping me at a distance; but that until she heard from Bessie, and could discover by her own observation, that I was endeavoring in good earnest to acquire a more sociable and childlike disposition, a more attractive and sprightly manner—something lighter, franker, more natural, as it were—she really must exclude me from privileges intended only for contented, happy little children."

4. "What does Bessie say I have done?" I asked.

5. "Jane, I don't like cavilers[2] or questioners; besides, there is something truly forbidding in a child taking up her elders in that manner. Be seated somewhere; and until you can speak pleasantly, remain silent."

6. A breakfast-room adjoined the drawing-room, I slipped in there. It contained a bookcase: I soon possessed myself of a volume. . . . I feared nothing but interruption, and that came too soon. The breakfast-room door opened.

7. "Boh! Madam Mope!" cried the voice of John Reed; then he paused: he found the room apparently empty.

---

1 nurse: servant in charge of the nursery; nanny

2 cavilers: those who object with little reason; quibblers

8. “Where the dickens is she!” he continued. “Lizzy! Georgy! (calling to his sisters) Joan is not here: tell mama she is run out into the rain—bad animal!”

9. “It is well I drew the curtain,” thought I; and I wished fervently he might not discover my hiding-place: nor would John Reed have found it out himself; he was not quick either of vision or conception; but Eliza just put her head in at the door, and said at once—

10. “She is in the window-seat, to be sure, Jack.”

11. And I came out immediately, for I trembled at the idea of being dragged forth by the said Jack.

12. “What do you want?” I asked, with awkward diffidence.

13. “Say, ‘What do you want, Master Reed?’” was the answer. “I want you to come here;” and seating himself in an armchair, he intimated by a gesture that I was to approach and stand before him.

14. John Reed was a schoolboy of fourteen years old; four years older than I, for I was but ten: large and stout for his age, with a dingy and unwholesome skin; thick lineaments in a spacious visage, heavy limbs and large extremities. He gorged himself habitually at table, which made him bilious,[3] and gave him a dim and bleared eye and flabby cheeks. He ought now to have been at school; but his mama had taken him home for a month or two, “on account of his delicate health.” Mr. Miles, the master, affirmed that he would do very well if he had fewer cakes and sweetmeats[4] sent him from home; but the mother's heart turned from an opinion so harsh, and inclined rather to the more refined idea that John's sallowness was owing to over-application and, perhaps, to pining after home.

15. John had not much affection for his mother and sisters, and an antipathy to me. He bullied and punished me; not two or three times in the week, nor once or twice in the day, but continually: every nerve I had feared him, and every morsel of flesh in my bones shrank when he came near. There were moments when I was bewildered by the terror he inspired, because I had no appeal whatever against either his menaces or his inflictions; the servants did not like to offend their young master by taking my part against him, and Mrs. Reed was blind and deaf on the subject: she never saw him strike or heard him abuse me, though he did both now and then in her very presence, more frequently, however, behind her back.

16. Habitually obedient to John, I came up to his chair: he spent some three minutes in thrusting out his tongue at me as far as he could without damaging the roots: I knew he would soon strike, and while dreading the blow, I mused on the disgusting and ugly appearance of him who would presently deal it. I wonder if he read that notion in my face; for, all at once, without speaking, he struck suddenly and strongly. I tottered, and on regaining my equilibrium retired back a step or two from his chair.

17. “That is for your impudence in answering mama awhile since,” said he, “and for your sneaking way of getting behind curtains, and for the look you had in your eyes two minutes since, you rat!”

18. Accustomed to John Reed's abuse, I never had an idea of replying to it; my care was how to endure the blow which would certainly follow the insult.

19. “What were you doing behind the curtain?” he asked.

20. “I was reading.”

---

3 bilious: having a bad temper—a condition formerly believed to come from having too much yellow bile, the fluid secreted by the liver to aid in digestion

4 sweetmeats: any sweet foods, such as cakes or candies

21. "Show the book."

22. I returned to the window and fetched it thence.

23. "You have no business to take our books; you are a dependent, mama says; you have no money; your father left you none; you ought to beg, and not to live here with gentlemen's children like us, and eat the same meals we do, and wear clothes at our mama's expense. Now, I'll teach you to rummage my bookshelves: for they *are* mine; all the house belongs to me, or will do in a few years. Go and stand by the door, out of the way of the mirror and the windows."

24. I did so, not at first aware what was his intention; but when I saw him lift and poise the book and stand in act to hurl it, I instinctively started aside with a cry of alarm: not soon enough, however; the volume was flung, it hit me, and I fell, striking my head against the door and cutting it. The cut bled, the pain was sharp: my terror had passed its climax; other feelings succeeded.

25. "Wicked and cruel boy!" I said. "You are like a murderer—you are like a slave-driver—you are like the Roman emperors!"

26. I had read Goldsmith's *History of Rome*, and had formed my opinion of Nero, Caligula,[5] etc. Also I had drawn parallels in silence, which I never thought thus to have declared aloud.

27. "What! what!" he cried. "Did she say that to me? Did you hear her, Eliza and Georgiana? Won't I tell mama? but first—"

28. He ran headlong at me: I felt him grasp my hair and my shoulder: he had closed with a desperate thing. I really saw in him a tyrant, a murderer. I felt a drop or two of blood from my head trickle down my neck, and was sensible of somewhat pungent[6] suffering: these sensations for the time predominated over fear, and I received him in frantic sort. I don't very well know what I did with my hands, but he called me "Rat! Rat!" and bellowed out aloud. Aid was near him: Eliza and Georgiana had run for Mrs. Reed, who was gone upstairs: she now came upon the scene, followed by Bessie and her maid Abbot. We were parted: I heard the words—

29. "Dear! dear! What a fury to fly at Master John!"

30. "Did ever anybody see such a picture of passion!"

31. Then Mrs. Reed subjoined[7]—

32. "Take her away to the red-room, and lock her in there." Four hands were immediately laid upon me, and I was borne upstairs.

---

5 Nero, Caligula: tyrannical Roman emperors described in *History of Rome* by Oliver Goldsmith

6 pungent: here, painful; sharp

7 subjoined: added to what has already been said

1. What is the main purpose of the novel's first paragraph?

   Ⓐ to introduce the narrator and explain her situation to readers

   Ⓑ to introduce the setting and establish an atmosphere

   Ⓒ to introduce the main characters and explain their relationships

   Ⓓ to foreshadow the novel's ending

2. In the first two paragraphs, what do the connotations of most of the adjectives emphasize about the narrator?

   Ⓐ her discomfort in the Reed household

   Ⓑ her scholarly nature

   Ⓒ her hopeful, dreamy nature

   Ⓓ her affection for her nurse, Bessie

3. Which word in paragraph 3 does Jane, the narrator, use sarcastically?

Ⓐ reclined

Ⓑ darlings

Ⓒ quarreling

Ⓓ happy

4. What impression of Mrs. Reed, when she is introduced in paragraph 3, is confirmed by her behavior later in the passage?

Ⓐ She is a warm, affectionate parent and a second mother to Jane.

Ⓑ She is a harsh, demanding parent, strict with her own children as well as Jane.

Ⓒ She is languid and self-indulgent, caring little about her own children or Jane.

Ⓓ She indulges her own children but treats Jane unfairly.

5. Consider John Reed's behavior in paragraphs 16 and 24. What explicit statement in Jane's narrative does that behavior best illustrate?

Ⓐ . . . he was not quick either of vision or conception. . . . (paragraph 9)

Ⓑ John had not much affection for his mother and sisters. . . . (paragraph 15)

Ⓒ He bullied and punished me. . . . (paragraph 15)

Ⓓ . . . the servants did not like to offend their young master by taking my part against him (paragraph 15)

6. Jane uses hyperbole in paragraph 15 when she says of John, "every morsel of flesh in my bones shrank when he came near." What feelings is she most clearly trying to convey with this figurative language?

Ⓐ her anger with John

Ⓑ her disgust with John

Ⓒ her fear of John

Ⓓ her bitterness at being unfairly treated

7. From the details near the end of the passage, what inference can the reader draw about the red-room mentioned in the last paragraph?

Ⓐ It is an upstairs room that is Jane's usual bedchamber.

Ⓑ It is a colorful, cheerful room.

Ⓒ It is an elegant, ornate room.

Ⓓ It is used as a place of punishment.

8. Which statement gives the best one-sentence objective summary of the passage?

Ⓐ Jane, a ten-year-old orphan, is bullied and mistreated by the Reed family, the relatives with whom she lives.

Ⓑ Mrs. Reed is a dreadful woman who treats her orphaned niece Jane terribly, and her son John is even worse.

Ⓒ Poor Jane does not want to be outside on a bitter winter day and prefers reading somewhere to escape her vile relatives.

Ⓓ No matter how horribly Jane's cousin John treats her, his mother and the rest of the household always unfairly take his side.

9. Which of these sayings expresses a theme most clearly conveyed by the details of this passage?

Ⓐ Blood is thicker than water.

Ⓑ What goes around comes around.

Ⓒ The apple never falls far from the tree.

Ⓓ Children should be seen and not heard.

10. From the details in the passage, which set of themes will the novel most likely explore?

Ⓐ poverty and creativity

Ⓑ childcare and love

Ⓒ crime and injustice

Ⓓ rural and urban life

Selection 2

Sonnet 29

by William Shakespeare

When in disgrace with fortune[1] and men's eyes
I all alone beweep my outcast state,
And trouble deaf heaven with my bootless[2] cries,
And look upon myself, and curse my fate,
Wishing me like to one more rich in hope,
Featured like him, like him with friends possessed,
Desiring this man's art, and that man's scope,
With what I most enjoy contented least;
Yet in these thoughts my self almost despising,
Haply I think on thee, and then my state,
Like to the lark at break of day arising
From sullen earth, sings hymns at heaven's gate;
For thy sweet love remembered such wealth brings
That then I scorn to change my state with kings.

---

1 fortune: luck; fate; success

2 bootless: useless; vain

11. In the structure of this sonnet, what do the first two quatrains (lines 1–8) do?

    Ⓐ state the narrator's discontent and then give specific examples of it

    Ⓑ state the narrator's discontent and then explain the chain of events that caused it

    Ⓒ state the narrator's discontent and then show how it can be eased

    Ⓓ state the narrator's discontent and compare and contrast it to the discontent of others

12. What structural relationship do the last six lines of the sonnet have to the first eight?

    Ⓐ They present a generalization about them.

    Ⓑ They show the effects of them.

    Ⓒ They show examples to support them.

    Ⓓ They present a contrast to them.

13. What does the simile in lines 11–12 convey about the effect that the person addressed has on the speaker?

    Ⓐ The person addressed brings joy and hope to the speaker's life.

    Ⓑ The person addressed has talents that prompt jealousy in the speaker.

    Ⓒ The person addressed shocks the speaker by appearing so suddenly.

    Ⓓ The person addressed underscores the speaker's hopelessness by performing a hopeless act.

14. What are the connotations of the word *wealth* in line 13?

    Ⓐ greed

    Ⓑ abundance

    Ⓒ showiness

    Ⓓ upper class

15. What are the multiple meanings of the word *state* in the last line of the poem?

Ⓐ "nation" and "ceremonial"

Ⓑ "territory of a nation" and "frenzy"

Ⓒ "status," "tizzy," and "to set forth in words"

Ⓓ "rank," "condition," and "realm"

16. What tone does the speaker convey in the last two lines of the poem?

Ⓐ a romantic, passionate tone

Ⓑ a sad, thoughtful tone

Ⓒ a happy, grateful tone

Ⓓ a nostalgic, wistful tone

17. Which statement gives the best objective summary of the poem?

Ⓐ Sometimes I am jealous of everyone and everything, but at least I know that you love me.

Ⓑ When I feel the worst kind of hopelessness, your love comforts me, even if in my heart I know it is hopeless too.

Ⓒ When I feel like a failure, I remember your love, and then I would not change places with a king.

Ⓓ When I feel like the worst kind of loser, I remember you love me, and it's much nicer to feel like I'm on top of the world.

18. Despite the textual evidence and inferences you can draw from it, what is one thing left uncertain in the poem?

Ⓐ the speaker's feelings at the start of the poem

Ⓑ the cause of the speaker's disgrace

Ⓒ the feelings that the person addressed has for the speaker

Ⓓ the cause of the change in the speaker's feelings

Selection 3

from Speech at the Brandenburg Gate

by Ronald Reagan

After helping liberate Germany in World War II, the Soviet Union set up a communist government in the eastern part of the country, which it controlled, and in the eastern part of the German capital of Berlin. At first, people could travel from East to West Berlin, and vice versa, through the historic Brandenburg Gate. However, so many Germans fled the communist East that in 1961 the East German government put a wall around it, shooting or jailing anyone who tried to break through to the West. Two years later, American President John F. Kennedy came to West Berlin to express solidarity with the people there in his famous Ich bin eine Berliner ("I am a Berliner") *speech. The wall stood for nearly three more decades, a symbol of the Cold War. In June of 1987, when the Soviet Union under Mikhail Gorbachev was beginning to ease some its totalitarian policies, American President Ronald Reagan visited Berlin and delivered the speech below.*

1. Chancellor Kohl, Governing Mayor Diepgen,[1] ladies and gentlemen: Twenty-four years ago, President John F. Kennedy visited Berlin, speaking to the people of this city and the world at the City Hall. Well, since then two other presidents have come, each in his turn, to Berlin. And today I, myself, make my second visit to your city.

2. We come to Berlin, we American presidents, because it's our duty to speak, in this place, of freedom. . . .

3. Our gathering today is being broadcast throughout Western Europe and North America. I understand that it is being seen and heard as well in the East. To those listening throughout Eastern Europe, a special word: Although I cannot be with you, I address my remarks to you just as surely as to those standing here before me. For I join you, as I join your fellow countrymen in the West, in this firm, this unalterable belief: *Es gibt nur ein Berlin.*[2]

4. Behind me stands a wall that encircles the free sectors of this city, part of a vast system of barriers that divides the entire continent of Europe. From the Baltic,[3] south, those barriers cut across Germany in a gash of barbed wire, concrete, dog runs, and guard towers. Farther south, there may be no visible, no obvious wall. But there remain armed guards and checkpoints all the same—still a restriction on the right to travel, still an instrument to impose upon ordinary men and women the will of a totalitarian state. Yet it is here in Berlin where the wall emerges most clearly; here, cutting across your city, where the news photo and the television screen have imprinted this brutal division of a continent upon the mind of the world. Standing before the Brandenburg Gate, every man is a German, separated from his fellow men. Every man is a Berliner, forced to look upon a scar.

5. President von Weizsäcker[4] has said, "The German question is open as long as the Brandenburg Gate is closed." Today I say: As long as the gate is closed, as long as this scar of a wall is permitted to stand, it is not the German question alone that remains open, but the question of freedom for all mankind. Yet I do not come here to lament. For I find in Berlin a message of hope, even in the shadow of this wall, a message of triumph.

6. . . . Where four decades ago there was rubble, today in West Berlin there is the

---

1 Chancellor Kohl, Governing Mayor Diepgin: Helmut Kohl, leader of West Germany, and Eberhard Diepgin, mayor of West Berlin, at the time of the speech

2 *Es . . . Berlin:* There is only one Berlin

3 Baltic: the Baltic Sea, north of Germany

4 President von Weizsäcker: Richard Karl von Weizsäcker, former mayor of West Berlin serving as president of West Germany at the time of the speech

greatest industrial output of any city in Germany—busy office blocks, fine homes and apartments, proud avenues, and the spreading lawns of parkland. Where a city's culture seemed to have been destroyed, today there are two great universities, orchestras and an opera, countless theaters, and museums. Where there was want, today there's abundance—food, clothing, automobiles—the wonderful goods of the Ku'damm.[5] From devastation, from utter ruin, you Berliners have, in freedom, rebuilt a city that once again ranks as one of the greatest on earth. The Soviets may have had other plans. But my friends, there were a few things the Soviets didn't count on—*Berliner Herz, Berliner Humor, ja, und Berliner Schnauze*.[6]

7. In the 1950s, Khrushchev[7] predicted: "We will bury you." But in the West today, we see a free world that has achieved a level of prosperity and well-being unprecedented in all human history. In the Communist world, we see failure, technological backwardness, declining standards of health, even want of the most basic kind—too little food. Even today, the Soviet Union still cannot feed itself. After these four decades, then, there stands before the entire world one great and inescapable conclusion: Freedom leads to prosperity. Freedom replaces the ancient hatreds among the nations with comity and peace. Freedom is the victor.

8. And now the Soviets themselves may, in a limited way, be coming to understand the importance of freedom. We hear much from Moscow[8] about a new policy of reform and openness. Some political prisoners have been released. Certain foreign news broadcasts are no longer being jammed. Some economic enterprises have been permitted to operate with greater freedom from state control.

9. Are these the beginnings of profound changes in the Soviet state? Or are they token gestures, intended to raise false hopes in the West, or to strengthen the Soviet system without changing it? We welcome change and openness; for we believe that freedom and security go together, that the advance of human liberty can only strengthen the cause of world peace. There is one sign the Soviets can make that would be unmistakable, that would advance dramatically the cause of freedom and peace.

10. General Secretary Gorbachev, if you seek peace, if you seek prosperity for the Soviet Union and Eastern Europe, if you seek liberalization: Come here to this gate! Mr. Gorbachev, open this gate! Mr. Gorbachev, tear down this wall! . . . .

11. As I looked out a moment ago from the Reichstag,[9] that embodiment of German unity, I noticed words crudely spray-painted upon the wall, perhaps by a young Berliner: "This wall will fall. Beliefs become reality." Yes, across Europe, this wall will fall. For it cannot withstand faith; it cannot withstand truth. The wall cannot withstand freedom.

12. And I would like, before I close, to say one word. I have read, and I have been questioned since I've been here about certain demonstrations against my coming. And I would like to say just one thing, and to those who demonstrate so. I wonder if they have ever asked themselves that if they should have the kind of government they apparently seek, no one would ever be able to do what they're doing again.

13. Thank you and God bless you all.

---

5 Ku'damm: local name for the Kurfürstendamm, famous Berlin boulevard lined with shops, hotels, and restaurants

6 *Berliner . . . Schnauze:* German for "Berliner heart, Berliner humor, and yes, Berliner slang," a slang known for its outspokenness

7 Khrushchev: Nikita Khrushchev, Soviet leader in the 1950s and 1960s

8 Moscow: capital of the Soviet Union (now Russia)

9 Reichstag: historic Berlin building where the German legislature had met in the past (and again began meeting in the 1990s, after German reunification)

19. What is President Reagan's main purpose in opening his speech with a reference to President John F. Kennedy's famous Berlin speech, made over twenty years before?

Ⓐ to emphasize that he is a traditional politician following in the footsteps of others

Ⓑ to show that he, a Republican, is willing to praise Democrats like President Kennedy

Ⓒ to remind his audience—especially younger members of the audience—of a time before Germany was divided

Ⓓ to stress America's longstanding commitment to a united, democratic Germany

20. What does Reagan's metaphor calling the Berlin Wall a "scar" (paragraphs 4 and 5) stress about the wall?

Ⓐ its height

Ⓑ its permanence

Ⓒ its mystery

Ⓓ its ugliness

21. What structure does Reagan use in organizing paragraphs 6–8?

Ⓐ chronological

Ⓑ cause-and-effect

Ⓒ order of importance

Ⓓ spatial

22. Which of these is a main reason that Reagan includes German statements in his speech?

Ⓐ to show that he has taken the trouble to become fluent in German

Ⓑ to express ideas about German life and culture that cannot be expressed as well in English

Ⓒ to again tie his speech to President Kennedy's Berlin speech, famous for including a German statement

Ⓓ to say something that his audience will understand, since virtually everyone in Berlin speaks German but probably very few speak a word of English

23. In the structure of Reagan's speech, what is the relationship between the main idea in paragraph 8 and the main idea in paragraph 10?

Ⓐ Paragraph 8 describes a situation, and paragraph 10 presents a contrasting situation.

Ⓑ Paragraph 8 describes a changing situation, and paragraph 10 states how to confirm the changes.

Ⓒ Paragraph 8 describes a current situation, and paragraph 10 states a possible cause of that situation.

Ⓓ Paragraph 8 describes a problem, and paragraph 10 states a solution to that problem.

24. Which phrase best describes Reagan's tone in the last 4 words of paragraph 10?

Ⓐ mournful

Ⓑ hesitant

Ⓒ demanding

Ⓓ sarcastic

Part II

Writing from Sources: Argument

Directions: Closely read each of the five source documents provided on pages 325 through 329 and write a source-based argument on the topic below. You may write notes in the margin as you read. Write your argument on separate paper.

Topic

Is the phenomenon of social networking beneficial or harmful to society?

Your Task

Carefully read each of the six source documents provided. Then write a well-developed argument, asserting a claim on the topic of social networking. Address at least one counterclaim. Support your ideas with specific and relevant evidence from at least three of the source documents.

Guidelines

Be sure to—

- Establish your claim on social networking.
- Evaluate the sources to identify any possible biases.
- Address at least one counterclaim.
- Use specific, relevant, and sufficient evidence from at least three of the sources to develop your argument.
- Identify the source that you reference by source document number and paragraph number(s) (for example: Source 1, paragraph 4).
- Organize your ideas in a logical manner.
- Maintain a formal writing style and objective tone.
- Follow the conventions of standard written English.

Texts

Source 1 (on page 325): *from* "Is Social Media Hurting our Culture" by Abby Johnson

Source 2 (on page 326): *from* "Social Networking Benefits Validated" by Karen Goldberg Goff

Source 3 (on page 327): *from* Response to the Question: Is MySpace Good for Society? by Nicole Ellison

Source 4 (on page 328): *from* Response to the Question: Is MySpace Good for Society? by Judith Donath

Source 5 (on page 329): *from* Response to the Question: Is MySpace Good for Society? by Martin Baily

Source 1

from Is Social Media Hurting Our Culture?

by Abby Johnson

1. With Facebook, Twitter, Pinterest, and other popular social websites woven into both our personal and business lives, it is clear that society has become dependent on social media. Technology companies and marketers are, of course, advocating this dependence since it opens up more opportunities for them.

2. Privacy activists, on the other hand, have touted that concerns exist, but the majority of users do not appear to be worried.

3. Most users simply enjoy the convenience and the fun that social media sites bring and don't think about potential implications. Andrew Keen is terrified by this attitude and expresses his feelings in his new book *Digital Vertigo: How Today's Online Social Revolution Is Dividing, Diminishing, and Disorienting Us*. . . .

4. Andrew Keen, . . . is known for his controversial opinion of the Web after writing *The Cult of the Amateur*, in which he warns of the harmful consequences of the Web 2.0 culture. His latest book, however, targets social media and the negative impact that it is having on society.

5. "*Digital Vertigo* is a warning about the loss of privacy of the inner self that social media is doing to us," said Keen.

6. Although his viewpoints have earned him nicknames such as the "Net's supreme cyber-grump" . . . he prefers to think of himself as a "cheerful pessimist." As he explained, he is not against the Internet or social media sites—he is, in fact, very active on Twitter—but he does think that we, as a society, take it too lightly.

7. "I recognize that the Web is the dominant reality . . . of the 21st century, but that doesn't mean that we should accept it unthinkingly," he said.

8. "As we retreat from real social things, and as we retreat from readily watching or listening to other people's ideas—music, movies, books," he continued, "we seem to be more and more preoccupied with broadcasting ourselves. And that, I think, is deeply narcissistic and ultimately doesn't reflect well on ourselves as individuals or collectively as a species." . . . .

9. "I'm not saying that . . . social networking is killing our species," pointed out Keen. "What I am saying is that we need to make the Internet more suitable for human beings."

10. "I'm worried that, what I would call the new collectivism of the social age—grouping the publicness of much discourse—is resulting in losing something essential about what it means to be human."

11. According to him, not all social networking is really social behavior. While there have been some very good uses of social platforms such as what we saw in the Middle East and in Russia, Keen believes that, many times, these so-called demonstrations are merely "an aggregation of individuals." For instance, he thinks this is why the Occupy Wall Street Movement hasn't developed into a viable political movement. . . .

12. "We all have a responsibility as social media users to understand that, when we reveal everything about ourselves . . . we are impoverishing ourselves," explained Keen. "We are taking away the best part of ourselves . . . the internal mystery of what it requires to build personality."

Source: "Is Social Media Hurting Our Culture?" by Abby Johnson. *WebProNews*, June 15, 2012. (http://www.webpronews.com/is-social-media-hurting-our-culture-2012-06).

Source 2

from Social Networking Benefits Validated

by Karen Goldberg Goff

1. Texting, blogs, Facebook, gaming and instant messages might seem, to some, to be just more reasons to stare at a computer screen.

2. Thinking like that is so 2008, any middle schooler will tell you. Now a study that looked at the online habits of 800 teenagers backs them up.

3. Researchers in the study, titled the *Digital Youth Project* and conducted primarily at the University of Southern California and the University of California at Berkeley, found that in our increasingly technological world, the constant communication that social networking provides is encouraging useful skills. The study looked at more than 5,000 hours of online observation and found that the digital world is creating new opportunities for young people to grapple with social norms, explore interests, develop technical skills and work on new forms of self-expression.

4. "There are myths about kids spending time online—that it is dangerous or making them lazy," says Mizuko Ito, lead author of the study, which will be the basis of a forthcoming book, "Hanging Out, Messing Around, Geeking Out: Living and Learning With New Media." "But we found that spending time online is essential for young people to pick up the social and technical skills they need to be competent citizens in the digital age."

5. Co-author Lisa Tripp, now an assistant professor at Florida State University, says technology, including YouTube, iPods and podcasting, creates avenues for extending one's circle of friends, boosts self-directed learning and fosters independence.

6. "Certain technical skills in the coming years are not going to be just about consuming media," she says. "It is also going to be about producing media. It is not just about writing a blog, but also how to leave comments that say something. Learning to communicate like this is contributing to the general circulation of culture."

7. That means anything from a video clip to a profile page is going to reflect the self-expression skills one has, so teens might as well practice what will say who they are.

8. Social networking also contributes greatly to teens' extended friendships and interests, Ms. Tripp says. While the majority of teens use sites such as MySpace and Facebook to "hang out" with people they already know in real life, a smaller portion uses them to find like-minded people. Before social networking, the one kid in school who was, say, a fan of Godzilla or progressive politics might find himself isolated. These days, that youngster has peers everywhere.

9. "This kind of communication has let teens expand their social circle by common interests," Ms. Tripp says. "They can publicize and distribute their work to online audiences and become sort of a microexpert in that area." The study found that young people's learning with digital media often is more self-directed, with a freedom and autonomy that is less apparent than in a classroom. The researchers said youths usually respect one another's authority online, and they often are more motivated to learn from one another than from adults. . . .

Source: "Social networking benefits validated" by Karen Goldberg Goff, *The Washington Times*, Wednesday, January 28, 2009 Read more: http://www.washingtontimes.com/news/2009/jan/28/social-networking-benefits-validated/#ixzz3Am6Q2ypA

Source 3

from Response to the Question: Is MySpace Good for Society?
by Nicole Ellison

1. I believe the benefits provided by social network sites such as Facebook have made us better off as a society and as individuals . . . . Anecdotal evidence of positive outcomes from these technologies—such as political activities organized via Facebook or jobs found through LinkedIn—is well-known, but now a growing corpus of academic research on social networks sites supports this view as well.

2. Over the last three years, our research team at Michigan State University has examined the use of Facebook by undergraduate students. Charles Steinfield, Cliff Lampe, and I have used surveys, interviews, and automated capture of the MSU Facebook site to try to understand how and why students use Facebook.

3. Our original motivation was to better understand why individuals would voluntarily use a site that, based on media reports, offered them only a way to disclose information they shouldn't disclose, collect hundreds of "friends" they didn't know, and waste time better spent studying. What we found surprised us. Our survey included questions designed to assess students' "social capital," a concept that describes the benefits individuals receive from their relationships with others. Undergraduates who used Facebook intensively had higher bridging social capital scores than those who didn't, and our longitudinal data show that Facebook use preceded these social capital gains.

4. Bridging social capital reflects the benefits we receive from our "weak ties"—people we don't know very well but who provide us with useful information and ideas. These students were using Facebook to increase the size of their social network, and therefore their access to more information and diverse perspectives. Our interview data confirmed these findings, with participants commenting on how . . . Facebook helped them maintain or strengthen relationships: they used the site to look up old high school acquaintances, to find out information about people in their classes or dorms that might be used to strike up a conversation, to get contact information for friends, and many other activities.

5. These aren't the kinds of Facebook activities you are likely to read about in the media, which have encouraged widespread public concern about Facebook use by young people. Yes, there have been cases in which students have shown poor judgment regarding their profile disclosures. However, tools that enable us to engage in online self-presentation and connect with others will be increasingly part of our social and professional landscape, as social network sites continue to be embraced by businesses, non-profits, civic groups, and political organizations that value the connections these tools support. . . .

6. Social technologies never have predictable and absolute positive or negative effects, which is why social scientists dread questions like these. In considering the effects of social network sites, it is clear that there are many challenges to work through—the increasing commercialization of this space, the need to construct strong privacy protections for users, and safety issues—but I believe the benefits we receive as a society provided by these tools far outweigh the risks.

Source: "Is MySpace Good for Society? A Freakonomics Quorum," by Stephen J. Dubner. *freakonomics.com*, Feb. 15, 2008.

Source 4

Response to the Question: Is MySpace Good for Society?

by Judith Donath

1. The good: social networking technologies make it easier to keep up with a large circle of acquaintances and meet new people. They provide a venue for online socializing, as well as for coordinating in-person meetings.
2. The bad: they devalue the meaning of "friend." Our traditional notion of friendship embraces trust, support, compatible values, etc. On social network sites, a "friend" may simply be someone on whose link you have clicked.
3. The ugly: for teens, who can be viciously competitive, networking sites that feature a list of one's best friends and space for everyone to comment about you can be an unpleasant venue for social humiliation and bullying. These sites can make the emotional landmines of adolescence concrete and explicit.
4. The big picture: social networking technologies support and enable a new model of social life, in which people's social circles will consist of many more, but weaker, ties. Though we will continue to have some strong ties (i.e., family and close friends), demographic changes, such as frequent household moves and the replacement of friends and family with market services for tasks such as daycare, are diminishing the role of social ties in everyday life. Weak ties (e.g., casual acquaintances, colleagues) may not be reliable for long-term support; their strength instead is in providing a wide range of perspectives, information, and opportunities. As society becomes increasingly dynamic, with access to information playing a growing role, having many diverse connections will be key.
5. Social networking technologies provide people with a low cost (in terms of time and effort) way of making and keeping social connections, enabling a social scenario in which people have huge numbers of diverse, but not very close, acquaintances. Does this makes us better as a society? Perhaps not—we can imagine this being a selfish and media-driven world in which everyone vies for attention and no one takes responsibility for one another. But perhaps it does—we can also imagine this being a world in which people are far more accepting of diverse ways and beliefs, one in which people are willing to embrace the new and different.

Source: "Is MySpace Good for Society? A Freakonomics Quorum," by Stephen J. Dubner. *freakonomics.com*, Feb. 15, 2008.

Source 5

Response to the Question: Is MySpace Good for Society?

by Martin Baily

1. Powerful new technologies provide great benefits, but they also change the way we live, and not always in ways that everyone likes. An example is the spread of air conditioning, which makes us more comfortable, but those who grew up before its invention speak fondly of a time when everyone sat on the front porch and talked to their neighbors rather than going indoors to stay cool and watch TV. The declining cost of information processing and communication represents a powerful new technology, with social networking as the most recent service to be provided at modest cost. It can be expected to bring pluses and minuses.

2. New social networking services are counted in our measure of G.D.P., and will likely show up as an increase in productivity. Their effect is not large enough yet to move the needle by much, but it will be in the data, although in a rather strange way. Sites such as Facebook are free to users, with the "price" of using the service being the online ads viewed. This is, of course, the same way we "pay for" most television programming. This approach provides only a rough estimate of the economic value of the service.

3. But will social networking sites really improve the quality of people's lives? The pluses include easier contacts with friends, and increased chances to make new friends and create a community, as well as find romantic relationships. Even the advertising may be a plus, because it is targeted to the particular interests of the user.

4. The minuses are that all of this sharing can be dangerous, through gossip and potential abuse of the services. Examples include reported suicides linked to malicious gossip circulated on a social network. Some people become addicted to life on the computer screen, and withdraw from personal contact — it's a long way from people sitting on the porch talking to friends and neighbors.

Source: "Is MySpace Good for Society? A Freakonomics Quorum," by Stephen J. Dubner. *freakonomics.com*, Feb. 15, 2008.

Part III

Text Analysis

Closely read this excerpt on pages 331–332 from a famous slave narrative published in 1789 and then write a text-based response of two to three paragraphs. In your response identify the author's main purpose and analyze how his word choice (diction) or the details he presents help him achieve that purpose. Use strong and thorough evidence from the text to support your analysis. Do *not* simply summarize the text. You may use the margins to take notes as you read and to plan your response.

Guidelines

Be sure to—

- clearly state the main purpose of the author.
- analyze how the author's diction or details helps him achieve his purpose.
- use strong and thorough evidence from the text to support your analysis.
- identify citations by paragraph number(s) (for example: paragraph 4)
- organize your ideas in a cohesive and coherent manner.
- maintain a formal style of writing.
- follow the conventions of standard written English.

Planning Notes

from The Interesting Narrative of the Life of Olaudah Equiano, or Gustavus Vassa, The African

by Olaudah Equiano

1. . . . At last, when the ship we were in had got in all her cargo, they made ready with many fearful noises, and we were all put under deck, so that we could not see how they managed the vessel. But this disappointment was the least of my sorrow. The stench of the hold[1] while we were on the coast was so intolerably loathsome, that it was dangerous to remain there for any time, and some of us had been permitted to stay on the deck for the fresh air; but now that the whole ship's cargo were confined together, it became absolutely pestilential. The closeness of the place, and the heat of the climate, added to the number in the ship, which was so crowded that each had scarcely room to turn himself, almost suffocated us. This produced copious perspirations, so that the air soon became unfit for respiration, from a variety of loathsome smells, and brought on a sickness among the slaves, of which many died, thus falling victims to the improvident[2] avarice, as I may call it, of their purchasers.

2. This wretched situation was again aggravated by the galling[3] of the chains, now become insupportable; and the filth of the necessary tubs,[4] into which the children often fell, and were almost suffocated. The shrieks of the women, and the groans of the dying, rendered the whole a scene of horror almost inconceivable. Happily perhaps for myself I was soon reduced so low here that it was thought necessary to keep me almost always on deck; and from my extreme youth I was not put in fetters.[5] In this situation I expected every hour to share the fate of my companions, some of whom were almost daily brought upon deck at the point of death, which I began to hope would soon put an end to my miseries. Often did I think many of the inhabitants of the deep[6] much more happy than myself. I envied them the freedom they enjoyed, and as often wished I could change my condition for theirs. Every circumstance I met with served only to render my state more painful, and heighten my apprehensions, and my opinion of the cruelty of the whites.

3. One day they had taken a number of fishes; and when they had killed and satisfied themselves with as many as they thought fit, to our astonishment who were on the deck, rather than give any of them to us to eat as we expected, they tossed the remaining fish into the sea again, although we begged and prayed for some as well as we could, but in vain; and some of my countrymen, being pressed by hunger, took an opportunity, when they thought no one saw them, of trying to get a little privately; but they were discovered, and the attempt procured them some very severe floggings.[7]

4. One day, when we had a smooth sea and moderate wind, two of my wearied countrymen who were chained together (I was near them at the time), preferring death to such a life of misery, somehow made through the nettings and jumped into the sea. . . .

5. In this manner we continued to undergo more hardships than I can now relate,

1 hold: ship's interior below the decks
2 improvident: lacking foresight or thrift; wasteful
3 galling: chafing
4 necessary tubs: vessels for body waste; toilets
5 fetters: chains
6 the deep: the sea
7 floggings: beatings with a lash or stick, given as punishment

hardships which are inseparable from this accursed trade.[8]

6. During our passage I first saw flying fishes, which surprised me very much: they used frequently to fly across the ship, and many of them fell on the deck. I also now first saw the use of the quadrant;[9] I had often with astonishment seen the mariners make observations with it, and I could not think what it meant. They at last took notice of my surprise; and one of them, willing to increase it, as well as to gratify my curiosity, made me one day look through it. The clouds appeared to me to be land, which disappeared as they passed along. This heightened my wonder; and I was now more persuaded than ever that I was in another world, and that everything about me was magic.

7. At last we came in sight of the island of Barbados, at which the whites on board gave a great shout, and made many signs of joy to us. We did not know what to think of this; but as the vessel drew nearer we plainly saw the harbor, and other ships of different kinds and sizes; and we soon anchored amongst them off Bridge Town.[10] Many merchants and planters now came on board, though it was in the evening. They put us in separate parcels,[11] and examined us attentively. They also made us jump, and pointed to the land, signifying we were to go there. . . .

8. We were conducted immediately to the merchant's yard, where we were all pent up together like so many sheep in a fold, without regard to sex or age. . . . We were not many days in the merchant's custody before we were sold after their usual manner, which is this:—On a signal given (as the beat of a drum), the buyers rush at once into the yard where the slaves are confined, and make choice of that parcel they like best. The noise and clamor with which this is attended, and the eagerness visible in the countenances of the buyers, serve not a little to increase the apprehensions of the terrified Africans. . . .

9. In this manner, without scruple, are relations and friends separated, most of them never to see each other again. . . . O, ye nominal Christians! might not an African ask you, learned you this from your God, who says unto you, Do unto all men as you would men should do unto you?[12] Is it not enough that we are torn from our country and friends to toil for your luxury and lust of gain? Must every tender feeling be likewise sacrificed to your avarice? Are the dearest friends and relations, now rendered more dear by their separation from their kindred, still to be parted from each other, and thus prevented from cheering the gloom of slavery with the small comfort of being together and mingling their sufferings and sorrows? Why are parents to lose their children, brothers their sisters, or husbands their wives? Surely this is a new refinement in cruelty, which, while it has no advantage to atone for it, thus aggravates distress, and adds fresh horrors even to the wretchedness of slavery.

8 trade: the slave trade

9 quadrant: instrument used to determine a ship's position

10 Bridge Town: now the capital of Barbados and spelled Bridgetown

11 parcels: groups

12 Do unto . . . you: an ethic in Christianity and many other faiths, called the Golden Rule and spoken by Jesus in the New Testament

Acknowledgments

Every effort has been made to contact all copyright holders. If we have omitted anyone, please let us know and we will include a suitable acknowledgment in subsequent editions.

"Dead Men's Path," copyright © 1972 , 1973 by Chiuna Achebe; from GIRLS AT WAR: AND OTHER STORIES by Chinua Achebe. Used by permission of Doubleday, an imprint of the Knopf Doubleday Publishing Group, a division of Random House LLC. All rights reserved.

"The Latin Deli: An Ars Poetica" is reprinted with permission from the publisher of "The Latin Deli" by Judith Ortiz Cofer (© 1993 Arte Publico Press-University of Houston.)

Excerpt from SNOW FALLING ON CEDARS by David Guterson. Copyright © 1995 by David Guterson. Reprinted by permission of Houghton Mifflin Harcourt Publishing Company. All rights reserved.

"Girl" from AT THE BOTTOM OF THE RIVER by Jamaica Kincaid. Copyright © 1983 by Jamaica Kincaid. Reprinted by permission of Farrar, Straus and Giroux, LLC. Farrar, Straus and Giroux, LLC.

Excerpt from "The Moment The Gun Went Off" from JUMP AND OTHER STORIES by Nadine Gordimer. Copyright © 1991 by Felix Licensing, B. V. Used by permission of Farrar, Straus and Giroux, LLC.

Excerpt(s) from THE READER by Bernhard Schlink, translation copyright © 1997 by Carol Brown Janeway. Used by permission of Pantheon Books, an imprint of the Knopf Doubleday Publishing Group, a division of Random House LLC. All rights reserved.

Excerpt(s) from BELOVED by Toni Morrison, copyright © 1987 by Toni Morrison. Used by permission of Alfred A. Knopf, an imprint of the Knopf Doubleday Publishing Group, a division of Random House LLC. All rights reserved.

Excerpt(s) from THE GOD OF SMALL THINGS by Arundhati Roy, copyright © 1997 by Arundhati Roy. Used by permission of Random House, an imprint and division of Random House LLC. All rights reserved.

From THE JOY LUCK CLUB by Amy Tan, copyright © 1989 by Amy Tan. Used by permission of G. P. Putnam's Sons, a division of Penguin Group (USA) LLC.

"The Red Convertible." Copyright 1984, 1993 by Louise Erdrich. In *Love Medicine* published by Henry Holt and Comp., 115 18th St., New York, NY 10011.

"Church Going" by Philip Larkin from *The Less Deceived (poems)*, Marvell Press, 1955, 4th edition, St. Martin's, 1958.

Excerpt from "The Jilting of Granny Weatherall" from FLOWERING JUDAS AND OTHER STORIES by Katherine Anne Porter. Copyright 1930 and renewed 1958 by Katherine Anne Porter. Reprinted by permission of Houghton Mifflin Harcourt Publishing Company. All rights reserved.

From *Another Time* by W. H. Auden, published by Random House. Copyright © 1940 W. H. Auden, renewed by The Estate of W. H. Auden. Used by permission of Curtis Brown, Ltd.

"This is Just to Say" by William Carlos Williams, from THE COLLECTED POEMS: VOLUME I, 1909-1939, copyright ©1938 by New Directions Publishing Corp. Reprinted by permission of New Directions Publishing Corp.

Excerpt(s) from BEHIND THE BEAUTIFUL FOREVERS: LIFE, DEATH, AND HOPE IN A MUMBAI UNDERCITY by Katherine Boo, copyright © 2012 by Katherine Boo. Used by permission of Random House, an imprint and division of Random House LLC. All rights reserved.

From N*ickel and Dimed in America* by Barbara Ehrenreich. Copyright 2001 by Barbara Ehrenreich. Published by Holt Paperbacks, Henry Holt and Company, 175 Fifth Avenue, New York, NY 10010.

Excerpt from A ROOM OF ONE'S OWN by Virginia Woolf. Copyright 1929 by Houghton Mifflin Harcourt Publishing Company. Copyright © Renewed 1957 by Leonard Woolf. Reprinted by permission of Houghton Mifflin Harcourt Publishing Company. All rights reserved.

From *Counting Coup: A True Story of Basketball and Honor on the Little Big Horn* by Larry Colton. Copyright 2000 by Larry Colton. Used by permission of Grand Central Publishing.

Excerpt from ALL DELIBERATE SPEED: REFLECTIONS ON THE FIRST HALF-CENTURY OF *BROWN V. BOARD OF EDUCATION* by Charles J. Ogletree Jr. Copyright 2004 by Charles J. Ogletree Jr. Used by permission of W.W. Norton & Company, Inc.

Excerpt from *The Spirit Catches You and You Fall Down: A Hmong Child, Her American Doctors, and the Collision of Two Cultures* by Anne Fadiman. Copyright 1997, 2012 by Anne Fadiman. Published by Farrar, Straus, and Giroux, 18 West 18th Street, New York, NY 10011.

Excerpt from THE IMMORTAL LIFE OF HENRIETTA LACKS by Rebecca Skloot. Copyright © 2010, 2011 by Rebecca Skloot. Used by permission of Crown Books, an imprint of the Crown Publishing Group, a division of Random House LLC. All rights reserved..

Excerpt from BORN ON A BLUE DAY. Reprinted and edited with the permission of Simon & Schuster Publishing Group, a division of Simon & Schuster, Inc. from the Free Press edition of BORN ON A BLUE DAY: Inside the Extraordinary Mind of an Autistic Savant by Daniel Tammet. Copyright © 2006 by Daniel Tammet. All rights reserved.

Excerpt from MADE IN AMERICA by Bill Bryson. Copyright © 1994 by Bill Bryson. Reprinted by permission of HarperCollins Publishers.

Excerpt from *The Devil's Highway: A True Story* by Luis Alberto Urrea. Copyright © 2004 by Luis Urrea. Published by Little Brown and Company, Time Warner Book Group, 1271 Avenue of the Americas, New York, NY 10020.

Excerpt from *Seabiscuit: An American Legend* by Laura Hillenbrand. Copyright © 2001 by Laura Hillenbrand. Published by Random House Publishing Group (A Ballantine Book).

Excerpt from *Theodore Rex* by Edmund Morris. Copyright © 2001 by Edmund Morris. Published by Modern Library, an imprint of Random House, Inc. New York.

Excerpt from *Tsunamis: Detection, Monitoring, and Early-Warning Technologies* by Antony Joseph. Copyright © 2011, Elsevier Inc. Published by Academic Press, an imprint in Elsevier, 30 Corporate Drive, Suite 400, Burlington, MA 01803

Reprinted with the permission of Simon & Schuster Publishing Group, a division of Simon & Schuster, Inc. from THE MAN WHO MISTOOK HIS WIFE FOR A HAT AND OTHER CLINICAL TALES by Oliver Sacks. Copyright © 1970, 1981, 1983, 1984, 1985 by Oliver Sacks. All rights reserved.

Excerpts from "Introduction" and "Blood, Mountains, and Burgers" from INNUMERACY: MATHEMATICAL ILLITERACY AND ITS CONSEQUENCES by John Allen Paulos. Copyright © 1988, 2001 by John Allen Paulos. Reprinted by permission of Farrar, Straus and Giroux, LLC.

Excerpt from *The Particle Garden: Our Universe as Understood by Particle Physicists* by Gordon Kane. Copyright c 1995 by Gordon Kane. Reading, Mass: Addison-Wesley (Helix Books).

"Ascorbic Acid" from NAPOLEON'S BUTTONS: 17 MOLECULES THAT CHANGED HISTORY by Peggy Le Couteur and Jay Burreson. Copyright © 2003 by Micron Geological Ltd. And Jay Burreson. Used by permission of Jeremy P. Tarcher, an imprint of Penguin Group (USA) LLC.

Excerpt from chapter III, The Beginnings of American, section I, The First Loan-Words, in The American Language, Fourth Edition, by H. L. Mencken. Copyright 1919, 1921, 1923, 1936 by Alfred A. Knopf, Inc. New York: Alfred A. Knopf. Fourth Edition corrected, enlarged, and rewritten, published April, 1936, reprinted fifteen times, seventeenth printing, November 1965.

"Imaginary Lines" (Chapter 1) in *Longitude: The True Story of a Lone Genius Who Solved the Greatest Scientific Problem of His Time* by Dava Sobel. Copyright © Dava Sobel, 1995. Used by permission of Walker Books, an imprint of Bloomsbury Publishing Inc.

"The Contest That Shaped Careers and Inspired Research Papers," by Steve Lohr Published in *Chance*, Vol 23, No 1, Winter 2010. Reprinted by permission of American Statistical Association.

"The Rise of the New Groupthink" by Susan Cain From *The New York Times*, January 13, 2012. Copyright © 2012 *The New York Times*. All rights reserved. Used by permission and protected by the Copyright Laws of the United States. The printing, copying, redistribution, or retransmission of this Content without express written permission is prohibited.

Excerpt from *All Deliberate Speed: Reflections on the First Half-Century of* Brown v. Board of Education by Charles J. Ogletree Jr. Used by permission of Published by W.W. Norton & Company, Inc.

"Reducing Obesity in America Calls for Tough Policies and a 'Sugar Tax'," by Shirley L. Smith. examiner.com, September 26, 2011. http://www.examiner.com/article/reducing-obesity-america-calls-for-tough-policies-and-a-sugar-tax

"Dying to Play" by Kevin Cook From *The New York Times*, September 12, 2012. Copyright © 2012 *The New York Times*. All rights reserved. Used by permission and protected by the Copyright Laws of the United States. The printing, copying, redistribution, or retransmission of this Content without express written permission is prohibited.

"Nutrition, Obesity, & Processed Food," Food Safety Fact Sheet, May 2012.

"Reducing Obesity in America Calls for Tough Policies and a 'Sugar Tax'," by Shirley L. Smith. *examiner.com*, September 26, 2011. *http://www.examiner.com/article/reducing-obesity-america-calls-for-tough-policies-and-a-sugar-tax.*

Excerpt from THE WORST HARD TIME: The Untold Story of Those Who Survived the Great American Dust Bowl by Timothy Egan. Copyright © 2005 by Timonthy Egan. Reprinted by permission of Houghton Mifflin Company. All rights reserved.

Ripley, Amanda. "The Case Against High-School Sports" *theatlantic.com*. *The Atlantic*. September 18, 2013. Web. 23 January 2014. Copyright 2013. The Atlantic.com as published in *The Atlantic Online*. Distributed by Tribune Content Agency. Used by permission.

Dr. Douglas Hartmann. "High School Sports Participation and Educational Attainment: Recognizing, Assessing, and Utilizing the Relationship." LA84 Foundation: University of Minnesota, 2008. Web. 23 January 2014.

Carnoy, Martin and Richard Rothstein. "What Do International Tests Really Show About U.S. Student Performance?" *epi.org*. Economic Policy Institute, January 29, 2013. Web. 29 January 2014. Used by permission of Economic Policy Institute.

"The Case for High School Activities." *nchsaa.org*. The National Federation of State High School Associations: 14–15. N.d., Web. 3 February 2014.

"Social Media Affecting Teens' Concept of Friendship, Intimacy" by Pauline Dakin. CBC News. *http://www.cbc.ca/news/health/social-media-affecting-teens-concepts-of-friendship-intimacy-1.2543158.*

Chris Woolston, "Health Benefits of Friendship," published on *healthday.com http://consumer.healthday.com/encyclopedia/emotional-health-17/psychology-and-mental-health-news-566/health-benefits-of-friendship-648397.html*. Used by permission.

"R U friends 4 real?" by Amy Novotney, *Monitor on Psychology*, Feb. 2012, Vol. 43, No. 2, page 62 in print edition. (http://www.apa.org/monitor/2012/02/friends.aspx). Copyright © 2012 by the American Psychological Association. Reproduced [or Adapted] with permission.

Excerpt from *The Meaning of Friendship* by Mark Vernon. Copyright © 2010 by Mark Vernon. Reproduced with permission of Palgrave Macmillan.

Excerpt From Roomies: A Novel About Friendship, First Loves, and Random Room Assignments by Sara Zarr and Tara Altebrando. Copyright © 2013 by Tara Altebrando and Sara Zarr. Used by permission of Little Brown Books for Young Readers.

Excerpt from "Grown Women Don't Need a 'Best Friend'" by Alice Robb from *The New Republic*, July 10, 2014. Used by permission.

Excerpts from "A Rose for Emily," copyright © 1930 and renewed 1958 by William Faulkner; from COLLECTED STORIES OF WILLIAM FAULKNER by William Faulkner. Used by permission of Random House, an imprint and division of Random House LLC. All rights reserved.

"The Far and the Near" by Thomas Wolfe. Copyright 1935 Thomas Wolfe. Renewed 1963 by Paul Gitlin Administrator, C.T.A. of the Estate of Thomas Wolfe. Reprinted by permission of McIntosh & Otis, Inc.

Statement of the American College of Physicians to the Senate Special Committee on Aging for the Record of The Hearing on the Impact of Direct-to-Consumer Advertising on Seniors' Health and Health Care Costs. September 29, 2005.

Kurt C. Stange, "Time to Ban Direct-to-Consumer Prescription Drug Marketing," *Annals of Family Medicine*, 2007 5:101-104.

"Maybe It's Time for Drug Companies to Drop TV Ads," by John LaMattina. From *Forbes.com*, February 15, 2012 © 2012 Forbes LLC. All rights reserved. Used by permission and protected by the Copyright Laws of the United States. The printing, copying, redistribution, or retransmission of this Content without express written permission is prohibited.

Alan F. Holmer, JD, "Direct-to-Consumer Prescription Drug Advertising Builds Bridges Between Patients and Physicians," *The Journal of American Medical Associations*, January 27, 1999, Vol. 281, No 4.

C. Lee Ventola, MS, "Direct-to-Consumer Pharmaceutical Advertising: Therapeutic or Toxic?" *Pharmacy and Therapeutics*, Oct 2011; 36(10): 669-674, 681-684.

"Is Social Media Hurting Our Culture?" by Abby Johnson. *WebProNews*, June 15, 2012. (*http://www.webpronews.com/is-social-media-hurting-our-culture-2012-06*).

Excerpt from "Social Networking Benefits Validated" by Karen Goldberg Goff, *The Washington Times*, Wednesday, January 28, 2009. *http://www.washingtontimes.com/news/2009/jan/28/social-networking-benefits-validated/#ixzz3Am6Q2ypA*.

Response to the Question: Is MySpace Good for Society? By Martin Baily. Used by permission of the author.

Response to the Question: Is MySpace Good for Society? By Nicole Ellison. Used by permission of the author.